The Face of Naval Battle

'RAN ships paste Japanese posts' by Roy Hodgkinson. (AWM ART22766)

The Face of Naval Battle

The human experience of modern war at sea

edited by
John Reeve and David Stevens

ALLEN&UNWIN

*This book is dedicated to all those who have suffered
from the reality of modern naval battle.*

First published in 2003

Allen & Unwin
83 Alexander Street
Crows Nest NSW 2065
Australia
Phone: (61 2) 8425 0100
Fax: (61 2) 9906 2218
Email: info@allenandunwin.com
Web: www.allenandunwin.com

National Library of Australia
Cataloguing-in-Publication entry:

The face of naval battle.

Includes index.
ISBN 1 86508 667 3
ISBN 1 74114 154 0 (hb)

1. Naval strategy. 2. Navies—Personnel management. I. Stevens, David. II.
Reeve, John.

359.22

Typeset in 10.5/12 pt Bembo Text by Midland Typesetters, Maryborough
Printed and bound by SRM Production Services, SDN, BHD, Malaysia

10 9 8 7 6 5 4 3 2 1

Foreword

THIS BOOK EXPLORES the individual and group experience of maritime combat in twentieth-century warfare. Such an agenda is an extensive intellectual task and I am pleased to see that the editors have adopted a thematic approach, achieving a balance between chronological periods, geographical areas and operational activities. Running throughout this volume, however, is the overall theme of the face of naval battle. The human dimension of naval warfare is essential and rich, but our lack of knowledge of that experience is still a serious gap in our naval history, which is only just beginning to be filled. Understanding the human factor in naval battle is critical for navies if they are to be trusted guardians of national and international interests in war and peace. We must never forget that while navies are highly complex technological organisations, a naval vessel and the weapons system it constitutes (or of which it is a part) is comprised not simply of equipment, but also of the men and women of its ship's company. Moreover, while the technology of war may change, and tactics and strategy may evolve, the vital human issues are eternal. Qualities such as courage, teamwork and determination to get the job done are as important now as they have ever been. As one of my predecessors once declared, a navy is a 'creation of nerves as well as steel; united with blood as well as rivets'.

It is this human element, this very real combination of nerves and blood, which has been indispensable in giving Australia's Navy such a proud tradition. Indeed, the period covered by this book coincides almost exactly with the life of our national naval force. It is important that we ponder the lessons of our history, that we record and discuss the hard-won knowledge and wisdom for which our predecessors, those who experienced at first hand 'the face of naval battle', paid such a high price. A better understanding of our history can help us prepare for the future, by assisting us better to ready our people for the undoubted shock of going into battle for the first time. The wisdom residing in the past has been paid for, by our own people and others, and we cannot afford to throw it away.

Naval leaders can be caricatured, sometimes justifiably, as technocrats in uniform, and they can easily become absorbed with the technical dimensions of navies at the expense of the human. Despite this, successful navies and great admirals have always understood the human factor. Admiral Cunningham's famous observation before the evacuation of Crete in which Australian ships were to play a distinguished role—that it would take three years to rebuild a lost fleet but 300 years to rebuild a tradition, and that therefore the Navy could not let the Army down—was above all a statement of values and attitudes and hence an appeal to the human factor.

Navies today talk much about how people are their most important resource, but it is too often the case that the human factor has been considered only after the *matériel*. Notwithstanding recent improvements I am fully aware of the difficulties we still face in attracting and retaining enough young men and women for the future force. I firmly believe that a proper understanding of the sacrifice and service of those who have gone before can help us in this ongoing task. It is the Navy's people who have made our history, and we have ample past experience and achievement on which to reflect and draw for inspiration.

There are many stirring stories in the following pages, as well as analyses aimed at better understanding the face of naval battle. In order for us to pursue our professional calling we must appreciate how and why our people and others performed these heroic deeds. Part of that understanding is an awareness of what is unique in naval warfare as well as those aspects that are part of the nature of warfare as a whole. Those of us now serving must remember and learn from these lessons as we promote and pursue the Navy's vital role in our future national security.

Vice Admiral C.A. Ritchie, AO, RAN
Chief of Navy

Contents

Contributors

Commodore Lee Cordner, AM, RANR   Lee Cordner entered the Royal Australian Navy in January 1968 as a Junior Recruit and was selected for officer training in 1970. As a Midshipman he saw operational service in the Vietnam War onboard the aircraft carrier HMAS *Sydney*. He later commanded HMA Ships *Betano* and *Bass* before qualifying as a Principal Warfare Officer in 1981. This was followed by exchange service in the Royal Navy. He served as the Executive Officer of the frigate HMAS *Darwin* and commanded HMAS *Sydney* 1990–92 during the Gulf War and an operational deployment in the North Red Sea. On promotion to Captain in 1994 he was appointed Director of Naval Warfare, then Director of Naval Current Policy and Plans. He commanded HMAS *Adelaide* 1997–99 as senior Captain in the Fleet. He was a member of the 'Tomorrow's Navy Team' before being promoted to Commodore in December 1999 as Director General Navy Strategic Policy and Futures. He is a graduate of the Australian Joint Services Staff College and the US Naval War College and holds Masters degrees in management and international relations. He separated from the Navy in 2001 to become Chief Executive Officer of the Centre for International Strategic Analysis, Claremont, WA.

Commodore Michael Dowsett, AM, RAN (Rtd)   Michael Dowsett joined the RANR in 1961 while completing his postgraduate dental studies. A graduate of Sydney University (MDS) and UNSW (MHPEd) he transferred to the permanent naval forces in 1965. He served in HMAS *Vampire*, HMAS *Derwent* and HMAS *Parramatta* during the period of Indonesian Confrontation. A variety of postings at sea and ashore followed including ANZUK Force Singapore, HMAS *Melbourne* and Service Conditions Branch, HQADF, culminating in his promotion to Commodore in 1990 as Director General Naval Health Services until his retirement in 1996. He has had a long-standing interest in naval history and was instrumental in re-establishing the HMAS *Cerberus* Museum in 1975.

Professor Bruce A. Elleman   Bruce Elleman is Associate Professor in the Strategic Research Department at the Center for Naval Warfare Studies, United States Naval War College, Newport, RI. He specialises in Chinese, Japanese and Russian History, East Asian International Relations and Chinese Military History. A graduate of the University of California, Berkeley, CA, and Columbia University, where he gained his PhD, he has taught at the Cheng Chih University, Taipei, Texas Christian University, Fort Worth, Texas, and Hunter College, New York, and was a research assistant at Columbia University. His published works include *Modern Chinese Warfare, 1795–1989* (2001), *Mongolia in the Twentieth Century* (1999) and *Diplomacy and Deception: The Secret History of Sino-Soviet Relations, 1917–1927* (1997). He has also completed a book entitled *Wilson and China: A Revised History of the 1919 Shandong Question*, which he intends to publish shortly.

Dr Andrew Gordon   Andrew Gordon has a PhD in War Studies from King's College, London, and currently lectures at the United Kingdom's Joint Services Command and Staff College near Swindon, Wiltshire. His specialist function is that of Naval Historian on the Higher Command and Staff Course. Dr Gordon served as a member of the Royal Naval Reserve from 1979 to 1994. His many publications include *British Sea Power and Procurement Between the Wars* (1988) and *The Rules of the Game: Jutland and British Naval Command* (1996 and reprinted 2000), which won both the Westminster Medal for Military Literature and the Longman *History Today* Book of the Year prize.

Rear Admiral Guy Griffiths, AO, DSO, DSC, RAN (Rtd)   Guy Griffiths entered the Royal Australian Naval College in January 1937 at the age of 13. He was made Chief Cadet Captain in 1939 and after graduation was posted to the Royal Navy where he joined the battlecruiser

HMS *Repulse*. In 1943 he joined the cruiser HMAS *Shropshire* and saw action in the South West Pacific, being awarded the DSC after the Lingayen Gulf operation. After the war he completed the Specialist Course in Gunnery at HMS *Excellent* and served as Gunnery Officer in the aircraft carrier HMAS *Sydney* during the Korean War. In 1952 he saw further action in Korea in the destroyer HMAS *Anzac*. After serving ashore in Canberra, and commanding HMAS *Parramatta*, he was promoted Captain and in 1965 took command of the new destroyer HMAS *Hobart*, seeing action in Vietnam and being awarded the DSO. He later commanded the aircraft carrier HMAS *Melbourne*, flagship of the Australian Fleet, and in addition to normal operations participated in 'Operation Navy Help Darwin' after Cyclone Tracy in 1975. He was promoted Rear Admiral in 1976 and served as both Chief of Naval Personnel and Flag Officer Naval Support Command, being made an Officer of the Order of Australia in 1979. He retired from the RAN in 1980 after 43 years' service. He is currently National Chairman of the Australian Veterans and Defence Services Council and a Director of the Australian War Veterans Trust.

Commander David Hobbs, MBE, RN (Rtd) David Hobbs joined the Royal Navy in 1964. As a Fleet Air Arm pilot he flew Gannets, Hunter and Canberra aircraft as well as Wessex Commando Helicopters, and he has served in the aircraft carriers HM Ships *Victorious*, *Hermes*, *Albion*, *Bulwark*, *Centaur*, *Ark Royal* (4) and *Ark Royal* (5). Commander Hobbs retired from the active list in 1997 and is presently Curator and Deputy Director of the Fleet Air Arm Museum at RNAS Yeovilton in the United Kingdom. His publications include *Aircraft Carriers of the Royal & Commonwealth Navies* (1996), *Aircraft of the Royal Navy Since 1945* (1982), a Naval Staff Study—*The* Invincible *Class and Their Air Groups* (1997)—and *Ark Royal—The Name Lives On* (1985). He has contributed to *The Battle of the Atlantic 1939–1945* (1994) and *Men of War: Great Leaders of World War II* (1992). He is writing a new book on British and Australian carrier operations and researching British carrier development in the post-1945 era.

Gordon Johnson Gordon Johnson left high school at 16 to join the RAN's Communication Branch, beginning his training as a telegraphist in 1940 at HMA Signal School, Flinders Naval Depot, Victoria. His first ship was HMAS *Hobart* and his experiences included service as a unit of the 7th Cruiser Squadron of the Mediterranean Fleet commanded by Admiral Sir Andrew Cunningham. Subsequent service included operations in the Singapore-Netherlands East Indies area during the initial Japanese advance, followed by the Coral Sea and Guadalcanal actions in company with the United States Navy. After serving for two years in *Hobart*, he spent time in HMA Ships *Moresby* and *Townsville*, first on patrol and escort duties off the Papua New Guinea coast and later sweeping for mines in Rabaul Harbour and the New Britain area. After the war, he served in the aircraft carrier HMAS *Sydney* from 1948 to 1949. Having left the RAN in 1949, his later career included time with the Civil Aviation Aeradio Service at Cocos Island, the Philips telecommunications company in Adelaide and the Commonwealth Public Service (CPS). He retired from the CPS in 1983 as a First Assistant Secretary and now lives in Canberra.

David Jones   A lifelong resident of Brisbane, since an early age David Jones has gained great enjoyment from observing the wide range of shipping using the Brisbane River. Married with two adult children, he retired in 2000 after a career in the Queensland Public Service. This has allowed him more time to pursue his long-standing interest in naval and maritime history. He is a member of the Queensland Maritime Museum and the Navy League, and has written two short books with nautical themes: *Patrol Boat Story* (with his brother Colin) (1972) and *The Whalers of Tangalooma* (1980).

Captain Peter Jones, AM, RAN   Peter Jones joined the RAN College as a 16-year-old Cadet Midshipman in 1974 and, after initial training as a seaman officer, specialised in gunnery. His subsequent service has seen him hold a variety of appointments in Australia and overseas, including command of the guided missile frigate HMAS *Melbourne* during sanction operations in the Persian Gulf. He became the inaugural Director of Naval Strategy and Futures in Naval Headquarters in 2000. He has written for a large number of professional journals, and is the editor (with T. Frame and J. Goldrick) of *Reflections on the RAN* (1991).

Lieutenant-Commander Malcolm Llewellyn-Jones, MBE, RN (Rtd)   After gaining a degree in mathematics, Malcolm Llewellyn-Jones joined the Royal Navy and served, mainly in the Fleet Air Arm, for 26 years. His career included the analysis of airborne anti-submarine tactics, both ashore and afloat. He commanded an Operational Flying Training Flight and a front-line anti-submarine helicopter squadron, where he introduced a new helicopter variant into the service, for which he was awarded the MBE. He retired from the Royal Navy as a Lieutenant-Commander in 1996 in order to take up an academic career. He is the author of two papers: 'The trials with HM Submarine *Seraph* and British preparations to defeat the Type XXI U-Boat, September–October 1944' and 'A flawed contender: the "Fighter Submarine", 1946–50'. He has given papers on the history of anti-submarine warfare at King's College, London, the Royal United Services Institution and the University of Greenwich. He is currently an historian with the RN's Naval Historical Branch.

Dr Peter Overlack Peter Overlack held a German Academic Exchange Scholarship and completed his PhD at the University of Queensland in 1995 on the East Asian Cruiser Squadron as an instrument of German 'world policy'. He has published numerous articles on naval and political history in such journals as *War & Society*, *The Australian Journal of Politics and History*, *The Journal of Strategic Studies* (UK), *The Historian* and *The Journal of Military History* (USA), as well as contributing to various books and giving seminars at German universities. Further details of his work are available from his Website at http://www.geocities.com/peteroverlack. He currently teaches secondary school and is active as an independent writer.

Major Russell Parkin Russell Parkin graduated from the Australian Army's Officer Cadet Training Unit in 1982 and was appointed to the Royal Australian Army Ordnance Corps, Army Reserve. After several regimental postings he graduated from the Reserve Command and Staff College and in 1989–91 served on full-time duty at the Directorate of Supply in Canberra. In 1990 he joined the Regular Army and after a posting as a Research Fellow to the Army's thinktank, The Land Warfare Studies Centre, he moved to the office of the Deputy Chief of Army. He holds a PhD in history from the University of NSW at the Australian Defence Force Academy (UNSW, ADFA).

Dr John Reeve John Reeve is Senior Lecturer and Osborne Fellow in Naval History at UNSW, ADFA. A graduate of Melbourne University (MA) and Cambridge (PhD), he has taught at Cambridge, Yale (as a Fulbright Fellow), Hong Kong and Sydney Universities, held visiting fellowships at Cambridge and London Universities and is a Fellow of the Royal Historical Society and a Member of the International Institute for Strategic Studies. He began his career as a political and diplomatic historian and for fifteen years has specialised in international, naval and strategic history, and contemporary maritime strategic affairs. His publications include *Charles I and the Road to Personal Rule* (1989), (as co-editor) *Southern Trident: Strategy, History and the Rise of Australian Naval Power* (2001) and many articles, essays, chapters, working papers and dictionary entries, including an essay on 'Asia-Pacific naval strategy 1500–2000' in Geoffrey Till (ed.), *Seapower at the Millennium* (2001). He is writing a study of early modern diplomacy and strategy and is an Associate Editor of the forthcoming *Oxford Dictionary of National Biography*.

Dr Peter Stanley   Peter Stanley is Principal Historian at the Australian War Memorial, where he has worked since 1980. He has been involved in the development of the Memorial's temporary exhibitions and permanent galleries, most recently the extensive new Second World War galleries. He has published widely in the fields of Australian and British military history, having written eleven books. His most recent three books reflect the breadth of his interests: *Whyalla at War 1939–45*, *For Fear of Pain: British Surgery 1790–1850* and, with Dr Mark Johnston, *Alamein: The Australian Story*. A life-long devotee of the novels of C.S. Forester, this is the first time he has tackled a naval historical subject.

Dr David Stevens   David Stevens has been the Director of Naval Historical Studies within the Royal Australian Navy's Sea Power Centre since retiring from the Navy in 1994. He joined the RAN College in 1974 at the age of 16 and after graduation spent time in a variety of Australian fleet units, eventually specialising in anti-submarine warfare. In 1984–86 he served on exchange with the Royal Navy and was one of the first Australians to conduct a Falkland Islands peace patrol. In 1990–91 he served on the staff of the Australian Task Group Commander during Operation DAMASK and the Gulf War. In 1992 he graduated from the Australian National University with an MA (Strategic Studies) and in 2000 he received his PhD from UNSW, ADFA. He is the author or editor of a number of books including *The Royal Australian Navy in World War II* (1996), *In Search of a Maritime Strategy: The Maritime Element in Australian Defence Planning Since 1901* (1997), *U-Boat Far From Home* (1997), *Maritime Power in the Twentieth Century: The Australian Experience* (1998), *Prospects for Maritime Aviation in the 21st Century* (1999), *Southern Trident: Strategy, History and the Rise of Australian Naval Power* (with John Reeve, 2001) and the third volume in the 'Australian Centenary History of Defence', *The Royal Australian Navy* (2001).

Dr Colin Wastell   Colin Wastell is currently Senior Lecturer in Psychology at Macquarie University, Sydney, and a member of the Psychological Society and the College of Counselling Psychology of the Australian Psychological Society. His research interests include the areas of trauma (chronic and acute), battle stress, medium- to long-term psychotherapy and personality disorders (including borderline) and DID, especially the function of dissociation. His published papers include 'Borderline personality clients in university populations' in the *British Journal of Guidance & Counselling*, and 'The impact of human agency on victimized survivors' in the *Journal of Interpersonal Violence*.

Michael Whitby   Michael Whitby is Chief of the Naval History Team at the Directorate of History and Heritage, National Defence Headquarters, Ottawa, and responsible for producing the three-volume *Official History of the Royal Canadian Navy, 1867–1968*. As well as co-authoring a forthcoming volume on *The RCN in the Second World War*, he has co-authored two histories of Canada's experience in the European theatre during the Second World War. He has co-edited a technical history of Canadian naval aviation and written several articles on naval history for international journals. Among other current projects, he is editing for publication the diary of Commander Frank Layard, RN, and preparing a biography of Vice Admiral Harry DeWolf, RCN. He has also served as a senior speech writer and policy analyst at Canadian National Defence Headquarters.

ACKNOWLEDGEMENTS

Most of the essays contained in this book originated as papers presented at the second King-Hall Naval History Conference held in Canberra in July 2001. The conference was jointly sponsored by the Royal Australian Navy in conjunction with the University of New South Wales at the Australian Defence Force Academy and the Australian Naval Institute. This book could not have been produced without the support, not only of the contributors, but of a variety of individuals and organisations. Particular thanks are due to Professor Peter Dennis, David Griffin, Debra Locke, Brett Mitchell and Joe Straczek, and to the Department of Veterans' Affairs, Screen Sound Australia, the Australian War Memorial ANZAC Foundation and the National Archives of Australia.

Illustrations, figures and table

ILLUSTRATIONS

FIGURES AND TABLE

Acronyms and abbreviations

AOC	Air Officer Commanding
ADF	Australian Defence Force
ADM	Admiralty Files, Public Record Office, Kew, London
AIF	Australian Imperial Force
AIR	Air Ministry Files, Public Record Office, Kew, London
AN&MEF	Australian Naval and Military Expeditionary Force
A/S	Anti-submarine
ASW	Anti-submarine Warfare
AW	Air Warfare
AWM	Australian War Memorial
BLO	Bombardment Liaison Officer
BPRS	Blackett Papers, Royal Society, London
C3	Command, Control and Communications
CAG	Carrier Air Group
CAP	Combat Air Patrol
CBALO	Carrier Borne Air Liaison Officer
CBALS	Carrier Borne Air Liaison Section
CCAC	Churchill College Archive Centre, Cambridge
CTG	Commander Task Group
DDG	Guided Missile Destroyer
CEC	Cooperative Engagement Capability
CVA	Attack Aircraft Carrier
DSO	Distinguished Service Order
EBO	Effects-Based Operations
ERGM	Extended Range Gun Munitions
FAA	Fleet Air Arm
HF/DF	High Frequency Direction Finding
HMAS	His/Her Majesty's Australian Ship

HMCS	His/Her Majesty's Canadian Ship
HMNZS	His/Her Majesty's New Zealand Ship
HMS	His/Her Majesty's Ship
IJN	Imperial Japanese Navy
INTERFET	International Force East Timor
IT	Information Technology
IWM	Imperial War Museum, London
JOOTS	Joint Overseas Operational Training School
JSF	Joint Strike Fighter
LPA	Landing Platform Amphibious
LSI	Landing Ship Infantry
LST	Landing Ship Tank
MOLE	Manoeuvre Operations in the Littoral Environment
NAA	National Archives of Australia
NAC	National Archives of Canada, Ottawa
NARA	National Archives and Record Administration, Maryland, USA
NATO	North Atlantic Treaty Organisation
NCW	Network Centric Warfare
NFCS	Naval Fires Control System
NGS	Naval Gunfire Support
NHC	Naval Historical Center, Washington, DC
NHD	Naval Historical Directorate, Canberra
NMM(G)	National Maritime Museum, Greenwich, UK
PBM	Principal Beachmaster
PLAN	People's Liberation Army Navy
PRO	Public Record Office, London
PTSD	Post Traumatic Stress Disorder
RAAF	Royal Australian Air Force
RAF	Royal Air Force
RAN	Royal Australian Navy
RANB	Royal Australian Naval Brigade
RCN	Royal Canadian Navy
RDO	Rapid Decisive Operations
RFC	Royal Flying Corps
RMA	Revolution in Military Affairs
RN	Royal Navy
RNAS	Royal Naval Air Service
RNAS	Royal Naval Air Station
RNM	Royal Naval Museum, Portsmouth
SDR	Strategic Defence Review

SWPA	South-West Pacific Area
UAV	Uninhabited Aerial Vehicles
USCGC	US Coast Guard Cutter
USN	United States Navy
USS	United States Ship
UUV	Uninhabited Underwater Vehicles
UW	Undersea Warfare
V/STOL	Vertical/Short Take Off and Landing

Part I

Setting the Scene

1 | Introduction

An anatomy of the face of naval battle

John Reeve

'My home would be in ships, and on the fascinating, deadly, unresting ocean.'
> Michael Thwaites, Australian veteran of the Battle of the Atlantic.[1]

'Sink, burn and destroy. Let nothing pass.'
> Admiral Sir Andrew Cunningham, RN, C-in-C Mediterranean Fleet, on the need to prevent German evacuation of Africa, 1943.[2]

'Ericson sighed again. "And we only sank three U-boats. Three, in five years."
> "We worked hard enough for them, God knows."
> "Yes." Ericson brooded, leaning heavily against a corner of the bridge where he must have spent many hundreds of hours. Out of the deep dusk he said—and after sixty-eight months it was still a shock to hear him use the words:
> "I must say I'm damned tired." '
> Nicholas Monsarrat, *The Cruel Sea*.[3]

'Which was the real world? The hard-bitten kill-or-be-killed life we led in the [USS] *Jack*—or the luxurious leisurely dinners . . . with their long philosophical discussions?'
> James Calvert, US Navy submariner in the Pacific during the Second World War.[4]

'Sweet is war to them that know it not.'
> Erasmus.[5]

3

BATTLE AT SEA has an ancient history. Just as human beings have used the seas and oceans they have fought upon them. Two-and-a-half millennia ago, at Salamis, 1500 war galleys—Greek and Persian—closed in mortal combat to decide the future of Greek civilisation. In 1588, in the English Channel, English galleons and a Spanish Armada fought ferocious gun duels to decide whether the Spanish superpower would rule over northern Europe. In 1805, off Cape Trafalgar, Nelson's ships ruthlessly crushed the combined fleet of France and Spain: the strategic seeds of Napoleon's defeat were sown. In 1944, at Leyte Gulf, the grey steel machines of modern naval warfare sliced through the waters of the Philippines to eliminate the Japanese fleet as an obstacle to American hegemony in the Pacific. We know these events as historic milestones and remember the names of the great naval captains: Themistocles, Drake, Nelson and Halsey. We know of the ships in and with which they fought, and can summon up their silhouettes to the mind's eye. But what do we know of the sailors and their commanders who sweated, fought, bled, suffered and died in these human catastrophes? We know little, and we ought to know more. Essentially ordinary people, caught up in the harrowing experience of war, their story is one of the great epics of human history. It holds lessons, moreover, of inestimable value for navies today: those military forces which venture upon the sea, praying for peace but preparing for war.

THE HUMAN FACTOR

People have always mattered most in the outcome of naval warfare. In the words of Wayne Hughes, today's best-known writer on naval tactics: 'Leadership, morale, training, physical and mental conditioning, willpower, and endurance are the most important elements in warfare'.[6] In the age of the sailing warship, the Royal Navy could go into battle with inferior (and fewer) vessels but superior men—and win. In 1916 however, at Jutland, despite its material superiority this elite force contained defects of organisation and training which impacted upon its performance. During the Second World War, when its equipment could be inferior, it had leaders of flair and imagination, aggressive and willing to innovate in areas such as night-fighting, and redeemed its reputation.[7] Nathan Miller, in a long and learned study of the Second World War at sea, concludes that it was not critical mass which gave victory to the Allied navies, but rather the quality of their leadership in the face of adversity.[8] Naval weapons systems have always depended upon the interface between people and material. Each can enhance or detract from the effectiveness of the other, but the best equipment is still unlikely to compensate for poor personal performance.

Navies down the generations have understood the human factor by tradition, rather than by precept or concept, and this is probably the wisest course. Human beings are habitual creatures, responding more to perceived realities and regular practicalities than to abstractions, no matter how profound. Traditions can be powerfully effective, therefore, especially successful ones. Lee Cordner, an Australian frigate captain in the Gulf War, has written of how history inspired (and warned) him during the demanding task of maintaining effectiveness in a war zone.[9] But traditions must be retrieved, understood, preserved, nurtured and propagated to continue the habits of success, especially in such a demanding area as military operations at sea. Past experience, moreover, has been dearly bought. In the words of a Falklands veteran, speaking about the naval aviators of the previous twenty years: 'it's on the blood, sweat and tears of those people that our expertise . . . was built. It only came from a lot of work, hard flying and, sadly, a lot of casualties'.[10] This book, therefore, has a twofold aim. It seeks to explore a critical dimension in the history of naval warfare, as well as a remarkable strand of human experience. It also seeks a better understanding of that experience for a practical purpose. Given the difficulty of simulating real war, historical lessons are priceless. Naval thought and policy, strategy, tactics and technology are nothing without the human factor, and navies must learn from history how to nurture it—for the sake of their people as well as of their professional success.

THE 'FACE OF BATTLE' HISTORICAL GENRE

The phrase 'the face of battle' was employed by Sir John Keegan a generation ago, as the title of a distinguished book in which he explored the varied facets of personal experience in the midst of combat on land.[11] Many subsequent writers on war have been haunted by Keegan's memorable opening sentence: 'I have not been in a battle . . . ', and by his interim conclusion: 'I grow increasingly convinced that I have very little idea of what a battle can be like'.[12] Can the experience of battle be imagined, or communicated to those who have not had it? There are differing views.[13] One veteran has told me of his belief that, with care, it can be imagined. Another maintains that it is impossible to communicate the terror of having another human being approach with the intention of killing you. There is a credible consensus among many that battle experience can only be known, in truth and reality, by having had it.[14] To think otherwise is arguably to demean a frequently intense and always uniquely personal experience, as well as to make light of formidable intellectual difficulties. Historically, however, all is not lost. We can travel a considerable distance by listening closely to those who have seen battle and by imaginatively reconstructing events from eyewitness accounts. Indirect experience indeed has a certain value, as Liddell Hart observed, in terms of its variety and extent.[15]

There is a growing and impressive literature, largely stimulated by Keegan's work, on the human experience of warfare on land.[16] With certain exceptions there has not been, however, a similar genre of writing about naval war. As Paul Kennedy has pointed out, 'writings upon "the face of battle" have found little echo in its naval dimensions'.[17] Why this should be is at first mysterious. Sea power has been, and remains, a major strategic factor in the shaping of the modern world. English-speaking societies in particular are the products of a great global maritime diaspora. Naval operations combine the inherent adventure of seafaring with the drama of war. The popularity of the novels of C.S. Forester and Patrick O'Brian testifies to the vast public interest in this combination of great themes. The audience is there, but can the story be readily told?

There are obstacles to recovering the personal experience of warfare in general. Operational security is essential and can be mandated long after the events concerned. Governments preserve support for military operations by sparing their peoples the horrors of truly vivid reportage. Veterans are often reluctant to speak, at least until late in life, of what they have seen, done, thought and felt, through a natural desire to expunge often traumatic memories. The public commemoration of war is thus inherently unreal in terms of battle experience. As Sir Max Hastings wrote of an American serviceman killed in Vietnam: 'The more remote this man became from the battlefield, from reality, the more honoured would be his carcass'.[18] This is not to deny that commemoration is powerfully invested with meaning, for veterans as well as others, but it is not in itself the meaning and reality of battle.

Finally, there is the difficulty of reconstructing after the event the often kaleidoscopic impressions of action and reaction, of sight, sound and smell, and of life-threatening emergency, all filtered through the lens of personal observation and frequently coloured by the effects of shock, injury and exhaustion—all this in an atmosphere which frequently plays tricks with the human sense of time. In addition, personal battle accounts are generally written after the fact, and are subject, to a greater or lesser extent, to the human inclination to rationalise and logically re-order.[19] Neither is the perspective of high command always helpful in glimpsing the face of battle. Admiral Cunningham (who like so many high naval commanders risked the perils of combat) said with candour as well as modesty: 'the best seats in any war are high up and at the back', presumably meaning they are safer and afford a view of the bigger picture.[20] But this kind of relative safety and strategic appreciation are not the same as the immediate reality of war.

THE FACE OF NAVAL BATTLE: THE VEIL OF INVISIBILITY

A further difficulty is apparent when we consider more closely the specifically naval dimension of warfare. History contrives to draw a veil of invisibility over the face of naval battle. Why is this so? It derives essentially from three factors: the nature of the events, the nature of those involved and the nature of what remains afterwards. Turning first to the events, in his keynote address to the King-Hall Naval History Conference in 2001, David Rosenberg pointed out how naval combat is tactically rapid.[21] Its action can be very fleeting and, even in the age of modern sensors, highly unexpected. It can be over, literally, in a flash, leaving less of an actual event to create an impression on human memory. Historically there have usually been relatively few witnesses to naval battle in comparison to land warfare. Many of these witnesses, moreover, have been killed in action or by the perils of the sea. One reason for the paucity of testimony to naval defeat and loss is that ships can sink rapidly and with very few survivors. One hundred per cent losses of the crews of downed submarines and aircraft are not uncommon. Non-combatant witnesses are very few or totally absent. Merchant crews caught up in maritime war (a de facto paramilitary force) have often been lost with their ships and, unlike those on land, naval actions are not usually observed by local populations.

Journalists are rarely present to report naval battles. Even in the Falklands, with accredited journalists in theatre and action in proximity to the shore, there was no direct reporting of the battle in Falkland Sound involving the loss of HMS *Ardent*. A Royal Naval surgeon wrote of the survivors:

> What these boys had done was place themselves between a well handled and hostile air force and our soldiers, who were trying to land on the shore. I think some of the ship's company were slightly anxious that there was no one around to recognize just what they had achieved.

Action messing, HMAS *Adelaide*, September 1940. 'There have been many books written by private soldiers, a few by Air Force rankers, and fewer by men of the Silent Service . . . there is a reason for this. That reason is the vehicle in which they go to war. Very few sailormen actually see the exploits they take part in.' Signalman Brian Sheedy, RAN, HMAS *Perth*. (RAN)

All the journalists were ashore with the Brigade commander and had missed all this.[22]

Here is an instance (convoy escort being another, and the evacuation of defeated armies yet another) of something navies frequently do, which is save lives rather than kill or destroy. In such situations naval forces are often highly professional, and their conduct highly honourable, but they lack the glamour of having 'accounted' for the enemy—not always their operational purpose.

What of the people involved in naval battle? A sailor's way of life and way of war are different from those of a soldier and distinct from the life of a civilian. Seafaring is a technical skill, with something of a separate language of its own. Sailors have traditionally lived in somewhat segregated coastal communities and, beyond these, on the seas and as transients in foreign lands; in other words, they dwell on the fringes of their domestic societies. They have not always gone to war in the same massed and demonstrable way as soldiers, nor have they always re-entered society in similar fashion. Theirs is but a partially visible and somewhat distinct sub-community and society is conditioned to their regular absence. Unsurprisingly, their stories of war penetrate society less readily. Naval officers are—to a great extent and increasingly—technocrats, with their professional standing resting upon arcane and often secret knowledge. They are not, in this sense, 'user-friendly' as sources of contemporary history. As Peter Stanley observes, sailors are not generally literary people, inclined to publish their stories, although there are exceptions.[23] Life at sea is not conducive to such activity. Modesty, taciturnity and discretion (hallmarks of 'the silent service') have traditionally been held up as naval virtues, and navies have frequently shunned publicity. The Royal Navy, for example, has had an historical tendency to dislike the press and at least one great admiral (Cunningham) was residually hostile to it.[24] An officer such as Mountbatten was unusual in seeking publicity for the Royal Navy during the Second World War.[25] Sailors and navies, in short, have for a variety of reasons not promoted their tales of the face of naval battle.

And what remains of naval battle after the event? Ships are sunk and those that survive, with few exceptions, are eventually sold off or scrapped. There are no walkable battlefields as such, and historical reconstructions are impractical on any scale.[26] Fewer visual images, such as photographs, remain of naval action (sailors are usually intensely occupied on a warship in battle), and few of those images we do have are of people. Submarines, indeed, usually have only a periscope view through which to photograph the battlespace. Sailors do not have the same access as soldiers to retrievable battle souvenirs. The personal effects and weaponry of their defeated enemies usually sink beneath the sea. Souvenirs are classic vehicles for human stories. (One thoughtful ship's captain in the Falklands engaged a war correspondent to collect pistols and bayonets for distribution among his crew: 'Every soldier and marine on the islands is busy collecting souvenirs. I've got several hundred men on this ship who've done just as much towards winning the war, but can't go ashore.'[27]) Ships successful in battle return home, and while their crews are often dispersed by transfer and replacement, or retire, the ships themselves become objects of technical fascination. Naval officers, historians and architects, procurement specialists and the naval equivalents of train-spotting techno-buffs study the vessels themselves, too often without reference to those who live and work in them. As David Rosenberg has observed, that great and indispensable work of reference *Jane's Fighting Ships* is a record of things and not people.[28] Even in the aftermath, the veil of invisibility obscures the face of naval battle.

LOOKING BEHIND THE VEIL

Can we peer behind the veil? There have recently been encouraging signs. The latest contribution in the slender series of writings exploring the face of naval battle is by Ronald Spector. His book *At War at Sea* is a highly successful investigation of 'the complex relationship between naval technology, operations, and human factors'.[29] With contextual sophistication and meticulous scholarship, Spector pursues this theme on a global scale. He concludes that the human factor is supreme in terms of skill in utilising existing (rather than the most advanced) naval technology. The amount of personal testimony which Spector has identified and deployed suggests one of the advantages enjoyed by twentieth-century naval historians: their period is marked by high levels of literacy among sailors, relative to earlier times.

The essays collected herein further attest to the sources available to those wishing to look behind the veil. This book is intended to assist in the development of a 'face of naval battle' historical genre. While international in scope it is also unique in bringing Australian material into play. Such material combines the continuity and traditions of a predominantly surface warship navy with the experiences of a smaller naval power ultimately rooted in the Asia-Pacific region. Andrew Gordon observes that naval warfare is best understood in terms of the continuum of naval operations.[30] This book involves the working assumption that the human experience of war at sea, while punctuated by intense episodes of battle per se, is also best understood as part of that operational continuum. The book spans the chronological period encompassing the industrial and post-industrial eras: from the coming of modern battleships and weaponry in the late nineteenth century to the contemporary world of the information and technological revolution. It aims to provide a balance of operational themes and to draw case studies from a variety of nations. Above all, its subject is people and the maritime military setting in which they have lived and died.

THE BACKGROUND AND LEGACY OF THE AGE OF SAIL

The great age of the sailing warship, culminating in Britain's naval supremacy in the early nineteenth century, is in many ways a vanished world. Its operational modes and way of battle have largely been consigned to history. When remembered, however, it throws the nature of modern naval warfare into clearer relief. It has also left a legacy with important continuities into the modern age.

Naval warfare under sail took place in what Nicholas Rodger has termed 'the wooden world'.[31] This world saw an eternal interaction of human beings with superbly crafted timber vessels. The resulting combination was one of military history's most effective weapons systems. As British line-of-battle ships closed to engage the enemy, their preparations reflected the interaction of timber and flesh.[32] Carpenters as well as surgeons set up their stations. The decks, vulnerable to fire, were sluiced with water and sprinkled with sand—the latter to give grip to bare feet, not least when the decks ran with blood. Magazines were secured against explosion and fire. Splinter netting was erected and loose timber cleared, for there was mortal danger to sailors from a hail of wooden splinters struck off by solid shot. With battle joined, the atmosphere in the gun decks was one of hellish confusion, even in a fleet which emerged victorious. According to a Royal Marine officer at Trafalgar, the atmosphere in the middle of three decks 'beggars all description: it bewilders the senses of sight and hearing . . . the guns recoiling with violence, reports louder than thunder'.[33] Other accounts paint the same picture of noise, smoke, confusion and terror. There being no system of triage, the wounded received treatment in the order they were brought to the surgeon. Rum might be issued to sailors after an action (the dangers of giving alcohol to men in shock being not then fully appreciated), but the immediate necessity was to repair and work the ship and deal with any changing weather conditions.[34]

How did this experience change in the 150 years from Trafalgar in 1805 to the Second World War and beyond? Fleet actions and ship-to-ship combat in the age of sail were set differently in place and time from more modern naval engagements. Sailing ship battles could only take place in fair weather and, like the early twentieth-century gun actions at Tsushima and Jutland, were usually one-day affairs. Damage to ships and men could often hardly be sustained beyond a matter of hours. Nelson himself said that Trafalgar was too warm work to last long.[35] Admittedly, this could be the case in modern engagements. Night fighting under sail, however, was technically dangerous and practised only on rare occasions, such as at the Nile in 1798. Tactically it was only facilitated well into the twentieth century by the coming of radar. Significantly, the arrival of strike air power—at and over the sea—meant that naval engagements were longer and their strain more sustained.[36] Sailing battles were fought in very close proximity, but modern, long-range guns, locomotive torpedoes and aircraft have made naval combat distant

'The Battle of Trafalgar, the fall of Nelson' by Denis Dighton. 'This was a busy time for us, for we had not only to endeavour to repair our damage, but to keep to our duty. Often during the battle we could not see for the smoke whether we were firing at a foe or friend, and as to hearing, the noise of the guns had so completely made us deaf, that we were obliged to look only to the motions that were made.' Seaman William Robinson, HMS *Revenge*. (National Maritime Museum, Greenwich BHC0552)

and impersonal. Hand-to-hand-fighting has become a thing of the past.[37]

Industrial age weaponry had a new destructive effect, even against industrial age vessels, which was different in kind and degree from what had gone before. It is credibly argued that sailing ship gunnery at the height of the Nelsonian era was essentially personnel-killing in its effect.[38] Wooden warships were difficult to sink by gunfire, although on occasion they could burn and explode (like the French *L'Orient* at the Nile). As Nicholas Tracy has observed, 'Nelson's tactics always emphasised the importance of using overwhelming concentration of power to destroy enemy morale and gun-deck organisation'.[39] While the fact remains that a sailing ship's morale was not readily broken by gunfire, it was physical damage and significant loss of life, rather than wholesale destruction of the platform, which usually disabled the ship as a weapons system. Twentieth-century weaponry enabled tactics which were primarily platform-killing through destruction and sinking. As a consequence, while human beings were not the major target, they could become casualties in new orders of magnitude, even when we allow for more sailors manning bigger ships. *Bismarck*'s destruction of HMS *Hood* in 1941, with just three survivors out of 1419 men,[40] is an extreme but not isolated example. Ronald Spector writes of 'a special horror in the kind of instantaneous mass death' which naval battle could now produce.[41] This would appear to be the major reason for the decline of surrender in modern naval warfare. Such niceties were essentially alien to the desire for total destruction at a distance.

General conditions of sea service had improved significantly by the beginning of the twentieth century and continued to do so over the next hundred years, even—as Guy Griffiths observes—between the 1940s and the 1960s.[42] Harsh corporal punishments, poor nutrition and primitive medical care were progressively eclipsed by social and democratic progress and better scientific knowledge. But while the sea remained an inherently dangerous place in the face of the elements and the enemy, there was one way in which it was more so by 1945. More sophisticated naval technology did not necessarily mean greater safety. The munitions, machinery and fuel which were part and parcel of modern warships increased the threat of deadly accidents in an unforgiving metallic world. More than 200 USN sailors died in just three such incidents in the late 1960s.[43]

Changes in the face of naval battle, largely driven by new technology, had thus created an even more destructive and dangerous environment at sea by the mid-twentieth century. The age of sail, however, has left its legacy. Key elements of the experience of naval warfare have hardly changed since the days of Nelson, even in the era of missile warfare. Leadership at various levels, including the sharing of risks by commanders, has remained essential to victory at sea in terms both of competence and effect on morale. Nelson was famous for the inspirational effect of his presence within a ship or a fleet. A seaman who fought at Trafalgar reflected: 'in fighting under him, every man thought himself sure of success'.[44] Great naval leaders of the 1940s such as Cunningham and the Australian Hec Waller, who made his name as a destroyer commander in the Mediterranean, were fighting sailors who led from the front, had a rapport with the men under them and communicated their confidence.[45] Beyond fleet and unit command, lower-level leadership has also been vital for operational success, as it was on the gun decks in the age of sail. Ronald Spector sees this as the critical leadership link in twentieth-century naval warfare.[46]

Human response to leadership is a component of human reaction to danger. In the potentially lethal environment of a modern warship in battle, often marked—as in earlier times—by material and human destruction, the same essential factors have kept sailors working their ships and operating their weapons: confidence in their leaders, small group dynamics, training and tradition, the discipline of having to perform tasks, the lack of a place of retreat and sheer physical courage. For such reasons the warship's morale is still relatively immune to enemy fire. The more protracted tasks of convoy escort, blockade and the exercise of sea control are still, as under sail, complex, demanding and arduous. Finally, there is the sea itself, liable to induce sickness and always demanding respect for its ability to act with violence. Even in the moment of victory, in the hour of his death, the prospect of a gale was high in Nelson's thoughts.[47] In such ways the face of naval battle has remained unaltered by time.

SURFACE WARSHIP WARRIORS

The crews of modern surface warships, descendants of the tars who manned the sailing line of battle ships, have never ceased to be at the sharp end of naval warfare.[48] What have been the salient features of their experience of naval battle?

As twentieth-century warships, seeking battle, approached for action, rising anticipation among their crews accompanied efforts to locate the enemy. The spectacle of fleets in movement could be memorable. Guy Griffiths, remembering the *Bismarck* chase, recalls it as an inspiring sight.[49] In the era before radar it was sharp-eyed lookouts who established contact.[50] Reflective men had, by this time, pondered their mortality and sought to come to terms with their lives, as Peter Overlack tells us Von Spee did before the Battle of Coronel.[51] Immediately before action, from Jutland in 1916 to the Falklands in 1982, there was palpable tension, deep fear and general attempts by men to mask the appearance of being afraid.[52] Admiral Sir John 'Sandy' Woodward wrote how each man has a different way of dealing with fear.[53] The expectation of probably being hit—as for the crew of *Ardent*, sent into Falkland Sound to draw fire—was terrifying.[54] For many sailors action was an unknown quantity as they awaited their baptism of fire.

Aboard a warship in action there are two worlds: above and below the deck. Each has its particular dangers and terrors. The visibility of air attacks to US sailors at Guadalcanal increased their sense of vulnerability.[55] Conversely, below the deck, it could be stressful being unable to see the action or know what was going on. This was the case in the Falklands as it had been, as Bruce Elleman observes, almost a century earlier.[56]

While men on the upperworks of a ship in action were directly exposed to enemy fire, those below decks and in the engine room could also suffer its effects in frightful ways—explosions in confined spaces, smoke, soaring temperatures and incoming water.[57] Engine-room spaces in a modern surface combatant can straddle the water line and be hit by missile or torpedo.[58] The noise of a naval action during the Second World War, when heard below decks, could be colossal and a cause of nervous breakdown. As Gordon Johnson recalls: 'There was the screaming whine of the ship's turbines, the blast of our guns, and Japanese bombs exploding, the latter like having your head in a 44 gallon drum while someone hits it with a sledgehammer'.[59]

Physically detached from the enemy, however, sailors in action have usually continued to work the ship. Such work is an antidote to panic and helps denial that the worst will happen.[60] Indeed, not having a job in a ship, for example, as a rescued survivor of another, can induce a sense of helplessness.[61] There have been remarkable examples of coolness aboard warships in action. A Royal Naval pilot above Falkland Sound spoke to the operations room of a ship below: 'I said: "What do you mean, wait?" He said: "Well, we've just had our ops room strafed with gunfire, with 30mm cannon. The man across the desk from me has lost the top of his head and I've been hit in the arm and I'm just collecting myself." '.[62] Commitment to the task in hand has largely derived from the realisation that it is a matter of 'kill or be killed'.[63] There can also be a fatalism about death, an acceptance that it may come regardless, which frees the mind for the job. 'You just become fatalistic. If a bullet's got your name on it, that's it.'[64]

Water is a better conductor of physical shock than air.[65] It is the combination of heavy artillery, bombs, torpedoes and missiles with such explosive potential which has made war at sea so awesomely destructive within the confined areas in which sailors serve. While some such as Vice Admiral Sir John Collins could be nostalgic for the old surface gun actions, for the era before submarines and aircraft threatened warships, the decks and spaces of the ships at Tsushima and Jutland could still become killing zones.[66] As Michael Dowsett relates, the sight of the *Emden* in 1914 was a shocking example of the state of a defeated ship in a gun action.[67]

ATTACK FROM THE AIR

The advent of massed air attacks at sea, sustainable for days, created environments on surface ships which were hellish in their lethality and psychological pressure. There was no safe place, for example, on a target carrier in the Pacific War.[68] The British carrier HMS *Illustrious*, caught by three dozen Stukas off Italy in 1941, was a picture of what large warships could suffer before the development of carrier task groups which could deal with land-based air forces.[69] There was noise, damage and destruction (both human and material), flooding and fire, burning fuel and exploding ammunition. The devastating effect of projectiles in enclosed spaces was an echo of the age of sail. Everywhere the metal of the ship was hot, with the engineering spaces reaching 140° Fahrenheit.[70] The ship survived. A comparable fate befell HMS *Ardent* in the Falklands: bombed and engulfed in fire and smoke. A Royal Naval surgeon watched from a helicopter: 'It's a sight I shall never forget. The fires of hell were burning in that ship'.[71] The ship was lost.

The evacuation of Crete in 1941 is probably the most dramatic case study of the effects of maritime strike against ships lacking air cover and adequate air defence. Cunningham's fleet suffered terrible losses while evacuating Allied personnel. One sailor became a casualty for every eight troops evacuated, 90 per cent of the naval casualties being deaths. Three cruisers and six destroyers were sunk, and two battleships, an aircraft

Japanese air attack in the Solomons, August 1942. '*Canberra* opened fire first and soon she appeared to be a ball of fire from her own gun flashes. As our tornado of fire burst amongst the Japs they seemed to shake their wings as if flipping water from their backs as they swooped down to torpedo range. It was a thrill, those roaring demons screeching closer with the seconds.' Yeoman Cec E. Price, USN, USS *Hovey*. (RAN)

carrier, two cruisers and two destroyers badly damaged.[72] The cruiser HMS *Orion*, which survived, had a bomb pass through her bridge and explode in the 4-inch magazine, causing 500 casualties among sailors and soldiers. The air attacks on the Mediterranean Fleet could be truly terrifying. While the first experience for a sailor could be shocking, second and subsequent episodes were dreaded in advance. The cumulative effect on an individual could be nervous exhaustion or breakdown. Simultaneously there could be extraordinary examples of gallantry. During the Crete evacuation, an Australian seaman, Ian Rhodes, carried on firing at a Stuka and shot it down as his ship HMS *Kashmir* sank.[73]

A further version of the terror of the air threat appeared in the form of the *kamikaze* in the Pacific War. According to an American sailor, the destroyer battle stations at Okinawa were 'as close to Hell as a man could get in this world'.[74] A later variation came in the shape of the anti-ship missile. Few individuals have witnessed a missile fired in anger approaching a ship. A Royal Naval officer in the Falklands found the experience mesmerising:

> They don't shoot Exocets at you in training . . . You don't actually see them coming head-on . . . I was transfixed by the missile coming at us . . . It was a sense of awesome power coming towards you . . . quite incredible. For ages afterwards I closed my eyes and that's all I could see, that sort of imprint on my mind.[75]

The missile, fired at the short range of twelve miles and travelling at 680 miles per hour, took a minute to reach the picket destroyer HMS *Sheffield*, which had shut down its electronic support measures—and hence part of its missile radar detection capability—to transmit communications by satellite. The only detection was visual, at less than a mile, with no time to fire decoys. The missile approached by the starboard bow and struck amidships without exploding. The impact ignited the missile's fuel, triggering an intense fire which caused dozens of casualties and the abandonment of the ship, which sank several days later.[76]

ATTACK FROM BENEATH THE SEA

As well as the drama of gun actions and the shocks of air attack, there was the protracted threat posed by submarines for escort crews and particularly for merchant seamen. Here was a whole dimension of naval battle which during the Second World War, for months and years, eroded and tested the endurance of surface sailors. Many merchant officers detested the physical strain of watch-keeping and convoy station-keeping.[77] This was combined with the anticipation of the unseen arrival of a U-boat wolf-pack, likely to attack at night and create a random wave of explosions, fires and sinkings. Escort and merchant crews were often expected to undertake a return voyage and relive the experience within a matter of days or weeks. There is no mystery in the inclination of naval personnel to relieve the stress with high living in ports such as Derry.[78] The most famous British submarine-killer of the War, Captain F.J. Walker, died in 1944 of 'overstrain, overwork and war weariness'.[79] Frank Layard, as Michael Whitby's human portrait shows, was in the same tradition. His willpower as an escort commander in the face of his own anxiety, stress and middle age was a sustained act of courage which symbolised the commitment of a generation to duty and the victory of their cause.[80]

The courage of merchant seamen, whose ships were the prime target of submarine warfare, was one of the human phenomena of the War. British Merchant Naval morale held up in the face of a higher proportional casualty rate than in any of the uniformed services. Merchant seamen received 6000 awards for gallantry.[81] Herein lies one illustration of the significance of the George Cross and George Medal as recognition for gallantry.[82]

JOINT OPERATIONS

All naval warfare is in a true sense 'joint', given the fundamental nature of the land–sea interface and its reinforcement by the coming of air power. But amphibious or joint operations in the more particular sense have a history as old as sea power. While the conduct of such operations has become more professional over time, modern historical experience has found them to be various, complex, difficult and often highly dangerous to all involved.

At one end of the operational spectrum, sailors have been at the lethal end of power projection against the land. The first Australian servicemen to die in action in the First World War were sailors, killed in the attack on the wireless station at Rabaul in 1914.[83] At the other end of the spectrum, navies have evacuated armies from land to sea. To evacuate a defeated land force under fire is surely one of the most difficult operations conceivable for a navy. Crete, as already mentioned, is a case in point. At Dunkirk the task was facilitated by the transfer of moral authority from ship to shore. Naval officers organised the beaches in the face of loss of cohesion and discipline among the troops. Neither destroyer crews nor soldiers, however, were practised at the work involved and initial progress was slow. German air and S-boat attacks caused ships, sailors and troops to be lost, but the operation turned into a remarkable success.[84]

Such joint operations required luck, mainly in relation to the weather. The 'miracle' of Dunkirk was the calm weather and water, together with helpful cloud cover.[85] Similar luck attended the British in the Falklands, with thick mist covering their main landing at San Carlos.[86] It was also human factors such as leadership, experience and specialist knowledge which brought success in such complex enterprises. Vice Admiral Bertram Ramsay's achievements at Dunkirk and on the naval side of the Normandy landings were based on his people skills, flexibility, improvisation and moral courage.[87] John Collins recalled the way in which the Allied landings in the South West Pacific created a pattern, one clearly honed by experience.[88] Specialist knowledge was invaluable in the Falklands, for example, when a Royal Marine officer, Ewen Southby-Tailyour, could share his expert knowledge of the coastline with planners and guide in the main landing force.[89] The cultural gap between military services, in terms of language and procedures, has been one of the hazards of joint operations.[90] This underlines Russell Parkin's point that such operations require specialist and cooperative training.[91] Such training should be predicated on the awareness that all involved are literally in the same boat. Historically this awareness has been too rare, coming *in extremis* and out of the experience of being under fire. 'Thank God we've got a Navy' said a British soldier to a sailor at Dunkirk.[92] A wounded Australian digger taken out of Tobruk aboard the destroyer *Vendetta* used similar words: 'Thank God for the Navy'.[93]

WORKING A SHIP

Working a ship at sea is a continuous task whether in action or not. Maintaining and sailing a warship has always required high levels of efficiency and commitment from its crew. As industrial age vessels and weapons evolved, sailors increasingly became skilled tradesmen who could not perform their tasks mindlessly. Boredom and fatigue are perennial pitfalls of life at sea. During the Pacific War (and other operations in the Asia-Pacific region) these dangers were compounded by heat and the travelling of vast distances. Such factors not only made the technical tasks of naval seamanship more difficult, but could be a threat to physical safety and military security and had to be guarded against.[94] Living conditions aboard ship gradually improved, but on smaller ships during the early twentieth century they could be hellish. The *Flower* class corvettes, made famous in the Battle of the Atlantic, lacked space, ventilation, adequate sanitation and protection from the elements.[95] Over the last generation, soldiers have often been impressed by the quality of life afloat. The war correspondent Sir Max Hastings visited British ships in the Falklands:

> Throughout the war, it was always an odd experience to pass from the primitive, muddy bivouacs of the men ashore into a warship cabin, decorated with books and family photographs, [and] tiny personal comforts . . .[96]

Such relative comfort, however, was no protection from the reality of war. One Royal Naval officer, having been evacuated from HMS *Sheffield* after the missile strike, was in the wardroom shower aboard another ship when the air raid warning sounded.[97]

Whatever the level or lack of danger or discomfort, ships have personalities essentially created by their captains and crews. Cunningham appreciated a very positive spirit aboard the light cruiser HMAS *Sydney* during the war in the Mediterranean.[98] A satisfactory living and working atmosphere aboard a warship derives ultimately from the mutual respect which is generated by performance of skilled and interdependent tasks.

SUNKEN SHIPS, LOST SAILORS AND SURVIVORS

Three likely fates generally befell ships sunk during the Second World War and their crews. A vessel might be destroyed instantaneously, with almost no chance of survival. As we have seen, the battlecruiser *Hood*, sunk by *Bismarck*, had virtually no survivors. Fatal damage might swiftly sink a ship but allow a significant survival rate. British destroyers bombed in the Mediterranean could sink in two minutes, or even less, although half the crew could survive. Otherwise a ship might sink relatively slowly, allowing what was usually an orderly abandonment such as Guy Griffiths recalls of HMS *Repulse*, sunk by Japanese aircraft off Malaya.[99] Meredith Dewey, a naval chaplain aboard the British cruiser HMS *Effingham*, related the very orderly and good-humoured abandonment of the ship off Norway in 1940. He had time to pack his suitcase, retrieve comforts for the troops and save the ship's communion plate.[100]

The maritime tradition was that the captain went down with a sinking ship, although how many did so by accident or design is unclear.[101] We can assume that many captains were lost immediately due to destruction of ships' bridges or swift sinkings. Others surely went down unintentionally: still fighting, trying to save the ship, or waiting for others to get off. Others were warriors willing to share the fate of their command. Hec Waller, lost aboard the cruiser HMAS *Perth* while engaging superior Japanese forces in the Sunda Strait in 1942, was probably in this category. Historically, sailors, and especially captains, have bonded with their ships and felt emotional loss when they have been sunk. A warship is a shared home in a hostile environment, a thing of professional pride and a symbol of national power. Few captains have been able to live at ease after losing their ships in action.

Having survived a sinking, sailors in the water were exposed to many new dangers. At Jutland, the fate of those floating could be grim: burns or injury could cause death or hasten drowning; men could be minced in passing ships' propellers or drowned in their wakes; and shells exploding in the water could kill swimmers.[102] Much of the evidence for experiences in life boats or rafts comes from the stories of merchant seamen in the Second World War. The chances of survival in such circumstances were generally good, and morale and cooperation were apparently the critical factors. Bad seas such as those of the North Atlantic were always a threat and could overturn small craft. Death, when it came in boats or rafts, came slowly and could involve mental as well as physical disintegration and collapse.[103] Cold and exposure—such as affected Argentinian survivors of the *Belgrano* sinking in 1982, drifting in sub-Antarctic waters—could still bring on heart failure even when modern survival clothing was worn.[104]

NAVAL WARRIORS IN NEW DIMENSIONS

Submariners

Sailors fought in two new dimensions as the twentieth century progressed—first below then above the sea—and the face of naval battle acquired new aspects.

Undersea life and warfare had particular and unique elements. Within the confines of submarines, there was of necessity a heightened informality and familiarity. U-boat captain Peter Cremer took care to select men who were natural team players.[105] Submarine work required considerable calmness and teamwork.[106] Even without the enemy it was a highly dangerous environment. Collective survival depended upon each individual performing every detail of his duty, which created close bonds among the crews of boats. Such bonds were one of the factors which sustained German U-boat morale during the 1940s despite a casualty rate of almost 70 per cent.[107] For such reasons, submariners have always considered themselves an elite.

Submarine life was and is conditioned by harsh physical facts. Internally, boats are essentially designed as engineering systems, almost completely occupied by weapons and machinery.[108] Such cramped quarters are not natural living spaces for human beings. Externally, the ominous weight of the sea itself can flood or crush the boat with no real prospect of human escape. Submariners recalling the interior of boats remember the smell—always one of the most evocative senses for human memory. Peter Cremer wrote of 'the characteristic U-boat fug: the stink of diesel oil mixed with cooking smells, the exhalations of fusty clothing and stale air'.[109]

Men also remembered the exhaustion they felt after actions and extended patrols. Cremer recalled the effects of a transatlantic patrol on the crew of his *U-333*. There had been lack of sunlight and fresh air,

> the tiring bridge watch in the wet and cold, the confined work around the diesels and electric motors, lack of oxygen when submerged, the lack of exercise and loss of appetite which occurred despite every culinary art, all this made extreme physical demands. Add to this the interminable depth-charge attacks to which we had been helplessly exposed when submerged, and even the strongest men emerged exhausted.[110]

In action submariners were the hunters, seeking to strike before their quarry could scatter and often exalting at their kills. But they could quickly become the hunted, working in the dark of a damaged boat and suffering the enormous tension of being under attack from the surface.[111] David Jones relates how in action a boat's crew had to remain in ignorance of what was happening.[112] A submarine could also be engaged in traditional combat on the surface. Peter Cremer remembered the horrors of a duel with a corvette in the Atlantic in 1942. Gun and shellfire riddled his conning tower and he suffered multiple wounds, surviving serious loss of blood and makeshift surgery, performed without anaesthesia by his unqualified chief engineer.[113] Lack of onboard medical facilities was a feature of early twentieth-century submarine life.

Naval aviators

Naval pilots and aircrew operating in the maritime environment faced a variety of challenges and dangers. Many of these were unique in naval warfare, deriving essentially from operating in a platform separate from a ship. Naval aviators could be involved in a variety of types of mission, principally combat air patrols, air combat, maritime strike, land attack, transport and evacuation. They could have the responsibility of defending or attacking capital ships such as carriers, as well as having to deal with the complications of operating over sea, land and enemy territory. They faced a threefold threat from the hazards of flying, the action of the enemy and the danger of the sea.

Naval air warfare put a premium on the human factor in the form of pilots, crews and their intimate control of their aircraft. What manner of men were they? Naval aviators were essentially volunteers, kept flying by group bonding, the lure of adventure and the challenge of flying off carriers. David Hobbs writes of how naval flying, with all its complications, required a particular kind of courage and 'can do' attitude.[114] Beyond the endurance and discipline needed to deal with the boredom of long maritime patrols, the qualities needed of a naval aviator were—above all—absolute nerve and confidence. In the words of a Falklands veteran, 'There cannot be the slightest element of self doubt when you are flying combat missions'.[115] Naval aviators could die or have friends die in training, but could not afford to think about it. During the Second World War flyers could anticipate heavy casualties. Fifty per cent losses were expected in the attack on Taranto in 1940,[116] but aviators had to deny death and carry on, aided by peer group pressure.[117] This kind of stoicism brought out their respect for the courage of enemy pilots.[118]

With their resolve in the face of danger, high degree of individualism and critical job of fleet defence, aviators became heroes and team champions among carrier crews. Japanese sailors applauded their pilots as they downed the first wave of American torpedo planes at Midway in 1942, in Walter Lord's phrase 'like a theater audience watching a superbly skillful performance'.[119] Conversely, flyers depended on carrier crews for all their support functions. Engineers and ordnance handlers performed arduous tasks for long hours, working under pressure amidst machinery and live explosives.[120] Aviators bonded with the ships and crews who needed their protection.[121]

Aviators faced awesome experiences in action. In air-to-air combat, although not seeing their enemy face to face, they were seeking to kill in an individual way unusual in naval battle. A British carrier pilot in the Falklands recalled the fear of real combat, with the need to kill or be killed: a need one could not anticipate in training. There was universal fear and the sense of the inevitability of death.[122]

'Plotting Room, HMAS *Nepal*' by J. Goodchild, 1945. 'To the men in radar plot, an air battle forty or fifty miles away was as personal a problem as one directly overhead; and, although tension mounted as raids came closer, there was always tension . . . they had to calculate risks, make instant decisions, and take immediate action on information that was often incomplete.' Lieutenant (j.g.) J. Monsarrat, USN, USS *Langley*. (AWM ART 22782)

Pilots who attacked surface targets, however, give more of an impression of professional detachment, of performing a mechanical task. This probably relates to their having significantly more mobility than their targets and to their becoming in a sense their own weapon. But such experiences could be alarming. Australia's Admiral Sir Victor Smith recalled leading the torpedo attack on the *Scharnhorst* early in the Second World War, flying Swordfish aircraft off the coast of Norway:

> . . . a rather frightening experience but on the other hand in a situation like that there is no option and you have to press on. I think that that probably sums it up. It is very alarming when you are on a committed course heading towards the target . . . you are in some respects a sitting duck. That does not make life very pleasant.[123]

Attacks on moored ships, as at Taranto or Pearl Harbor, could be similarly hair-raising. A pilot required great skill to manoeuvre his aircraft as a delivery system, precision to hit particular targets in particular ways and raw courage to fly into enemy fire without being distracted. Besides the risk of being shot down there was the danger of misjudgement and crashing.[124] Sometimes the elation of the attack and the ruthless commitment to achieving a kill could cause indifference to one's own fate. An American divebomber pilot, having scored a direct hit on a Japanese carrier at Midway, found himself not caring when he seemed likely to crash while returning to the USS *Yorktown*. He survived.[125] After action, aircrews had the problem of locating their ship: a small speck in the vastness of the sea. The relief at finding the carrier was coupled with the challenge of a deck landing before one was 'home again'.[126]

Casualties among aviators could be very high. They were almost 100 per cent among the first American strike wave at Midway. Besides falling foul of enemy fire, aircraft could run out of fuel, often over the sea. The fuel factor therefore weighed heavily on the minds of aircrew. The US Navy flyers sent to find the Japanese carriers in the Philippine Sea knew they had insufficient fuel to return safely to their ships. To press on with their mission took formidable courage and some men were lost at sea.[127] Aviators ditching at sea or shot down over land could be taken prisoner. Not all were as fortunate as Sub-Lieutenant MacMillan and his observer Chief Petty Officer Hancox, two RAN flyers forced down in Korea and rescued from the air while under fire.[128] In the face of the multi-plicity of risks, however, many naval aviators were still inspired by the experience of flying: by its beauty, skill and exhilaration, all epitomised by a perfect deck landing.[129]

NAVAL COMMAND

While aspects of command are common to the various dimensions of war, certain factors have been unique to naval warfare or had heightened importance within it. Warships—as instruments of graduated force and as national symbols—have long had very significant diplomatic use. In peace and war the naval commander has often had to be a diplomat, in the tradition of officers such as Nelson, Perry and Cunningham.[130] In action he has had considerable and sobering responsibilities, in command of an expensive strategic platform and set of capabilities as well as of its crew. The penalty for failure is peremptory: the loss of the ship, which cannot be rallied like a broken infantry battalion. A natural pitfall of naval command has therefore been operational conservatism, and protection of a fleet or vessel at the expense of its use. Overcom-ing this inhibition is critical, and the best naval commanders have therefore been known for their remarkable degree of aggression. Much of Nelson's legacy boils down to the example of his ruthless desire to shock and annihilate the enemy.

There have been further complications for command at the unit and fleet level: the need to deal with people as well as technology (there is a certain parallel here with the air forces); the problem of both navigating and using a highly mobile weapons system, usually simultaneously; the need for individual initiative while being highly (and increasingly) integrated within a larger force; the need to consider often vast geographical areas; the need to comprehend the interrelationship of increasingly diverse vessel types; the imperative of increasingly rapid decision-making in battle in the context of technological change; and all this while being mindful of the need for inter-service cooperation and understanding— a fundamental consideration for a force which operates primarily as a critical enabler.

There is also the physical positioning of the naval commander. Radio made shore command feasible at the higher strategic level, as practised successfully by Ramsay at Dover (during Dunkirk), Horton at Liverpool (in the Atlantic)[131] and Nimitz in Hawaii (during the Pacific War). Such positioning, however, was not generally a feature of modern naval warfare. The fleet commander has usually had the advantages (often difficult to combine in command on land) of a frontline view and full communications at his disposal, enabling greater directness of control.[132] The necessary price is the regular presence of high-ranking naval commanders in the combat zone. Von Spee, like many senior naval commanders, died a warrior's death in battle.[133] Collins was severely wounded when a *kamikaze* struck the bridge of the cruiser HMAS *Australia* at Leyte in 1944.[134] Sustained physical courage has remained a prerequisite, and in this little has changed since the days of Nelson.

Locating enemy vessels at sea, at the strategic level, places a premium on intelligence. The ability to use it flexibly, as Cunningham did before Matapan,[135] could be vital. In seeking to make contact with the enemy at the operational level, initiative could be a cardinal virtue as Andrew Gordon makes clear.[136] It was at this level that the British Grand Fleet arguably failed at Jutland.[137] At this level also, the advent of air reconnaissance and radar were breakthroughs, before which commanders had to rely solely upon eyesight at surface level. Conditions at sea can deceive the untrained eye, so experience was essential and good vision (like Cunningham's) a great asset.[138] Having placed the enemy, aggression was the key. One of Cunningham's staff officers wrote of his usual behaviour in the presence of the enemy:

ABC's burning desire to get at them and utterly destroy them would at once become evident . . . He would pace one side of the Admiral's bridge, always the side nearest the enemy; the speed of advance of the battleship was never fast enough for him . . . This mood was known colloquially among the staff as the 'caged tiger act' . . . It was always, for all beholders, an inspiring example of single-minded concentration on the one object of getting to close grips with the enemy.[139]

As Wayne Hughes concludes: 'The tactical maxim of all naval battles is *Attack effectively first*'.[140] At every point in the progression, from contemplating action to seeking out and engaging the enemy, the value of initiative and flexibility—and the need to encourage them—is demonstrated by history. Cunningham's brief verbal instructions to Collins in 1940, when he left Alexandria before winning the victory at Cape Spada, contrast somewhat with the 70 printed pages of operational instructions issued by Jellicoe to the Grand Fleet during the First World War.[141]

Fatigue and stress have always taken their toll on naval commanders, whether as a result of the intensity of fleet chases and engagements, the protracted strain of convoy duties and blockades, or simply the pressure of great responsibilities while commanding ashore. After a period of less than a year which saw Nelson's starring role in the victory at Cape St Vincent, the defeat at Tenerife and the loss of his arm, and his unfinished search for Napoleon's expeditionary force in the Mediterranean, he wrote in 1798 of the vulnerability of 'my too irritable nerves'.[142] Nimitz was depressed and suffered insomnia for several months after assuming command in the Pacific.[143] After six months of continuous combat duty, Halsey was hospitalised with shingles in 1942.[144] Walker's death in 1944, after years of strain, has already been mentioned.

In order to mitigate the cumulative effects of sea-riding, loneliness, complex decision-making and danger upon a middle-aged commander, it was necessary to have strengths and consolations. Nelson had a religious sense of duty, extraordinary physical and moral courage, and many people (including the women in his life) whom he loved.[145] Cunningham had great energy and stamina, ruthlessness, incurable optimism and an infectious sense of humour, although even he would be mentally drained after six years of war.[146] Ramsay had an admirable ability to delegate and rest, even in the midst of national crisis.[147] Nimitz tossed horseshoes, listened to classical music, walked and swam, had dinners at which shop-talk was banned and delegated anything with which anyone else could deal.[148] Keeping a written confessional in the form of a diary or correspondence proved an effective solace for naval commanders at various levels, as the cases of Von Spee, Layard and Woodward all attest.[149] Of all aspects of naval command, it is stress and fatigue which most closely resemble the effects of war in other environments.

In addition to preserving his own morale, the naval commander must sustain that of others. Like other military commanders he must be an actor, a therapist and a communicator. Cunningham was famous as a booster of the tired or defeated, filling his house with them. One of his destroyer commanders recalled being made to lie on the floor after dinner and throw ping-pong balls into the light shade: 'I wrote home to my family saying I felt certain we would win the war'.[150] At sea, however, there are more unique aspects of inspirational naval command. For example, within the limited confines of a vessel it is feasible to keep crews informed of developments.[151] With the assistance of modern internal broadcast systems this became practicable even aboard large vessels in the midst of action. People perform better when they are aware of the place of their work in the wider picture.

More broadly, commanders at sea (at least at the level of unit command) have a scope and a need for interaction with their crews suggesting a contrast with war on land. Navies are relatively small human communities with fewer subordinates to know, brief and sustain. Their working spaces are more confined and their command atmosphere necessarily more relaxed than those of armies. For such reasons individual ships have personalities in a way infantry battalions do not. While naval commanders have not always been approachable or humane, they have had to interact with their people and set the tone in immediate and personal ways. On joining an escort vessel in the Atlantic in 1941, Michael Thwaites found himself well satisfied with his captain and quickly deduced that they would have a happy wardroom, and hence probably a happy ship.[152] Even at fleet level, Woodward in the Falklands had confidence in his picket destroyer captains whom he knew personally and well. He spoke to them frequently, which boosted their morale (and his).[153]

THE FACES OF NAVAL, LAND AND AIR BATTLE COMPARED

We can notice immediate similarities between battle experience at sea, on land and in the air. Sailors, soldiers and airmen are all vulnerable to the effects of climate and weather. All are required to deal with their fear in battle and to function amidst the din and confusion of combat; all must sometimes face the need to kill or be killed; and all can be surrounded by the bodies of the dead and wounded. A soldier in a tank, like his compatriots in naval vessels and aircraft, is vulnerable as part of a weapons system which can be targeted as a whole. Above all, serving personnel in each environment are motivated by similar small group dynamics: the bonding based upon mutual confidence in the face of danger, as well as the individual's fear of appearing before his peers to have been disabled by fear itself.

Naval and land battle

There are, however, factors distinguishing the experience of sailors from that of soldiers. Sailors are not treated as beasts of burden, as has been the lot of soldiers through the ages. Unlike soldiers they do not suffer the exhaustion of marches, nor the same effects of hunger and thirst.[154] A fundamental point is that their attitude towards the enemy and to combat is necessarily different. Armies are trained to engage with human enemies which, even in counter-terrorism, have a human face.[155] While recognisable as an animated being, that enemy must also be depersonalised to legitimate the act of individual killing, which can occur in face-to-face combat.[156] As (then) Major Chris Keeble of the 2nd Battalion, the Parachute Regiment, described the battle at Goose Green in the Falklands: 'You close up towards the trenches. You throw grenades, you fire your weapon, you bayonet. It's savage gutter fighting. Everything you've ever experienced before is nothing like it. It is basic killing.'[157] History suggests that, despite its horror, human beings can positively embrace licensed face-to-face killing.[158] In modern warfare distance and chaos can blur this individual violence but still allow great technical satisfaction, and the act of killing for the first time can still be a major personal event.[159]

This kind of experience is alien to modern battle at sea, where even in combat between ships and piloted aircraft there is detachment. A British ship's captain in the Falklands said of Argentinian air attacks:

> At that stage I didn't think about the pilots who were bombing me. As far as I was concerned they were aircraft that were trying to hit my ship and it was very much a military action to try and shoot those aeroplanes down. I didn't think of it in personal terms at all. That's one of the things about being in the navy. It's not quite as personalised as jumping into a trench with someone and trying to kill him.[160]

Sailors, by extension, do not generally suffer the stress felt by soldiers under bombardment when they cannot act or reply, since they can usually do one or both, although there can be a significant exception in the case of a submarine suffering a depth-charge attack.[161]

Ships in action become targets in terms of the capabilities they possess and the areas they command, not the ground they hold. The basic reason for the fierce discipline to which soldiers are subject is the need to overcome the human instinct to fly from danger and, in the military sense, to hold ground. When this discipline is threatened under fire, troops can bunch, panic, be paralysed, or run.[162] Sailors—confined, preoccupied, often having to fight or die and with nowhere to run—comparatively rarely succumb to panic or breakdown.[163] Similarly, combat refusal does not generally occur at sea on any scale, nor does the sailor seek or rejoice in a 'Blighty' wound which will take him to safety for he remains in the battle line.

These distinguishing features of naval battle derive from the hostile environment of the sea. Within it, aboard the vessels themselves, there is an intensely human atmosphere for they are without many animals (horses, by contrast, being long-standing elements of war on land).[164] At the same time, while civilians—especially merchant seamen—suffered grievously from the U-boat campaigns, this human world afloat has been generally spared their presence. Almost as much as in the desert of North Africa, trauma is lessened in naval warfare by not having to witness the mass suffering of non-combatants.[165] Compassion is exhausted faster than courage. Naval warfare is marked by the essentially singular interaction of professional military personnel with 'the cruel sea'.[166] This interaction occurs continuously and has a life of its own, regardless of the state of military operations.

The sea has an undeniable romance and natural wonder. Many have written of the brilliant, myriad aspects of its beauty. In the words of a long-serving naval officer: 'over my years at sea I have seen God's creation in all its splendour and in all its fearful power'.[167] Respect for that power is ingrained in those who have seen hurricanes, fogs, icy decks, freezing waters and high seas which can sweep men overboard into darkness.

The sea is more powerful than war. Atlantic weather could stop U-boat operations, forcing boats to submerge 50 metres to be still.[168] Such weather was more often the enemy for escort crews than was the *Kriegsmarine*. Allied sailors had frequently to alternate between fighting the waters and fighting the U-boats without rest.[169] Most sailors, wrote Admiral Sandy Woodward, are superstitious: surely a consequence of living in the presence of the power of the sea.[170] (Sailors often speak of their belief in luck and lucky ships, and Collins even entitled his autobiography *As Luck Would Have It*.)[171] The enterprise of going to sea thus creates a perceptible bond between sailors, as David Stevens relates.[172]

This can cause understanding between navies often to be better than between compatriot navies and armies.[173] This bond very often survives combat between navies at sea. While examples of chivalry in land warfare are far from unknown, such cases exist in abundance in naval history. Examples include Captain Glossop's care for the wounded of the defeated *Emden* in 1914 and Collins' rescuing of the survivors of the Italian destroyer *Espero* in 1940 at the risk of his own ship.[174] Even amidst the total war of the Battle of the Atlantic, the captain of a Norwegian vessel torpedoed by Cremer's *U-333* recalled the U-boat commander's very humane attitude towards his opponents: 'He behaved according to the code of seamen who take no oath on it but know: help one another when in trouble at sea!'.[175] Naval warfare is unique in having a third participant, one which is always neutral—the cruel sea, which answers to no human being.

Naval and air battle

There have been obvious similarities between the battle experience of naval aviators and that of operational air force personnel. As in naval aviation, there is no air force flying career free of the life-threatening danger of accidents in training and war.[176] Those pilots who fly fighter aircraft are attracted to flying as an adventure. They function in a form of war in which the fighter is dependent upon his base support and faces the intense, highly skilled and individualistic nature of fighter combat, with the need to kill or be killed. A fighter pilot has, ultimately, sole responsibility for his fate in the air.[177] Hence for fighter pilots of both services, lack of experience, fatigue and loss of nerve have all proved fatal.[178]

There are also similarities between the experiences of sailors in surface warships, submariners and air force aircrew. Aircrew, like sailors, have a dangerous environmental enemy: in their case, height. Flying, like seamanship, is itself a technical discipline on which a warfighting capability is built. War in the air, therefore, like war at sea, depends upon a critical interface between people and technology, and aircrew are part of a weapons system which, like ships, can be targeted as a whole. Like sailors they must deal with the dangers of machinery and explosive or combustible materials. There are also small group dynamics. Historically, bomber crews have been highly interdependent teams comparable to the crews of small ships. Sailors on warships, closed up at action stations, have resembled bomber crews in their aircraft approaching enemy territory.[179] Flying has been comparable to submarine service in that lives have depended upon complex engineering systems.[180] The painstaking style of operational flying and avoidance of unnecessary risk which were required for the survival of RAF Bomber Command crews during the Second World War are very similar to the discipline of submarine life.[181] Under attack, both platforms have often survived by retreating into their dimension. For a bomber, that was height, for a submarine, depth.

Like sailors, both bomber and fighter aircrew have been personally detached from the destruction and killing they have performed. A member of Bomber Command asked 'Was this fighting? There was no anger, no red lust, no struggle, no straining muscles and sobbing breath; only the slight movement of levers and the rattle of machine guns . . .'.[182] A member of RAF Fighter Command recalled: 'When you . . . [were] shooting at another aircraft it never occurred to you that there were people in it. It was an *aircraft* you were shooting at'.[183] In a famous passage describing his first kill in a Spitfire, Richard Hillary concluded: '[a fighter pilot] has none of the personalized emotions of the soldier, handed a rifle and bayonet and told to charge . . . The fighter pilot's emotions are those of the duellist—cool, precise, impersonal'.[184]

Similarly, when on the defensive their experiences have been comparable, particularly those of bomber and warship crews. Second World War bomber formations were like fleets in the days before radar, with lookouts whose ability to spot the enemy was a matter of life and death.[185] They were also like convoys, in which the sight of an aircraft being shot down could be observed from other platforms and be a reminder to their crews of their own vulnerability. In sinking ships, as in downed aircraft, loss of the platform meant instant mortal danger. Aircrew, indeed, could also end up ditched in the sea where they might die.

There have been, however, fundamental differences between naval and air war and their impact on human beings. Flying, as an adventure, is akin to going to sea in the combination of freedom, danger and technical challenge involved in emancipation from the earth. It is not, however, a way of life in the manner of going to sea for sustained periods, being continually isolated in the face of an awesome natural environment. Flights remain episodes and flying time is measured in hours, rather than days, weeks, months and, effectively, years, as is the case for sailors at sea. The essential conditioning factors of naval warfare therefore do not apply in the air. Aircraft are not homes as ships are, housing continuous and substantial human communities. Neither do they require the same kind of endurance on the part of their occupants to maintain them safely even in the midst of military operations.

This is no reflection on the historical courage of aircrews, who have been tested in different ways. That courage is underlined by a further factor—specifically in bomber forces—distinguishing war in the air from war at sea. Allied bomber forces during the Second World War apparently suffered heavier losses of personnel through stress induced by actual operations than navies. While psychological casualties were insufficiently understood (many RAF Bomber Command personnel being classified 'LMF' or 'Lacking Moral Fibre'), the concentrated strain to which aircrew were subject was undeniable, and the result was emotional carnage. While morale held up generally in Bomber Command, evidence suggests that approximately one man in seven was lost to operational flying 'for morale or medical causes'.[186] Several factors suggest themselves as joint causes of this high rate of attrition. There was the nightly terror of the battles in the skies over Germany; the daily disjunction between these and the peace of the English countryside; and the knowledge among aircrew that the statistical odds against their surviving a full tour of operations were formidable.[187] The cumulative effect on the bank account of individual courage, as Lord Moran put it, was ultimately to empty it in many cases, irrespective of any moral issue.[188] The closest naval comparison to this experience is the high casualty rate, over 65 per cent, among U–boat crews during the Second World War.[189] Generally speaking, however, the factors eroding bomber crew morale did not apply to naval warfare, despite high casualty rates in certain ships and operations and the horrors of various kinds of actions. While navies have suffered psychological casualties, tragic for the individuals concerned, the nature of naval battle has meant that this has not become a problem on such a devastating scale.

AT SEA, WAR ETERNAL

Despite the significant contrasts between war at sea and in other environments, the face of naval battle exhibits the eternal features of war in every age. They run the gamut of personal experience from the time of the sailor's departure for war to the aftermath of his return. There have always been professional warriors, such as Von Spee, who have looked forward to battle and seen it as glorious.[190] For others, going to war has held out the prospect of experiences frequently attractive to the young: a sense of purpose, responsibility, comradeship, physical fitness, travel and exotic sights.[191] Jim Calvert recalled the enthusiasm which greeted the news that the USS *Jack* would be based in Australia: 'We were young and strong, and this was adventure'.[192] There is also the abiding nexus between love and war, as well as the moral quandaries resulting from distance and personal separation. Jim Calvert and Michael Thwaites have written of their complex experiences in forming romantic attachments in foreign ports.[193]

Confronting the reality of battle has always been a personal watershed. As Malcolm Llewellyn-Jones writes here, it is extremely difficult to simulate in peacetime the danger and confusion of war. In the words of a Royal Marine recalling the Falklands, 'No amount of training can prepare you for it'.[194] In anticipation of battle, religion is a traditional consolation. One Australian naval veteran remembers the voyage to the Gulf War, during which religious services were well attended. On the way home they were not.[195] There is also naval evidence that the ancient link between war and narcotics—epitomised in the age of sail by the Royal Navy's issuing of 'grog'—survived into modern times. In the words of David Tinker, a Royal Naval officer aboard the destroyer HMS *Glamorgan* who was killed in action in the Falklands, 'The best thing to do is to have a few wets before an attack. I'd had a drink before the Exocet attack and the pulse rate stayed very normal . . . '.[196] Above all, according to so many testimonies, there is fear—fear of danger and of one's own reaction to it. In action, in Calvert's words, one can be 'scared to death'.[197] Some men also feel pride in the stories they will be able to tell.[198] Peter Cremer was of the view that real courage comes after being wounded, when one returns to the fight having suffered and knowing that it can indeed happen to oneself.[199]

While sometimes in naval warfare men feel satisfaction in revenging their losses, there can also be honour and humanity in the aftermath of battle, indeed even in the midst of it.[200] A Harrier pilot in the Falklands, taken prisoner, shook the hand of the Argentinian soldier who apparently shot him down.[201] An Argentinian naval doctor recalled cooperative arrangements for wounded prisoners: 'We had periodic encounters with the British hospital ship *Uganda* north of San Carlos . . . Within the drama of war we had the paradox of being allowed to meet with the English doctors, to transfer wounded prisoners, in a specially designated zone which was an area of peace in the middle of war'.[202]

Of course, as in all war, there have been psychological casualties of naval battle, just as there have been physical ones. Dr Scott, Chaplain aboard HMS *Victory* at Trafalgar, may well have been suffering from post-traumatic stress in being haunted for years by the horrors he witnessed.[203] Shellshock, breakdowns and insanity affected sailors subjected to sustained air attacks during the Second World War.[204] As Guy Griffiths has written, the early twentieth century did not recognise post-traumatic stress disorder (PTSD). Its recognition as a war-related medical condition came out of the years following the Vietnam War.[205]

As Colin Wastell tells us, PTSD is now better understood and battle stress can affect anyone.[206] The clear implication of this is that psychological casualties are real and honourable ones. They are part of the tragic price paid for duty, service and victory in war. Since unit cohesion and leadership are ameliorating factors in a sufferer's recovery from post-traumatic stress, naval personnel may well have an advantage in recovering from these after-effects of conflict.

War ages and changes human beings. Corvette sailors, very young men, visibly aged during the Battle of the Atlantic.[207] Tom Parks, after submarine service in the Pacific, felt old at 24.[208] Admiral Sandy Woodward relates how the attack on HMS *Sheffield* showed the British Task Force that one can get badly hurt in action. At the time he wrote: 'I do not think I shall ever be quite the same again, and I am not very happy about it . . .'.[209] He found that fighting had hardened his heart. Naval veterans have spoken of how being close to death changes one's attitude to life, bringing human, family and moral concerns to the forefront.[210] Three weeks before his death David Tinker wrote: 'Here, certainly, the material things are unimportant and human things, values, and ways of life are thought about by everybody'.[211] Some men conclude that war is not only hell, it is absurd.[212] Others, like Ben Bradlee who served in a USN destroyer in the Pacific, recall a character-building and mind-broadening process.[213]

Such life-changing experiences cause veterans to feel detached from public celebrations when they return home, even in victory. There is a sense that one cannot explain such experiences to others, that only comrades will understand.[214] It is this ultimate gulf of understanding which is at the basis of the respect and curiosity we feel towards those who have been under fire and more generally to war. It also underpins the bonds between veterans. War is a world unto itself for it is a function of passion, tribalism and secrecy, and of conduct, especially killing, which in other circumstances society would find unacceptable. When veterans remember, moreover, many tend to recall the totality of their experience, which could include humour, romance, comradeship, courage, elation, boredom, stupidity, fear, trauma, death, food, sleep, weather and, for sailors, the sea.

THE FUTURE

Prediction involves taking intellectual risks, but it can be useful if done with care and in the context of emerging trends. Three main factors are likely to condition the face of naval battle in the foreseeable future: technological, social and strategic change. History has always seen such change, but at the end of the twentieth century it accelerated enormously. Its interaction with powerful continuities, such as the human factor, will determine how navies fight in future and how sailors experience naval warfare.

Exponential developments in such areas as sensor, stealth, computer networking and precision weapons technologies are creating a new context for naval warfare, one which promises vastly increased awareness and strike capabilities. They also imply a need for greater speed in tactical decision-making.[215] Such extraordinary technical progress will have its teething problems: constriction of the operational time factor will place greater demands on personnel;[216] there is the danger of data confusion and overload, of incoming information beyond the ability of human beings to digest and act upon it;[217] and modern communications at this level may have problematic effects on the human sleep cycle.[218] In short, personnel will be stressed in the face of operational friction and danger, just as they always have been. Fear and stress can cause people to misinterpret instruments and misuse technology, as would appear to have happened in 1988 when the Aegis cruiser USS *Vincennes* shot down an Iranian airliner over the Persian Gulf.[219] Of course, technology can fail, for whatever reason, creating further friction—as occurred with the delay in launching land attack missiles from the USS *Wisconsin* at the opening of the Gulf War.[220] This new war of systems will also create more expert sailors and require a different culture of command.[221] The challenge for future naval commanders will be to master new technologies while remembering and sustaining the human factor. This is in addition to dealing with the complex new media and legal environments.

Social change has always affected navies. The early twentieth-century world of instinctive obedience and deference has gone, and command structures now operate within the context of a more democratic, educated and questioning society. There has been further dramatic change in the form of women asserting their equal role in society. While women have always been part of naval warfare in indirect and informal ways, they now serve as fully-fledged sailors and officers in operational zones. As elsewhere in society, so too in the naval environment, the influence of women inevitably creates change in important and subtle ways which will only become apparent with time, and to which adjustment must be made. Various successful captains of warships have voiced their support for mixed gender naval roles.[222]

Terrorism and asymmetric warfare (attempts to change the operational game, usually in the face of greater force) are far from new, and conventional naval operations are likely to remain fundamental. But the resort to terrorist attack in the face of the vastly superior technology of the dominant superpower, and the potential use of weapons of mass destruction, creates new risks for navies and their people. In something of a reversal of traditional attitudes, the sea may well come to be seen as a place of refuge and ports as dangerous. Strategic agendas for power projection from the sea imply greater proximity to land and littoral waters and are potentially complicated by asymmetric threats. Navies must equip their people to deal with a new combination of threats mounted both by conventional and unconventional forces.

In human affairs there is always continuity, and in the face of such changes the human factor will remain incontestably vital. The ultimate challenge for navies will be what it always has been: to combine reliability with imagination in their people. As Peter Jones concludes, there will always be the age-old elements of naval battle: human beings, the fog of war and the cruel sea.[223] And war at sea will remain war. It is one of the mercies of naval warfare that it has caused vastly fewer casualties, in absolute terms, than other modes of conflict in modern times. Pain and loss are ultimately personal, however, and rightly resist any such quantitative analysis. In the end only two facts matter about war and two naval veterans can remind us of them. Alfred Thayer Mahan wrote: 'War is violence, wounds, and death'.[224] John F. Kennedy pondered, at the height of the Cuban missile crisis, how in war the brave and the young die.[225] War involves suffering, and war affects mainly the young. Lest we forget.

2 | Operational command at sea

Andrew Gordon

THIS CHAPTER IS NOT an academic treatise on how to command a ship in wartime. The naval reader would find that offensive, and there is nothing I could suggest that is not described (with greater authority) in a number of memoirs, outstanding among which is Roger Hill's *Destroyer Command*. A quite junior officer in 1939, Hill commanded a range of escort and fleet destroyers in the Second World War. Among other things, he endured Russian convoys, including PQ17, nursed the tanker *Ohio* into Malta during Operation PEDESTAL (the attempt to relieve the island in 1942) and grounded his Asdic dome off Omaha Beach on D-Day. He knew the whole gamut of success and failure, of enervating self-doubt and rage at being messed about by shore staff. At the end of the war, nervously and physically exhausted, he left the Navy, emigrated to New Zealand and became a casual dockyard labourer.

Then there is an excellent booklet called *Your Ship*, issued to Royal Navy commanding officers, the RAN's *Command Guide*, and no doubt similar official publications in other navies. I might also mention that I come to write this chapter soon after watching the most recent television production of *Hornblower*, which brought to mind how novelists and scriptwriters have no doubts about their ability to differentiate between good and bad ship command, a state of certainty which academics might well envy. It is clearly not so simple. History suggests that (for example) madness yoked to government service can have its sublime uses in desperate times.

INTUITION AND OPERATIONAL COMMAND

To raise the level (as the exam question demands) to what is now known as the 'operational' plane, I would want to take a long, hard look at those so-called 'generals-at-sea' who, in the English Civil War, adapted with some success to fleet command. Were they able to see the wood *despite* the trees precisely because they knew little of the specialist paraphernalia and methods of seamanship, and had perforce to leave the technical stuff to their subordinates?

Leaving that disconcerting thought hanging, I will list nine examples of inspired command, many of them no doubt familiar:

- Commodore Nelson's decision in 1797 to take HMS *Captain* out of the line at the Battle of Cape St Vincent without waiting for the admiral to tell him to do so, to block a Spanish fleet movement which the whole British line would have been too unwieldy to intercept. Equally telling was Admiral Sir John Jervis' approval of an action which some of the fleet's captains considered indisciplined.
- Rear Admiral Sir David Beatty's decision in 1914 to press closer than planned into the Heligoland Bight in support of his light cruisers which (as it happened) would have been in deep trouble had the battlecruisers not turned up when they did.
- Commodore Reginald Tyrwhitt's decision in 1916, when he caught the first signals of the Battle of Jutland, to sail his destroyers from Harwich without waiting for orders to do so. Once at sea he told the Admiralty what he was doing, and was promptly ordered home, for reasons more of Admiralty huff than operational sense.
- The captain of HMS *Cumberland*'s similar decision in 1939 to curtail a boiler clean in Port Stanley and head north, based on overheard wireless reports of the pocket battleship *Graf Spee*'s sighting 1000 miles away, enabling him to arrive off the River Plate several hours sooner than subsequent Admiralty orders could have allowed.
- Captain John Collins' decision in 1940 to delay HMAS *Sydney*'s foray into the Gulf of Athens, so as to remain in close-ish support of destroyers sweeping westwards through the channel between

The loss of HMS *Queen Mary* at the Battle of Jutland, 31 May 1916. '. . . at 4.23 the *Queen Mary* was obliterated by an 800 feet high mushroom of fiery smoke; in this case I remember seeing bits of her flying up. As I watched this fiery gravestone, it seemed to waver slightly at the base, and I caught a momentary but clear glimpse of the hull sticking out of the water from the stern to the after funnel.' Lieutenant Stephen King-Hall, RN, HMS *Southampton*. (RAN)

Greece and Crete. The result was the action off Cape Spada. When Admiral Cunningham asked him how he got there so soon, he said 'Providence guided me, Sir'; to which the reply was: 'Well, in future you can continue to take your orders from providence'.[1]

- Air Marshal Bowhill's decision in 1941 to deploy a Coastal Command reconnaissance aircraft to an area further south and west than the Admiralty had requested, in search of the missing German battleship *Bismarck*. (Bowhill had started his military career as a naval officer.)

- Captain Philip Vian's decision, when *Bismarck* was reported, to disregard his orders to find and escort HMS *Rodney* and to head for the enemy. Significantly, at the Admiralty, the First Sea Lord, Admiral Sir Dudley Pound, deemed it unnecessary to tell him to do so.

- Commander Graham Stoke's decision in 1941 to press on at full speed with his four destroyers when a group of Italian cruisers and destroyers were reported ahead of him near Cape Bon, in spite of orders to avoid trouble because his own ships were cluttered with passengers and stores for Malta. He just happened to be nurturing a private theory (which he proceeded to validate) that four destroyers could sink two cruisers in the dark.

- Lieutenant Alastair Mars' decision, at the time of Operation PEDESTAL, to shift the submarine HMS *Unbroken* to a position 40 miles away in the Lipari Islands, because he reckoned Italian cruisers would 'waypoint' there rather than the headland on the coast of Sicily where he had been ordered to station himself. He was thinking through the terrain, with the outcome that he torpedoed two cruisers with a left and a right.

These were all operational decisions which the respective commanders would have been legally justified in *not* taking (and they would have had top cover for doing so). They were, in varying degrees, both risky and lucky decisions. They involved disobedience or insubordination or (at the least) initiative. Most of them were taken before contact had been established with the enemy, to expedite contact with the enemy: in other words in *operational* rather than *tactical* mode.

The famous photographer Henri Cartier-Bresson coined the phrase 'decisive moment' to explain his skill. He would wait (one imagines) sphinx-like, observing events around him, watching for a moment in which his subject's character and significance would be betrayed at their most pronounced. He would then press the shutter. There is a useful parallel concept here, even if it cannot be stretched very far; and the factor, I would suggest, which separates the captains-of-war from the captains-of-ships (to borrow a Churchillism) must be the ability to recognise when a decisive moment has arrived, and the preparedness (if necessary) to 'take their orders from providence' to initiate the necessary exploitative or preventive action.

The Germans (naturally) have a word which is almost fit for purpose here: *Fingerspitzengefühl*. This, apparently, means 'an intuitive understanding of the battlespace, which causes the hair on the back of one's neck to rise when something is amiss', or closely similar. It is a more exact description of (for example) Captain Johnny Walker's uncanny ability to sniff out U-boats than what I am attempting to describe here, but the element of intuition or instinct is important in both cases. The next question is whether intuition can be taught. I do not know the answer to that; but people can certainly be indoctrinated with opportunism, and with that comes the habit of leaving one's mental antennae firmly on and switched to 'receive'. As Admiral of the Fleet Lord Fisher once remarked, 'Any damned fool can obey orders'.

INHIBITORS TO GOOD OPERATIONAL COMMAND

Let me move on to look at some of the issues and conditions which are liable to get in the way of good operational command. One question which I can pose and then step carefully around is whether the above sort of talent for operational command is not out of date, picturesque, romantic and irrelevant in the twenty-first century. The cutting-edge, up-to-the-minute, digitised 'systemisers of systems' will probably say 'Probably'—or, at least, 'It is of such diminished importance that we don't really care'. But we will come to them.

First, there is the contemporary phenomenon of written doctrine. One recent change is that the armed forces are today beset by doctrine publications. In periods of stability, the usages and avowed purposes of the military are likely to be too habitual and too well-known to require articulation. The fire brigade doesn't need a glossy doctrine publication to explain to the taxpayer what it's for. By contrast, any spasm of strategic change will get military institutions scrambling to establish new bearings in unfamiliar surroundings, and to reposition themselves in relation to other defence organisations.

We all know that two eras have recently, simultaneously, ended: the 100-year-long age of great power competition and its subset, the 45-year Cold War, with its Dr Strangelove succession of nuclear-exchange theories. A consequence of this, in the mid- to late 1990s, was a sudden spasm of doctrinal jockeying. Given that written doctrine has a track record of bridging gaps between reality and aspiration, it is unsurprising that the Royal Air Force (for example) was more familiar with the state of being defined by it than was the Royal Navy. Few sailors welcomed the word doctrine (they had done alright for 350 years without realising they had any), and they approached it nervously, as one would a rattlesnake in one's cabin. It has sinister religious-historical connotations, and sounds ominously like official real-world-denial (we will come back to that). But it also resonates with intellectual one-upmanship, and if *they* (the Marine Corps, the Army, the RAF, *whoever*) were waving it about, then so must we.

It quickly proved its worth. It is hard to imagine that the Royal Navy would have done so well in the 1997–98 *Strategic Defence Review* (SDR) without the crumple-zone of *The Fundamentals of British Maritime Doctrine* (BR 1806)[2] in front of it, and without all the head-banging and phrase-coining which went into its production. It helped to frame an articulate maritime case to a degree unknown for 100 years, and eased the United Kingdom into the twenty-first century somewhat ahead of many of our neighbours and allies. To borrow a device from Professor Richard Holmes, SDR nudged the British into deciding that they wanted to be a *whale* after all, after two generations of trying, rather unconvincingly, to be an *elephant*. And, where those two promised aircraft carriers were concerned, it promised to settle old scores from the 1960s in a most gratifying manner.

The second edition of BR 1806 is even better: that is, thinner and more joint, with less 'we can do anything' public relations padding—more secure, one might say. But there are flaws. Our current order of battle of doctrinal statements seem to me to have several bear-traps or disconnects which we are ushering through what is purported to be a rigorous analytical filtering process, and which may impact on our future war-fighting performance by putting distracting, and possibly plain wrong, keynote expectations into our operational commanders' heads.

A very big potential flaw is that we may be hypothesising about future warfare according to what suits us institutionally or financially. The US Marine Corps are doing that on stilts. Written doctrine is full of corporate aspirations and survival wheezes. One can argue that such considerations are merely part of the real world; but, equally, there are many past instances, analysed by Professor Theo Farrell, among others, of how they can depart from the real world.

- For example, the only defence threat facing the Irish Free State in the inter-war years was the possibility of invasion from Ulster by a Britain at war with Germany and desperate for naval bases in the west of Ireland. The only realistic way of deterring the United Kingdom was to prepare for a sustained guerrilla war. Yet the tiny Irish Army deemed guerrilla warfare to be beneath professional soldiers, and set about shaping themselves into a microcosmic, under-equipped, semi-trained copy of the British Army, with little hope of winning a contest with the real thing.
- In the same period, the Air Force needed an independent role for reasons of institutional survival and thus uselessly equipped the country for ineffective strategic bombing at huge financial and (in wartime) strategic cost to the country.
- The US military, in their air campaign against North Vietnam, tried to treat that country as if it were an industrialised European state, because that was on record as having worked for them in the past.
- Various interpretations of the Soviet threat served US defence–corporate interests very well during the Cold War.

- The Royal Navy's current enthusiasm for out-of-area power projection may not be unconnected with the glittering prizes of those two promised carriers.

Published doctrine, therefore, may help secure funding, but it by no means guarantees that requirements defined through corporate necessity will find operational validation the next time the shooting starts.

Another flaw is that BR 1806 and other doctrinal market stalls are making our likely responses transparent to prospective enemies. Villeneuve, the French commander in 1805, could only guess what was being hatched in HMS *Victory*'s great cabin before the Battle of Trafalgar.[3] Today, however, he could have on his cabin bookshelf the whole range of official doctrine books by which our officer corps is supposed to be guided.

Another arguable flaw is that there is a certain amount of shirking the business of separating principles, processes and product. An example,

'HMAS *Sydney* in action with Italian cruiser off Cape Spada' by Frank Norton. '[We did not expect the] devilish cheek of the Australians, who rushed into the fight with the greatest contempt for the enemy's longer range, and neatly hit the *Bartolomeo Colleoni* on a vital spot almost immediately after opening fire. From that moment the battle was over.' Captured Italian officer, *Bartolomeo Colleoni*. (AWM ART23692)

in my view, is the familiar acronym C3 (or whatever is the current extravagant multiple). C3 has always been brandished about as a sort of Holy Trinity of equals, but a couple of seconds' thought will reveal that the first two elements, Command and Control, are essential functions of war-fighting, while the third, Communications, is merely a means to an end—and not the only means, for Doctrine is another way of obtaining effective Command and Control, and shares that task in erratically varying proportions *with* Communications. So C3 is composed of two functions and an enabler, or two oranges and a banana, and thus contains an insidious virus which we should sort out before elaborating upon the acronym.

Another issue of more concern to the Army perhaps, is that our doctrine founts trumpet the virtues of 'Manoeuvre Warfare', while forecasting (no doubt correctly) that future conflicts are almost certain to be fought by coalitions. They seem to miss the point that, owing to technical and cultural incompatibilities, coalitions will probably have to fight in accordance with their operational common denominator which, whether we like it or not, will be attritional warfare. So we educate our future commanders in the mantras of an approach to war-fighting which is not the one they are most likely to have to use in practice. The desideratum of 'Manoeuvrism' is obviously most accessible in single-nation operations: are we all expecting to refight the Falklands?

Another matter is the failure to reconcile the optimistic lip-service paid to the potential for devolution of command offered by digitisation, with the near certainty that it will have exactly the opposite effect. This issue is more skillfully dealt with, or perhaps evaded, in *Australian Maritime Doctrine*[4] than it was in the first edition of BR 1806. But in British doctrine we certainly appear to be saying one thing while doing the opposite. What opportunity is there for a future John Collins to take his orders from providence if he is trussed up in a complex network of systems interdependency? Does it matter? Will future wars be fought by systems managers rather than by warriors? If so, let's come clean, and not continue to pretend otherwise. But more on that, or related areas, anon.

Another flaw is the promise implicit in the digitised vision: the mirage of universal interoperability within an *ad hoc* task force or coalition which happens to be thrown together in response to a crisis. The purveyors of RMA (the Revolution in Military Affairs) technology depend for their livelihoods on the unceasing need for upgrades and catch-ups. If they ever allow us to achieve, for any length of time, the level pitch of interoperability they will be starving the goose which lays their golden eggs. So it is a safe bet that they will not.

A further flaw is that the Western, Aristotelian, approach to warfare, life and the universe, evidenced (certainly) in British military doctrine, may not be mirror-imaged by a future adversary. An opponent with a glacial sense of destiny, no democratic electoral cycles and an un-Rousseauesque disregard for the individual may not be so readily checked by the Clausewitzian chess moves of Western planning methods. There is little point in training our future leaders to finesse campaigns against people just like us, as we are discovering in the aftermath of 11 September 2001.

Yet another flaw is *British Maritime Doctrine*'s shotgun adoption (for reasons of joint operational theory) of inappropriate Army jargon into the naval war-fighting scenario: *tactical, operational* and *strategic* may be easily separable levels of land warfare, but they are often *not* so in warfare at sea. In that respect, maritime doctrine contains a certain amount of clutter or disinformation which a naval operational commander will have to see his way past if he is not to discredit the whole. The good which comes from this is that, having spotted such incongruities, naval officers tend to address the publication with a medium-sized salt-cellar handy beside them.

I might now mention my overriding problem with the written doctrine industry which has very firmly got its feet under the defence table in the United Kingdom. It now constitutes a vested interest which is avoiding the robust scrutiny to which all vested interests should be subjected. There would seem to be no officially-recognised end to its usefulness—or, rather, the industry itself will not offer even a working definition of the limits of the utility of their product. Until they do this, it seems to me that the integrity of their business must be placed in doubt. It is high time their 'Happy Time' was drawn to a close, for the damage they could do to operational command philosophies potentially exceeds any benefits they can offer.

HISTORY AS A REALITY CHECK

In allowing an historian to sound off about the practices of the naval profession, this chapter would have been seen as pretty radical a few short years ago. There has recently been a discernible sense among British naval officers that they have left the Service's history somewhere—they can't quite remember where—and that they would rather like it back. In part, historians have been rehabilitated by the ending of the Cold War, while the Cold Warriors have taken their place in the attic.

A similar resurgent interest in history pervaded the Navy on the eve of the First World War, when there was, at long last, a vague opinion that the technocrats had got out of their box and were corrupting matters of operational doctrine; that is, that they were behaving like masters instead of servants (or service providers). Part of the problem has been that the Navy, the world's first wholly-mechanised force, has always been a highly technocratic service, and the midwives of new technology almost always oversell the revolutionary nature of their deliveries.

I am sometimes accused of transplanting apparent truisms from the Victorian era to the beginning of the twenty-first century. I will give you a parable from 700 years ago. In 1303 two of my distant ancestors, one Alexander de Insulis and his son, Angus Og, fought a sea battle against each other in the Sound of Mull on the West Coast of Scotland. They each had a fleet of galleys. I do not recall what they were fighting over—one of them was supporting Robert the Bruce's bid for kingship, and the other was not, or something like that—and I must confess that historians bicker about the alleged facts.

Alexander's flagship (so the story goes) had the innovation of a hinged rudder instead of a steering oar, making it more manoeuvrable. Junior's flagship attempted to ram, but Senior was able to turn inside and they brushed past each other. One may imagine stones, abuse, bottles, and so on passing between the two. But as they passed, one of Junior's oarsmen is said to have shoved the flat of his oar between the rudder and the rudder post of the enemy, whereupon the oar broke but the blade stuck, rendering the enemy flagship unmanoeuvrable and leading to Senior's defeat. This is alleged by some to be the origin of the expression 'to stick one's oar in' (a family tradition I endeavour to keep up).

Now that picturesque tale, supposing it to be true (and even if it isn't), illustrates that new technology is likely to bring with it vulnerabilities which its purveyors may not have thought about, and certainly haven't advertised. The next time two fleets (or armies) meet in combat they will do so in the thrall of a wealth of new technology which has never been really tested in anything like 'symmetrical' warfare. It is timely to recall the words of a certain Royal Navy captain in 1908: 'we must never allow practice to become overwhelmed by theory',[5] and yet it is probably already too late. The worry is that today's technocrat, exercising immense power without ultimate responsibility, is steamrolling operational doctrine in the direction in which his vested interests lie. Operational doctrine is, rightly, the prerogative of the practitioner, not of the theorist. The practitioner must decide, from a full awareness of his options, how he wants to operate and the technocrat must help him operate in the way he wants.

It is much easier to defeat an enemy who is secure in the certainty of his technical solutions. In the Second World War the German U-boat arm under Admiral Karl Dönitz institutionalised its unshakeable faith that the Enigma cipher machines had made wireless communications unbreakable. It was taboo to question the W/T (wireless telegraphy) reporting practices which were operationally essential to U-boat wolf packs. The result is well-known, but the key point is that it was not so much a matter of our codebreakers at Bletchley Park *winning* the Battle of the Atlantic, but of the German signals establishment *losing* it.

Perhaps today all is sweetness and light. Perhaps I am hopelessly misinformed and overstating the problem. But it is reasonable for the taxpayer to suppose that the C3 regime with which practitioners enter the next conflict, for better or worse, has their full consent and approval. The U-boats' C3 regime did *not* have the consent and approval of the practitioners—many had instinctive misgivings about it. But only the most successful, teflon-coated aces (such as Otto Kretschmer) could stand up to Dönitz and disregard their signalling schedules. 'What has the airforce ever done for me?' Kretschmer asked when he refused to transmit daily weather forecasts for the benefit of the *Luftwaffe*.

A senior, retired British admiral recently illustrated to me the point about technocracy. I mentioned to this celebrated officer, a gifted mathematician with a profoundly technical approach to every problem, that I was due to give a paper in Australia on the subject of operational command at sea, and asked if he would help my turgid thought processes. He said it was very simple. 'You only have to deal with the last 30 years: before then it was quite different. Since then, all ships in a group have been Net-linked in a task-sharing, information-sharing manner which has greatly enhanced the efficiency and flexibility of the whole.'

I said, fine, admiral, but in the long view of history the computer linking of warships is new only in the scale of its promise and in its technical processes. And I can say with a high degree of certainty that, during the First World War, John Jellicoe and David Beatty would have fallen on Netcentricity with glee and used it in doctrinally opposite ways: the former would have grasped it enthusiastically as a device of central control which absolutely precluded any ship's deviating from the orchestrated script, whereas the latter would have used it as a device for collaboration and *ad hoc* task switching. And it would have been Beatty's force which would have retained some cohesion (but admittedly only some) when the system broke down.

THE ROLE OF INSTITUTIONS

Even the most complex command-system technologies do not (yet) necessarily preclude doctrine from being personality-influenced at the very top; but our personnel selection policies might.

There is a well-authenticated peacetime inclination to select our future warrior-commanders from an already self-selected pool of able technicians and administrators. Risk aversion tends to be built into the merit-and-reward system of most peacetime military institutions, and those who keep tidy desks and tight budgets and never give cause for questions to be asked in parliament are not likely (other things being equal) to be the most adept at confounding the Queen's enemies or recognising a decisive moment—or, if they are, it's a fluke (and one which reflects no credit on the institution).

It is difficult for servicemen, Active List or retired, to debate this subject without descending into anecdote and personal grievance. It provides an attractive explanation for the career disappointment of the many officers who must far outnumber those who can ever reach high rank. Among warrior-commanders, Andrew Cunningham (1943–46) was not a great First Sea Lord; Nelson would probably have been hopeless.

It is reasonable to suggest that in the modern world of intense public scrutiny, corporate strategies and internal markets, an officer cannot reasonably expect to reach senior rank without well-developed bureaucratic abilities. People have probably always said this. And while one must not turn the thing on its head and suggest that administrative and warrior skills are mutually exclusive (Beatty, Mountbatten and Collins were all effective Chiefs of Naval Staff), one must also recognise that they are *not* synonymous, and that peacetime offers very little opportunity to identify, practise and develop the skills of war-fighting. And it is a vicious circle, for the preferment of risk-averse officers and a risk-averse culture boosts the obsessive quest for certainty to ever greater heights and creates ever greater susceptibility to the snake-oil theorists.

I will end by returning to the Royal Navy's innermost historical comfort zone, Horatio Nelson. Although the Immortal Memory—celebrated every Trafalgar Night—originally referred to 'Lord Nelson and all who lost their lives at Trafalgar', it has long become implicit that the gathering is to celebrate Nelson. Even people with zero comprehension of joined-up history are aware of his iconography. A friend of mine in the Naval Reserve had a civilian job for a while as 'chief officer' of the wool-clipper *Cutty Sark*, long preserved in a dry dock in Greenwich.

Most of his time was spent in the care and maintenance of the rigging and so on, but he did mingle with the tourists, and on more than one occasion he was asked to point out the spot where Nelson fell. He would point vaguely and say 'Just over there'.

In his time, Nelson's effect on the collective imagination of the British public was almost supernatural. It was the embracing of a saviour-figure credited with the ability to work miracles. His death at the moment of his highest achievement hardly diminished the Messianic metaphor, that last doctrinal meeting of captains in *Victory* approximating to the Last Supper. With just one, recent, exception, the national outpouring of grief for Nelson remains without parallel in the record of British behaviour. And now, on each successive 21 October, a sort of naval Ascension Day, we reaffirm his immortality with ritual and ceremony.

For the Royal Navy, however, this deification of Nelson is wrong-headed, and lazy. I can see why it is attractive, for it imposes no inconvenient disciplines on the institution. The man was a genius, and that is apparently the way we won the Napoleonic Wars: obliging destiny delivered the saviour, and all was well. The whole heroic saga can be kept in the wardroom silverware cupboard, regularly polished and often admired, but kept separate from the daily, bureaucratic business of running a modern navy. It is caffeine-free tradition.

We can also rest assured that he would not have troubled the appointers much in today's service: he was frail and often sickly (certainly *sea*-sickly); he was a patriotic fanatic (and fanaticism *is* rather gauche); he not infrequently made a fool of himself ashore with outlandish hats and bizarre foreign decorations; his ships were scruffy, and his handling of them not all it might have been; his attempts at joint operations were disastrous; his private life would have delighted the tabloids; and his travel-expense claims were decidedly dodgy. For a multitude of reasons, therefore, it appears we can celebrate him without much risk. But that is, narrowly, missing the point.

Nelson was merely (if one can use such a word) the ultimate in a generational succession of sea-going officers whose command of their profession influenced the future political and cultural geography of this planet. Trafalgar was merely (that word again) the last in a succession of six fleet victories—with no defeats—in eleven years. Had Nelson become a parson, like his father, one cannot seriously postulate that Britain would thereby have lost the war at sea. The Captains' and junior Flag Lists were jostling with competent and self-confident men, gradu-ates of the same empirical school of combat, who were ready, able and eager to take command and to win. One of them, Sir John Orde, challenged the Earl of St Vincent to a duel in a quarrel which began with St Vincent's appointment of Commodore Nelson instead of Orde to command the Mediterranean Squadron (Jervis wisely declined to attend).[6] After Trafalgar, Villeneuve famously, and with only slight exaggeration, said: 'To any other nation the loss of Nelson would have been irreparable; but in the British Fleet off Cadiz, every Captain was a Nelson'.

Now, of course, Nelson's own contribution to that state of affairs was considerable. But even he, being asked to choose his officers in 1805, had been able to hand the Navy List back to Lord Barham with the words: 'Choose yourself, my Lord, the same spirit actuates the whole profession; you cannot choose wrong';[7] and the Immortal Memory should rightly be of the institution which took Nelson to sea, enthused him, conditioned him and promoted him in spite of all his unofficer-like qualities. This was the Navy which did not clutter his thought processes with an array of distracting, smart-sounding and possibly misleading doctrinal precepts, whether borrowed from the Army or not—the Navy which, learning from innumerable empirical mistakes, had got its culture, doctrine and practices so lined up with its operational tasks as to become the most successful military institution since the Roman Legions. But that would be potentially more subversive, and thus less readily indulged, than remembering a unique genius.

CONCLUSION

So what, then, is the keystone of successful operational command at sea? I suppose that if there is a coherent thread in all that I have written it is that there are no easy answers to the question of what good practice in operational command at sea should look like in the twenty-first century, or to the question about where it is most likely to come from (or rather, the nature of the soil from which it is most likely to grow). There are, however, clear inhibitors of good operational command at sea, some of them so insidious, so culturally climatic, that one may not actually be aware of them.

We may be proffered simple answers—formulas for universal application—by impressively smart people, with business-speak words, who have thought about it only in two dimensions, or by those snake-oil merchants who have manifestos and agendas, which will not include sharing the blame when it all goes to rats.

But while effective individuals cast in the role of commanders are hugely important, and are the visible embodiment of an institution getting it right, it is not just them. And it is not just culture, which on past performance is more likely to be prohibitive than permissive of the effective application of force in any emergent set of circumstances. And it is not just deliberate doctrine, which cannot be a holistic enough term, one which has been getting rather too many free lunches recently and needs to have its box defined, preparatory to being put in it.

It is the nature of the surrounding institution, which embraces and counter-balances all of these things, which ultimately matters. To get it reliably right at the operational level of command in the next spasm of yet-unknowable emergencies will be immensely difficult, and will demand an institutionally joined-up, doctrinally uncompromised and uncluttered approach to the delivery of Command product to the time and place where it is likely to matter. We do not have these conditions today.

Part II

Aspects of the face of naval battle

3 | Western advisors and Chinese sailors in the 1894–95 Sino-Japanese War

Bruce Elleman

IN THE POST-COLD WAR ERA, Western military experts frequently point to China as America's next major rival for naval dominance in the Pacific. What is largely overlooked in these estimations, however, is that the Chinese Navy has engaged in only one full-scale 'modern' naval battle against a foreign opponent. This battle—known alternatively as the Battle of the Yellow Sea or the Battle of the Yalu—was the first major naval battle since the Austro-Italian Battle of Lissa in 1866, and took place on 17 September 1894 during the Sino-Japanese War. The Chinese Imperial Navy lost, and by most accounts lost spectacularly, its maiden modern naval engagement. Arguably it was this Chinese defeat that really gave Japan full control over Korea.

This chapter will focus on the individual and group experience of foreign advisors and Chinese sailors during this crucial battle, as well as on the relationship of that experience to the Chinese Imperial Navy's operational effectiveness. Of the seven foreign advisors (three Germans, three Englishmen and an American) employed by China's Beiyang or Northern fleet, two were killed, four were wounded and only one—an engineer who worked below deck—escaped completely unscathed. The three best-known advisors were a German soldier, Constantin von Hanneken, an English sailor, William Ferdinand Tyler, and an American sailor, Philo Norton McGiffin. By examining the accounts of these three foreign participants, then comparing them with contemporary Chinese sources, this chapter will seek to investigate pertinent historical lessons in relation to:

- the division of China's Navy into separate regional fleets;
- the effectiveness of Chinese naval command and control;
- the battle experience of officers and sailors; and
- the impact of Western technology on the military performance of the Chinese Navy.

The aim of this investigation is to compare and contrast the situation of China's fleet in 1894–95 with that of the People's Liberation Army Navy (PLAN) of today. Notable similarities between the problems China's Navy experienced in 1894 and today include a division of the PLAN into separate regional fleets, serious questions about the effectiveness of the PLAN's command structure, a notable lack of battle experience and the PLAN's recent purchases of foreign-made equipment such as the *Sovremenny* Class destroyers and *Kilo* Class submarines. If the Chinese Navy had to engage a foreign navy in battle today or in the near future, would it face similar experiences and a similar fate to that of the Chinese Imperial Navy in 1894?

FOREIGN ADVISORS AND THE CHINESE IMPERIAL NAVY

Constantin von Hanneken, a German gunnery expert by training, was the highest-ranking foreign advisor in the Beiyang fleet. After ten years in the Chinese service, he was appointed in 1889 to design the defences at Weihaiwei (later Weihai), on the southern shore of the Yellow Sea. He later designed the defences at the Port Arthur (Lushun) naval base on the northern shore. In July 1894, von Hanneken was a passenger on the *Gaosheng*, the first Chinese ship to be sunk off Korea during the Sino-Japanese War. After swimming to shore, he made his way back to China, where he was appointed to be the naval advisor to, and later the co-admiral of, the Beiyang fleet, in conjunction with Admiral Ding Ruchang. His memoirs have recently been edited by Rainer Falkenberg and published under the title *Constantin von Hanneken: Briefe aus China 1879–1886*.[1]

The second highest-ranking foreign advisor was William Ferdinand Tyler, a Sub-Lieutenant in the British Royal Naval Reserve and an officer of the Chinese Imperial Maritime Customs. After war erupted in Korea, Tyler left the Customs Office and volunteered for the Chinese Imperial Navy. At first he was assigned to be naval advisor and personal secretary to von Hanneken, but he later became co-commander with Li Dingxin of the Chinese flagship, the 7430-ton *Ding Yuan*, one of the two modern battleships that China had purchased from Germany. William Tyler published his memoirs under the title *Pulling Strings in China*.[2]

Finally, the foreign co-commander of the other German-built battleship, the *Zhen Yuan,* was 31-year-old Philo Norton McGiffin, an American graduate of the US Naval Academy. When McGiffin was unable to obtain a commission in the US Navy due to force reductions, he travelled to China in 1885 to advise the Beiyang fleet. At first he was an instructor at China's Naval Academy at Tianjin, then in 1890 he became Superintendent of a new Naval Academy at Weihaiwei. After war broke out with Japan, McGiffin was assigned to the *Zhen Yuan*. Following the Battle of the Yellow Sea, McGiffin wrote numerous descriptions of the engagement for the American press. Much later, his personal papers were collected and edited by his niece, Lee McGiffin, in the book *Yankee of the Yalu*.[3]

Assisting von Hanneken and Tyler in the *Ding Yuan* was a British artillery instructor, named Nicholls, and a German engineer named Albrecht. Assisting Philo McGiffin in the *Zhen Yuan* was a German gunnery expert, Heckman. Meanwhile, another British engineer, Purvis, was in the cruiser *Zhi Yuan*, which sank during the battle.[4]

Taken together, the memoirs of von Hanneken, Tyler and McGiffin provide a wide range of detailed information about the Chinese Imperial Navy, its preparations for battle and the battle itself. Examination of these three accounts also allows us to evaluate the organisation of the Chinese Imperial Navy, its command structure, its overall battle readiness and, finally, the military effectiveness of the Chinese Imperial Navy's foreign-bought technology.

THE DIVISION OF THE CHINESE IMPERIAL NAVY INTO FLEETS

Before turning to accounts of the Battle of the Yellow Sea, it is important to set the historical stage and describe the structure and composition of the Chinese Imperial Navy. To do this, it will be necessary to discuss the formation of China's first modern navy in the mid-nineteenth century. At this time China was ruled by the non-Han

Manchus, the founders of the Qing dynasty. Fearful of losing their grip on the Imperial throne, the Manchus created a navy which was weak and divided. Although structuring the navy into separate fleets may have protected the Manchus from the dangers of mutiny or a naval-led coup, this approach would have disastrous military consequences.

China began to build a modern navy in the 1860s. It is not widely known today that by the early 1890s China's Imperial Navy was ranked eighth in the world, with a total of 65 ships, compared to Japan's eleventh ranking with only 32 ships. Immediately prior to the Sino-Japanese War, one British admiral even claimed that China's Imperial Navy 'would prove more than a match for the Japanese at sea; in fact, the Japanese would not be in it'.[5]

In the 1890s, however, the Chinese Imperial Navy's overall size and weaponry was offset by several factors. Most important of these was that it was divided into separate regional fleets. Responsibility for this development is often given to Ding Ruchang (1823–82), a coastal defence strategist who argued that China's Imperial Navy should be divided into Northern, Central and Southern fleets. The Northern Fleet would protect the Yellow Sea from the Liaodong peninsula to the Shandong peninsula. The Central Fleet would protect the eastern seaboard and the entry to the Yangzi River near Shanghai. Finally, the Southern Fleet would protect Fujian and Guangdong provinces.[6] According to a slightly different interpretation by Richard Wright, the division may be traced to 1861 when China established two High Commissioners for Trade in Tianjin and Shanghai. The northern was called the Beiyang, or 'North Ocean', office, while the southern was called the 'Nanyang,' or 'South Ocean', office.[7]

In any event, by the late 1870s the Chinese government had ordered the development of several modern naval fleets, based at Guangzhou, the Fuzhou Naval Yard in southeast China and along the Yangzi River. Meanwhile, in the north, Li Hongzhang was the head of the Anhui Army, which had born the brunt of the fighting against the Taiping, the Nian and the Muslim rebellions, and he soon became responsible for forming the Beiyang Navy in China's northern waters.[8]

Although these regional fleets should have cooperated closely with each other, in fact they all too often refused to cooperate in times of war. This problem was most evident in the mid-1880s, when the Beiyang fleet refused to come to the aid of the Nanyang fleet during the Sino-French war. Although the leader of the Beiyang fleet, Li Hongzhang, argued that Japan might take advantage of the Beiyang fleet's absence to attack, by refusing to assist the Southern fleet he doomed it to destruction. During 1894, in the midst of the Sino-Japanese War, the Southern fleet returned the favour. In partial repayment for their de facto neutrality, the Japanese even allowed one of the few ships from the Southern fleet—named the *Guangxi*—to depart Weihaiwei Harbour unharmed after the fighting was over.[9]

Some accounts have argued that dividing China's Imperial Navy into separate fleets was intended to protect China from surprise attack by potential enemies. As we have seen, however, the non-Han Manchu leaders were more concerned about possible anti-government uprisings or coups should the separate fleets ever be merged into one. For the sake of political safety, therefore, there was little central control over the regional navies. Government policy appeared to be that the fleets compete with, rather than assist, each other.

Furthermore, within each separate fleet there was a notable lack of central authority. As described by Tyler, the Beiyang fleet was like a 'machine' whose 'complexity lay in a vast muddle of diverse motives and ideals'. Instead of efficiency, from the Viceroy down to the director of the arsenal, the interlocking 'wheels revolved to no general purpose but only to their own'. In the midst of this confusion, there could be no 'homogeneity of purpose', but only a 'monstrously disordered epicyclic heterogeneity'.[10] The lack of a unified naval structure, both to connect the various fleets and to direct them efficiently, proved an enormous disadvantage to the Chinese.

CHINESE COMMAND AND CONTROL

During the Sino-Japanese War, the prospects of Chinese naval success were hampered by the generally poor performance of China's naval command. In particular, many accounts suggest that Admiral Ding Ruchang's inept leadership doomed the Chinese Imperial Navy to a rapid defeat. China's naval problems ran much deeper, however, with an inadequately-trained officer corps and endemic corruption in the area of weapons and ammunition procurement. All these factors contributed to China's defeat.

Admiral Ding was a soldier—a former cavalry officer—rather than a sailor by training, and had little technical knowledge of ships. According to Tyler, the Chinese commander was given a co-admiral so as 'to save Admiral Ding from summary decapitation, in case of a reverse', the traditional practice in China.[11] His co-admiral, the German advisor von Hanneken, also was not a trained sailor but, according to a *North China*

Philo McGiffin after the Battle of the Yalu, September 1894. 'Commodore Lin was our captain, but he was not to be seen at Yalu . . . I kept on hearing a curious noise going on below me in the conning tower every time there was a lull in the firing, and going down there . . . I [fell] over . . . Lin, lying flat on his stomach, cursing and grovelling, and praying for all he was worth.' Commander Philo McGiffin, *Zhen Yuan*. (USN Naval Historical Center)

Daily News report of the period, von Hanneken was actually listed as being in command of the Chinese fleet.[12] Although Tyler was very complimentary, describing von Hanneken as a 'man of long and trusty service with the Chinese and of great capacity and daring', he also truthfully remarked on 'the burlesque touch of his position, for he [von Hanneken] was also no sailor'.[13]

The admiral and the other high-ranking Chinese officers were woefully deficient in familiarity with modern naval strategy and tactics. One of the most obvious differences between the Chinese and Japanese fleets at the outset of the battle was in their tactical deployment. On the day of the battle Admiral Ding's ten ships were sailing in what has widely been described as a ragged wedge-shaped formation.[14] This unified formation did allow the battleships to use maximum firepower, but greatly reduced the manoeuvrability of the Chinese fleet as a whole. The Japanese, in contrast, divided their 12-ship fleet into two squadrons: the First Flying Squadron under Rear Admiral Tsuboi Kozo and the Principal Squadron under Vice Admiral Ito Sukeyuki. Although the Chinese fleet was substantially larger in tonnage than its opponents, this tactical decision played to the Japanese fleet's faster speed and greater mobility, giving it a crucial advantage.

Tyler described the Chinese formation as a 'coup' by the *Ding Yuan's* Captain Liu Buchan, since Admiral Ding and von Hanneken had formerly decided on using the 'Line Ahead of Sections', which would have put the flagships out ahead of the remainder of the fleet. According to Tyler, Liu made this change to save his own skin: 'With the battleships in the centre and the weakest vessels on the wings, the enemy would give the latter first attention; it would be a respite for a time, for an hour perhaps or more; it would avoid the immediate concentrating fire on his ship that would result from Line Ahead'.[15]

Tyler further reported that since it was too late to change the signals, he advised Admiral Ding and von Hanneken to retain this formation. Thus, the Chinese fleet went into battle with the incorrect formation.[16] During the battle, the Chinese zigzag, wedge formation, or crescent shape—depending upon which source one relies—made it difficult for the individual ships to manoeuvre, and once communications were disrupted it also made the ships easy targets. After the battle, Chinese accounts attempted to 'pass the buck' by blaming the foreign advisors. Instead of pointing at Captain Liu, these accounts claimed that Admiral Ding had initially ordered a different fighting formation but was overruled by Tyler, identified as the foreign captain of the Chinese flagship, whom they claimed hoped to protect his own ship by placing it in the centre.[17]

THE BATTLE

On the day of the battle, the sea was calm and the weather clear. The Japanese first reported smoke on the horizon at 10.50 am and Vice Admiral Ito ordered his fleet to close with the Chinese at 12.05 pm. The Japanese First Flying Squadron was in the lead and steamed at full speed toward the centre of the Chinese formation, but gradually veered to port so that it could attack the Chinese flank. Meanwhile, at 12.50 pm the Japanese Principal Squadron steamed in front of the Chinese formation and began to manoeuvre around behind it. The ships in the Principal Squadron bore the brunt of China's initial artillery attack when they were still 6000 metres away. These first shells missed, and five minutes later the Principal Squadron formed its own wedge-shaped formation and began firing at 3000 metres.

China's problems were compounded by the fact that Admiral Ding had been injured in the opening exchange, hurt by the blast from his own flagship's guns. Again, the main source for this is Tyler. In his account, as the two fleets closed Admiral Ding gave the order to Captain Liu to alter course to starboard to protect their starboard flank and bring the two Chinese battleships into a position to make first contact with the Japanese. Liu disobeyed this order and Tyler, after hurling a curse, hurried to advise Ding. The Admiral was standing on the temporary wooden flying-bridge, which extended over the muzzles of the 10-inch barbette guns. As Tyler reached Ding's side Liu gave the order to open fire. In Tyler's words: 'That bridge was quite well named: it flew, and so did Ding and I'.[18]

A main tactical goal of the Japanese fleet was to damage the Chinese flagship and hence destroy the enemy's cohesion. Within minutes of the battle's opening a shell from the Japanese flagship *Matsushima* damaged the upper half of the *Ding Yuan*'s central mast, disrupting Admiral Ding's ability to signal his fleet. Then a lucky Japanese shot hit the helm room of the *Ding Yuan*, killing two men and destroying all the signal flags. This put paid to any further communication between the flagship and the remainder of the Chinese fleet. To add insult to injury, another Japanese shell knocked over the flagship's main mast. This led to the Admiral's flag falling to the deck, which merely increased the level of organisational confusion.

Taking advantage of the Chinese ships' lack of communications, the Japanese Principal Squadron dispersed and surrounded their opponent's fleet, firing continuously at the main group. In the face of such intense short-range fire the Chinese fleet also split up. Since the Chinese ships were now on their own, several turned on one of the weakest of the

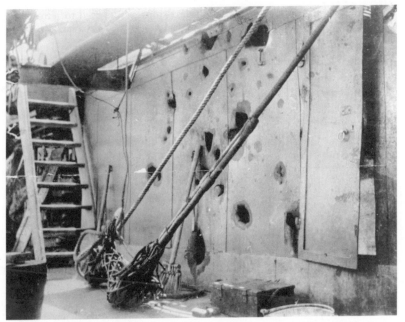

Battle damage to *Zhen Yuan*, September 1894. 'My van and main squadrons subsequently attacked the *Ding Yuan* and *Zhen Yuan* from both sides simultaneously. The former was soon in flames forward. My van then proceeded in chase of the runaway vessels, and sank the *King Yuan*, the main squadron still engaging the *Ding Yuan* and *Zhen Yuan*.' Vice Admiral Ito Sukeyuki, IJN, HIJMS *Matsushima*. (USN: NH 61993)

Japanese ships, the 600-ton gunboat *Akagi*. Her main mast was soon destroyed and her captain killed, but although apparently doomed, the Flying Squadron intervened and the *Akagi* managed to limp away to safety. The Chinese severely damaged two other smaller Japanese ships and achieved a 12-inch hit on the *Matsushima*, which devastated her gun crews, but this proved the limit of their success.

By failing to remain in formation and coordinate their fire against the principal Japanese ships, the Chinese fleet suffered heavy losses while the Japanese fleet weathered the engagement without the loss of a single vessel. In fact, during the four-and-a-half hours of battle, the Japanese quick-firing cannon poured thousands of shells into the Chinese ships. The battleship *Zhen Yuan* reportedly sustained over 400 hits during the course of the engagement, surviving only because the Japanese shells could not pierce her 14-inch armour. Nevertheless, a total of four Chinese ships were sunk and there were over 1000 Chinese casualties.[19]

After the battle, the surviving Chinese ships were forced to retreat to Port Arthur for repairs. Later the fleet relocated to Weihaiwei, which unfortunately did not have repair facilities. Although the Beiyang fleet still existed in name, it had lost some of its best ships and its reputation had been severely damaged. More importantly, the Japanese fleet now dominated the sea routes between China and Korea. This strategic position gave the Japanese a virtual free hand to conduct further land operations during the remaining months of the war. Surrounded by the Japanese both on land and at sea, Admiral Ding decided that the tactical situation was hopeless. On 12 February 1895 he surrendered. Later that day, Ding and two other high-ranking officers committed suicide to atone for their failure.

Because Ding's suicide was considered by the Japanese to be an honourable ending for a defeated commanding officer, his body was sent to Qifu for burial. As the ship bearing his body departed the harbour 'the Japanese men-of-war lowered their flags and fired their guns in honor of the late Admiral'.[20] Perhaps as a result of his suicide, Ding's failings as a commander have been glossed over in most Chinese and Japanese studies of the war.

BATTLE EXPERIENCE OF OFFICERS AND SAILORS

Although much of the blame for the Chinese defeat must rest with Admiral Ding, the less than professional behaviour of more junior Chinese officers cannot be ignored. Although there were many examples of individual bravery, the average Chinese officer was poorly trained and ill-suited for battle. According to Philo McGiffin's descriptions, most of the officers came from the 'mandarin class', and so were 'soft from good living and almost indifferent to learning gunnery or navigation'. Seeing their military rank as merely a 'status symbol', they took little pride in their profession and had no personal loyalty to the Navy.[21] In the heat of battle, many of these officers fled, or hid below decks.

Accounts of the battle vary widely but, not surprisingly, a lack of discipline seems to have been a major problem. Certainly, the training and professionalism of the Chinese crews proved in most cases to be below expectations. According to one account, a junior officer serving in the *Yang Wai* had a rather unique way of getting his stokers to shovel coal faster. On the one hand, he had several cases of gin, and would hand around bottles to the sweating coolies to urge them to work harder. On the other hand, however, he held a thick rubber club and 'whenever a man lagged he beat him with it until he picked up his shovel again'.[22]

By contrast, the foreign advisors, like Philo McGiffin in the *Zhen Yuan*, drilled their sailors relentlessly and were usually given credit for whatever discipline existed. McGiffin ordered the Chinese 'powder monkeys' to disperse ammunition at regular intervals, so as to avoid high concentrations of munitions. Sailors holding 50-pound powder bags were lying prone on the deck of the ship, 'waiting to spring up and pass it on when it should be wanted'.[23] McGiffin's biggest concern, however, was defective shells, many of which were found to contain black sand instead of gunpowder.[24]

In every ship the sailors' nerves were tense. This was especially the case below deck, since they could not 'see the approaching enemy, [and] nothing was known, save that any moment might begin the action, and bring a shell in through the side'.[25] Once the battle actually began, however, the Chinese sailors reportedly became more confident. Notwithstanding the critical comments passed by other foreigners, McGiffin himself found ample evidence of courage and fighting spirit. He lavished particular praise on the crew of the *Lai Yuan*:

> About the middle of the fight the *Lai Yuan* caught fire aft, and burned fiercely. The broadside guns could not be manned, being surrounded by flames; but the bow guns were worked steadily, while the crew persistently fought the flames on the quarter-deck. Below, in the engine-rooms, with ventilators stopped on account of fire overhead, and, in darkness, receiving orders only by voice-tube transmitted from the deck through the stoke-hole, the engineers stood their duty, hour after hour, in a temperature bordering on 200°. After several hours the fire was extinguished; but these brave men were in several cases blinded for life, and in every instance horribly burned and disfigured . . . [26]

It should be noted that medical facilities of any sort were minimal and, according to one report, the surgeon on the *Yang Wai* constantly carried an 'atomizer with prussic acid'. After determining that his wounds were hopeless, the surgeon would spray 'the poison into the man's mouth and nostrils' and he would quickly expire. As elucidated by an anonymous reporter: 'There were very few of the wounded who were not put out of their misery by the surgeon's atomizer'.[27]

RELIANCE ON NEW TECHNOLOGY

A further explanation for China's poor showing was its Navy's incomplete and uncoordinated adoption of Western technology. Many of the Chinese ships were built in Europe and were armed with a wide variety of guns. This meant that there was little consistency in requirements between different ships, greatly exacerbating the problem of supplying proper ordnance.

In his in-depth study of the Chinese fleet, Chia-chien Wang has determined several reasons, including scientific and technological, that led to its failure. Wang concluded that when 'considering all aspects— industry, science and technology, personnel, and finance—China at the time was quite unqualified to support a modern navy'.[28] This was perhaps best shown in the midst of battle, when the officers' and crews' insufficient training with their newly-purchased Western equipment contributed to their rapid defeat and destruction.

McGiffin also mentioned examples of technology being unsuited to the conditions. For example, the steel gunshields covering the four 12-inch Krupp guns on the *Zhen Yuan* were removed since, according to McGiffin: 'As they revolved with the guns a shot might easily jam them, and being too thin to keep out any but light machine gun missiles, they would have served only as man traps, since shells which might pass directly over the barbette and on when meeting no resistance, if intercepted by these shields, would have penetrated and, bursting, have filled the entire closed space with flame and fragments'.[29]

Undoubtedly Chinese government corruption also played an important role in the outcome of the battle. Corruption was rife at all levels of the Navy, from captains who pocketed funds intended for the repair and upkeep of their ships to senior officers implicated in schemes to sell cartridge gunpowder on the black market and replace it with coal dust. The autocratic Qing court was also to blame for the widespread corruption. According to one account, an estimated $12 million in naval funds had been diverted by the Empress Dowager between 1889 and 1894 to refurbish the Summer Palace in Beijing and to build a floating 'Marble Boat'.[30]

Inadequate supplies of ammunition, however, were perhaps the greatest problem. The Chinese had more large-calibre guns, yet Tyler has described how, due to corruption, the fleet's entire inventory of large shells consisted of only three projectiles several weeks before the battle.[31] By 5 pm on the day of the battle, the 6-inch shells were gone and most of the 12-inch shells were also used up. In the *Zhen Yuan*, there were only three 12-inch shells left and these were loaded into the last three functioning guns. Fortunately for the Chinese, the Japanese did not realise how little ammunition was left, and the battle ended at 5.45 pm as sunset approached. This allowed the surviving Chinese ships to limp back to their main base at Port Arthur.

The Japanese attack on Port Arthur, November 1894. 'We hear that our combined squadrons have fought gallantly in the Yellow Sea and have gained a great victory, and it is apparent that they will henceforth hold the command of the enemy's seas. Deeply appreciating the services of our officers and men, we feel devoutly thankful for the wonderful results which they have obtained.' The Emperor Meiji. (Australian National Maritime Museum, Sydney)

According to J.C. Perry, the major reason for Japan's rout of China was that 'the Japanese fleet was newer and far better equipped than the Chinese. The quick-firing guns of the Japanese cruisers gave them immense advantage over their foe'. But another reason also appears clear: the Japanese 'men were far better trained and disciplined' than the Chinese.[32] In the end, it was Japan's more effective use of their foreign-made ships and weapons which turned the tide of battle.

PARALLELS BETWEEN PAST AND PRESENT

There are various similarities between the Chinese Imperial Navy of 1894 and the PLAN of today, including: the division of China's Navy into separate fleets; poorly maintained command and control; lack of proper battle experience in officers and sailors; and misuse of Western technology. All these deficiencies could potentially have a negative impact on the military performance of the current Chinese Navy.

The PLAN is now ranked as one of the largest fleets in Asia and its maritime mission has recently been described as evolving from a role of static coastal defence to one of 'active offshore defence'. This includes a new strategy 'to assert China's role as a regional maritime power, to protect coastal economic regions and maritime interests, and to optimise the Navy's operations for national defence . . .'.[33] In early April 2001,

Zheng Ming, Director of the Armament and Technology Department of the Chinese Navy, cautioned in a PLA magazine that China must enhance its maritime awareness. In particular, he stressed that the 'PLA must speed up the modernisation of its naval forces so that China can transform from a large oceanic country into a strong ocean power at an early date'.[34]

As in the 1890s, however, the PLAN is still hampered by an outmoded fleet system. Likewise, today's PLAN is commanded by officers with little or no actual battle experience, official corruption is rampant and it is not clear whether the communist leaders have been willing to devote the resources needed to turn the Chinese Navy into a world-class fleet. Specifically, there is no firm schedule for the construction of a Chinese aircraft carrier, which many PLAN commentators have suggested would be necessary for China to possess a true 'blue water' capability.

The PLAN is divided into three separate fleets. The Northern Fleet is headquartered in Qingdao, the Eastern Fleet is based in Ningbo and the South Sea Fleet is based in Zhanjiang. The PLAN has begun to discuss the need to increase unified training but only recently has there even been the suggestion that the various fleets should actively 'conduct combined operations together'.[35] Each fleet, however, has a specific geographical area for which it is responsible. Specifically, the Northern Fleet must defend the capital, the Eastern Fleet is responsible for the Diaoyu (in Japanese, Senkaku) islands and the Taiwan Strait, and the South Sea Fleet is focused on the Spratlys and the South China Sea. Therefore, considering the vast differences in their responsibilities, and acknowledging that the current communist government might be concerned about uprisings and coups, it is an open question whether these three fleets could actually merge and work together as a single unit in times of crisis.[36]

Current Chinese command and control is also suspect. As in 1894, naval commanders must report to army generals in charge of the military districts under which the fleets must operate. Although training levels have vastly improved, modern-day PLAN commanders may encounter similar tactical problems as Ding, especially since the Chinese Navy does not engage in as much live-fire training as its Western counterparts.

Many commentators also acknowledge that the officer corps of the PLAN is weak in terms of its loyalty. In a pattern which would be all too reminiscent of China's earlier naval encounter, the modern-day PLAN may well experience widespread desertions. Certainly, as China's economic reforms have proceeded, the pay and conditions of Chinese naval personnel have diminished in relative terms. This may well under-mine the loyalty and fervour of the officer corps, a situation which would undoubtedly have a serious negative impact on their actions under fire.

Finally, the purchasing of foreign-made equipment can engender problems. This dilemma may affect the contemporary Chinese Navy, since much of its high-tech equipment is being procured from abroad, particularly from Russia. These purchases include diesel-electric submarines and SSN-22 Sunburn surface-to-surface missiles (3M80E *Mosquito*) for use on its *Sovremenny* Class missile destroyers. According to some reports, China currently possesses only 54 of these missiles, a totally inadequate number if the PLAN were actually to use these ships in battle. In addition to serious problems with maintenance and repair, it is not altogether clear whether PLAN officers and men have received sufficient hands-on training or adequately translated manuals to be able to use these weapons effectively.

The repair of foreign-made equipment remains a critical problem. In late March 2001, it was reported that China had signed a contract with Russia for a pre-repairs inspection of a diesel submarine which China had bought from Russia two years previously. The Chinese Navy decided that the submarine should be repaired at the Zvezda shipyard, located in Bolshoi Kamen, after examining Zvezda, the Amur shipyard and the Dalzavod shipyard during 1999. Certainly, this extensive search for a proper facility would suggest that China cannot undertake such repairs itself.

There is thus a probability that the PLAN suffers from some of the same systemic problems which plagued the Imperial Navy in the last modern Chinese naval engagement. In time of war these limitations could have drastic consequences. If there were ever a naval battle between the PLAN and another of the world's major navies, the outcome might well exhibit certain parallels with the Battle of the Yellow Sea. Although the Chinese are well-known for studying and learning from their own history, what is as yet unclear is whether they realise that, as in 1894, these histori-cal parallels could have a significant negative impact.

4 | The commander in crisis

Graf Spee and the German East Asian Cruiser Squadron in 1914

Peter Overlack

THE EMPHASIS IN much historical writing on the theme of the commander in wartime deals with issues well into the period of hostilities. But what of the decisions which must be made before hostilities commence? What will be the best course of strategic action? How does the commander ensure that his force will be most effective? How does he maintain fighting efficiency and morale under conditions of material deprivation and restricted communications? This chapter examines these questions in light of the situation faced by the German East Asian Cruiser Squadron before August 1914, and the factors which influenced its commander, Vice Admiral Maximilian Johannes Maria Hubertus Reichsgraf von Spee.

THE MAN AND HIS COMMAND

Spee was born in 1861 and entered the Imperial Navy as a cadet at seventeen. Early photographs show a serious young man, tall and lean. Posted as Artillery Officer to the armoured ship *Bayern*, he specialised in heavy gunnery. In later years he suffered intensely from rheumatism, aggravated by a fever caught in Kamerun while serving as Harbour Commander in Duala. In 1899 he was promoted to *Korvettenkapitän* (Lieutenant-Commander), and saw active service in China with the Cruiser Squadron then commanded by the Kaiser's brother, Prince Heinrich, with whom he worked closely as Admiralty Staff Officer. From 1908–10 Spee was Chief of Staff North Sea Naval Stations. This was a crucial coastal defence position and he reported directly to the Kaiser. In January 1910 he was promoted to Rear Admiral, and returned to a sea command in the armoured cruiser *Yorck*.

In September 1912, Spee was promoted to command of the East Asian Station, considered one of the most prestigious commands in the Imperial Navy as it represented German power in a region of increasing strategic importance. Significantly, the distance from home provided the Squadron Chief with a considerable degree of autonomy. Conversely, the degree of responsibility was also much higher. On 4 December 1912 Spee assumed command of the Squadron in Shanghai from Vice Admiral Günther von Krosigk. In early 1913 he had an audience with the Japanese Emperor and this, along with his interest in Chinese politics, sharpened his interest in diplomacy and Germany's position and future in Asia. In November 1913 he was promoted to Vice Admiral.

While possessing a strong sense of self-discipline, and exhibiting methodical ways in an orthodox naval career, Spee's memoranda and letters show he was not averse to independent and creative thinking. He had a perceptive grasp of world affairs and the currents of international diplomacy, and was occasionally critical of the *Realpolitik* that Germany was pursuing. While he supported Navy Secretary Alfred von Tirpitz in his drive to build a battleship-based fleet, this did not prevent him from recognising the potential of cruisers within wider naval warfare.

Spee personified the highest ideals of the German officer corps. He was known as a tough but fair commander, and woe betide any junior officer who submitted an insufficiently prepared report or proposal. His letters show the wide range of his interests, from politics to literature and botany. Austere in his personal life, he indulged in few of the luxuries his status made available, and at every opportunity sought to avoid the round of social engagements which came with his official position. Spee was a serious thinker, perhaps in this sense too introverted, and there is sometimes a streak of melancholy in his writings. He was a devout Catholic and placed his trust in God when confronted with a difficult situation. Above all, his letters show a deep humanity and a concern for the welfare of the men under his command.

The letters Spee wrote to his family, principally to his wife Margarethe (Grete) and daughter Huberta, found their way by circuitous means through neutral countries to Germany.[1] The working of the naval postal system is itself an interesting story. The first wartime post from the East Asian Cruiser Squadron was taken at Ponape on 6 August 1914. To avoid it falling into the hands of the occupying Japanese forces, the post-master gave it into the care of the Capuchin Mission, where it was buried in a metal case under the church floor until 1923, when it was finally forwarded to Germany. At Pagan in the Marianas the collier *Markomania* received more post, but this was lost when the British captured the vessel. Before departing Eniwetok in the Marshall Islands on 22 August, the Squadron's post and despatches were given to the cruiser *Nürnberg* which went to Honolulu before rejoining the Squadron on 6 September. There was no further opportunity for post until the Squadron reached Easter Island in mid-October, when a collier was sent to Valparaiso in Chile. The next opportunity was in Valparaiso on 13 November, after the victory at Coronel, and the final post was sent from Peñas Gulf in Chile on 26 November 1914, the date on Spee's last letter to his wife.

The German Cruiser Squadron was based at the port of Tsingtao in the leased territory of Kiautschou in northern China. The Squadron's wartime orders were to attack merchant vessels, lines of communication and, to a limited extent, coastal fortifications, with the aim of halting exports of raw materials and foodstuffs to Britain via the Suez and Cape routes. The East Asian command was strictly organised into regional Stations with assigned light cruisers and gunboats, while the armoured cruisers ranged over the entire expanse of the Indian and Pacific Oceans. Adequate facilities for coaling and provisioning were essential for the effective operation of cruisers in wartime and throughout the 1890s the German Navy had been surveying remote harbours and anchorages. Contractual arrangements were also made with German shipping companies to convey coal, food and munitions from neutral and Australian harbours to the Squadron's warships. When hostilities were declared these merchant vessels would be converted into armed auxiliary cruisers, which would assist the Squadron in wreaking havoc on Anglo-Australasian trade and shipping.[2]

In 1914 the Squadron comprised the sister ships *Scharnhorst* and *Gneisenau*, armoured cruisers of 11 420 tons, with eight 21-cm and six 15-cm guns, and a maximum speed of 23.5 knots. Although the total armament was not heavy for ships of this size, its range and accuracy was to prove useful. The two armoured cruisers were supported by the light cruisers *Leipzig*, *Nürnberg* and *Emden*. Attached to the Squadron, and patrolling the Australian Station, was *Cormoran*, a light unarmoured cruiser of 1600 tons. The Squadron maintained a high standard of training and gunnery, so much so that when the two armoured cruisers competed for the naval gunnery prize at Kiel, they were the two finalists for the Kaiser's Gold Medal. Although many members of the Squadron's crews were relieved in May 1914, their replacements were fully trained and almost all the original officers remained.

THE FIRST STAGES OF WAR

At the end of 1913 Spee wrote of the strategic importance of the Pacific region. Its central position and numerous hiding places made it an ideal area for ongoing commerce warfare. His task was clear: 'We have to appear as a unified force where the mercantile traffic comes together, before important harbours, or in much frequented straits'.[3] Contact with enemy forces always had to be anticipated.

The Squadron's plans for 1914 were to take it on a lengthy tour of duty. *Scharnhorst* and *Gneisenau*, with the collier *Titania*, departed Nagasaki on 28 June for the Caroline and Marshall Islands. This was to be followed by stops at Samoa, Fiji, Bougainville and New Guinea before returning to Tsingtao at the end of September. On 28 June a Serb nationalist, Gavrilo Princip, assassinated the Austrian Archduke Franz Ferdinand, and Spee received the first news of rising political tensions in Europe at Truk on 7 July 1914.

Spee's greatest fear materialised immediately. Britain provided Japan with the basis to enter the war when Whitehall requested assistance under the terms of the 1902 Alliance. The Royal Navy's China Squadron was too weak to blockade Tsingtao and would have been pinned down and unable to protect British shipping in East Asia. The Japanese, however, had more far-reaching plans and advocated an attack on Tsingtao. *Emden* remained based there, with its commander, *Fregattenkapitän* Karl von Müller, as Senior Officer. His initial intention was to disrupt Russian commerce in the straits of Tsushima and towards Vladivostok, before sailing to Pagan to join Spee.[4]

Spee's personal observations reveal his thoughts on the developing situation. On 2 August, in a letter to his daughter, he wrote that the prospect of a war involving all Europe was 'unmentionably saddening, and my thoughts are quite mixed, all here, all there'. He evidently believed war was inevitable, and while at Ponape visited the Capuchin Fathers 'to prepare myself for the most serious eventuality'. *Scharnhorst*, he remarked, had been put on a war footing, and all unnecessary items removed to shore and stored. Spee concluded that 'We all rest in God's hand . . . whatever may come will come regardless, and we have to come to terms with it . . . If we fall, then it is in the service of a good cause'.[5]

Spee was unaware of Germany's convoluted diplomatic exchanges with Japan. He had been informed that Japan would stay neutral if no attack were made on British Asian territory. The Station Officer at Shanghai, however, believed that Japan would attack regardless. He based this on reports of steamer movements bringing reservists from Canton and Hong Kong to Shanghai for travel to Tsingtao.[6] On 17 August Foreign Minister Gottfried von Jagow received from the Japanese chargé d'affaires the ultimatum which would have such far-reaching effects. Given Japan's treaty obligations to Britain, Germany should immediately withdraw from Japanese and Chinese waters all warships and armed vessels, and disarm those which could not be withdrawn. No later than 15 September, Germany should deliver 'the entire leased territory of Kiaochow, without condition or compensation . . .'. If by noon on 23 August no German response indicating unconditional acceptance had been received, Japan would be 'compelled to take such action as deemed necessary' to meet the situation.[7] Hence were set in motion the events which would determine the fate of the East Asian Cruiser Squadron.

Logistical problems needed careful attention. Loading at sea from colliers and at some of the remoter atolls would be an ongoing technical and physical challenge. In August 1914 at Ponape, *Scharnhorst* and *Gneisenau* had full bunkers and colliers, but Spee was well aware that under existing circumstances he would not be able to obtain sufficient coal for extended operations. He noted in his War Log:

> The cohesion of the Cruiser Squadron, including the auxiliary cruisers, imposes a very difficult if not impossible demand on the coal supply. Thus a division of the force must be considered through which the different trade routes can be threatened. The armoured cruisers should remain hidden as long as possible, so that the enemy is constantly required to reckon with an encounter, and accordingly detach a strong force . . . The seeking out of enemy forces only comes into question . . . when we are superior.[8]

This strategy could be altered according to circumstances. There was always the possibility that the British 'on political grounds . . . will suddenly attack us from the rear . . . I have to keep the Squadron's presence hidden'. Its location had to remain a point of conjecture for the Allies.[9] The Cruiser Squadron indeed appeared to have been swallowed up by the vast expanse of the Pacific, which worried the Allies. Spee had thus already achieved one of his strategic aims. Colonel William Holmes, who led Australia's New Guinea Expeditionary Force, observed that although he believed the larger German warships had gone southeast, 'until they are accounted for, and in the absence of the Australian Fleet, merchants will not risk the loss of shipments'.[10]

At this time Spee was without *Leipzig* and *Dresden*. *Leipzig* was in Mexican waters and received news of Germany's mobilisation at Mazatlan on 2 August. Her orders were to attack the large 'Empress-class' steamers which carried Anglo-Canadian trade to East Asia. On 17 August *Leipzig* entered San Francisco to coal, but encountered difficulties and departed after 24 hours, heading south. Coal was finally loaded at Guayamas in the Gulf of California. Entering so deep into the narrow gulf was a calculated risk for the captain, *Fregattenkapitän* J.S. Haun, who wrote in a letter to his wife on 2 September: 'We lack coal, coal, coal, and the worst is, our opponents know this . . . Entering Guayamas was very uncomfortable for me, but I am out of the trap now'.[11] The task was not made easier by the extreme heat. Coal was procured again on 3 October near Callao from a Kosmos Line steamer. Meanwhile *Dresden* had commenced her homeward voyage from St Thomas in the Caribbean with full bunkers on 31 July. The next day came orders to implement cruiser warfare. On 21 August off Rio de Janeiro *Dresden* was joined by the gunboat *Eber*, which had come from West Africa, and a second supply ship.

STRATEGY AND OPERATIONS: SPEE'S OPTIONS AND MOVEMENTS

Spee recognised that although his Squadron was approximately equal to its British counterpart, two factors could quickly change this—Japan's entry into the war and the arrival of the battle cruiser HMAS *Australia*. By joining with *Australia*, the British China Squadron could at any time establish an unconditional superiority over German forces. Thus a major consideration had to be avoiding the Australians while still conducting attacks on commerce until inevitably the Squadron was forced to retreat to safer waters. On 2 August the flagship *Scharnhorst* received a telegram based on advice from Consul-General Richard Kiliani in Sydney that in the event of war *Australia* and three cruisers would patrol the Australia and China Stations.[12]

Vice Admiral Graf von Spee. 'Count Spee is running short of munitions; he can scarcely last in a long battle; it would be a miracle if he broke through. The whole of America is aiding Britain and France, and if *we* get a little coal there is a great outcry. It is contemptible injustice towards us . . .' Grand Admiral von Tirpitz, State Secretary of the Imperial Naval Office. (P. Overlack)

What options did Spee have? Given the difficulty of obtaining coal and the uncertainty of the whole situation, it was difficult for him to assess the most effective course of action. The Squadron's earlier position at Ponape, while central to the German possessions, was far removed both from Tsingtao and the secondary base at Rabaul. Neither was it within striking distance of any frequently-used merchant shipping route. Spee assumed that a continuous supply of coal would be sent from San Francisco, but difficulties created by the American authorities caused a change of plan. *Nürnberg* arrived at Ponape on 6 August and, after recoaling, the Squadron headed for Pagan in the Marianas, arriving on 11 August. Here Spee was joined by *Emden* as well as the auxiliaries *Prinz Eitel Friedrich* and *Cormoran*. (The latter was the captured steamer *Rjäsan* of the Russian Volunteer Fleet, outfitted as an auxiliary cruiser and re-named after *Cormoran* which had been laid up in Tsingtao.) Considerable supplies, including live cattle, came with the steamers. In what were to be the last such moments, the doctor on *Gneisenau* wrote that after a day of loading there was an enjoyable gathering with coffee and music in the salon of the North German Lloyd steamer *Yorck*.[13]

Spee's War Log and his letters to his wife reveal his frustration at being unable to engage the enemy directly, although he did accept that this could only be undertaken in favourable circumstances. His prime task was to stop trade, and he had to consider where the Squadron would be most effective. Returning to Tsingtao was ruled out by the possibility of Japanese entry into the war. Attacks on shipping across the Pacific could be supported by coal and provisions carried by German steamers from the ports of the Philippines and the Dutch East Indies. Working against this course of action was the number of supply ships required, which would limit the Squadron's mobility and flexibility—factors Spee rightly saw as his major advantage. Such a large German presence would attract *Australia*, and eluding the battle cruiser remained a determining factor in weighing up his options. Nevertheless he wrote optimistically that 'It is not easy to find a vessel in these extensive waters, provided the coal supply is there'.[14]

With the support of the colonial bases, coal depots at remote island anchorages and radio stations in New Guinea and other points in the Pacific, the Squadron was capable of operating against trade routes over a vast area of Southeast Asia and the Pacific. Should Japanese activity preclude this, a less promising but safer area of operations lay off the North and South American coasts, the latter carrying the bulk of Australian meat transports and most of New Zealand's products destined for Britain. Spee advised the German Admiralty of his likely approach on 4 August:

> In view of Japanese conditions for neutrality, regard it as necessary in event of war with England, providing coal supply suffices, to leave the East Asian Station and either conduct cruiser warfare in Indian Ocean or return home around South America. In this event, I request coal supply in Chile be organised.[15]

Germany had made considerable efforts to cultivate the Chileans over the years, and their neutrality was not expected to be enforced strictly in wartime.[16]

That same night the Squadron received news of Britain's declaration of war. Spee's immediate dilemma was that he should not provide Japan with an excuse to attack Tsingtao. His War Log noted that in order to protect Tsingtao, the Cruiser Squadron would not attack British territory in East Asia. Spee now had to decide on the best course of action: advancing to the Indian Ocean and commerce warfare against shipping on the Suez and Cape routes, or to South American waters and the wider Atlantic.[17] He considered his options carefully:

> For cruiser warfare the region west of Colombo to Aden comes into first consideration, where the East Asian and Australian routes (meat supply

to England) come together; otherwise the Australian coast. The English advance southward leads to the conclusion that they assume this will be our course of action, and are heading south in order to unite with the Australian Squadron and sweep us out of the way. The best thing for them would be to hold us on the Station as fully as possible, or even to force us into Tsingtao.[18]

This important document shows the real possibility of the Cruiser Squadron attacking in full strength in Australasian waters. If he had to depart the region, Spee was determined to inflict as much damage as possible before he left.

A thrust into the Indian Ocean presented the Squadron with the difficulty of obtaining coal when its reserves had been consumed, as there were neither neutral harbours nor connections with agents west of the Dutch Indies. An advance to the west coast of America, however, would make both available. Following his departure from Pagan, and lacking any reliable news about Japanese intentions, Spee wondered whether his decision to head east was the correct one. Would operating in the Indian Ocean be more effective given the frequency of enemy shipping, despite the greater difficulties of supply involved?[19] All efforts were now made to discover Japanese intentions by maintaining radio contact with Tsingtao via *Cormoran* and *Emden*.[20]

On 10 August a telegram from Knorr in Tokyo reported that, on the basis of conversations with his counterparts, it appeared certain Japan would side actively with Britain and that a declaration of war could be expected.[21] The decisive factor in Spee's evaluation of options was a disjointed telegram received on the night of 12–13 August, which contained only the words 'Tokyo . . . declaration of war . . . withdrawal to Chile, as enemy fleet appears departing for Pacific. Naval Attaché'.[22] The Japanese cruiser *Tone* and four torpedo boats had left the home islands the previous day, six cruisers and eleven torpedo boats were ready to depart and *Australia* was evidently heading for Hong Kong. Prospective operations in the whole region south of Tsingtao were looking less feasible every day.

The German Squadron reached Pagan on 12 August. The same day the pivotal radio station on Yap was put out of action by bombardment from the cruiser HMS *Minotaur*.[23] Spee met with his commanders the following afternoon. Having lost the most valuable link in his chain of communications, it would be extremely difficult to locate enemy forces in the vicinity which in turn would greatly disrupt planning. Spee nevertheless acknowledged his good luck to this point, noting that no enemy warship had been encountered, coal had been obtained from a German steamer and that there remained opportunities for attacking trade.[24] So far there had been no disruption of the Squadron's mobilisation, and not one supply vessel had been lost to the Allies—perhaps because they had been repainted in the same colours as British steamers. Spee agreed to Müller's proposal that *Emden* be detached to conduct independent attacks in the Indian Ocean. While an attempt at widespread commerce warfare in the Indian Ocean was considered pointless because of the lack of reliable coal supplies sufficient for the whole Squadron, Spee judged correctly that *Emden* would be able to resupply herself from captured steamers, operate for longer periods and be more effective alone.[25] The Squadron sailed again at 1800 on 13 August, radio signals from *Australia* and other British ships having been detected.

Meanwhile in Berlin on 17 August, the day of Japan's ultimatum, there took place a somewhat depressing meeting on the defence of Kiautschou, chaired by Acting Admiralty Chief of Staff *Konter-Admiral* Behncke and attended by five officers with experience on the East Asian Station.[26] While Tsingtao was lost in any event, they agreed that the Cruiser Squadron could still attack the nearest enemy force and inflict considerable damage. The alternative was for Spee to transfer his whole operation to another ocean, in which case an immediate attack on either British or Japanese forces was not required. If the Squadron were to enter the Atlantic it could not only damage British trade, but also maintain freedom of movement for much longer with the supply and intelligence support arrangements already in place in Central and South America.[27] The final decision, however, rested entirely on Spee's shoulders.

Spee thought it pointless to expose the Squadron to danger before it had contributed anything to the war effort and considered the best course of action would be to keep his whereabouts hidden for as long as possible. As a 'fleet in being' (Spee used the English phrase) its mere unlocated existence could disrupt Anglo–Australasian trade, and later it could choose the optimum time and place for a direct engagement.[28] Spee also decided against entering the Indian Ocean. Even if coal supplies were to make it through enemy lines, the Squadron would still be in the impossible position of resupplying where there were neither neutral coaling harbours nor intelligence agents available.[29] A move to the American coast would provide both, while the Japanese were unlikely to follow for fear of antagonising the United States.[30] Spee interpreted news of the assembly of British forces between Hong Kong and Shanghai to mean that they were waiting for the Squadron to return to Tsingtao. The Germans had sent deliberately misleading radio transmissions to encourage this belief.

Still, *Kapitän zur See* Gustav Otto Maerker, the captain of *Gneisenau*, wrote that 'It is pointless to manoeuvre here against England, Japan, France, and Russia . . . not even the Admiralty Staff knows where we are. Certainly we are already given up for sunk, like the "Goeben" and "Breslau" '.[31] The lack of up-to-date intelligence was a major preoccupation. On 18 August Spee lamented that the only news he had received was of a successful small-scale attack on the British fleet in its home waters and of the battle for Louvain in Belgium. In the Pacific, the British, French and Russians had united their fleets, which boded ill for his Squadron, as it was weaker than this Allied force if it remained together. On the night of 17–18 August, Nauru radioed the position of the Australian Squadron 'heading in full strength to the colonies where we were expected'.[32] Still foremost in Spee's mind was that:

> The English Australian Squadron has as flagship the 'Australia', which alone for the Cruiser Squadron is such a superior opponent, that it must be avoided. In [any] . . . situations the presence of torpedoboats makes the whole situation more difficult.

He also expressed apprehension about the continuity of radio communications,

> . . . which until now has done everything . . . Without it I would know nothing of the War, but it appears that the Yap Station has fallen into enemy hands, for since the 12th it has no longer been functioning. Perhaps I will gain some news from a captured ship.

Spee remained unsure of the sustainability of his operations, and his isolation seems to have put him in a somewhat pessimistic mood: 'Great laurels are not to be achieved, given the conditions. One does one's best . . . Whether my present plans are correct only the future will validate'. The inactivity to which the Squadron was reduced took its toll, and Spee was hard-pressed to maintain morale. Ship life was monotonous. The Chinese cooks and coolies had been put ashore and the crews had to perform their tasks. Combat preparation imposed considerable physical hardships, with the sealing of all openings adding to the hot and claustrophobic atmosphere inside the ships. No lights burned at night, increasing the feeling of gloom. 'The night is no man's friend, and the thoughts that come to one are not exactly uplifting, but I hope that everyday life will accustom us to them.'[33]

During the night of 24 August, Apia radioed openly that Japan had declared war. Five days later Spee wrote to his wife that 'it is quite pointless to remain in East Asian waters, and so I will move from here'. He saw his task as to attack commerce until *Australia* forced the Squadron to change its area of operation.[34] This would entail some cat-and-mouse activity, as he would have to avoid direct contact and any damage which would impair his ships' ability to function for a lengthy period. Nevertheless, on arrival at Apia on 14 September, Spee had hoped to find enemy warships 'which I would have fought gladly, but the nest was empty'. He did not know how many troops were occupying Apia and saw any landing there as pointless, since the enemy would only return once he had departed. Once again the lack of opportunity to join battle annoyed and frustrated him. His thoughts turned to the European front: it would be more productive for Germany to let Austria go and come to an agreement with Russia. Returning to his immediate concerns, he wrote: 'I do not believe I will come into contact with enemy warships in the immediate future'.[35]

The Squadron continued southward and, following a zigzag course, arrived at Nukahiva in the Marquesa Islands on 26 September. Spee wrote to his wife on 1 October, their 25th wedding anniversary, that he had celebrated the day with his sons Otto and Heinrich who were serving in *Nürnberg* and *Gneisenau*. Despite the demands of war there was time for a human touch: he had found with his breakfast the gift of a small silver chocolate dish. Spee also wrote of his recent venture to Tahiti in the hope

SMS *Nürnberg* destroys the Fanning Island Cable Relay Station, 7 September 1914. '. . . our cruisers were everywhere and nowhere. They seemed to mock all of the enemy's exertions. For a long time no English merchantman dared sail in South American waters . . . the English were touched in their most sensitive spot—their moneybags.' Seaman Richard Stumpf, SMS *Helgoland*. (AWM P02564.002)

of finding an enemy warship. Fired upon by the shore battery, he shelled it and sank the gunboat *Zelée*. The town of Papeete was partly destroyed in the exchange. Happily he had just taken custody of some 10 000 francs from the French administration's treasury and could re-provision from the closed Marquesan government stores and a trading company. He had often expressed fears about the security of the post, and did so again, noting that this letter was entrusted to a coaling steamer. The constant uncertainty aggravated the loneliness of command, and Spee told his wife that 'I long for news of you all but that is a forlorn hope . . .'. He enjoyed the company of *Nürnberg*'s captain, Schönberg, but added, 'I am missing social contact very much here on board. The evenings are extremely tedious, as we extinguish the lights. It is too hot to sit in closed rooms, everything is uncomfortable. One cannot escape the coal grime . . .'.[36]

The tedium and strain continued unabated. On 13 October Spee could only report that since leaving the Marquesas the Squadron had lapsed into inactivity. The days passed listlessly and the natural beauty of the islands, which under other circumstances would be explored and appreciated, held little attraction. Radio provided Spee's sole immediate link to the outside world, albeit mostly from Allied transmissions. Otto von Spee wrote on 11 October that his new occupation was as a journalist, spending the nights culling the radio reports for news that his father would read the next morning and 'decolouring' the pro-British accounts.[37] Providing further balance were the newspapers received up to the end of September which showed Germany's position as not unfavourable. The news of the taking of Antwerp by German troops lifted the crews' spirits, as did the knowledge that *Emden*'s successes had caused insurance premiums to rise for merchant shipping in Indian and East Asian waters.[38] Otto likewise noted the aggravation caused the British by captures at the hands of German cruisers. This was more than could be said for the work of his Squadron: 'I have seen very little of the enemy, one could say—nothing! And this more than two months after the War beginning. It is quite depressing . . .'.[39]

On 10 October 1914 the Admiralty Staff transmitted the General Operational Order that cruiser warfare was to be conducted vigorously. France should soon be suffering shortages of coal and grain, and the interdiction of these imports was a high priority. Hindering this task for the Squadron was the fact that Britain, unable to prevent 'the highly embarrassing activity of our cruisers', was attempting to cut off their supplies by exerting diplomatic pressure on neutral countries. Berlin authorised Spee to cease commerce attacks when he considered a suitable impact had been made, and directed him to proceed home with all the converted auxiliaries he could assemble. As far as the Admiralty Staff was concerned, there was but one option for Spee: 'If he can no longer hold out he should push through home . . . The united ships are so strong that they will be superior everywhere'.[40]

The situation was further complicated by Japan's occupation of Yap and Jaluit, and by 20 October the Japanese were in the Mariana, Marshall and Caroline Islands. The two Japanese Pacific Squadrons were using the Marshalls and Carolines as bases, and a third squadron, consisting of three armoured and two unarmoured cruisers, had been formed for operations in the Indian Ocean. On the American Pacific coast, the armoured cruiser *Idzumo* under Rear Admiral Moriyama (which had been in Mexican waters since the end of 1913 overseeing Japanese trade) was supporting the British cruisers *Newcastle* and *Rainbow* in tracking *Nürnberg* which had moved to the Peruvian coast. The Japanese armoured cruiser *Azama* and the older battleship *Hizen* were preventing *Geier* from leaving Honolulu where she had retreated for repairs. It was clear that the East Asia Squadron would have to leave the region as it now faced the Allied superiority in numbers which Spee had feared all along.

Spee was isolated, cut off from supplies and caught between Japanese and Anglo-Australian forces. For the Squadron's main body, however, the many remote Pacific anchorages still offered a chance to leapfrog to neutral Central and South American countries, especially Mexico and Chile where German influence was considerable. They also offered good opportunities for recoaling, communicating with Berlin and frequent merchant shipping to attack. Spee's War Log noted that the Squadron's unlocated Pacific presence would require the Allied forces to divide and patrol a wide area; the uncertainty as to Spee's whereabouts would still have a damaging effect upon trade.[41] Spee had requested 5000 tons of coal be sent from Honolulu to Valparaiso, and an additional 10 000 tons with stores to other Chilean ports. He also arranged for coal, oil and stores from La Plata and New York to be sent to Pernambuco in Brazil to facilitate the Atlantic leg of the return voyage to Germany.[42]

Naturally, his concern about a continuous supply of coal permeates Spee's observations.[43] It was essential that the Squadron obtain as much coal as possible in South America, to enable the ships to sail straight to the Canary Islands—hence the attempted movement of coal from Australia via the Dutch Indies, the Philippines and San Francisco. This was not without difficulty, since the Dutch were not cooperating under Japanese pressure and Germana agents in Australia, such as Consul Johannsen in Newcastle, were under close observation. The *Cannstadt*, interned in Brisbane, had been destined to rendezvous with the

Squadron in Samoa and be outfitted as an auxiliary cruiser 'to harass the Dominion and Commonwealth trade'.[44] Her loss, one of many, was a complicating factor. In San Francisco the Vice-Consul was being investigated by the Justice Department for shipping supplies and coal to Valparaiso.[45] By the end of November, Ambassador Bernstorff in Washington reported that although the Consuls and Naval Intelligence agents had been working round the clock to facilitate despatch, they were encountering increasing difficulties due to British complaints to the Chilean government about its loose observance of neutrality. The departure of supply ships and the Squadron's presence at the Chilean Juan Fernandez Islands had also provoked British complaints about the abuse of neutrality. It now appeared that the Chilean Foreign Minister would prevent all German supply steamers from departing.[46]

Radio contact enabled *Dresden* and *Leipzig* to join the Squadron at Easter Island by 14 October. As Spee had news from Chile that Admiral Sir Christopher Cradock's Squadron (with the armoured cruisers *Good Hope* and *Monmouth*, the protected cruiser *Glasgow* and the auxiliary *Otranto*) could well be awaiting him, he took the precaution of having *Dresden* scout the area first, with orders to attack with torpedoes. When nothing was found, coal, and cattle for fresh meat, were loaded under extremely difficult conditions. Despite the demands of command, Spee was more relaxed since the island's isolation provided some protection. In a more optimistic mood, the Admiral and Otto took time to marvel at the great stone figures. In a letter to his brother, Spee wrote that there was still little to report. Again he lamented the lack of German-sourced radio news and tartly observed that this was hardly a situation appropriate to the technical advances of the 1900s.[47]

The next leg of the Squadron's journey, to the island of Mas a Fuera in the Juan Fernandez group, was undertaken at slower speed and with intensive war preparations. Spee wrote on 27 October that his goal was Chile. There he expected to find Cradock's Squadron and perhaps more ships of which he was as yet unaware: 'If it comes to battle, trusting in God I hope for victory. It will not be easy and I will need some luck'. This seemed to reflect the German situation on the western front, and he commented on the hard battles on the Belgian coast which were hindering operations against France. In a reflective mood, Schönberg commented on the common celebration of four officers' birthdays that 'It was exactly the atmosphere I wish for my ship: no "hurrah"-mood, but the refined quiet mood of soldiers who have come to terms with their lives and await each battle with joyful expectation. With this a common understanding and trust. I have the firm belief that whatever is demanded of this ship will be produced, come what may'.[48]

Spee expected assistance from the large German community in Chile, but was aware of the strong Allied influence upon neutrals. His dwindling coal stocks were reaching a critical level: 'If our needs cannot be met, then I am vulnerable'.[49] Writing to his daughter, he observed that he had imagined war to be quite different from what he had so far experienced, but this was due to the 'very unique conditions in which we have to work'. He drew strength from the belief that 'In such times there is something uplifting in the thought that the whole nation stands shoulder to shoulder for the common goal . . . we should trust in God that he will grant us victory in our just cause'.[50]

VICTORY AND DEFEAT: CORONEL AND THE FALKLANDS

God's favour seemed to be confirmed in Spee's mind when, on 2 November, he described in great detail his victory over Cradock at Coronel. This engagement has been analysed in several major studies, but aspects of Spee's account are insightful:

> Yesterday was All Saints' Day and for us a lucky one. I was heading south along the coast when I received news that an English cruiser had entered the small coastal harbour of Coronel. Since according to international law a ship has to depart within 24 hours I contemplated taking it . . . When I was informed that two ships had been sighted, I ordered the other cruisers to rejoin me, for it was clear that they were the enemy . . . I began to narrow the distance and at five miles opened fire . . . I had so manoeuvred that the sun in the west would not hinder our sight . . . My ships fired quickly and had great success . . . *Good Hope* and *Monmouth* experienced many fires on board, and on the former there was a tremendous explosion causing it to appear like a firework against the dark evening sky, glowing white with green stars showering down above *Scharnhorst* . . . As darkness fell I had narrowed the distance to 4500m and then turned, renewing fire . . . The guns had battled for 52 minutes . . . [*Nürnberg*] gave a heavy broadside and finished [*Monmouth*] off with artillery fire. *Monmouth* sank, and unfortunately the heavy seas prevented any attempt to save its crew . . . So we have won and I thank God for the victory. We were protected in a marvellous way, and have no losses to complain of.

Good Hope and *Monmouth* went to the bottom with over 1000 men. Herein lies one of the great moral issues facing any commander in battle—to what extent and under what circumstances can and should he rescue enemy personnel? The Germans were later incensed that at the Falklands, Sir Doveton Sturdee made no attempt to rescue survivors, arguing that because they had not surrendered, he was under no obligation to do so. At Coronel the weather was an extenuating circumstance, as accepted by the British Admiralty in its public statement issued on 6 November. A German account observed that 'There was a terrible sea running, and ships rolled heavily. At times the seas were breaking right over the foremost turret'.[51] It is a reflection on Spee's character that he retained his humanity in the stress of war conditions. Even the *Sydney Morning Herald* wrote in 1935 that he was 'a fine man, a great friend of Cradock in peace time'. At the festive dinner in his honour in Valparaiso, he had refused the toast 'Damnation to the British Navy', replacing it with 'To a gallant enemy'.[52] Understandably, after the uncertainties of the previous months, Coronel provided a great boost to morale. Otto von Spee wrote that:

> We have achieved this victory over an opponent who was at the beginning in no way inferior to us from a gunnery point of view. It is particularly pleasing that the superiority was in men and not in material.[53]

Admiral Spee continued that the enthusiasm of the crews was now indescribable, and he could sense their desire for further victories: 'You can scarcely imagine the joy that is expressed here, finally we have been able to contribute to the glory of our arms . . .'.[54] Coronel's significance lay not so much in the material success or that, for a short time, the Germans had regional naval supremacy, but in the lesson to the world that the Royal Navy was not invincible. Spee's charisma and leadership qualities enabled him to extract the maximum effort from his crews. His tactical ability, combined with the experience and professionalism of his gunnery officers, seemed irresistible. The legend was being built.

In what would be his final letter to his wife, Spee exhibited a mixture of pride and foreboding. He told her of his being awarded the Iron Cross First and Second Class, and of 300 Second Class for the Squadron, including his two sons.

> That is a great joy for the crew . . . they have a share in the glory and it is better than to wait until the return home, for who knows whether they will still be with us . . . How our next undertakings will develop lies in God's hand, and if I too have a place there, then I tell myself that the possibilities are so numerous that I have to be prepared for everything . . .[55]

Spee sensed that after the long voyage across the Pacific and the stunning victory of Coronel his luck might run out. With some foreboding he referred to the rose petals strewn before him when he landed at Valparaiso as being 'Flowers for my own Squadron's funeral'.[56] For the Allies at this point, as long as Spee's Squadron was at large it constituted a danger which must be quickly dealt with. If it operated unchallenged in southern and mid-Atlantic waters merchant shipping would be severely disrupted, and in these early months of the war this was a significant British concern. After the defeat at Coronel, it was clear that not only the safety of trade but British prestige and influence with neutrals were at stake. Indeed the Chilean Naval Chief, Vice Admiral Goni, known to be pro-British, told Spee that 'as a naval man he could only wish the Squadron luck'.[57] Spee finally achieved direct contact with Berlin through the Naval Attaché in Buenos Aires. Tirpitz made it clear that he was opposed to the risk of any second engagement, and stated his preference for the Squadron to return to Europe. *Dresden* was to precede it, coal in South West Africa and, after bombarding occupied Swakopmund, return to operate in the Indian Ocean.[58]

Developments in the Pacific indicated that Spee's decision to head for South America was the right one. The route provided his only chance to obtain much-needed coal both by capture and through agents, and as a 'fleet in being' to force his enemy to divide their search operations, distracting them from other important undertakings, most notably, the transport of Australian troops to Europe. Why then did Spee make the fatal decision to attack the radio station and arsenal on the Falklands instead of proceeding into the wider Atlantic and home, a decision which mystified Berlin?[59] There was certainly no operational consensus among Spee's commanders. The captains of *Dresden*, *Gneisenau* and *Leipzig* proposed avoiding the Falklands, heading instead for the Plate estuary to attack trade before making for the mid-Atlantic. Schönberg of *Nürnberg* and *Kapitän zur See* O.W. Fielitz, Spee's Chief-of-Staff, however, agreed with their admiral's proposal for a second strike against the British.

Between 3 and 6 December the Squadron continued its journey towards Cape Dos Bahias, stopping at Picton Island to load coal from the captured Canadian ship *Drummuir*. Immediately after this, Spee called a conference at which he confirmed his plan to attack the Falklands. He did not explain his reasons, but clearly he believed in the need to destroy the sole British repair facilities in the Southwest Atlantic, and to hamstring British intelligence by eliminating the radio station at Port Stanley. This would not only disrupt British operations, but enhance those of the German Squadron in its pursuit of cruiser warfare across the Atlantic to South Africa. Spee also saw his actions as part of the larger war at sea, drawing British forces from European waters and hence assisting the operations of the High Seas Fleet. He sensed that time was running out. Would his most effective contribution to the German war effort be made by commerce warfare or by engaging the enemy directly?

There was also a more subjective factor at work. Spee was a warrior, who by nature preferred traditional fleet combat to attacking merchant shipping. This is most clear in those letters to his wife detailing his progress through the Pacific, when every opportunity was taken to attack and thus justify the Squadron's existence. To ensure that it had an overtly effective role in the war appears to have been Spee's prime motivation. This attitude was shared by his son Otto who wrote, even after Coronel: 'God grant that soon we do [the English] some considerable damage'.[60] One must also recall Spee's words after Coronel, that 'finally we have been able to contribute to the glory of our arms'. He was above all a man of action. As a young man he wrote that:

> I don't like doing things slowly, perhaps that is a result of my calling which is a hard one. It is not so much duty, but responsibility which is hard to bear. If you act wrongly it is often better to go on than to try and get back to the right path . . . the loss of time is often fatal.[61]

In the South Atlantic, Spee reckoned with encountering only inferior or at most equal forces. It does not seem to have occurred to him that the British could or might despatch so quickly fast, modern battle cruisers from the Home Fleet to deal with his Squadron. Spee lacked fresh intelligence: he was unaware of the war situation in Europe, particularly the inactivity of the High Seas Fleet, and his mistaken belief that there was naval action in European waters may account for his not considering internment in a neutral harbour—a course not lacking in precedence or honour. Given that the British battle cruisers were in Port Stanley before Spee arrived, it was a major error not to send one of his light cruisers ahead to determine precisely what force awaited him. If he had done so, the British must have pursued, and he would again have succeeded in splitting an enemy force to his advantage by binding it to a search action.

The reports collated by the German Consul-General at Buenos Aires provide the most accurate picture of the Squadron's final moments. It would appear that when Spee became aware that he was facing two *Invincible* Class warships he sought to avoid an engagement, but the superior speed of the British ships forced him to battle.

'The Last Man', SMS *Leipzig*, 8 December 1914. 'As solid as a rock he stands, steadfast and erect/With his mighty Seaman's arms he, one last time/Waves the flag for his Fatherland./And as the hull goes down into the sea/With both arms, the flag waves he./And as his head is swamped by sea/Out of the waters an arm with the flag is seen.' Heinrich Röser. (P. Overlack)

Graf Spee decided to sacrifice 'Scharnhorst' and 'Gneisenau' by engaging, thereby providing a possibility to save the small cruisers . . . the last radio message that 'Dresden' received from 'Scharnhorst' and 'Gneisenau' stated that the ships intended to attack with torpedos. From English radio transmissions the commander of 'Dresden' deduced that at 7p.m. 'Scharnhorst' and 'Gneisenau' had been sunk . . . they could no longer continue the battle when their ammunition was expended . . . unable to defend themselves, they sank to the deep after the crews gave three hurrahs for His Majesty the Emperor and the German Fatherland . . . 'Leipzig', bombarded and burning, hoisted the flag on the bow, and it was observed that a sailor held this out broadly as the ship went down.

Dresden managed to escape, but only temporarily, for in March 1915 she was scuttled in Cumberland Bay in neutral Chilean waters. At the Battle of the Falklands the Germans lost 2200 men against the British loss of seven killed and twelve wounded. The battle, however, was not without damage for the British: *Invincible* took 22 hits, two under the waterline. The Consul-General ended his report with the observation that 'this battle indeed has fostered the idea of German superiority, for the English needed five hours to defeat the Germans with a tenfold superiority. They only achieved it when the Germans' ammunition expired'.[62] The propaganda value of Spee's exploits should not be underestimated. Despite the loss, neutrals were impressed with German naval power, and the 'Spee legend' achieved almost mythical proportions in Germany. The production of mementos, postcards and assorted collectables bolstered public morale considerably.

CONCLUSION

Spee achieved much with relatively little. By splitting his forces while in the Pacific, he ensured that each part posed a threat, and the Squadron's success increased with the maintenance of mobility, as *Emden* demonstrated. It is one of the chances of history that the British force arrived at the Falklands the very night before Spee's planned attack. Had his coaling stop at Picton Island not been delayed for three days, Spee would have had a relatively free hand in the Atlantic. There are no official documents shedding light on Spee's deliberations from 4–8 November, and no eyewitness accounts of *Scharnhorst's* last moments as she went down with all hands. The only indication of Spee's last thoughts is a flag signal to *Gneisenau* answering her captain's query as to whether Spee was still alive, since for some reason his admiral's standard had fallen to halfmast during the battle. *Kapitän zur See* Maerker received the response that Spee was well and that 'You were quite correct'—a reference to Maerker's opposition to the Falklands undertaking. Spee's was certainly a cool mien in the face of impending death.

In the final analysis, Spee's fate was determined both by circumstance and the inherent defects of the system in which he operated. Plans were formulated and support measures taken, but the means to ensure their effective implementation suffered from periodic neglect and penny pinching by Berlin. Despite Spee's best efforts to create an effective force, in the immediate prewar years the Squadron became increasingly subordinate to German European concerns. Spee suffered from the customary lack of understanding in politicians and bureaucrats that they should lead by delineating the boundaries of strategic planning, setting out goals and limits of armed forces' deployment and adequately providing material support.

Despite his impetus to fleet action, Spee maintained his belief in the efficacy of cruiser warfare to the end. Indeed Admiral Sir Herbert Richmond agreed that the damage to commerce at the beginning of the war, and the greater harm done later by submarines on trade routes, 'are both traceable to an . . . acceptance of the theory that a *guerre-de-course* must fail, without examining the reasons supporting the theory'.[63] Spee's exploits caused something of a renewed debate over naval strategy. In his capacity as official war historian, Admiral Erich Raeder later suggested that the task of the German Navy in seeking equality with British forces in the North Sea was aided by the distraction created by the Cruiser Squadron. That this advantage was not exploited after the despatch of British ships to the south Atlantic, and that the High Seas Fleet remained locked up in Kiel and Wilhelmshaven, was arguably due to the incompetence of the naval leadership. Perhaps the final vindication of commerce warfare came in 1915, when its old advocate Admiral Viktor Valois recommended attacks on Britain's Atlantic supply routes by means of flexible units.[64] Because the task was carried out by submarines rather than cruisers it opened a new chapter in the centuries-old saga of *guerre-de-course*, but that is another story.

> *Schlaft ruhig Ihr Helden*
> *Tief in der See,*
> *Wir werden's vergelten.*
> *Hurra! Graf Spee.*

Fritz Seydel, Naval Cadet, 13 years

> 'Sleep peacefully you heroes,
> Deep in the sea,
> We shall avenge you.
> Hurra! Graf Spee.'

5 | Sailors and seaborne soldiers in the defence of Australia, 1914–2001

Russell Parkin

THE HISTORIAN GEOFFREY BLAINEY observed in 1988 that Australians had become a nation of islanders who devalue sea power. He noted that older Australians would immediately recognise the role which Singapore and the Battle of the Coral Sea had played in the nation's history. Writing near the end of the Cold War, however, he believed that strong historical forces had 'eroded Australia's interest in what sea power can do to protect or harm us' and caused sea power to fade from the public imagination.[1]

But the events of 1999 in East Timor and Australia's subsequent leadership of the International Force East Timor (INTERFET) once again highlighted the importance of sea power to an island continent. Without sea power, INTERFET's operations in East Timor would have been vastly more difficult and complex, especially in such key areas as force protection, mobility and logistics.

Viewed in retrospect, however, East Timor was simply the latest in a number of twentieth-century operations requiring close cooperation between Australia's naval and military forces, a cooperation that has occurred more frequently than is generally realised. This chapter provides something of a survey of such operations—a much neglected aspect of the Australian experience of warfare—discussing each briefly.

The chapter concludes with some observations about the common characteristics of these experiences, which perhaps may be useful in planning similar future operations.

SEA AND LAND POWER IN DEFENCE OF AUSTRALIA'S INTERESTS

The ability to project military power by means of a combined sea and land force seems a very logical capability for an island continent to develop. Such a combination of forces provides a very flexible range of military options, a fact quickly recognised by those charged with planning the defence of the new Commonwealth of Australia. In December 1901, the Barton Government appointed a British officer, Major-General Sir Edward Hutton, as the General Officer Command-ing the Australian Military Forces. The following April, Hutton submitted a report to the government on the defence of Australia, and did not hesitate to remind that government that it must look to '. . . the defence of Australian interests outside Australian waters'. He believed that 'It [was] hardly consistent with the present development of Australia as a young and vigorous nation to neglect her responsibility for defence outside Australian waters, and in the robust period of her youth thus to rely entirely upon the strong arm of the Mother Country'. It followed that 'for the defence of Australian interests wherever they might be threatened the first essential was the sea supremacy, which was guaran-teed by the Royal Navy. The second was the possession of a Field Force capable of undertaking military operations in whatever part of the world it might be desired by Australia to employ them'.[2]

From the Army's perspective, these words were to be proven prophetic. While successive twentieth-century governments conceived of the Army's role in national security as that of local or continental defence, the Australian Army has never yet had to defend Australia in this manner. Instead it has been primarily an expeditionary force and the RAN has been a close partner in its operations.

THE AUSTRALIAN NAVAL AND MILITARY EXPEDITIONARY FORCE, 1914

Few people now recall that Australia's first independent military operation was a successful joint campaign by elements of the RAN and the

Commonwealth Military Forces which seized German colonial possessions in New Guinea. Between mid-August and early December 1914, this brief campaign secured Australia's Pacific trade routes by denying the Germans use of their chain of regional wireless stations, intended to direct an anti-shipping campaign. The Commonwealth had already committed 20 000 men to the formation of the Australian Imperial Force (AIF), but it agreed readily to create the smaller Australian Naval and Military Expeditionary Force (AN&MEF) to counter the serious potential threat posed by German surface raiders operating from New Guinea.

The force comprised six companies (500 men) of the Royal Australian Naval Brigade (RANB), a battalion of infantry (1023 men), two sections of machine guns, a signals section and elements of the Australian Army Medical Corps. These forces were placed under the command of Colonel William Holmes, DSO, VD, officer commanding the 1st Australian Brigade. Rear Admiral Sir George Patey, RN, commanded the ships supporting the operation. His fleet would eventually comprise the cruisers HMAS *Australia*, *Encounter* and *Sydney*, a transport, *Berrima*, the destroyers HMAS *Parramatta*, *Yarra* and *Warrego*, and the submarines *AE1* and *AE2* with their tenders *Upolu* and *Protector*.[3] The later arrival of the French cruiser *Montcalm*, commanded by Rear Admiral Huguet, made the campaign a coalition as well as a joint operation.

One of the most remarkable aspects of the expedition was the relative speed with which it was mounted. The decision to raise the force was taken in early August 1914, and *Berrima*, with her escorts, sailed from Sydney on 19 August. Simultaneously, Admiral Patey co-ordinated the convoying of a similar force from New Zealand to seize German Samoa. As a result of the latter operation, *Berrima* did not rendezvous with all the other elements of the force until she reached Port Moresby. The whole fleet assembled on 9 September near Rossel Island, to the south-east of the New Guinea mainland, where Holmes and Patey made final plans for the attack.

The first troops to go ashore in enemy territory on the morning of 11 September were two RANB landing parties, each 25 men strong. They were landed at Kaba Kaul and the main German settlement of Herbertshöhe respectively, to locate and capture the German wireless station in the vicinity. The party at Kaba Kaul soon located the wireless station at Bitapaka, which was also the main German defensive position.[4] By mid-morning, however, this small force was facing serious opposition and had to be reinforced by two companies of the RANB, supported by an Army machine gun section. The *Sydney Morning Herald* reporter F.S. Burnell recorded that as the reinforcements left *Berrima*,

Midshipman Veale, RANR, at Rabaul, September 1914. 'By the sound of rifle fire ahead we knew we would soon be in the thick of it . . . my party and I caught up with the front-line just as Lieutenant-Commander Elwell, RN, had been shot dead while leading what was the first bayonet charge by a British force in World War I. Thus I became one of the first 100 Australians to go into action.' Midshipman R.S. Veale, RANR, AN&MEF. (RAN)

they were 'pursued by the envy of every other man on the military side of the expedition'.[5]

After a series of small but sharp engagements, the wireless station was captured on the morning of 12 September, with the loss of six dead and four wounded: the first Australian casualties of the war. Enemy casualties were unknown, but nineteen Germans, including three officers, and 56 native constabulary were taken prisoner.[6] Eight naval personnel (five officers and three enlisted men) were recommended for bravery awards for their roles in the fight for the wireless station. The citation for the award of the Distinguished Service Order (DSO) to Lieutenant R.G. Bowen, RAN—he eventually received a Mention in Dispatches—indicates that the Navy was quite accustomed to conducting operations ashore:

By his disposition of skirmishers [he] discovered what was virtually an ambush, and by capturing the 3 Germans in command, utterly demoralised the native force and probably averted a disaster to the small party of Naval Reserves. Later on, the scheme of attack drawn up by him & Lieutenant Hill [Gerald Hill was also recommended for the DSO] proved to be sound, and eventually brought about the surrender of the trench. [He] Was slightly wounded.[7]

The successful attack on the wireless station demoralised the German authorities and made further resistance pointless. Two days later, early in the morning of 14 September, the *Encounter* shelled the ridge behind Herbertshöhe then, in the afternoon, four companies of infantry, with supporting machine guns and a 12-pounder artillery piece, marched unopposed on the settlement of Toma. On the morning of 15 September, with *Montcalm* newly arrived in the harbour, Dr Haber, the Acting Governor of Rabaul, surrendered the colony.

Although brief and small in scale, the expedition against Rabaul demonstrated clearly the value of joint forces in the defence of Australian regional interests. To echo General Hutton, it showed the usefulness of troops who could go anywhere and of a fleet capable of carrying and supporting them. Between mid-September and early December 1914, small elements of the AN&MEF took control of the German settlements at Madang, New Ireland, Nauru, the Admiralty Island Group and the Solomons. This highly successful joint operation has unfortunately been overshadowed in the national memory by Australia's participation in the British-led landings at Gallipoli the following year. While Gallipoli undoubtedly contributed to Australia's sense of nationhood and cemented an enduring link between the civil community and the armed forces, it was nonetheless detrimental to Australia's development of a clear understanding of its strategic circumstances. The value of close cooperation by naval and military forces in the defence of Australia was largely forgotten. For the remainder of the First World War the services would operate separately, aside from those occasions when RAN ships convoyed elements of the AIF to and from the Middle East and Europe. With only rare exceptions, the trend towards single service operations continued during the inter-war period.

INTER-WAR COOPERATION BETWEEN NAVAL AND MILITARY FORCES

In 1935, on a weekend just ten days before the twentieth anniversary of Anzac Day, Tasmanian militia forces of the 40th Battalion took part in an amphibious landing exercise at Blackman's Bay, south of Hobart. The assault was launched from the cruisers HMAS *Canberra* and HMS *Sussex*, the Australian Squadron's two most powerful ships. A local newspaper report painted a light-hearted picture of the soldiers 'storming' ashore in the miserable conditions of a steady downpour. A photograph shows sailors in neat white shorts steadying the bow ropes of boats, towed ashore by cutters from the two naval vessels, while enthusiastic militiamen disembarked gingerly via planks suspended from the bows. Such rudimentary amphibious techniques harked back to 1915, with the only touch of modernity—and reality—being supplied by an Air Force seaplane making mock attacks on the landing forces.[8]

The whole event was indeed remarkable for the air of unreality surrounding it. The good-humoured tone of the newspaper story was echoed in the official reports. Rear Admiral W. Ford, RN, commander of the Australian Squadron, remarked on how '. . . the exercise was entered into whole heartedly by all concerned. I understand that the military thoroughly enjoyed their stay onboard . . .'.[9] The unopposed landing had been watched by interested crowds of civilians who turned out in large numbers despite the weather. Perhaps the most striking feature of the whole affair, given its timing, is the absence of even a hint of irony in the contemporary reports. The press and the military alike seemed totally unconcerned that, almost twenty years after Gallipoli, the best Australian forces could do was stage a small-scale replay of the fateful landings. Admiral Ford's report to the Naval Board concluded that '. . . useful experience was gained by naval personnel, particularly by Australian officers and men, few of whom had taken part in an exercise of this nature, and an excellent liaison was established between the Army and Navy. It is in this latter respect that such an exercise is so valuable'. Despite Ford's acknowledgment of the value of joint exercises, the landing at Blackman's Bay was the only one of its type held in Australian waters during the inter-war period. Considering what Australian naval, land and air forces would face during the island campaigns of the Second World War it was poor preparation indeed.

The legacy of the First World War and the inter-war period, as far as the Army was concerned, was a distortion of the relative value of land, sea (and later air) forces in the defence of Australia. Belief in the ability of a fleet operating from Singapore to defend Australia negated the need for detailed inter-service training and cooperation by the Australian Forces. Reliance on 'Fortress Singapore' was so complete that it decided the calibre of coastal defence guns (9.2-inch, rather than 15-inch) in Sydney, Melbourne, Newcastle and Fremantle, much to the frustration of Army leaders.[10] The chief importance of Singapore, however, was that it offered Australian politicians a cheap option for national defence. In the decade before 1939, the bulk of Australia's meagre defence spending was devoted to the RAN—approximately double that expended on the land forces.[11] The RAN's role was to cooperate with the Royal Navy in imperial defence. It was not designed for local defence (i.e., the defence of the Australian continent), which was left to the Army and Royal Australian Air Force. This was a huge burden for these two small, poorly-equipped and under-trained services to take on. By 1939, twenty years of financial negligence by both conservative and Labor governments had created fierce inter-service rivalries, leaving the three Australian services poorly placed to cooperate in national defence. In addition, with the outbreak of war commitments to imperial defence in the Middle East stripped Australia of her best naval and land forces. When Japan attacked in the Pacific in 1941, the forces available for national defence were extremely limited.

TRAINING FOR AMPHIBIOUS OPERATIONS

During the first six months of the Pacific War, the Japanese conquered a vast area to the north of Australia in a series of carefully planned, well-executed and rapid amphibious operations. This enemy occupation of the northern approaches was an event which Australian defence planners had long feared, but done little to counter.[12] As they recovered from the physical and psychological shock of the Japanese assaults, Australia's leaders realised that recapturing these conquered territories would require the closest cooperation between all three services so as to master the techniques of amphibious warfare. In March 1942, the Deputy Chief of the General Staff, Major-General S.F. Rowell, noted that there were at least two steps which could be taken to re-establish a ring of island bases to the north and north-east of Australia:

(i) planning for the provision of special equipment, including landing craft and air landing equipment, and
(ii) the establishment of a School of Combined Operations.[13]

At this stage, planning was all that could be done since in early 1942 no amphibious equipment or training facilities existed in Australia. Virtually the only amphibious asset the Australian Army possessed was a handful of officers, from the 6th and 7th Divisions, who had attended courses at the British Combined Training Centre at Kabrit, in Egypt.

The first steps to commence amphibious training were taken in April 1942. Three officers—Commander F.N. Cook, DSC, RAN, Lieutenant-Colonel M. Hope, a British artillery officer, and Major A. Rose, an Australian Army officer—undertook a rapid but extensive reconnaissance of Australia's east coast to find suitable training areas. Their survey suggested three sites: Port Stephens, north of Newcastle in New South Wales; the Toorbul Point/Bribie Island area north of Brisbane; and the San Remo/Trinity Beach area just to the north of Cairns. Major amphibious training establishments were developed in each of these locations during the war. At Port Stephens, for example, the sheltered waters of Salamander Bay offered the rare combination of calm water close to surf beaches, ideal for the conduct of basic and advanced landing exercises. Consequently, the area was soon the site of two major amphibious training establishments: HMAS *Assault* and the Joint Overseas Operational Training School (JOOTS).

Rear Admiral Daniel Barbey, USN, arrived in early 1943 to take command of Amphibious Forces in the South-West Pacific Area (SWPA). Well before this, however, the Australian training establishments had begun to grapple with the complexities of amphibious warfare. Adding to the difficulties faced by these early planners was the fact that any amphibious operations on the part of the US/Australian coalition would involve three services from both nations. Problems existed at the most elementary level, since the two nations employed different basic terminology. Indeed, instead of the word 'amphibious', the Australians used the British term 'combined operations'.[14] When it came to fundamentals, however, American and British doctrines were remarkably similar, varying only slightly in operational methods. Nevertheless, even small differences of terminology and style were sufficient to create friction between the coalition partners, and the operational focus of the JOOTS meant that conflict between national methods was bound to emerge there first.

Much of the criticism of American methods came from British, New Zealand and Australian officers with experience in combined operations in Europe and the Middle East. At the core of this criticism was the view that the Americans were too rigidly theoretical, and that instruction at the JOOTS was based on 'rather out of date theory from American Army text books'.[15] The reports of British officers seconded to Australia to assist with the establishment of amphibious training, such as Lieutenant-Colonel Walker of the Royal Marines, are filled with frustration at being unable to institute what they considered to be useful training. After one exercise involving the RAN's Landing Ship Infantry

(LSI) HMAS *Manoora* and the USN's APA (large amphibious transport) USS *Henry T. Allen*, Walker wrote acerbically:

> It was quite a good exercise but, all the same, there is a lot which they [the Americans] could learn from us [the British]—if only they would! . . . What worries us is the American unwillingness to learn anything from British methods or to let the Australians and British have any say in running preparations for amphibious ops. For instance: *Manoora* was made to lower her boats empty and to go through that fatuous American boat-circling drill before the boats left to go inshore; from the beach we could hear the roar of landing craft engines five miles out to sea for one hour before the 0200 hrs landing.[16]

Despite these initial problems, under Barbey's able leadership American and Australian forces soon overcame their differences and eventually conducted 56 successful assault landings between late 1943 and the end of hostilities in 1945. In these operations, *Manoora* and the other two RAN LSIs, HMAS *Westralia* and HMAS *Kanimbla*, were one of the success stories of inter-Allied cooperation.

The spirit of improvisation which prevailed during the early days of training is captured in *Spearheads of Invasion*, the wartime memoir of Lieutenant-Commander W.N. Swan, RAN.[17] Swan served in *Westralia* from early 1942, when it was converted from an Armed Merchant Cruiser to become an LSI. HMAS *Assault's* role in training landing craft crews and beach teams made it a logical base for the three LSIs, each of which was capable of carrying a battalion of troops. Together they could transport an Australian Brigade Group or an American Regimental Combat Team, both formations of approximately 5000 troops, making them important assets in the Allied war effort in the Pacific. Swan remained with *Westralia* throughout the war, and recorded the stories of his ship's participation in seven of the key landing operations carried out by American and Australian Forces in New Guinea, the Netherlands East Indies and the Philippines.

THE NEW GUINEA CAMPAIGN: INTERSERVICE COOPERATION AND THE CONDUCT OF AMPHIBIOUS OPERATIONS

Two sets of factors made the SWPA ideal for the conduct of amphibious operations. The first was geographic with the region's numerous islands, most of them mountainous and almost all covered with dense tropical rainforests. The second arose from the difficulties of military operations in this harsh physical environment. The Kokoda Campaign had indicated the wide range of problems—operational, logistic and medical—involved in land operations conducted in the tropics. Largely to overcome these problems, General MacArthur and his staff evolved a strategy making maximum use of air and sea power. Instead of fighting their way along the northern coast of New Guinea, Allied forces began a series of amphibious landings in mid-1943 with the object of seizing or building airfields. These were then used to cover the next operation further along the coast. This strategy required close inter-service and Allied cooperation.

One of the first amphibious operations in which Australian troops took part was the assault on Lae by the 7th and 9th Divisions—Operation POSTERN. This was a truly joint operation, involving an amphibious assault from the east by the 9th Division in conjunction with an air landing operation from the north-west by the 7th Division. Naval participation included a brief bombardment of the landing beaches by five US Navy destroyers, one of which also acted in the fighter direction role for Allied aircraft. The ships were divided between two assault beaches, codenamed Yellow and Red. Two destroyers were allocated to Yellow Beach, while the larger Red Beach had three.

Naval bombardment was co-ordinated by Australian Army artillery officers acting as Bombardment Liaison Officers (BLO). Major N.A. Vickery, the BLO in USS *Lamson*, noted that while the American crew were generally cooperative, their knowledge of this type of operation was 'superficial'. According to Vickery, the Americans were 'unwilling to depart from set and standard ideas on procedure' and 'did not seem to appreciate the Army's problems'.[18] The BLOs soon proved their worth when the initial bombardment of the target area was 1500 yards out of line, partly due to the inaccuracy of the ships' radars. Fire was adjusted using map readings supplied by the BLOs and the fire missions then proceeded as planned. Other minor problems arose when the USN ships did not answer the Army's call for fire, leaving the troops wondering whether the requested support would arrive.[19] Brigadier R.N.L. Hopkins, the Australian Liaison Officer with Admiral Barbey's 7th Amphibious Force, listed several areas in which the Australians and their allies could make improvements for future operations. He concluded, however, that the landings on the morning of 4 September 1943 were carried out on schedule, and that complete surprise was achieved against the lightly-held Japanese positions.

At Aitape during July 1944, No. 100 Squadron, RAAF, and its attached Army Unit, 11 Australian Air Liaison Section, provided aerial observation and direction for naval gunfire support (NGS) of ground operations. The squadron's Bristol Beauforts had not been used in this role prior to the operation, but the skilled aircrews and their air liaison section proved adaptable. The naval personnel were indeed fulsome in their praise of the high degree of cooperation provided by the squadron, which enabled very accurate missions to be fired against suspected enemy headquarters, troop concentrations, supply areas and communications facilities. As 11 Australian Air Liaison Section's Captain K.A. Coventry wrote in his report on the operation: 'the ships' captains and gunnery officers were emphatic that they had never before experienced such simple and accurate observations or had better communications with the spotting aircraft'.[20]

The extent and prevalence of inter-service cooperation in the SWPA was a necessary response to the unique problems imposed by the theatre. Units of all the armed forces undertook long periods of training before participating in amphibious assaults. With experience came the realisation that the complexity of such operations required the development of specialised units in all three services. Towards the end of the war the Australian 1st Corps, with air and naval support, undertook three large-scale amphibious operations against the Japanese-held island of Borneo, the last of which took place on 1 July 1945, with the landing of the 7th Division at Balikpapan.

BALIKPAPAN

The landing at the important, oil-exporting port of Balikpapan had been the subject of a dispute between the Australian military and US naval planning teams. The Australians wanted to land troops on top of the objective and had selected landing beaches in the Klandasan area. They considered that an early success would reduce the duration of the campaign and thus the ground troops' casualties. Attacking the centre of the enemy's defences would disorganise them and permit key points to be seized rapidly.[21] It was a plan that involved a calculated risk, but at this stage of the war the Japanese had altered their defensive tactics. They no longer used the bulk of their forces to cover the landing beaches. Most of their troops were now held back so that even when the assaulting forces secured a beachhead, they had still to fight for every inch of ground. The USN planners had wanted to land near Sepinggang, where ships could stand closer in to the shore and away from the strongest Japanese coastal artillery defences. This, however, would have required the 7th Division to make an approach march of over ten miles, fighting all the way. The Navy eventually agreed to the Army's plan, and a preliminary bombardment by both air and naval forces was conducted over 30 days to soften up the coastal guns and anti-aircraft defences.

In addition to the preliminary bombardment, the display of firepower on F-Day, 1 July 1945, was the heaviest ever witnessed by Australian troops during the war. Malcolm Uren recalled:

> Never had the Australians seen such destructive forces let loose by their side. The air and sea shook and reverberated to the crashing discharge of hundreds of naval guns . . . Whole buildings and trees were tossed grotesquely in the air, to fall back shapeless and shuddering . . . all the time the Japanese guns continued firing but without much effect. The Air Force added its quota to the inferno until it seemed nothing could possibly live on or near those belted beaches.[22]

This was a measure of how far the US forces and their Australian allies had come in only three years, as was the wide variety of specialist RAN and Army units which went ashore with the first waves of assaulting infantry.

Gavin Long, the Australian official historian of the Second World War, comments on the 'multitude of specialist units and detachments which existed at this stage of the war'.[23] The RAN's LSIs each had a Landing Ship Detachment (LSD) of the Royal Australian Engineers. These men assisted with the loading and unloading of ships, and had by this time reached a very high degree of efficiency. In a previous operation, the LSD commander in *Kanimbla* recorded that the launching of all ship's boats had taken under fourteen minutes and that 972 men, 44 vehicles and 100 tons of stores and equipment had been discharged in just over two hours.[24] In *Westralia*, Commander A.V. Knight, RAN, had already noted that the LSD on his ship had proven to be 'a very definite asset' contributing 'greatly to the general efficiency shown in all the operations in which the ship has participated'.[25] In addition to the three LSIs, by 1945 the RAN had a flotilla comprising six LSTs (Landing Ship Tank), representing a significant allocation of resources to another specialist amphibious task.

On the beach, both RAN and Army units assisted with the rapid unloading and turnaround of landing craft and the dispatch of men and equipment towards the front line. RAN Commando groups would go ashore with the first waves of the assault to signpost the beaches, delineate various landing areas and perform any other naval tasks which were required. The Principal Beachmaster (PBM) was an RAN officer

Assault on Balikpapan, 1 July 1945. 'There was an air of tension both among the embarked troops and my boat's crew. We knew from the determined *kamikaze* attacks that we could expect fierce resistance from the Japanese, but my main concern was to ensure that we reached the line of departure at the correct time and make a good run in.' Midshipman James Hume, RAN, HMAS *Kanimbla*. (AWM 018812)

charged with guiding and supervising all craft which landed during the operation. The role of the Army Beach Groups was to unload the landing craft. These integrated areas of responsibility required a high degree of inter-service cooperation. Following the Tarakan Operation in May 1945, the RAN's PBM had reported that 'complete harmony' had existed between him and his Army counterpart in the 2nd Australian Beach Group throughout the operation.[26]

Assessing the Balikpapan Operation, Rear Admiral Albert Noble, USN, wrote in his after-action report:

> In spite of the many nationalities and military services involved in the operation, there was little difficulty experienced in the preparation and planning for this operation. Minor differences in organisation and methods of operation were quickly adjusted by adoption of the other's ideas, or, when necessary by compromise.[27]

The spirit of inter-service cooperation developed in the Pacific campaigns had left its mark on the Australian services well before the end of the war. A 1943 paper on the post-war defence of Australia written by the Deputy Chief of the Naval Staff, Captain R. Dowling, noted:

> The whole trend of modern attack warfare in the Pacific is towards combined operations [i.e. joint operations]. By definition this involves the participation of naval units . . . Thus any plan for a post-war naval force must include landing craft for amphibious training. For the same reason an amphibious force, patterned on the United States Marine Corps, is a most desirable naval contribution to combined operations.[28]

The lessons of the Pacific War were not lost on post-war Australian defence planners. In February 1946, the Australian Chiefs of Staff drew up their appreciation of the nation's strategic circumstances. As they saw it, 'The strategic choices open to Australia were isolation or cooperation with other nations'.[29] They rejected what they termed the fallacy of isolation, because as 'an isolated continent with a small population and limited resources, [Australia] is unable to defend herself unaided against a major power', concluding that an isolationist policy of continental defence would only lead to disaster, and hence that national security policy '. . . must be built upon cooperation with other nations'. It followed that the nation's preparations for war '. . . must be such that her forces can cooperate with those of other nations [and that] overseas commitments may be necessary and in fact unavoidable in . . . a future war'.[30] To meet the requirement for credible forces to contribute to coalition operations, the appreciation called for a force structure in which the three services were organised and trained to provide a mobile joint task force based on permanent personnel, rather than specially-raised forces or militia. Key aspects of the recommended force structure were a fleet train capable of maintaining a task force operating in the Southeast Asian littoral, Army units trained for amphibious operations to take and hold forward operating bases and an air component with not only fighters and bombers but also sufficient strategic transport assets to support the other services.[31] The next involvement of Australian naval and military forces in an international conflict resulted directly from this post-war policy of developing joint forces for coalition operations.

THE RAN CARRIER AIR GROUP IN THE KOREAN WAR

Three squadrons from the RAN's Fleet Air Arm (FAA) served in the Korean War and demonstrated the value of forces well versed in the techniques of joint operations. Carrier aviation was a new capability for Australia and one directly related to the 1946 Chiefs of Staff Appreciation. The first of two aircraft carriers, HMAS *Sydney*, was commissioned in mid-December 1948, and 32 months later the FAA was at war. In the period between its formation and setting sail for Korea on 31 August 1951, the carrier air group (CAG) was involved in anti-submarine warfare (ASW) exercises, combat air patrol (CAP) for the fleet and naval gunnery control exercises. These were practised on cruises in the Pacific and Indian Oceans and from the airfield at HMAS *Albatross*, the Naval Air Station near Nowra, New South Wales. Embarked with the CAG was an Army Carrier Borne Air Liaison Section (CBALS) tasked with assisting in the training and briefing of aircrews in such matters as targets, battle damage assessment, map reading, escape and evasion techniques, and procedures for directing naval gunfire.

On her arrival in Korean waters, *Sydney* was due to take over from the British carrier HMS *Glory*. *Glory* had been working as part of the USN's Task Force 77, which was primarily engaged in Operation STRANGLE: the ultimately unsuccessful campaign of interdiction against communist supply routes. The naval aircraft involved in these missions attacked roads, bridges, railway tunnels, enemy troop concentrations, supply dumps and convoys. *Sydney*'s CAG would perform all of these missions which, like the RAAF's ground attack missions, commonly took place at altitudes of between 60 and 3000 metres. The presence of the CBALS was vital to the successful conduct of such missions. When *Sydney* sailed for Korea, 71 CBALS, which had a normal complement of one officer, a warrant officer and a corporal driver, was augmented by the officer from 72 CBALS, Major Max Simkin, because of the high tempo of naval air operations. Simkin flew ahead to Japan to conduct reconnaissance for the CAG, leaving Major Gordon Hardcastle as the Carrier Borne Air Liaison Officer (CBALO) charged with conducting the work-up training for the pilots during the passage.

The daily drills in target location and gunnery direction undertaken by *Sydney*'s squadrons paid immediate dividends when she began operations in October 1951. Following a mission in which pilots from *Sydney* had directed the 16-inch guns of the battleship USS *New Jersey*, the carrier's commanding officer, Captain D.H. Harries, RAN, received a signal complimenting *Sydney*'s pilots for the accuracy of their target spotting and high sortie rate.[32] Lieutenant-Commander G.F.S. Brown, RAN, a Sea Fury pilot from No. 808 Squadron, later described his personal experience of providing gunnery spotting observations:

We'd find the targets or the land forces would give them to us. The targets were mostly heavy guns or important store dumps. . . . The bigger the ship the better the result. I remember spotting for an American cruiser which was 15 miles off shore and getting wonderfully good results. . . . Those heavy shells landing plunk into the targets from an invisible source miles out to sea was indication enough that we had complete command of the sea. The enemy's only answer to these tactics was wonderfully good camouflage.[33]

The Sea Furies carried out their first Close Army Support missions on 21 October. These were performed with the British Commonwealth Division, and although the pilots initially experienced difficulty with communications, targets of enemy troops were accurately bombarded and strafed. Simkin noted in the CBAL War Diary that 'This type of mission is very popular with the pilots who are anxious to do as much as they can for their "brown" brothers'.[34]

As operations continued, the carrier's Sea Fury and Firefly aircraft were engaged in a range of other tasks, including photographic reconnaissance, bombing of enemy supply lines, CAP and support for search and rescue missions flown by USN helicopters. The Korean War saw the first large-scale use of helicopters for such missions. The American pilots of these aircraft frequently took considerable risks and many doomed RAN and RAAF pilots owed them their lives and freedom. Another innovation to assist downed aircrews was introduced by *Sydney*'s CBALOs. Using red and yellow fluorescent panels, each about a metre square, pilots could communicate with circling aircraft to inform them as to whether their crews were injured as well as the direction of enemy fire. The system was so effective that it was soon adopted by RAAF No. 77 Squadron and promulgated for use by Headquarters, US Fifth Air Force.[35]

The *Sydney*'s experienced CBALOs also ensured that the battle damage reports submitted by the RAN pilots were as accurate as possible. Notes written by the CBALOs in early December 1951 advised the pilots that in assessing enemy troop casualties:

> . . . a rocket must be seen to strike a known number of troops before we accept them as being killed. Consequently, our estimates are a minimum, for when large concentrations of troops are attacked, many unobserved casualties must result. [This] system gives a much truer picture of the damage done to the enemy than the rather grandiose claims made by some other air units operating in this theatre.[36]

Sydney and her air group 'won themselves an excellent reputation with both the United Nations Naval Command and the British

Commonwealth soldiers fighting the battle in the trenches'.[37] The role played by the CBALS in this success was significant. In particular, the two officers influenced the performance of the CAG on a daily basis, as they briefed and debriefed the aircrews, and gathered target and other intelligence to assist with future missions. Captain Harries recognised their efforts and the excellent work they had done 'since long before the ship came to Korea'.[38] Together with the RAN pilots they helped to train, the Army ALOs formed an effective joint service team. By the time *Sydney*'s patrols ended in late January 1952, her CAG had achieved a very high sortie rate (2366 in four months). Once again, thanks to the exceptional performance of a relatively small unit, Australia was able to make a significant contribution to a coalition. For the loss of three pilots and nine aircraft, *Sydney*'s CAG was estimated to have killed 1428 troops and destroyed 47 rail bridges, four road bridges and 1000 buildings.[39]

THE LONG DECLINE OF AUSTRALIAN NAVAL/MILITARY COOPERATION

The Cold War period of the mid-1950s to the 1980s saw another decline in cooperation between the Australian armed services. Key reasons were the routines of peacetime and the low-intensity conflicts of the period (the Malayan Emergency and the Vietnam War), which allowed few opportunities for regular training in joint operations. For almost three decades single service issues and operations dominated the concerns of the whole Australian Defence Force (ADF).

For a period after the Second World War limited joint training continued in the Port Stephens area. In general, however, the post-war era was one of retrenchment. Budgetary pressures turned the minds of service leaders inwards and sapped their commitment to large-scale joint training activities. Among the first retrenchments were the many specialist units required for amphibious warfare. The RAN's 10th Flotilla, comprising six LSTs, was disbanded in 1951. Even when such units survived, their resources were greatly reduced and they were often allocated to reserve components.

Only rarely did instances of joint service cooperation occur, most notably after *Sydney* was converted to a fast troop transport in the early 1960s. Her 22 voyages to Vietnam again underlined the value of the strategic lift capabilities of the Navy, as she transported the bulk of the Army's Task Force to and from the war zone. Building on this experience, in May 1973 *Sydney* participated with troops and helicopters in the first exercise in which each Australian service operated as a self-contained force from the same platform. Further development plans were shelved, however, after the former carrier was paid off for disposal in November 1973.

Notwithstanding significant reorganisation and frequent calls for better co-ordination, the period following the Vietnam War saw single service issues continue to dominate. With no clearly-defined threat, strategic guidance drifted towards the fallacy that the ADF should be only concerned with continental defence. During the 1980s, the Kangaroo series of exercises was conducted to practise the use of joint forces in the direct defence of Australia. While relatively large-scale undertakings, these exercises were highly choreographed and their chief value consisted in keeping alive the broad concepts of inter-service cooperation. By the mid-1990s, despite much hard work and goodwill from all three services, the ADF possessed few joint assets, only rudimentary joint doctrine and no clear concept for the conduct of joint operations.

From the mid-1990s, however, a series of economic and political crises in the Asia-Pacific region gave fresh impetus to inter-service cooperation, largely by illustrating the need for Australia to adopt a maritime strategy as the only effective safeguard for her national inter-ests.[40] A corollary of this new strategic direction was the need for the Navy and the Army in particular to give fresh thought to the problems of amphibious operations. At the same time, following the Navy's acqui-sition of two USN *Newport* Class amphibious ships and the Army's decision to return to service a limited number of amphibious cargo lighters (LARC-V), the ADF's small amphibious capability received a significant boost. Between 1999 and 2001, both Navy and Army have given serious attention to the development of operational concepts for this rejuvenated capability.

DIFFICULT AND PRACTICAL PROBLEMS—TOWARDS AN AUSTRALIAN AMPHIBIOUS FORCE

In 1950 Lord Tedder, reflecting on the problems of national defence planning, offered advice which might well have been formulated with Australia in mind:

> Awkward questions of relative priority will always arise, but in the final stages of a war they rarely have the critical urgency they have at the outset . . . Surely it is the problems of the early stages of the war which

we should study. Those are the difficult problems; those are the practical problems which we and every democratic nation have to solve.41

Since 1999 the ADF has begun to examine the questions of relative priority posed by the unstable international security environment. Faced by the formidable range of variables required by ongoing peacekeeping operations and commitments to the war on terror and homeland defence, no national security policy can possibly meet all eventualities. As in the past, however, the creation of balanced joint forces will provide the government with the widest range of options to meet the threats that may arise. Recognising this, the then Lieutenant-General Peter Cosgrove told a conference on amphibious operations in 2000 that 'increasingly Australia's amphibious capability is being viewed as a capability of first resort'.[42] As he had cause to recall, in East Timor the presence of sea power, including amphibious elements, provided INTERFET with force protection, mobility and significant sustainment capabilities.

While the materiel—ships, aircraft and other equipment—necessary for amphibious operations has increased over recent years, this build up

HMAS *Labuan* unloading vehicles in East Timor, September 1999. 'The persuasive, intimidatory or deterrent nature of major warships was not to me as the combined joint force commander an incidental, nice to have "add on" but an important indicator of national and international resolve and most reassuring to all of us who relied on sea lifelines.' Major-General P.J. Cosgrove, Commander INTERFET. (RAN)

has been accompanied by corresponding doctrinal and organisational developments. The two most significant documents are the Navy's *Amphibious and Afloat Support Force Element Group Master Plan* and the Army's *Concept for Manoeuvre Operations in the Littoral Environment* (MOLE). The RAN plan links strategy and capability to the peacetime requirement to justify them financially. While this may make it unexciting reading, the document makes a cogent business case for the maintenance and development of the ADF's amphibious capability. The Army's MOLE paper is more conceptual in style, in line with its aim of making a significant contribution to the development of an ADF joint warfighting doctrine. Within the MOLE concept, the littoral region becomes the area from which offensive operations are projected and in which defence is conducted. In line with the joint nature of the concept, offensive and defensive operations are conducted utilising the striking power of the Air Force, the mobility of the Navy and the holding power of land forces.

This progress in both the technical and doctrinal areas is just a beginning. As this chapter has demonstrated, after 1945 Australia had an amphibious capability, which it chose to reduce for reasons of economy and policy. Few would regard the two LPAs (Landing Platform Amphibious), HMAS *Manoora* (II) and HMAS *Kanimbla* (II), which form the core of current capability, as more than an expedient medium-term solution. Maintaining and developing a capability for amphibious operations within a maritime strategy is a task for all three services. There are important questions of air defence, air support and logistics that must still be addressed but, above all, priorities for funding, procurement and replacement of key equipment must be resolved if this newly rejuvenated capability is to become a potent joint force.

CONCLUSION

The century just ended has seen Australia's defence policy come full circle. The Howard Government's White Paper, *Defence 2000,* echoes General Hutton's recommendation that Australia's defence outlook must consider 'the defence of Australian interests outside Australian waters'. As experience has shown, achieving this requires the creation of credible joint forces. Yet from Rabaul in 1914 to East Timor in 1999, Australia's employment of its armed forces has repeatedly been on an *ad hoc* basis in reaction to crises, rather than as part of a well-considered strategic policy. When a crisis subsides, forces created at great cost are dismantled or downgraded, because of either the frugality of peacetime defence preparations or shifts in policy direction.

During the early stages of almost all of its twentieth-century conflicts, Australia has been required to employ naval and land forces in the national defence. All too frequently these forces were ill-prepared for deployment beyond the nation's borders. The difficult and practical problem which Australia's defence planners have repeatedly failed to solve in peacetime is the creation of balanced joint forces tailored to the nation's geo-political circumstances and capable of defending not only national territory but also national interests.

One of the few clearly discernible trends of the post-Cold War period has been the requirement to project armed forces into remote areas and sustain them there, often for lengthy periods. Sea power has the unique ability to project, protect and sustain. If the ADF continues to learn the lessons of its history and develops its amphibious capability, it will be better prepared for the challenges of future deployments. For the Australian Navy this means that, in the twenty-first century, its inspiration will probably be Corbett, rather than Mahan. The Army, in Sir Edward Grey's words, will be the projectile which the Navy fires from the sea, and cooperation between the ADF's sailors and seaborne soldiers is likely to retain the same high priority it has so often had in the past.

6 | The treatment of casualties from the *Sydney–Emden* action

Michael Dowsett

THE FIGHT BETWEEN HMAS *Sydney* and SMS *Emden* on 9 November 1914 was the first action of an Australian warship in open battle with an enemy. Fought with neither interference nor interruption the engagement was celebrated in the Allied press as proof of the Australian sailor's fighting spirit and as a worthy opening page in the young nation's battle history. Although the particulars of the tactics and progress of the action have since received a number of detailed treatments, far less attention has been paid to its aftermath.[1] Making specific use of the contemporary records created by *Sydney's* Senior Medical Officer, Surgeon Leonard Darby, this chapter seeks to review the face of naval battle from a somewhat different perspective. The medical aspects of the *Sydney–Emden* action are not simply of dramatic historical interest, they are equally useful as food for thought for naval operational planners today.

HMAS *Sydney* (I) was a Town class light cruiser built in the United Kingdom and commissioned in 1913. Her main armament consisted of eight 6-inch guns and she had two torpedo tubes. In late 1914 the ship was under the command of Captain J.C.T. Glossop, RN, and had a complement of 390 men. As was the case more generally in the fledgling Australian Navy, most of the senior positions on board were held by officers and senior sailors on loan from the Royal Navy with a proportionately larger number of ratings recruited and trained in Australia. Of these some 60 were from the training ship HMAS *Tingira*, many of them only 16 years old.

Born in Tasmania, Leonard Darby joined the RAN in 1912 at the age of 23 and had been with *Sydney* since her commissioning. He was assisted by Surgeon Arthur Todd from Tamworth, NSW, who had joined the Navy in August 1914, aged 24. Two Sick Berth Stewards were the other permanent members of the medical organisation. Their sickbay was on an upper deck and, being unprotected, was not used in action. Instead, two emergency operating theatres were prepared in well-separated stokers' bathrooms situated not quite below the waterline and off the tunnel (or 'tube') which ran up the centre of the ship. These spaces were relatively small (3.7m x 2.4m x 2.1m), but well-protected above by two decks and on the sides by armour and coal bunkers. In action the surgical parties and stretcher-bearers were positioned in the fore and aft ammunition lobbies.

THE PRELUDE TO THE ACTION

On 1 November 1914 Convoy 1—carrying the Australian Imperial Force's first contingent of 21 528 troops and 7882 horses—sailed from Albany for the Middle East. Delayed by concerns as to the whereabouts of the German Pacific Fleet, the 38-ship convoy was heavily escorted by the two Australian light cruisers *Melbourne* and *Sydney*, the British armoured cruiser HMS *Minotaur* and the Japanese battle cruiser *Ibuki*. *Minotaur* was senior ship of the escort but a week after leaving Western Australia she was called away to other duties, leaving *Melbourne* in charge of the convoy.

Sydney's opponent, the German cruiser *Emden*, had been operating in the Indian Ocean for two months prior to the action, in which time she had sunk 25 allied steamers, a Russian cruiser and a French destroyer. On the night of 8 November, unaware of the presence of the ANZAC convoy, she crossed its route less than 40 miles ahead. The next morning she arrived off Direction Island in the Cocos group intending to destroy the island's cable and wireless station and thereby disrupt communications between England and Australia. At 0600 *Emden* landed an armed party of three officers and 40 ratings to carry out the task.

Just after 0630 on 9 November, *Melbourne* intercepted a distress call from the cable station and ordered *Sydney* to detach and investigate.

DIE EMDEN AUF DER JAGD

SMS *Emden* and victim, 1914. '[we] had a queer sensation when we had to destroy [merchantmen] and saw them sinking. . . . The bow would settle down, the masts would touch the water, the propellers would stand up in the air, the funnel would blow out the last steam and coal dust; for a few seconds the ship would stand upright, and then like a stone shoot vertically to the bottom.' *Kapitänleutnant* H. von Mücke, SMS *Emden*. (P. Overlack)

Emden's commander, Karl von Müller, seeing smoke on the horizon initially thought it to be from his collier, the *Buresk*. He subsequently identified the vessel as a British warship but, believing his foe to be one of the comparatively light cruisers of the East Indies Squadron, he elected to engage and reluctantly left his landing party on Direction Island to complete the destruction of the British facilities.

THE BATTLE

Sydney, however, was without doubt a superior opponent. She was both faster and larger, displacing 5400 tons compared with *Emden's* 3600 tons. Moreover, while *Sydney's* 6-inch guns fired 100lb shells, *Emden's* ten 4.1-inch guns could reply with only 38lb shells. Captain Glossop in *Sydney* decided to open fire at 9500 yards, a distance he believed to be beyond *Emden's* effective gun range. His technical information was proven wrong when *Emden* opened fire at 10 500 yards and the salvo burst in the sea just 200 yards from his ship. Within minutes two shells had hit *Sydney's* after control platform, wounding three men, while one hit the range finder on the foremost upper bridge and killed the operator. Other shells killed or wounded personnel on *Sydney's* disengaged side and set fire to cordite charges. One pierced the forecastle deck, exploding without loss of life.

Sydney took longer to find the range and her fire was at first less effective. However, her superior speed and armament allowed Glossop to control the action and a succession of hits on *Emden* resulted in the destruction of the German cruiser's wireless installation and the loss of her steering gear and both range finders. The forward funnel collapsed overboard, followed by the foremast carrying with it the primary fire-control station. Whole gun crews were swept away and, with the landing party still stranded ashore, there were no reserves to replace them. By 1100 *Emden* was heavily damaged and burning fiercely. With only one gun still operable and his torpedo room flooded, von Müller considered that he could do no further damage to his opponent. He decided therefore to run his ship onto the reef at North Keeling Island 'in order not to sacrifice needlessly the lives of the survivors'.[2]

Gun drill in HMAS *Sydney,* 1914. 'Showers of shells poured down on us, soaring the funnels and other deck superstructure away, some gun crews were entirely killed and blown overboard by the air pressure of the passing shells. Some were practically torn to pieces by exploding shells. Those blown into the sea were drowned immediately. Time to attend to the wounded was none.' Third Officer, SMS *Emden.* (RAN)

Below decks in *Sydney*, Surgeon Darby had been preparing for action since 0730 and then found himself busy throughout the engagement:

On sighting smoke at 9am I went round the guns and control stations to see if the first aid bags were correct, thence to the sickbay to ascertain if anything useful had been left behind but before I could get below to my station our guns opened fire.

The *Emden* soon hit us and within 5 to 10 minutes from the commencement of the action the first wounded man was brought below . . . the first man had a fracture of the right leg and thirteen shell wounds. He was in great pain and I gave morphia, ordering the sick berth steward to attend to the wounds and put on a splint rapidly because now a constant stream of wounded men came down who required urgent attention. The second case was shot through the chest and was bleeding freely . . . pads and tight bandages were rapidly applied, a large dose of morphia being given . . . Before this case was attended to another was brought down who had various shell wounds . . . and two others who were very badly wounded . . . one of these soon died. In the meantime two more men had been carried down and all available space near my station was taken up so I gave orders to some of the stretcher party to give first aid assistance and to convey wounded—who were temporarily dressed—to the wardroom and to place them on beds and blankets from the cabins . . . The wardroom was only protected by thin armour but space had to be cleared near the theatres and this was the only available space.

We were now clear around our station and I went aft to see the wounded in the wardroom on the way passing Surgeon Todd's station. He had all this time been equally busy, and had been handicapped by the fact that on four occasions his sick berth steward had fainted.

During the action the space below seemed like a mad inferno. The 'tube' was full of men belonging to the ammunition and fire parties and at the best of times there is little room here. All the time we knew not how the fight was going—we could only hear orders for ammunition and the continual rapid fire of our own guns. At one time when we heeled over and the operating table took charge it seemed as though the ship had been badly hit, but we soon found out that this was only due to a sudden alteration of course.[3]

Emden went aground at 1115. Glossop disengaged and chased after the *Buresk* which had come up during the action. The *Emden* survivors were initially shocked by *Sydney*'s sudden departure:

. . . to our great indignation [*Sydney*] turned and steamed full speed away an unworthy act of a victor to do as we all expected help for our wounded, . . . as many had their legs and arms hanging down smashed and only connected by sinews with their body which was covered by blood and dirt. Nearly all articles used for bandages were destroyed and we had to use our shirts to dress our wounds, some cut their limbs fully off with a knife and dressed the stumps with rags from their underwear. Not even freshwater was available as all our watertanks were smashed also the distilling engine.[4]

For *Sydney's* medical staff, meanwhile, the sounding of 'Cease fire' had brought some brief respite from 'two solid hours' of working 'in a confined atmosphere of 105 F':

> The strain had been tremendous and SBS Mullins who had done wonderfully well with me started off to faint but a drink of brandy saved him and I was very glad of a similar drink at the time. Our clothes were saturated with blood and perspiration and altogether it had been a terrible two hours of high tension. We had been ably assisted by the first aid party and especially by Tilbrook Off Std RAN, Holley MAA RN, Paymaster Norton RAN and Chaplain Little RAN.[5]

Sydney's wardroom was rapidly equipped as a hospital while the sickbay was simultaneously prepared as an operating theatre so that the actual extent of the injuries could be determined. This took some considerable time, as the medical staff was exhausted and the sickbay itself had been flooded with water from the fire mains. Moreover, supplies of clean water had to be obtained from the galleys since ten minutes after firing began the water that came through the bathroom and sickbay taps became muddy and useless. Instruments and dressings had still to be sterilised. At the same time there were many necessary interruptions due to the needs of the wounded and all through the afternoon and evening German sailors were being picked up out of the water:

> The wardroom now contained eleven cases, most of whom were restless and in pain . . . Fresh doses of morphia were administered and iced water, soda water and brandy to the various cases as thought fit . . . Our constant attention was now taken up by two very severely wounded men . . . one of these men died two hours after being wounded.[6]

THE GERMAN SURRENDER

Overtaking *Buresk* shortly after noon, Glossop was unable to prevent the German crew from scuttling their ship and thus avoiding her capture. By 1600 *Sydney* had returned to *Emden* and Glossop was surprised to see her still flying the German ensign. An exchange of signals was inconclusive and he closed in to 4000 yards and reluctantly fired two further salvoes. The ensign immediately came down and was replaced by a white sheet on the quarterdeck.[7] As soon as *Emden* surrendered Glossop went back to collect two boats which had been left behind to rescue those *Buresk* sailors still in the water. Returning to *Emden* for the second time he sent one of the boats, manned by a German crew, with a message that he would come back the next morning. Glossop felt obliged to return to Direction Island to check on the situation. The German landing party had completed the destruction of the wireless station which was now without any form of communication with the ship. At the same time, Glossop was not sure that *Emden* had been acting alone as the whereabouts of another German cruiser, the *Königsberg*, had yet to be determined. Darby continued his account:

> Until midnight we were attending to the wants of the patients. The two sick berth ratings were sent to bed at 10pm thoroughly worn out and Surgeon Todd and myself took 4 hourly watches from midnight with the assistance of the first aid parties and volunteers to do the nursing.[8]

Glossop reached Direction Island too late in the evening to make a landing and lay off all night ready to deal with the *Königsberg*, should she appear. He proceeded to the cable station the next morning to find that the German landing party had already escaped in a commandeered schooner. (After an epic sea and overland journey they would eventually reach the safety of the German Embassy in Istanbul.)

HELPING THE GERMAN CASUALTIES

Having ascertained the extent of the damage at Direction Island, Glossop could now consider the rescue of the remaining German survivors. Recognising the need for additional medical help, Glossop embarked Dr H.S. Ollerhead, the Eastern Extension Telegraph Company's surgeon, and two assistants and then set course for North Keeling Island and the beached *Emden*. By this point *Sydney's* sickbay had been rigged up as a theatre and, with Surgeon Todd acting as anaesthetist and Dr Ollerhead assisting Surgeon Darby, the medical staff performed operations on two Australian wounded.

> Our chief difficulties were lack of space and trained assistance and we had used up all the sterile towels on the day of the action. The shortage of trained theatre staff caused delay in the preparation of the theatre

between each case. Later in the day we organized a theatre staff from volunteers. They helped to clear up, held basins, handed stores and dressings and did much remarkably useful work with a composure that was astonishing, as they were present at many bloody operations, to which none of them previously had been in any way accustomed.[9]

By 11 November *Sydney* had returned to *Emden* and arrangements were made for trans-shipping more than 200 German prisoners, including about 70 wounded. All available stretchers, hammocks and cots were sent to the *Emden* with a party under Dr Ollerhead and he did not return until the last patient left the ship some five hours later. The state of affairs aboard the German cruiser was, according to Ollerhead, truly awful. Dead and mutilated men were lying in heaps with large, blackened flesh wounds. The ship was riddled with gaping holes and it was difficult to walk about the decks as she was gutted with fire except for right forward. A large surf was running, and the lowering of wounded into *Sydney*'s boats was complicated by the fact that *Emden*'s davits were damaged and could not be used.

The best arrangements possible under the circumstances were made for the receipt and immediate treatment of the German wounded as they arrived on board *Sydney*. All blankets and beds were drawn from stores and most of *Sydney*'s officers went without. As the wounded came inboard they were carried to the temporary hospital in the wardroom where Surgeons Darby and Todd attended the most serious cases and directed the first aid parties with the simpler dressings. There was an attempt to keep the sickbay clear for surgical operations but this too had to be used as a dressing station owing to the overcrowding in the adjacent corridors and spaces. Soon there was scarcely room to move.

Some 40 of the 70 wounded received on board were classified as serious. Some had shattered limbs, others whole body burns and several were stone deaf. A man was lucky if he had less than three shell wounds and many presented horrible sights:

> . . . by this time the wounds were practically all foul and stinking and maggots $\frac{1}{4}$ inch long were crawling over them. ie only 24 to 30 hours after injury. Practically nothing had been done for the wounded sailors.
>
> In cases where large vessels of the leg or arm had been opened we found tourniquets of pieces of spun yarn or a handkerchief or a piece of cloth bound round the limb above the injury. The majority had been put on by the patients themselves.[10]

One of *Emden*'s two medical officers, Doctor Johannes Luther, had survived the battle but, in Darby's words:

[he] was a nervous wreck having had twenty four hours single handed with so many wounded on a battered ship with none of his staff and very few dressings, lotions and appliances . . . The other surgeon's action station had been in the tiller flat aft and when the ship was badly struck fire broke out whereupon he went up on deck and was blown overboard slightly wounded. He managed to get ashore and during the night lay helpless and exhausted and dehydrated. After much persuasion he got a sailor to bring him some salt water of which he drank a large quantity and straightaway became raving and died.[11]

After the most urgent cases were dealt with the theatre was cleaned up and operations recommenced at 1800. The first case taken was a German whose right leg had been almost severed above the ankle. He was followed by an Australian Ordinary Seaman with over thirteen separate shell wounds, most of them severe. The operating teams consisted of *Sydney*'s two surgeons, Dr Ollerhead and Dr Luther. During the evening Luther had to be sent to bed, a rest which he needed badly. He was followed by the two Sick Berth Stewards, who were also thoroughly exhausted. Darby, Todd and Ollerhead, with the assistance of three volunteers, continued until 0430 on 12 November. After a spell of over 40 hours without sleep, Surgeon Darby recorded that his team 'retired to rest after a cup of Bovril'.[12]

Meanwhile, the remainder of the Germans from the *Emden* who had gone ashore at North Keeling Island, some of them wounded, were also brought on board and *Sydney* returned to Direction Island to land Dr Ollerhead. Darby was fulsome in his praise: 'I cannot lay too much stress on the great assistance so generously afforded by the Eastern Extension Company's surgeon. He was always cheery and energetic throughout the 24 hours he was with us and he kindly left behind some instruments, lotions and dressings'.[13]

THE VOYAGE TO COLOMBO

Much to Darby's relief, *Sydney* then set off for Colombo at high speed. The medical staff attended to the fresh batch of wounded and, soon after sailing, another four surgical operations were completed with Darby, Todd and Luther rotating their roles. The remainder of the day was taken up with cleaning and dressing wounds and setting fractures under anaesthesia but they had by no means been able to get up to the theatre all the cases which required careful and thorough attention. The number and offensive state of the wounds added to the difficulties. At one point the sick berth attendant was overcome and had to be sent on deck for an hour to recover. According to Darby, '50 per cent. of the staff were *hors de combat*'.[14]

Two large wards were set up by utilising the wardroom and the waist deck, and various special wards were established in officers' cabins given up by their owners. *Sydney's* wounded were nursed in the wardroom but were sometimes carried up on deck since it was very hot below. The German wounded filled the waist deck and, while cooler there, they were exposed to heavy rain despite the erection of extra awnings and side curtains. *Sydney's* Chaplain supervised a special duty party to look after the feeding of patients and additional volunteers from both ships' companies were organised to assist in the nursing. The sickbay was in constant use for the ongoing treatment of surgical cases and the movement of wounded to and fro was very difficult owing to the steep ladders, small hatchways and narrow passages.

On 12 November Glossop was advised that an armed passenger liner, the *Empress of Russia*, had been despatched to help with the wounded and take on board the German prisoners. That evening Darby and Luther assessed which patients should be transferred. It was thought advisable to retain the most severe cases of the German wounded and all of *Sydney's* men, for although the *Empress of Russia* had fine accommodation and plenty of bedding she had only two surgeons and one sick berth rating. The transfer was effected over two hours in calm weather on the morning of 13 November and a total of 60 patients and 100 prisoners were moved together with the eighteen Chinese crew members of the *Buresk*. A fresh supply of blankets was obtained and most of *Sydney's* used bedding was thrown overboard due to its filthy condition.

Sydney now had more space and during the afternoon and the following day the opportunity was taken to restore the ship to as clean a state as was possible. Each of the 25 remaining patients was thoroughly reviewed. The decks were washed down every morning and every patient who could be was moved with his bedding and replaced when his position was dry.

Sydney arrived at Colombo at 1000 on Sunday 15 November. The ships of the AIF convoy were at anchor in the harbour and many troops were on deck to witness her arrival. As a gesture of compassion to *Emden's* wounded, Captain Glossop had requested that there be no cheering for the victors of the battle. After much delay ashore the military authorities took over the wounded, filling the military hospital and sending the rest to the civil hospital. The departure of the wounded left *Sydney* in a most unsanitary and dangerous condition and it was some days before this could be remedied as she spent two days coaling, an exercise involving nearly all on board. Everywhere was well scrubbed out, but the deck coverings in the wardroom, sickbay and starboard corridor had to be scraped, 'as they were thick with marine glue, which was unavoidably fouled by dressings and discharges from wounds'.[15] The Colombo health authorities were then brought aboard and they sprayed every living space with disinfectant. In getting this done Darby faced some difficulty with and reluctance from Glossop:

> . . . the Captain did not attach sufficient importance to it and was most anxious to put to sea as soon as we had coaled. There was only a slight outbreak of septic throats after but I was frightened of an outbreak of erysipelas which fortunately did not occur.
>
> At 9am Thursday we left Colombo after having gone through a very trying 10 days and the whole of the staff was worn out and could very well have done with a rest instead of which we put to sea and had another operation on the first day out.[16]

THE AFTERMATH

Surgeon Darby summarised his views of the action and its aftermath in his journal:

> It would be very difficult to imagine a more trying set of circumstances for the medical staff of a cruiser in action where so many wounded would be rescued. Had the *Emden* sunk before she reached the beach our work would have at least halved itself as many wounded must have drowned. Thus we had an abnormal list in the enemy ship added to our own list of wounded. The ship was overcrowded and most unsuitable at any time as a hospital ship; we were delayed 48 hours around the scene of the action and we were 4 days steaming at 18 knots from the nearest hospital.[17]

Nonetheless, the operations were expertly carried out and, despite their poor condition and the initial delays in their treatment, only four of the German wounded died on board *Sydney*. Glossop's Report of Proceedings singled out three factors for special praise:

(i) The resourcefulness of the young surgeons in making the very utmost use of their very limited space and accommodation for the demands of an overwhelming influx of cases of terrible injuries . . . and their astonishing endurance through such an ordeal of continuous exertion and anxiety;

    (ii)   the adaptability of the sailors, whose naval training and intelligence enabled them to render valuable aid to the medical staff; and

    (iii) the humane consideration shown to the German wounded who received equal attention and care with our own wounded.[18]

Von Müller later made specific mention of the great care taken of his wounded, while Prince Franz Josef of Hohenzollern noted in his book *Emden*: 'One can only say that in this connection an enormous amount was done, and the medical personnel put itself to all conceivable trouble to help the wounded and as far as possible alleviate their pains'.[19]

    Sydney returned to her home port, Sydney, in July 1919 after active service in the Atlantic, the West Indies and the North Sea. She had been absent for more than five years. Surgeon Darby had remained on board until January 1918. Following the war he continued to serve. He was promoted to Surgeon Commander in 1922 and to Surgeon Captain in 1927 as Director of Naval Medical Services. Many beneficial changes were made during his tenure of office and the RAN Medical Branch began to emerge as an independent organisation. Deviations from Royal Navy procedures more suited to Australian conditions were introduced. Specialisation by Naval doctors was encouraged, the Dental Branch was expanded and specialised training of sick berth sailors introduced.[20] Darby retired from the Navy in 1946. Surgeon Todd transferred to the Retired List in 1917.

    Dr Luther was interned in England until May 1916 and then repatriated to Germany. He later served in the Naval Hospital at Hamburg, the battleship *Rheinland* and the cruiser *Hamburg*. He retired from the German Navy in 1919.[21] The survivors of SMS *Emden* were granted permission by the Prussian Government to change their surnames to Emden and most chose to do so.

MEDICAL LESSONS LEARNED

Surgeon Darby and his staff performed well in extremely difficult circumstances. But how would a modern RAN warship fare in the aftermath of a tragedy on a similar scale—say an explosion and fire in a peacetime Indian Ocean transit with a casualty list of 20 wounded and four deaths in a two-hour period? In many ways fairly similarly—the essential difference would be the possibility of aero-medical evacuation by ship's helicopter to an airfield at Cocos Island for further transport to a mainland hospital. But what if the helicopters were not available, if the

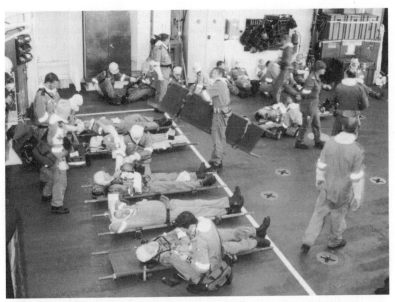

Training for casualty treatment, Operation SLIPPER, November 2001. 'The capability of a ship's medical staff to rapidly and effectively treat their wounded is not only a major morale factor, but also enhances a vessel's fighting abilities. Those of us deployed to the Gulf knew that our medical teams could handle anything.' Lieutenant-Commander J.H. Straczek, RANR, HMAS *Kanimbla*. (RAN)

flight deck were damaged, or if the ship were several hundred miles further westward?

A wartime scenario might introduce further limitations. The ship's helicopters might not be able to be released from their primary operational role and, in any case, their patient lift capability could be markedly reduced. Experience in the Second World War was that it was not always possible to transfer wounded to higher levels of medical support. After HMAS *Australia*'s first encounter with *kamikaze* aircraft in October 1944, 30 serious cases were forced to remain on board for six days. Despite the presence of two hospital ships in the vicinity the risk of submarine attack made their transfer impossible.[22]

Although the on-board management of patients today would be made easier by the availability of sophisticated monitoring systems, antibiotics, fluid replacements and more effective anaesthetics, the main problems faced by Surgeon Darby would also be faced by his successors.

In 1914 *Sydney* carried two medical officers in her complement. The present-day fleet unit would have only one in such a deployment.

The physical exhaustion experienced by those in *Sydney* in 1914 would be mirrored today. Darby was well-served by trained first aid teams but he had to supplement these with volunteers as the number of wounded increased. The tasks of monitoring patients following treatment, of dressing wounds and of feeding patients were and are manpower-intensive. In today's minimally-manned vessels, Ships Medical Emergency Team personnel are a scarce resource and may also be required to fill their primary roles.

Surgeon Darby also noted the delays in the treatment of wounded due to the need to re-sterilise instruments and disinfect the operating theatre between patients, despite the availability of pre-prepared packs. A similar situation would occur today. Furthermore, Darby's experience of working in extremes in temperature and patient discomfort could readily be replicated in any ship of today's fleet. Air-conditioning units can easily be damaged and alternative access to ventilation may be even less than in 1914. A final point to note is Darby's comment that his planning for the treatment of casualties was made difficult because 'we knew not how the fight was going'.[23] This is surely a lesson for present-day commanders: all must be kept informed, not just those fighting the battle.

7 | The aircraft carrier

The experience of its conception, procurement and operation

David Hobbs

THE PROBABILITY THAT AIRCRAFT would operate from specialised warships at sea was widely prophesied in the late nineteenth and early twentieth centuries. Among others, Clement Ader and Victor Lough-head wrote of aircraft carriers which would form the core of future fleets. Both recognised the need for the ships to be designed around flight decks and aircraft support facilities but, significantly, they saw aviation as adding new weapons and capabilities to an existing form of warfare and not as a new and separate force.[1] In 1912 the shipbuilding firm of William Beardmore proposed a design for an aircraft-carrying ship to the Admiralty. This featured a long flight deck, with workshops and hangarage either side connected, over the deck, by a bridge from which the ship would have been controlled. With the wisdom of hind-sight, we can see that the ship would have been inoperable. Fortunately, therefore, the Admiralty declined to order such a ship until it had gained more experience of aircraft operations.[2]

The procurement of warships built or converted to carry aircraft was pragmatic, with each step based on practical trial and discovery. The US Navy was the first both to launch and recover an aircraft using plat-forms built on to warships. The German Navy was the first to see the value of rigid airships for reconnaissance in support of the fleet at sea, although it was not permitted to purchase any until Count Zeppelin's designs had proved their utility. France, Italy, Spain, Japan and Russia all experimented with ships modified to operate hydro-aeroplanes (as seaplanes were then known), but between 1908 and 1918 it was the Royal Navy which led the field in the development of aviation and the integration of aircraft into the operational capability of its fleets.

Early British interest centred on airships, since their endurance, radius of action and potential load-carrying ability far exceeded that of contemporary aircraft. HM Rigid Airship Number 1 was ordered in 1909 but broke up on being extracted from its shed in September 1911. This setback, coupled with a change of leadership at the Admiralty, led to a shift in focus to 'heavier than air' winged aircraft, and prompt steps were taken to evaluate them at sea.[3] In January 1912 a Short biplane, piloted by Lieutenant Samson, was launched from a downward-sloping ramp over the bows of the battleship HMS *Africa* moored in Sheerness Dockyard. In May 1912 the same pilot took off from a more level ramp constructed on *Africa*'s sister ship *Hibernia* which was under way in Weymouth Bay. The success of these demonstrations led to the conversion of the cruiser HMS *Hermes* to operate seaplanes in the 1913 fleet exercises. This in turn led to the procurement of HMS *Ark Royal* in 1914 as a specialist seaplane carrier for the operational fleet.[4]

THE FIRST WORLD WAR

Seaplanes were presumed to be the ideal aircraft for naval use since the oceans could form their runway. They proved insufficiently robust, however, to cope with even minor sea states and, if they did succeed in getting airborne, their floats proved too heavy and cumbersome to allow the performance required to intercept Zeppelins or carry a meaningful offensive load. Seaplane carriers were used as mobile bases, and in early campaigns such as the Dardanelles and the *Königsberg* action allowed an aviation infrastructure which could not otherwise be provided. It rapidly became apparent that carriers needed to move with the fleet, but in this they were hampered by the need to stop: first to lower their aircraft on to the water and then to recover them.

A number of fast merchant ships such as *Riviera*, *Empress* and *Engadine* were taken up from trade for conversion to seaplane carriers in 1914. It was hoped that their speed would enable them to catch up with the fleet after operating aircraft, but this was not to prove practical. The pragmatic approach even survived the outbreak of war and these ships were rushed into service, with the addition of the simplest of canvas hangars and extended booms to operate aircraft. It was not until 1915, after benefiting from their early wartime experience, that they were given more thorough conversions.[5]

At first, the tasks assigned to aircraft were not new and they performed functions which even Nelson's captains would have understood. Flank marking for long-range gunnery was expected to be important, thus preventing enemy aircraft from providing their fleet with a similar service grew in importance as the war progressed. Aircraft carriers developed because aircraft could not operate where they were needed without them. Nothing has changed.

The possibility of using aircraft to extend the influence of sea power over inland targets was first tested in 1914 against the airship sheds believed to be at Cuxhaven.[6] It was proven four years later when

First take off from a warship platform, June 1917. 'I was prepared to fly off a deck 15 feet long . . . there was a long silence as each man turned over in his mind the implications. One could almost hear them wondering if I could really do it. If so, then aeroplanes could be carried in fighting ships and we had the Zeppelin beaten. My claim was quickly established . . .' Squadron Commander F.J. Rutland, RNAS. (FAA Museum)

aircraft from HMS *Furious* destroyed two Zeppelins in their sheds at Tondern. Frustration at the German use of Zeppelin reconnaissance to avoid battle when necessary led, at first, to fighter seaplanes being deployed to counter them. When these proved ineffective, however, wheeled fighters capable of taking off from small platforms were embarked on seaplane carriers and light cruisers. These were 'one-shot' weapons which could not land back on their parent ship and had to ditch near the fleet if they could not fly to a friendly shore. While reconnaissance types were considered important, the failure prior to Jutland to sail the Grand Fleet's seaplane carrier HMS *Campania*, due to a minor signals error, illustrates that they were not yet considered vital. Admiral Sir John Jellicoe and his staff appeared ready to accept such an *ad hoc* arrangement but his successor, Admiral Sir David Beatty, demanded a more extensive and aggressive use of aircraft.

The Grand Fleet Aircraft Committee, set up in late 1916, asked for more aircraft-carrying ships to be built as fleet units and, to save time, these were to be conversions of incomplete hulls. The number of new aircraft types was to be kept to a minimum by employing existing machines already in service with the Royal Naval Air Service (RNAS) ashore. These included the Sopwith Pup fighter and the 'One-and-a-half Strutter' spotter/reconnaissance aircraft. As the potential of carrier-borne aircraft became clear, Beatty and his staff planned to use them to attack the High Seas Fleet in its defended home ports, a form of warfare dating back to before Sir Francis Drake and his fireships. To achieve this, they asked for an aircraft capable of taking off from a carrier deck while carrying an 18-foot torpedo weighing nearly a ton, and of landing back on board after the mission. The result was the Sopwith T1 (subsequently named the 'Cuckoo' because it was designed to lay an egg in someone else's nest).

Attack at source was an altogether more sophisticated approach to naval aviation. It demanded flush-deck carriers and large numbers of aircraft, not just the handful needed for 'one-shot' defence. The increasing importance of the role of the carrier squadron was recognised by the appointment of Rear Admiral R.F. Phillimore as Admiral Commanding Aircraft Grand Fleet in January 1918.[7] By late 1918 his squadron included HMS *Argus*, the world's first true carrier, and the converted cruisers HMS *Furious* and HMS *Vindictive* as well as several smaller seaplane carriers. The rapid growth of the torpedo attack force demonstrates how the RNAS was well-placed, within a technologically advanced 'parent' service, to call on established weapons experts and engineers. In both areas the RNAS benefited from the evolution of tactical and technical ideas to a far greater extent than a separate service would have done.

Although there is no single moment when an air navy was born, by 1918 aviation was such a fundamental part of operations that no fleet could seriously contemplate sailing without air support. The impact of embarked aircraft on the First World War was more evolutionary than revolutionary, but in a dynamic way which changed the nature of naval battle forever. Shore-based aircraft and their integration into the fleet command structure was an important aspect, and one which was not fully understood until it was lost after the formation of the land-orientated Royal Air Force. No other navy in the world had come close to the Royal Navy's understanding of aircraft and their potential. It is, therefore, surprising that at the very moment when success was evident for all to see, the momentum was lost.

BETWEEN THE WARS

On 'All Fools' Day' 1918, the RNAS and Royal Flying Corps (RFC) were amalgamated to form a unified air service known as the Royal Air Force (RAF). This was a political act intended to calm public fears generated by German air raids on London, not the result of study into how aircraft had contributed to the actual conduct of war. Produced under the nominal authority of the Prime Minister, Lloyd George, the report was the work of one man, the South African General Smuts, who took account of the views of some senior officers in both services. Admiral Beatty had, at first, been receptive to the idea of a unified air service but, by October 1918, when it was too late, he was complaining that the new Air Ministry was 'failing to provide for the growing requirements of the Air Force units attached to the Grand Fleet'. Similar ideas proposed in the United States had not survived open public scrutiny.[8]

Paradoxically, the RAF was formed before technology had delivered the hardware which would make aircraft capable of operations independent of established naval and military forces. In the harsh post-war economic climate, therefore, it might not have endured had its leaders planned to do merely what the RNAS and RFC had done. To survive, the air marshals had to argue a case for strategic substitution warfare in which bombers would replace battle fleets and armies. A bizarre confrontation emerged in many countries wherein proponents of 'air power' actually opposed the use of tactical aircraft by navies. In the

United States, calls by General William 'Billy' Mitchell for a unified air service caused intense controversy. Both the Navy and Army Boards saw this as going 'much too far' and 'not the best approach to the aviation problems of the country'. Despite the hyperbole used in some quarters, the US administration managed to retain a rational approach.

The debate did force the US Navy to formalise the status of aviation within the service. Funds to convert the collier *Jupiter* into an experimental carrier, renamed the USS *Langley,* were approved in 1920. Equally important, a Bureau of Aeronautics (BuAer) under Rear Admiral William Moffett was authorised in 1921, charged with 'all that relates to designing, building, fitting out and repairing naval and marine corps aircraft'. Throughout the next ten years Admiral Moffett would fight and win political battles to keep aviation within the Navy. Adequate funding was provided for new carriers and their aircraft, and the roles and capabilities of aircraft within a balanced navy were identified. As Norman Friedman has observed, this period gave US carrier aviation organisational, institutional and individual foundations which have endured to this day. Barred politically from this approach, the Royal Navy was forced to rely upon an *ad hoc* arrangement with a separate service administered by a separate Air Ministry, and the USN gained a lead in air matters which it has never lost.

Progress in the USN stemmed from the driving force of men such as Commodore Joseph Reeves, who was instructed in 1925 to develop the 'strategy and tactics of the air in its relation to the fleet'. By introducing deck parks, arrester wires, crash barriers and Landing Safety Officers, sometimes against the advice of embarked pilots, Reeves doubled the number of aircraft in *Langley,* improved their sortie generation rates and gave her an operational capability. In the same year General Mitchell accused the Navy and Army of 'incompetency, criminal negligence and almost treasonable administration of the national defence'.[9] For this he was court-martialled and ceased to be a factor in the debate about aviation. President Coolidge set up a President's Aircraft Committee chaired by a prominent lawyer, Dwight D. Morrow, to advise on the best way forward. The 'Morrow Board', as it became known, took extensive evidence and rejected calls for a unified air force. Further, it recommended that only pilots should be given command of aircraft carriers and naval air stations. This encouraged many senior officers, some in their late forties, among them the future Admiral 'Bull' Halsey, to learn to fly and ensured that, in the next war, US carriers would be commanded by officers who knew how best to fight their commands. Progress after 1925 was helped further by a cycle of 'war games' involving BuAer, the Naval War College and operational fleets.[10]

In Britain it proved much more difficult to progress carrier aviation. It is difficult to understand how the theory of strategic bombing generated so much attention, while areas such as anti-submarine warfare, of such critical importance in the recent war, were sidelined. The bomber lobby dismissed the valuable tactical lessons learned by the RNAS in support of convoy protection as being largely irrelevant. Most had to be re-learned after 1939.

As the technology of naval warfare improved in the 1920s and 1930s more complex aircraft were required. The Air Ministry was responsible for all aircraft development in the United Kingdom, and although they did not deliberately provide second-rate aircraft, they did regard naval aircraft as fulfilling a secondary function. Naval requirements were seen as being a 'complication' on what they considered a 'normal' design. (This was not good design philosophy and would not have been possible in the USA and even Japan, where carrier aviation also soon surpassed the Royal Navy's efforts.)

Between 1918 and 1939 the Admiralty and the Air Ministry shared control of aircraft embarked in Royal Navy ships. From 1924, however, the Admiralty paid for the aircraft and provided 70 per cent of pilots and all observers and telegraphist air gunners. The Admiralty always retained operational control while the Air Ministry had administrative control, including the training of aircrew and the procurement of aircraft and equipment. Any technological initiatives had to be scrutinised by a series of joint committees, few members of which had any practical experience of sea flying. Operationally, however, the Royal Navy stayed ahead of the USN in multiple carrier operations, which were regularly practised in the Mediterranean.[11] When war came again, however, the pressure of events caused carriers to be deployed piecemeal, preventing the Royal Navy from putting much of its hard-won knowledge to practical use.

The Master of Sempill, a man experienced in the design and testing of naval aircraft during the First World War, led the British Mission to Japan which taught the Imperial Japanese Navy (IJN) how to operate a naval air arm. The Japanese considered the future role of naval aviation to be so important that the light carrier *Hosho* was commissioned in 1921, even before her contemporaries *Hermes* and *Langley*.[12] The influence of the RNAS is easily discernible throughout the expansion of the IJN's air component and gives tantalising glimpses of what the Royal Navy might have achieved. Little is written in English about Japanese plans, but analysis of their progress shows that the Japanese saw carriers, together with fast battleships, as forming a raiding force, a concept well suited to warfare in the vastness of the Pacific Ocean. They made steady progress and gained valuable combat experience in operations against China.

The German Navy is an example of a failed carrier force. The long-awaited *Graf Zeppelin* was finally launched in 1938 and incorporated many unique ideas for operating aircraft in rough weather, although not all were good. Plans for her completion were initially delayed by *Luftwaffe* opposition and then by the naval staff's concerns over the vulnerability of carriers, given the sinkings of HMS *Courageous* and HMS *Glorious*. The Germans, however, lacked adequate understanding of modern sea war as well as the determination possessed by the British to make naval aviation work. The case of the *Graf Zeppelin* provides historians with two 'what ifs'. What if a complete carrier battle group, instead of *Bismarck*, had sailed into the Atlantic in May 1941? Worse still, what if the Admiralty's enthusiasm for air power had been less and the RAF had succeeded, as did the *Luftwaffe* in Germany, in removing aircraft carriers from Britain's order of battle?[13]

From the outset, aircraft operated from ships other than aircraft carriers. The Royal Australian Navy (RAN) is an example of a fleet which was quick to recognise the value of aircraft at sea, but lacked the resources to centralise them in a carrier. RAN cruisers serving in the Grand Fleet during the First World War were among the first to be fitted with aircraft platforms, and many of the early experiments were carried out in the battle cruiser HMAS *Australia*. When the ships returned to Australia after the Great War, the loss of their aircraft was keenly felt, and attempts were made to establish an Australian Naval Air Service. These ended with the establishment of the Royal Australian Air Force (RAAF) in 1921, when the new Service was charged, like its British counterpart, with providing seaplanes for reconnaissance and spotting which were capable of operating from cruisers. The seaplane carrier HMAS *Albatross* was the result partly of political pressure to provide shipbuilding work in Australia when heavy cruisers were ordered from Britain. It was also a response to Admiralty advice that the Australian Squadron must be self-sufficient in aircraft. The Seagull V/Walrus was designed to meet Australian criteria for a cruiser aircraft, and shows how seriously the RAN took aviation.[14]

The Washington Treaty of 1922 affected every navy, but especially the Royal Navy with its large fleet of small, prototype carriers. Although there was scope in the treaty for building new ships, the British could not afford this until 1935 when they laid down the new HMS *Ark Royal*. Both the USA and Japan were better placed, with huge battleships and battle cruisers already under construction; these could be converted into carriers under the treaty rules. Thus USS *Lexington* and USS *Saratoga*, both over 40 000 tons at full load and capable of 33 knots, boosted the USN's operational capability when completed in 1927. At first they were seen as too big, but their ability to carry air groups large enough to demonstrate the value of strike warfare and to cope with the larger aircraft due in service after 1930 would make them invaluable. The *Akagi* and the *Kaga*, completed in 1927 and 1928 respectively, gave Japan a similar advantage. The Royal Navy had only the large light cruisers *Courageous* and *Glorious* to convert, both of which were just half the size of the American ships and capable of carrying only half the number of aircraft. In addition, with more available tonnage, the Americans and Japanese were better able to experiment than the British. After the small USS *Ranger,* the superb *Yorktown* and *Essex* Classes resulted from the USN's ability to try different hull forms in order to achieve the best compromise. They stand as the best carrier designs of their era.[15]

In the 1930s, after the experimental years, carrier aircraft were seen to have real operational capability. In 1931 Rear Admiral R.G.H. Henderson was appointed Rear Admiral Aircraft Carriers, to act as the focal point for the development of carrier tactics in the Royal Navy. He was not a pilot but had commanded *Furious*, and believed in the use of aircraft for fleet operations. With six carriers he was able to carry out trials with multiple-carrier task groups, but still did not fully appreciate the value of getting large numbers of aircraft airborne quickly enough to carry out simultaneous attacks on enemy ships. Although Henderson did not realise it, his biggest problem was that the British did not know how far behind their rivals they had slipped. Because the RAF view was that carrier flying was difficult, and impossible in the face of land-based air opposition, senior naval officers presumed that every navy found it so and failed to challenge this lack of drive. Even naval aircrew failed to see the shortcomings of this approach since they were imbued with RAF doctrine during training. That there was a lack of a Reeves or Moffett was only realised in the late 1930s when Sir Thomas Inskip, like Morrow an eminent lawyer, was appointed Minister for Defence Co-ordination. In a judgment subsequently known as the 'Inskip Award' he stated that naval aircraft and their crews were 'a great deal more than passengers in a convenient vehicle', that 'a pilot in the Fleet Air Arm will no longer be an Air Force Officer' and that the Admiralty should 'enjoy a more decisive voice in settling the type of machine suitable for naval use'. He gave the Admiralty two years to take over full control of the aircraft which flew from ships and their shore support. With much help from the Air Ministry, control was handed over two months early.[16]

The appearance of high-performance bombers in the late 1930s led to fears that visually directed interceptions by single-seat fighters would not be practical. The Royal Navy, therefore, moved away from fighter defence of the fleet and reduced the number of embarked fighter aircraft. The Americans and the Japanese, with their larger air groups, did not recognise the same problem. The Royal Navy increased its fighter complements again when radar revolutionised fleet air defence, pioneering its use to maximise the capability of embarked fighters. All navies agreed on the potential vulnerability of carriers to attack by aircraft or superior surface units. In response they created the balanced task force—using mutually supportive ships of various types to counter the threats. The Royal Navy, guided by Admiral Henderson as Comptroller in charge of new construction, produced the most radical solution. In the period of re-armament after 1936, it would have been easiest to produce more *Ark Royals*. But Henderson chose instead to build the *Illustrious* Class, which substituted armour for hangar space with a consequentially smaller air group.[17] A larger air group would have been impractical to man and equip anyway, since the Royal Navy did not yet have the resources. Another of Henderson's creations, and an example of how far the Admiralty was prepared to go to overcome Air Ministry opposition to carrier construction, was HMS *Unicorn,* described as a maintenance carrier but fully capable of operational flying. Such a ship was found to be necessary during the fleet concentration in the eastern Mediterranean at the time of the Abyssinian Crisis in 1935. This same crisis saw planning for a possible strike on the Italian Fleet in its base harbours, harking back to the Grand Fleet plans of 1918; plans which would prove useful when Italy declared war in 1940.

In 1939 the carrier navies differed in equipment and doctrine. Both the American and Japanese naval air arms were far larger than the British. Both had had time to integrate fast carrier task forces into their fleet battle plans, and were supported by industrial and training bases that had been indoctrinated into naval requirements for many years. The British lacked these advantages, particularly a naval air industrial base which understood what was required in carrier aircraft. All the Royal Navy possessed was a recently gained Air Branch, determined to show how well it could perform. War, when it came, did not resemble the political expectation and Air Branch staff found themselves required to do far more than they or their admirals had anticipated.[18]

THE SECOND WORLD WAR

The first Axis aircraft to be destroyed by the British in the Second World War was shot down by a fighter from HMS *Ark Royal* on 26 September 1939. The last was despatched likewise by fighters from HMS *Indefatigable* on 15 August 1945. In the intervening years British carriers fought in every theatre of war and in every conceivable role. Far from fearing land-based air attack, they proved able to dominate battle space and take sea power inland to attack strategic as well as tactical targets.[19]

The Royal Navy expected its carrier aircraft to 'find, fix and strike' enemy surface units. It equipped air groups with TBR (torpedo/ bomber/reconnaissance) aircraft and a few escort fighters trained to fight in a 'Jutland style' fleet action. The campaign in Norway of April–June 1940, however, highlighted the reality rather than the theory of modern war. The Germans relied heavily on land-based aircraft after the first landings by sea. The British had no planned air expeditionary capability and the brunt of providing air support for the Army fell on carrier-borne aircraft, first from *Furious*, then from *Ark Royal* and *Glorious*. *Furious* was ordered to sea in haste, some time after the heavy units of the Home Fleet. In order to make the rendezvous, her captain sailed without his fighter squadron rather than taking time to embark it. Would a cruiser captain have sailed without ammunition in similar circumstances? Aircraft were not yet seen as vital for fleet air defence, and carrier captains were not necessarily 'air minded'.

The campaign saw the first significant warships sunk by air attack in wartime, the British destroyer HMS *Gurkha* on 9 April and the German cruiser *Königsberg*—sunk by naval dive-bombers disembarked temporarily at RN Air Station Hatston—on 10 April. Fairy Swordfish carried out the first co-ordinated squadron attacks on shipping with torpedoes, dive-bombed German troops and airfields, and even flew combat air patrols. Blackburn Skua fighter/dive-bombers showed impressive versatility, bombing and strafing ships and shooting down a number of bombers despite their poor performance record and light armament.[20] Lieutenant W.P. Lucy, DSO, RN, commanding officer of 803 Naval Air Squadron, became one of the first Allied 'aces' on this unlikely mount.[21] HMS *Glorious,* the second British carrier loss, was wrongly employed ferrying a handful of RAF Hurricanes from Norway back to the United Kingdom. The campaign in Norway had a major impact on future operations and training due to the loss of so many of the Navy's valuable trained aircrew. The USN studied the campaign in detail and later made use of its lessons when planning operations in the Pacific.

Italian battleship *Conte Di Cavour* at Taranto on the morning of 12 November 1940. 'And so we jink and swerve, an instinct of living guiding my legs and right arm; two large clear shapes on our starboard side are monstrous in the background of flares. We turn until the righthand battleship is between the bars of the torpedo sight, dropping down as we do so. The water is close beneath our wheels, so close I am wondering which is going to happen first—the torpedo going or our hitting the sea— then we level out, and almost without a thought the button is pressed and a jerk tells me the "fish" is gone.' Lieutenant M.R Maund, RN, HMS *Illustrious*. (FAA Museum)

The attack on the Italian Fleet in Taranto harbour in November 1940, by aircraft from HMS *Illustrious*, would be highlighted in even the shortest account of the aircraft carrier in naval battle. Theory became fact when half the battle fleet was sunk or disabled by only a handful of biplanes bravely flown by men determined to prove their cause. As we have seen, the attack was based on plans drawn up during the Abyssinian Crisis, for the use of a force of carriers. Yet due to the strictures placed on naval aviation after 1918, only 21 obsolescent aircraft from a single carrier were available for the attack. The fact that these few achieved what they did was a magnificent, if officially unrecognised, feat of arms. The tactic proposed by Beatty's staff officers in 1918 was now justified, and the power of a fleet at sea had been brought to bear on an enemy who would not leave his harbour for a conventional fleet action. The airborne torpedo was proven to be a formidable 'ship killing' weapon in the hands of expert aircrew. The 'what might have been' had the carrier force not been enfeebled after 1918 can be imagined.[22]

The determination of the 'Men of Taranto' to succeed can be judged by the role of Lieutenant George Going, DSO, RN. At noon on 11 November, he was the observer in a Swordfish forced to ditch owing to fuel contamination. Rescued by a boat from the cruiser HMS *Gloucester*, and realising that he might miss the attack on Taranto that night, he pleaded with the captain to get him back to *Illustrious*. Respecting his enthusiasm, the captain had him flown back to the carrier in *Gloucester's* Walrus amphibian.

Piloted by Lieutenant E.W. Clifford, RN, George Going's aircraft, L5F, was one of the last to launch as part of the second strike. Unfortunately its wingtip was damaged when it hit L5Q as both aircraft moved to the centre of the flight deck. It was optimistically struck down into the hangar for repairs at 2145 while, for the second time that day, Going made his way to the bridge to plead with senior officers for the chance to take part in the battle. Supported by Commander James Robertson, RN, the Commander 'Flying', he won his case. Repairs to two broken wing ribs and torn fabric took only 20 minutes, then Clifford and Going took off alone and set a heading for the target. They arrived over Taranto as the last aircraft of the second strike were departing and selected a target for their bombs amid the chaos below them. They carried out a classic dive-bombing attack on the cruiser *Trento,* straddling it and scoring at least one hit which penetrated the armoured deck. Unfortunately, however, their bombs were defective and none of them detonated. They made it safely back to *Illustrious.*

On 10 January 1941, dive-bombers of the German Fliegerkorps X attacked *Illustrious* east of Malta, causing severe damage and heavy casualties, including 83 dead and more than 100 wounded. George Going went to help fight fires in the hangar and, finding the officer-in-charge of the damage control party dead, he at once took charge and was assisted by many pilots and observers. Lieutenant Clifford, his pilot in L5F, was among the dead and Going lost a leg as a result of the injuries he received. Lieutenant Going was awarded the DSO in May 1941 in the second list of awards for the Battle of Taranto. In his book on Taranto, Admiral B.B. Schofield later related how one of Going's fellow officers described him as 'the bravest man I ever met'. [23] Going died in July 2001.

To state that the Japanese 'learnt' from Taranto underestimates the independent progress in naval aviation made by the IJN. The British success surely would have strengthened their resolve, but preemptive strikes had been a feature of the Russo-Japanese War in 1905, and 'attack at source' had been a widely-used feature of naval warfare for centuries. The Japanese may well have adopted the idea of offensive action from the Sempill Mission. They were certainly aware that carriers were vulnerable to air attack if caught with aircraft re-fuelling and re-arming on deck (as, indeed, would happen to them at the Battle of Midway).

How much more sensible, therefore, to strike the first blow against an unprepared enemy in harbour than to risk battle on the high seas. Attacking Pearl Harbor was, for the Japanese, the best option for a quick and successful war against a superior enemy. The attack was very much the product of their own painstaking planning.

In England, early war experience changed the perception that carriers were an adjunct to the battle fleet. The unexpectedly wide range of tasks they were called upon to perform; the loss of the capital ships HMS *Prince of Wales* and HMS *Repulse* to air attack; the failure of aircraft to defeat the German 'Channel Dash' by *Scharnhorst* and *Gneisenau*; and the failure of the RAF to deliver capability to match its pre-war claims— all this led the Admiralty to review its carrier policy. The resultant Future Building Committee of 1942 recommended a massive increase in carrier construction. The committee also relaxed the restrictions on aircraft size which had limited the ability of aircraft manufacturers to deliver machines up to the standard of those procured by the USN.[24]

The recommendations were taken up enthusiastically, and large-scale carrier orders were placed to new designs at the expense of battleship and cruiser construction. These included seven new fleet carriers and 24 light fleet carriers, built to a novel design incorporating mercantile features to allow faster construction by a wider range of shipyards. The full package proved beyond the scope of British industry and five of the fleet carriers, including the three massive ships of the *Malta* Class, plus four of the light fleet carriers, were cancelled at the end of hostilities. In truth, these ships would have made little impact on the war, but they operated with great success in the post-war navies of the British Commonwealth and other countries.[25]

Escort carriers had been considered and rejected in Britain before the war, because the scale of open-ocean U-boat warfare had been underestimated. Wartime plans to build or convert such ships from mercantile hulls failed at first, owing to opposition from the Ministry of War Transport which would not release hulls from the merchant building program. HMS *Audacity*, a former German prize, was converted to become the first escort carrier and demonstrated the dramatic impact of such a ship on the business of convoy protection. The lessons learned are seen most clearly in the Royal Navy's *Fighting Instructions*. The 1939 *Instructions* discounted naval aircraft for ocean convoy defence, recommending instead small escort forces and evasive tactics. Revised instructions issued in 1945 stated: 'carriers with a convoy provide a tactical air force for its defence'. MAC (Merchant Aircraft Carriers) Ships supplemented the escort carriers.[26]

THE SECOND WORLD WAR IN THE PACIFIC

The Pacific War gave the most powerful demonstration that aircraft had come to dominate naval warfare. Fought across an ocean which covers approximately half the earth's surface, it involved logistical support distances vastly in excess of those in the European War. Japan and the United States had seen each other as potential enemies for over twenty years and planned accordingly. Both were constrained by the same treaties, the USN more so by the potential need to fight in the Atlantic as well as in the Pacific. Japan was able to concentrate on one main adversary and, while being inferior in battleships, the IJN had deliberately built up powerful air-striking forces, both sea- and land-based working to a common doctrine. The Japanese aim was to upset the traditional reckoning of naval strength and in this they succeeded.

By 1940, both navies had developed carrier flying to a high degree of tactical efficiency, the Japanese pilots given a keener edge by operational flying over China. The six carriers which attacked Pearl Harbor on 7 December 1941 embarked 450 aircraft. Against them, the USN had seven carriers capable of embarking up to 600 aircraft. To conserve their carriers' strike potential the Japanese embarked large numbers of scouting floatplanes in their cruisers, up to ten in each of the *Tone* class and a total of up to 60 in the Combined Fleet by 1941. These had a search radius in excess of 500 miles and an endurance of up to nine hours. In both the Royal Navy and the USN carrier aircraft carried out reconnaissance, with a consequent reduction in strike potential. Moreover, Japanese naval fighters such as the Zero had a distinct combat edge at the outbreak of war, although US industry rapidly produced a number of excellent designs with which the enemy could not hope to compete. Nor could Japanese shipbuilders rival the dozens of superb *Essex* Class carriers and literally hundreds of escort carriers which began to leave US builders' yards from 1943.[27]

After the period of rapid Japanese expansion, carriers played a crucial role in the consolidation of Allied resources before the period of unremitting offensive action which began in mid-1944. The Royal Navy, having defeated German and Italian opposition in Europe, participated in this phase by deploying carriers to form a British Pacific Fleet to fight alongside the USN. Never more than a quarter of the size of the US Pacific Fleet, the British were used to operating from an extended chain of bases and struggled to build up the logistic support fleet they needed in this type of warfare. It took over a year to create and relied heavily on main bases and airfields set up in Australia.[28]

At first the US carriers had been unable to concentrate as there were too many strategic assets to defend, but at the Coral Sea and Midway battles they did so with decisive strategic results. Fast carrier task forces, together with the Jeep carriers which supported amphibious landings, made the island-hopping campaign possible. American industry delivered materiel at a rate which the Japanese could not match. With the materiel came many thousands of trained men. American aircrew and sailors learned quickly in action, and their leaders rose swiftly on their merits to command of these forces. The quality of the whole fleet rose dramatically in consequence and, as historian David Brown has observed, the USN's Fifth/Third Fleet—with its associated Marine Corps formations—was probably the most efficient and effective instrument of war in the pre-nuclear age.[29]

THE NUCLEAR AGE

After 1945, the British and US Navies rapidly ran down their wartime carrier fleets. Carrier aircraft were, however, recognised as the core of a modern fleet's effectiveness and, as a result, many smaller nations planned carrier squadrons of their own, leaning heavily on British experience. They found the light fleet carriers, many of which were now surplus to British requirements, to be ideal units. Ships were exported to Canada, Australia, France, Holland, India, Argentina and Brazil. The Royal Navy saw problems in operating the post-war generation of jets from its relatively small carriers but overcame them with the invention of the steam catapult, the angled flight deck and the mirror landing sight: ideas subsequently adopted by every carrier navy.[30]

Despite the key role played by carrier fleets in the recent war, the advent of atomic weaponry led many to believe that this was the catalyst which would make strategic bombing effective, and that bombers really would now render fleets obsolete. The creation of the US Air Force in 1947 added weight to the argument as it sought to procure the B36 bomber to carry the atomic deterrent. The rival Navy plan—to operate P2V atomic bombers from super carriers of the *United States* Class—was defeated in Washington and the lead ship of the class was cancelled, following bitter political arguments, only weeks after it was ordered.[31]

The Korean War was to prove the air power theorists wrong yet again about naval aviation. The American carrier USS *Philippine Sea* and the British carrier HMS *Triumph* were both in Far Eastern waters and able to bring tactical aircraft to bear before land-based aircraft could be deployed.

Arming a Firefly on board HMAS *Sydney*. '23 October 1951—The [Firefly] flight bombed a rail tunnel at YC 194107 using once again a low level attack. Two bombs were neatly placed inside the tunnel collapsing the roof and another two bombs fell at the entrance cutting the line and causing the side of the cutting to collapse—thus covering what remained of the line.' Major M.B. Simkin, HMAS *Sydney*. (RAN)

They brought their own logistic train with them, could find their own good flying weather and were capable of providing concentrated force when and where required. They could also cover Formosa while there were fears that communist attacks might spread beyond Korea. The communists proved incapable of finding the Allied carriers, let alone attacking them. One-third of all tactical air missions in the three-year war were flown from the decks of American, British and Australian carriers. Korea proved that carrier navies would have a critical role in 'minor' wars, and both the USN and the Royal Navy deployed modernised carrier battle groups with second-generation jets.

The RAN deployed an efficient operational carrier, HMAS *Sydney*, only three years after establishing an embryo Fleet Air Arm—an outstanding achievement.[32] The carrier conducted seven operational patrols off the west and east coasts of Korea, each of some nine flying days in length. The various roles undertaken by *Sydney*'s three squadrons of Sea Fury and Firefly aircraft included armed reconnaissance, army cooperation, naval gunfire spotting and combat air patrols. The enemy's lines of communication were the most frequent targets and the carrier was credited with the destruction of at least 66 bridges, two locomotives, 159 railway trucks, 2060 houses and 495 water craft. As the logbook of one Firefly observer recorded, 'all bridges in our area were out. No vehicular traffic could move and the enemy was confined to moving supplies by hand at night'.[33]

After Korea, American and British carriers maintained strike potential in the Mediterranean and Atlantic fleets. At Suez in 1956, Royal Navy fighters flew two-thirds of the strike sorties and helicopters carried out the first 'live' vertical envelopment in history. French carriers saw action off Indo-China and American carriers saw extensive service throughout the Vietnam War. Less well-known actions include the Indian Navy's use of the carrier *Vikrant*'s battle group during the Indo-Pakistan war of 1971. Beyond overt conflict, there have been numerous occasions where the presence of a carrier has deterred aggression. British examples include Lebanon in 1958, Kuwait in 1961 and Aden in 1967.

The value of the West's strike carrier forces was, perhaps, best appreciated by the Soviets, who expended considerable resources in attempting to counter their potential. Bombers, surface ships and submarines, all armed with missiles, were intended to combat NATO carrier operations in the North East Atlantic. Once the USN had 'super carriers' of the *Forrestal* and subsequent Classes, culminating in the magnificent *Nimitz* Class, it could deploy high-performance aircraft such as the F4 Phantom and F14 Tomcat in a forward strategy aimed at defeating this Soviet capability. Bombers from the same ships could strike at Soviet bases, if necessary with nuclear weapons. Had deterrence failed, such battles in the northern seas would have been on a scale greater than Midway or the Philippine Sea.[34]

By the 1970s, attention was focused on the cost of defence, with carriers and their air groups attracting particular attention. As a result, nations such as Canada and the Netherlands opted out of carrier aviation. In Britain the cost of carrier ownership was initially kept down by the modernisation of wartime hulls such as HMS *Victorious* and HMS *Eagle*. Successive attempts to build new ships culminated in the TSR2 versus CVA01 debate of 1966, reminiscent of the US B36/*United States* battle twenty years earlier. Both were instances of competition between land-based air forces and naval carrier-borne squadrons for the role of conducting traditional maritime operations. The British Naval Staff added to their own difficulties by stressing the importance of carrier 'escorts' including a cruiser, thus heightening political fears that the carriers were vulnerable to attack. The USN's use of the term 'Battle Group' to describe ships and aircraft with complementary functions was a more politically astute use of the English language. Worse, since the British Naval Staff had overplayed the need for early replacement of all existing carriers by emphasising their importance east of Suez, the decision to withdraw from the Far East obscured the true value of aircraft carriers and weakened the political will to build what were to be known as the *Queen Elizabeth* Class. With the running down of the British strike carrier force, RN aspirations to contribute to the forward strategy came to an end, and the USN was left as the arbiter of Western sea control.

Fortunately for the Royal Navy, however, it was able to build three small carriers of the *Invincible* Class capable of operating a few V/STOL (vertical/short take off and landing) Sea Harrier fighters as well as helicopters although, short-sightedly, they lacked AEW (airborne early warning) capability. Together with the former CVA (attack aircraft carrier) HMS *Hermes*, HMS *Invincible* made the Falklands campaign of 1982 possible. Retention of even this reduced capability had been a close-run thing. In 1981, Britain offered to sell *Invincible* to Australia as a replacement for HMAS *Melbourne,* ending years of Australian debate that mirrored arguments in the United Kingdom and the USA. After the Falklands War, Australia did not hold the United Kingdom to the deal and *Melbourne* was scrapped without replacement. Had the sale gone through, it is interesting to speculate what steps Australia would now be considering towards a replacement ship.

There is a myth that 'Harrier Carriers' need not be as large as their conventional cousins. In fact, Harriers carry less and have a smaller radius of action than CTOL (conventional take off and landing) aircraft, so larger ships are needed to carry more of them to perform the same tasks. While V/STOL aircraft do not require catapults or wires, they cost more to build and use small engine production runs which lack logistic support partners. They are, therefore, more expensive to operate on a through–life cost basis.

THE FUTURE

Participation in intervention operations after the end of the Cold War has re-awakened British interest in operating large carriers. In fact, dozens of such ventures were actually carried out in the post-war years,

Lieutenant-Commander M.S. Blissett, RN, Falklands 1982. 'Blissett saw four Skyhawks crossing below him, from left to right. He called a break to starboard as the Argentine aircraft passed underneath and finished up ahead of his leader . . . and about 800 yards behind the Skyhawks . . . Both naval pilots fired a Sidewinder and both scored hits, Blissett's target exploding, while [the other] caught fire and went out of control . . .' David Brown, Head of the RN Historical Branch. (FAA Museum)

in which carriers proved ideal with their global reach, combat persistence and operational flexibility. At the time, British politicians discounted such operations as peripheral and focused on the potential for major land war in Europe. Now that prospect is removed, operations similar to those carried out during the last 50 years are wrongly regarded as new. Revived interest in carriers has led to British investment in the JSF (Joint Strike Fighter) Program as a full partner. A decision on whether to fund the USN 'tailhook' version of the design or a V/STOL version has yet to be taken, but it is interesting to reflect that the former meets both the Royal Navy Future Carrier Borne Aircraft requirement and the RAF Future Offensive Aircraft System. Other than the more limited ability of air forces to deploy, what is the future difference between navies and air forces?

The new British carriers are to be 'Joint' ships capable of operating both Army and RAF aircraft, mirroring 40-year-old plans for *Queen Elizabeth*. Indeed, the similarity is even more marked since the JSF program resembles the British Hawker P1154 project of the same period. Both Royal Navy and RAF versions of the P1154 were meant to go to sea as de facto Joint Strike Fighters. The loss of the *Queen Elizabeth* Class in 1966 damaged the Royal Navy more than any hostile force has done in 60 years.

The USN continues to operate the world's largest carrier fleet but with a reduced number of general-purpose aircraft types centred on the F/A18. As far as one can see, its carrier future is secure, whereas the Royal Navy has many obstacles to overcome before the new carriers recommended in the recent Strategic Defence Review become reality.

Since the decommissioning of *Melbourne*, the RAN's Fleet Air Arm has been virtually an all-helicopter force but these rotary-wing aircraft are world class, capable of operating from the majority of platforms and in a wide spectrum of roles.[35] Like other navies, the RAN needs aircraft to perform its tasks and is, in effect, a form of mobile air force. For the second time, the global 'carrier club' is expanding with both Brazil and India buying viable second-hand ships and expanding their fixed-wing capabilities.

CONCLUSION

The battle group centred on an aircraft carrier has the broadest range of capabilities of any force across the spectrum of naval and air power. It is a self-contained and self-supporting system ready for action. It is effectively independent of overseas bases, infrastructure or the political vacillations of foreign governments. In a time of tension the carrier group can wait out of sight in the vastness of the ocean but be capable of striking instantly when called upon to do so.[36] In peacetime the presence of an aircraft carrier on a port visit is an awesome display of national power which can be immensely useful in a variety of diplomatic ways. Anyone who has watched a USN carrier arrive in port would have to agree.

During the twentieth century only three navies, those of Britain, the United States and Japan, demonstrated the independent ability to design, build, man, equip with aircraft and take into action a significant carrier force. Other navies operated carrier fleets but relied on purchases and training from overseas. Some navies failed to achieve viable carrier forces at all.

Nothing dates faster than a prediction of the future, but an intelligent human operator in an aircraft capable of a variety of uses operating from a mobile base surely has a more certain future than many other weapon systems. Navies have proved indisputably that they carry out this task effectively, and emerging network technology will make them even more efficient. Command and control already comes from a joint national headquarters and the way carriers are controlled is changing and will inevitably continue to change as forces are integrated nationally and internationally. The time has now come to expose the fallacy expressed by protagonists of 'air power' that aircraft can only operate within their own narrow operational remit. If rational arguments prevail, the twenty-first century will see three-dimensional capability spread to every facet of warfare operating from both fixed and mobile bases, by whatever name the politicians allow the latter to be known. Aircraft carriers, unlike other weapons systems which have become outdated, thrive on new technologies which further enhance their capabilities. The fusion of naval and air warfare which they represent will cause several navies to reconsider their requirements for future operations.

8 | The Second World War, Korea and Vietnam

A personal perspective on naval battle

Guy Griffiths

THE SECOND WORLD WAR—HMS *REPULSE*

In early March 1941, I was one of five RAN midshipmen who joined the battle cruiser HMS *Repulse* of 1916 vintage. We had sailed from Sydney in a merchant ship in late December 1940, initially appointed to the cruiser HMAS *Australia* which was somewhere near the United Kingdom. Two days out of Glasgow we sighted a pair of aircraft. We began waving to them and it was not until they were nearly on top of us that we realised they were German Heinkels. One dropped a bomb, which hit the deck then bounced over the side before exploding and both strafed the superstructure of our vessel before departing. Thankfully they had caused no casualties and little damage, but the incident brought it home to us that we were truly at war.

When we arrived in Britain, about mid-February, *Australia* was off the Cape of Good Hope escorting a convoy to the Middle East. So we joined *Repulse*, and were given some hammock space in the midshipmen's accommodation down aft. In those days in the older ships there may have been a general broadcast system for 'This is the Captain Speaking' messages but captains seemed less inclined to chat. Moreover, some 60 years ago midshipmen were not renowned for having a sound understanding of strategic and tactical situations, and one tended to remain in the dark about most matters.

Repulse was in the Clyde on 22 May 1941, about to escort a WS ('Winnie Special') convoy to South Africa and the Middle East. The plan changed, however, and even before we had topped up with fuel we sailed at full speed northward to rendezvous with Admiral Sir John Tovey in the battleship HMS *King George V*, the newly-commissioned aircraft carrier HMS *Victorious*, four cruisers and seven destroyers off Cape Wrath, Scotland, early on 23 May. The word was about that the German battleship *Bismarck* was out—the British capital ships HMS *Hood* and HMS *Prince of Wales* were ahead—and all ships were headed to intercept. There was a high state of excitement on board *Repulse*, that the ship would get her first opportunity to fire her 15-inch main armament against an enemy (she had not been present at Jutland).

The 23rd of May was a fairly clear day with a strong nor-westerly blowing, and we were steaming into it at 27 knots, *King George V* leading *Victorious* and *Repulse* with the cruisers and destroyers on the screen. It was indeed a fascinating picture of sea power. At breakfast the next day it was difficult to understand that *Hood* had been sunk—maybe someone mentioned three survivors—it was all very sobering. The CinC altered course to the south-west and forced on to intercept. We expected to meet *Bismarck* in the early hours of 25 May, and never had the night lookouts executed their task more zealously. The day dawned with no sign of the enemy, however. The shadowing cruisers HMS *Norfolk* and HMS *Suffolk* had lost *Bismarck* and her accompanying heavy cruiser *Prinz Eugen* at 0300, and later records show that we crossed about 50 miles ahead of her track at about 0600.

At gunroom level we were not engaged in deep discussions about the vulnerability of battle cruiser against battleship, nor worried about the age of our main armament, which was controlled by an Admiralty fire control clock of ancient mark (a product of the development, or confused development, of gunnery fire control in the Royal Navy before and during the First World War).[1] Nor could we analyse Vice Admiral L.E. Holland's tactics in *Hood*: closing the enemy on the bow, so as to prevent full broadsides from both ships, and concentrating fire on *Prinz Eugen*. Fortunately, as records would show, *Prince of Wales* had ignored the order and engaged *Bismarck*, scoring three hits, an important result, but this would not be known until after 1945.

By noon on 25 May *Repulse* was short on fuel and was detached. Vice Admiral John Hayes (or, as he was then, Lieutenant Hayes, our 'Snotties Nurse') wrote in his book *Face the Music*:

> The anti climax for *Repulse* was debilitating. Keyed up for action, hopefully to have been an actor on the stage, we must now vanish into the wings. We crept away at economical speed to Conception Bay where we arrived with only a bucket of oil remaining.[2]

'Frustration' could have headed daily orders, but after that initial blow we were in Halifax, the lights were on and Canadian hospitality was most enjoyable.

Some seven months later our fine old ship prepared for a second opportunity to fire that main armament against the enemy—in a quite different environment: calm tropical waters. Tropical conditions were not recognised by Royal Naval architects during the First World War and afterwards, and air-conditioning was probably regarded as an unnecessary luxury for sailors.

Much has been written about the deployment of *Prince of Wales* and *Repulse* to Singapore in late 1941.[3] Hindsight shows that Admiral Sir Tom Phillips, and Force Z as we were known, was placed in a 'Mission Impossible' situation and, under the circumstances, he took the only course open to him, that of deploying against the Japanese force covering the landing in Northern Malaya, but he had no sea- or shore-based fighter protection or reconnaissance.

When we sailed, late on 8 December 1941, I believe the feeling in the gunroom reflected the mood in the ship—keen to get into action—but we were quite oblivious of the air threat. In their book *Battleship*,[4] Middlebrook and Mahoney record personal testimony of survivors of both ships, which reveal that many had feelings of apprehension on sailing. But these are flashes of hindsight written some 35 years after the event. Since no letters, which would have provided a fairly accurate record, were posted after sailing, I believe we have to look at the later assessments with some reservation. On the other hand, that twist of Kipling probably applied to a midshipman:'If you can keep your head when all about you are losing theirs—then you don't understand the problem my son!'

There is little doubt that the captains and senior officers of the two capital ships understood the tactical problems facing Force Z, but it is unlikely that they were aware of the extent of the Japanese air threat. On sailing, Captain W.G. Tennant told the ship's company of *Repulse*:

> We are off to look for trouble. I expect we shall find it. We may run up against submarines, destroyers, aircraft and surface ships. We are going to

carry out a sweep to the northward to see what we can pick up and what we can roar up. We must all be on our toes.

Tuesday 9 December 1941 dawned cloudy with low visibility, ideal for maintaining the element of surprise, but this was lost when, unbeknown to us, a Japanese submarine sighted the force about noon, and then enemy aircraft were sighted in the late afternoon.

(When Professor Arthur Marder visited Australia in 1979 and addressed the Imperial Services Club in Sydney, he was puzzled about what Captain Tennant would have been thinking on 9 December, and hoped that I could help. I thanked him for his question and reminded him that at the time I was a midshipman, and that it was not the custom for senior captains to confide their innermost thoughts to their midshipmen.)

With the element of surprise lost, Admiral Phillips called off the operation at 2015 on 9 December and headed for Singapore. He diverted to Kuantan to investigate a report of a Japanese landing which proved false: we investigated a tug and barges and then at 1015 on the next day, 10 December, were again sighted by a Japanese reconnaissance aircraft.

Just after 1100 the first high-level bombing attack began from starboard. The ships were turned together to starboard, masking the anti-aircraft guns. The port batteries had a glimpse, but then a turn together to port masked them. One bomb hit *Repulse* and it was 40-love to the Japanese. My action station was in the forward high angle control position (HACP) about three decks down, where I was aligning a cursor with a range plot to predict fuses for our four ancient 4-inch HA guns. At 1144–46 during the second attack—by torpedo bombers—both ships acted independently. *Repulse* successfully combed nineteen torpedo tracks, but *Prince of Wales* received two hits which virtually disabled the ship. 'Not under command' balls were hoisted at 1210.

Captain Tennant made the first report of enemy forces and indeed the first signal from Force Z since leaving Singapore at 1158. Admiral Phillips had maintained strict radio silence: no one in headquarters ashore knew where we were.

The next attack took place between 1220 and 1230. In a torpedo attack on both ships *Prince of Wales* received four hits. Twenty twin-engined Bettys, each with one 450-pound warhead torpedo, attacked *Repulse*. Captain Tennant could no longer dodge the fish and we took five hits between 1222 and 1225. Down in the HACP, one felt the hits and experienced the sensation that someone had removed the boat's plug.

Destroyer and HMS *Repulse* survivors, 10 December 1941. 'I was getting groggy from the oil fuel fumes. I could see in the distance the destroyer coming up and I knew this was my last chance, but I was slowly dropping off. [What] saved me was my mouth getting numb, and with a start I remembered the terrible time I'd had once as a boy at the dentist, I began to strike out with fresh vigour.' Ordinary Seaman Ian Hay, RN, HMS *Repulse*. (AWM P02018.058)

'Abandon ship' was ordered at 1225, followed by an orderly but tense evacuation up the ladders to the main deck abreast 'B' turret, where scuttles were open on the mess deck and the heavy list to port still allowed one to clamber up and get out, to slide down the starboard side and enter the water, and to realise that shoes are a handicap when swimming. *Repulse* sank at 1233 and 508 men (39 per cent of the ship's company) were lost. *Prince of Wales* sank at 1320, with the loss of 330 men. Survivors were picked up by our destroyers, HMS *Electra*, HMS *Express* and HMAS *Vampire*, and were returned to Singapore.

The expression 'picked up by destroyers' tends to dismiss lightly that vital phase of being in the water as a fortunate survivor. One cannot touch the bottom and the destroyer seems too far away. The sea around you is covered in some debris, one group of sailors are on a carley float singing, and heads are dotted about everywhere, some in the thick oil slick. Those who reach the destroyer are faced with the problem of getting aboard by clambering up lines, scrambling nets or ladders. The wounded have great difficulty, especially those suffering from burns. With some, it was a case of passing a line under the arms and being hoisted away by the destroyer's crew on the deck above. St John's Ambulance rules are discarded.

The midshipmen were sent back to Colombo, where we had four days' survivor's leave before joining the battleship HMS *Revenge* in Trincomalee. The diagnosis 'Post Traumatic Stress Disorder' had not been coined in those days, counsellors were unheard of and life just went on. A number of the officers and sailors who remained in Singapore became prisoners of the Japanese and theirs is a shocking story.

The highest award made after the action which saw Force Z sunk was 'mentioned in despatches', which included a number of posthumous awards. One was for Midshipman Robert Ian Davies, RAN. His citation reads: 'This very gallant young officer was last seen firing an Oerlikon gun at enemy aircraft when he and the gun mounting were slowly submerging'. I feel there is a case for an HMAS *Davies* in the not too distant future.

THE SECOND WORLD WAR—HMAS *SHROPSHIRE*

My next experience of naval battle was as a lieutenant in the heavy cruiser HMAS *Shropshire*, during service with the US Navy's 7th Fleet, covering numerous amphibious landings from New Britain to the Philippines between November 1943 and January 1945.[5] We belonged to Task Force 74, consisting of the Australian ships *Australia, Shropshire, Arunta* and *Warramunga*, three American 6-inch cruisers, and several American destroyers. We moved into the big league on 21 October 1944, with the landing in Leyte Gulf which was followed within the week by the Battles of Sibuyan Sea, Cape Engano, Surigao Strait and Samar. All these actions come under the collective title of 'The Battle for Leyte Gulf', which remains the largest naval battle in history. *Shropshire*, under the command of Captain C.A.G. Nichols, RN, was involved in supporting the landing at Leyte and in the Battle of Surigao Strait.

Let me set the scene. In a non-air-conditioned ship with a crew of over 1200, life was cramped and uncomfortable in the relentless tropical heat. The standard of food bordered on the deplorable. It was uninteresting and lacked nutrition, being mostly tinned or dehydrated, and fresh vegetables were virtually non-existent. On return to Manus after Leyte after a long no-vegetable period, Captain Nichols reported: 'We had hoped ample vegetables would be available [on our return] but only sufficient for 3 meals in each ship were received'. The mail service to RAN ships was also deplorable, being consistently irregular with long gaps between deliveries. Once despatched from Australia, it seemed delivery was purely by chance.

At the Leyte landing we participated in the bombardment and felt we were good at it. We were also initiated into countering air attack, and the *kamikaze* strike on *Australia* next door to us on 21 October helped to focus the mind. That good ship lost 30 killed and 76 wounded and had to retire for repairs, escorted by HMAS *Warramunga*. Our long-range reporting of enemy aircraft surpassed that of any American ship in the force, and our call sign 'porthole' was highly respected. We could use our main 8-inch armament in barrage fire against attacking aircraft and succeeded in splashing one or two, but the deterrent effect was splendid—for us.

We were overawed at the size of the pre-landing forces assembled in Manus and Hollandia and en route to Leyte. At the Battle of Surigao Strait the sight of tracer ammunition, hosepiping towards the enemy from six battleships and seven cruisers on the crossed 'T', is something I will never forget. Likewise the blinding flash of our own broadsides which initially drew attention from the enemy.

During the week beginning 20 October, we were at action stations for 146 hours out of a total of 168. The next week it was 98 hours, making a grand total of 72.6 per cent of two weeks spent at action stations. HMAS *Arunta*, in company with us, would have done much the same. Moreover, do not forget the stokers, engine-room crews and all those below decks. After Surigao Strait, where they contributed to the successful outcome of the engagement, the ship's company stood tall and morale was good. But action messing was lousy. We were lucky that the Japanese Admiral Takeo Kurita withdrew his central attack force from the Battle of Samar Island.

It is important to remember that there was a total of thirteen RAN ships in the Leyte and Lingayen Gulf operations; the four in our task force, three survey ships—HMAS *Gascoyne* saved *Shropshire* from a *kamikaze* attack—three infantry landing ships, which received high praise from the US command, and three supply ships.

The Lingayen Gulf operation involved an even greater landing force than Leyte and more exposure to enemy attack. The bombardment force and escort carriers departed Leyte Gulf on 3 January 1945, passed through a quiet Surigao Strait and on 4 January headed north-west, with the islands of Panay and Negros to starboard. The first air attack later that day sank the escort carrier USS *Omaney Bay* and set the pattern for the rest of the operation. On 5 January *Australia* received her first *kamikaze* hit and suffered another 25 men killed and 30 wounded.

From 6–9 January the bombardment force began softening up the landing area. There were frequent *kamikaze* attacks and *Australia* was hit another four times. Several other ships were lost or damaged. From later records it appears that on 6 January some 27 suicide planes took off from airfields in the Philippines, of which twelve hit their targets and seven scored near misses.

My action station in *Shropshire* was Air Defence Officer (Port)—a ringside seat. On 6 January I had the singular view of a Zeke diving out of the sun—presenting radial engine and wings only—and the result seemed inevitable. A few seconds later there was a glimpse of the starboard fuselage. He passed within feet of the ADP (Air Defence Position), just over the Bofors on 'B' turret, and crashed into the sea just off the starboard bow.

Throughout those four intense days *Australia* conducted scheduled bombardments and she received many congratulatory signals when she departed for much-needed repairs. Captain J.M. Armstrong, RAN, reporting on his ship's company, said: 'They were steady under attack and action to repair and make good damage was taken promptly and efficiently'. This was a masterly understatement. In all *Australia* suffered 39 killed and 56 wounded in the Lingayen campaign. *Australia's* Gunnery Officer at the time was Lieutenant R.I. (Peter) Peek, later Vice Admiral Sir Richard Peek, Chief of Naval Staff.

In *Shropshire* our good luck continued, supported by good air defence. Morale remained high but, understandably, some began to doubt our ability to survive. But we did, without damage or loss of life. As one can imagine, the ship's company were subjected to boredom between operations, particularly when anchored in Seeadler Harbour, whereas in action they experienced anticipation, apprehension and fear in the face of suicide air attacks. Consider the qualities required in guns crews to keep firing until the attacking aircraft is destroyed, banks away, or flies on until hitting the ship. Ironically, the concept of stress seems to be a modern discovery.[6]

THE KOREAN WAR—HMAS *SYDNEY* AND HMAS *ANZAC*

I next experienced naval battle while serving as Gunnery Officer in our aircraft carrier HMAS *Sydney*, which was deployed with the United Nations' forces in Korea from August 1951 until February 1952, and became the first dominion carrier in action. The naval battle involved air operations against enemy troop concentrations, supply dumps and supply lines, communications and coastal shipping. We also provided close air support to the Commonwealth Division, carried out gunfire spotting for surface ships and flew combat air patrols. The battle at sea also involved riding out Typhoon Ruth and operating in sub-zero temperatures. During the deployment, our two Sea Fury squadrons and one Firefly squadron flew over 2300 sorties and lost eleven aircraft and three pilots. A considerable number of aircraft were damaged by flak and small arms fire, which kept the smash-repair shop busy.

Morale was high throughout the deployment. The ship's company knew that *Sydney* was fulfilling the strike and air defence missions she was designed for and various congratulatory signals were received. This time the mail arrived regularly and the food, while hardly gourmet, was better than that of those earlier years. The deployment also confirmed the ability and endurance of the Australian sailor. Aircrews showed courage and tenacity in flying operations, and all departments in the ship worked hard to support the squadrons through a very unpleasant Korean winter.

In November 1952 I was back in Korea in the destroyer HMAS *Anzac*, looking forward to another winter. Our tasks were those for

HMAS *Sydney* in Typhoon Ruth, 14 October 1951. 'When relieved, [the aircraft handlers] would come below looking like drowned rats, many of them collapsing from sheer physical exhaustion. I remember Leading Airman Reg Holton coming down from the flight deck, soaked and bruised and saying: "I think we have had it. If it gets any worse, I don't think any of us will see tomorrow".' Alan Zammit, canteen staff, HMAS *Sydney*. (RAN)

which a destroyer is well known: interdiction of enemy positions, supply lines and depots, blockading against coastal craft, assisting in holding friendly off-shore islands and screening aircraft carriers. All this while avoiding the pancake ice floes. Like *Sydney*, *Anzac* fulfilled her tasks and morale was good. Again one experienced the can-do attitude of the RAN sailor, although no-one enjoyed the winter. What were our main problems? We lacked suitable cold weather gear and operated from an open bridge. One still wonders how sailors survived in the Arctic convoys during the Second World War.

As Gunnery Officer, my main problem was the gunnery fire control system. We had managed to buy the Royal Navy's Flyplane Mk 2 and twin 4.5-inch turrets, but the Flyplane Mk 2 was never meant to fly! It was consistently unreliable, and thank goodness we were not exposed to air attack. The 4.5-inch twin turret was an untidy and uncomfortable package of messy hydraulic systems—a maintenance nightmare. It was also unreliable and was not user-friendly in hot or freezing weather. The RAN had purchased the system in spite of the fact that we had already witnessed—under battle conditions in the Second World War—the effectiveness of the American MK 37 system and their twin 5-inch turrets.

Commanding Officer of HMAS *Hobart*, Captain Guy Griffiths, RAN, Vietnam, August 1967. '. . . undeterred by frequent, vigorous, accurate enemy shore fire, HOBART was responsible for the destruction of numerous enemy installations, earning an enviable reputation as an aggressive, eager, and dauntless member of the United States Seventh Fleet. The outstanding team work, courage and professionalism displayed by *Hobart* officers and men reflect great credit upon themselves and the Royal Australian Navy and were in the highest traditions of the Naval Service. P.R. Ignatius, Secretary of the US Navy.' (G. Griffiths)

THE VIETNAM WAR—HMAS *HOBART*

My last exposure to naval battle came during the Vietnam War, while in command of a new *Charles F. Adams* Class guided missile destroyer (DDG), HMAS *Hobart*. In March 1967 *Hobart* was deployed to join the US 7th Fleet for a six-month tour of duty. Our ship was built in Bay City, Michigan, and commissioned in December 1965. After achieving good results in trials and shakedown in the USA she arrived in Australia in September 1966, and participated in the joint RN/RAN exercise SWORDHILT off the New South Wales coast in November. *Hobart* confirmed her superiority over the Royal Navy's *Hampshire* Class destroyer, which had also been a contender for procurement. The result of this brief but satisfactory history was a well-trained crew with high morale. They knew they were serving in a ship which had commendable capabilities and were confident of meeting the challenges ahead.

As in Korea, the air and submarine threats were low, but a high degree of readiness was essential. Our duties included naval gunfire support and carrier screening, as well as 'Sea Dragon' operations. The latter involved interdiction of coastal shipping and bombardment of shore targets—at last we had a gunnery system which could shoot accurately with a high degree of reliability. The more we achieved the greater became the dedication and teamwork of the ship's company. Since *Hobart* was the only 'foreign' in the 7th Fleet, the ship's company quickly developed a competitive spirit in every aspect of operations. They worked hard, and the working week averaged at least 105 hours on operations.

Our achievements rested upon various factors. The ship, its weapons systems and their capabilities have already been mentioned. Mail arrived regularly. Food was either good or very good. Quarters were cramped for the 330 men onboard, but air-conditioned living quarters provided a reasonable quality of rest off watch. Most importantly, I had an outstanding ship's company.

CONCLUSIONS

Here follow some personal observations based upon these experiences of naval warfare. First, there is the matter of organic seaborne air power. In the past there have been tragic examples of its lack. When naval forces are deployed in harm's way beyond the range of land-based air cover—which is not very far—and are without naval air power, the consequences can be costly in terms of lives and equipment. I hope we have the guts to face this present deficiency in our force structure when we awake from our coma and talk about air power at sea, and I hope that the Army is interested. Perhaps someone will have the courage to admit that allowing Australian seaborne air power to lapse in the early 1980s was indeed a mistake, and will also have the courage to take early corrective action. On the other hand, if seaborne air power is now no longer necessary in strategic and tactical roles, then please invite me back to the classroom to learn about the practical alternatives.

Second, the man, and now also the woman, remains the greatest single factor in achieving optimal operational effectiveness with the materiel capabilities available. Everyone knows this. Defence planning over the last decade or so, however, indicates that this factor has been overlooked in the context of economic rationalist theory. But in naval operations and battle it is still the people who will experience boredom, anticipation, apprehension, fear, terror and sacrifice.

Third, the strategic blunders of the past demonstrate clearly that governments are not experts in military strategy. The political direction of conflict without regard to military advice has produced tragic consequences. Governments have a fundamental responsibility to provide appropriate military capabilities when they deploy servicemen and women in harm's way, or in situations which might easily escalate into conflict. National security measures require much more than fine plans in policy papers: it takes political courage to maintain and implement these plans. It is the Australian sailor's misfortune that all too often rhetoric has not matched reality.

9 | Aboard HMAS *Hobart* in the Java Sea area in 1942

Gordon Johnson

DURING THE TWO YEARS of my service in the modified *Leander* Class cruiser HMAS *Hobart*, the dates of 15 and 25 February 1942 live vividly in my memory as the days which, for me, were truly representative of the 'Face of Naval Battle'. The images of those days' events are as clear to me, as I write, as they were then—more than 60 years ago. I was an eighteen-year-old naval telegraphist.

Hobart was engaged in a defensive struggle in the Java Sea area against numerous attacks by large numbers of Japanese aircraft. She did of course survive to fight again at the Coral Sea and Guadalcanal actions later in 1942, but was sidelined for seventeen months for repairs after being torpedoed in the Pacific on 20 July 1943. Before describing the concentrated air attacks on *Hobart*, I will recall briefly the situation in which *Hobart* became involved leading up to the agonies of events in Singapore and Java.

ESCAPE FROM SINGAPORE

Hobart arrived in Singapore on 5 January 1942 under the command of Captain H.L. (Harry) Howden, RAN—coming directly from the Mediterranean where she had been a unit of the 7th Cruiser Squadron

HMAS *Hobart* sails as Singapore burns, 2 February 1942. 'The "Hobart" was in yesterday—just back from the Med. And they were all for going back there. They thought that it would be like a rest cure after this. I'm getting a bit jumpy now and am quite honestly scared stiff. All sorts of sounds seem to be that of bombs falling and I either jump about a foot in the air or just freeze . . .' Crew member, HMAS *Bendigo*. (G. Johnson)

of the Mediterranean Fleet. This was a month after the Japanese attack on Pearl Harbor. Singapore Roads seemed peaceful enough, but the city was being bombed intermittently, including leaflet raids, and the Japanese Army was already advancing rapidly down the Malay Peninsula.

As described elsewhere in this book, the Royal Navy's capital ships HMS *Prince of Wales* and HMS *Repulse* had been sunk 26 days previously south of Kuantan, Malaya, by Japanese aircraft. There was an air of concern pervading *Hobart*. The question on everyone's mind was: 'Where are our own aircraft?'. The Japanese bombers seemed to be operating with impunity.

Almost immediately after her arrival, *Hobart* set out again to participate in escort work. Supplies and troops were still being brought to Singapore, and the ship did not secure alongside again until 1 February 1942, two weeks before the surrender. By this time the situation had deteriorated alarmingly. The Japanese were close to the Johore end of the Causeway, and Singapore—now being bombed almost continuously—was very much a beleaguered island fortress. From our berth in Keppel Harbour on the south side of the island the scene around us was one of utter chaos.

Hobart departed the next day, 2 February, with the British destroyer HMS *Tenedos*. We had embarked about 100 evacuees including some survivors from *Prince of Wales* and *Repulse*. As we pulled out of Keppel, Singapore was a burning island and it was obvious to us that it was doomed. Our destination was Tanjong Priok, the harbour for Batavia (now Jakarta) in the Netherlands East Indies.

Near Banka Island on 3 February *Hobart* and *Tenedos* fought off a number of Japanese aircraft which were attacking the lone merchant ship *Norah Moller*. She had been hit amidships and was already dead in the water and burning. *Hobart* took off her wounded and passengers— a total of 57 including women and children, many of whom were shockingly burned. That evening we buried some at sea. More of *Norah Moller's* survivors succumbed before we arrived at Tanjong Priok on 4 February 1942.

Telegraphist Gordon Johnson extends a hand to the survivors of *Norah Moller*, 3 February 1942. 'Our doctors had an awful time. The sick bay, even of a cruiser, is such a little place when a large number of casualties pour into it. For days and nights Dr Lockwood and his fellow doctor and assistants slaved over the hurt people, doing all that was humanly possible.' Chief Petty Officer R.A. Blain, RAN, HMAS *Hobart*. (G. Johnson)

Between 4 and 14 February, *Hobart*—in company with various Royal Navy ships (including the 8-inch cruiser HMS *Exeter* and destroyers HMS *Jupiter*, HMS *Encounter* and HMS *Electra*) and other vessels—carried out sweeps in the Banka and Gaspar Strait areas searching for reported Japanese surface forces. The only outcome of these operations was, however, to expose ourselves to fairly frequent attacks by Japanese bombers.

'BLACK SUNDAY'

The air attacks, while determined and involving some near misses, proved to be more of a 'pipe opener' compared to what was soon in store for us! On 14 February *Hobart*, as ordered, arrived in Oosthaven (East Harbour) in southern Sumatra and became part of a strike force which included the Dutch cruisers *De Ruyter*, *Java* and *Tromp*, Dutch destroyers *Van Ghent*, *Banckert*, *Piet Hein* and *Kortenaer* and the United States destroyers *Bulmer*, *Barker*, *Stewart*, *Parrot*, *Edwards* and *Pillsbury*, and HMS *Exeter*. A Dutch officer, Rear Admiral K. Doorman, flying his flag in *De Ruyter* was in command.

The strike force sailed from Oosthaven during the afternoon of 14 February to intercept a reported force of Japanese cruisers and destroyers north of Banka Island. There was an air of excitement mingled with tension aboard *Hobart* as this sizeable Allied naval force proceeded at speed to meet the enemy. An encounter was expected to occur sometime on Sunday 15 February.

The Dutch destroyer *Van Ghent* ran aground early next morning and Admiral Doorman ordered *Banckert* to stand by and take off her crew. At about 9 am, *Hobart* went to the second degree of readiness, and closed up to action stations 30 minutes later. By this time Japanese aircraft were shadowing the force.

At about 11 am the Japanese bombers began their attacks, which continued unabated until dusk. It was a day of almost continuous anti-aircraft gunfire—including shooting by our 6-inch main armament—and of crunching bomb explosions. The ship turned sharply and heeled steeply. *Hobart*'s 72 000-shaft horsepower turbines whined in protest as the port or starboard engines were telegraphed from full ahead to full astern—or vice versa—as she dodged the bomb loads aimed at her. The strike force maintained 24 knots for much of the time, steaming in two lines ahead, but with ample distance for manoeuvring without fear of collision. One of *Hobart*'s Chief Petty Officers

Attacks on HMS *Exeter*, 'Black Sunday', 15 February 1942. 'All I did was ceaselessly to help rush shells to the guns and lie flat when the bombs were falling. It was either one or the other. *Hobart* was shaking from shock after shock, constantly pinging from the smack of shell splinters, every few minutes each man wondering "Will this one mean the end?" We prayed for darkness to come.' Chief Petty Officer R.A. Blain, RAN, HMAS *Hobart*. (G. Johnson)

spoke for us all when he described our escape: 'Again and again bombs fell just ahead or just astern of *Hobart*; we simply raced through the splash the bombs made. Only our captain's split second manoeuvring saved us again and again. We swore by Captain Howden. The confidence we had in him was as strong as our faith in the ship'.[1]

All the larger ships of the strike force had their turns as targets for the Japanese, but *Hobart* was in fact the most targeted of all the ships that day. She survived at least 260 bombs dropped, of which 74 were classed as near misses. A total of 128 enemy bombers came at us, attacking in waves of nine or 27 aircraft flying in formation. At one stage *Hobart* was so blanketed by the spray of explosions that *Exeter* piped 'Stand by to pick up *Hobart*'s survivors' (*Exeter* informed us of this later that day when the situation had quietened down). Sunday 15 February 1942 thereafter became known to the ship's company as 'Black Sunday' while Banka Strait was re-named 'Bomb Alley'. This was also the day that Allied forces in Singapore surrendered.

Captain Howden's own report of 'Black Sunday' summed the situation up quite well. He wrote:

> There have been occasions when I had to call for the most violent manoeuvring of the main engines and the instant answer resulted in the ship swinging in a manner I hardly thought possible. I found it necessary to go from 24 knots ahead to 24 knots astern on one engine while going full ahead on the other. The bombs fell close enough for me to see the ugly red flashes of their burst and feel the heat of their explosions across my face—the ship steamed clear.[2]

ESCAPE FROM JAVA

Hobart was back at Tanjong Priok on 16 February to refuel and reammunition. In company with *Electra* we sailed again five days later to escort the SS *Orcades* through Sunda Strait, returning to Tanjong Priok on 25 February and securing alongside the oiler *War Sirdar*. At 10.30 am, just as pumping from *War Sirdar* began, 27 Japanese aircraft attacked both ships. Sixty bombs straddled the both of us with one passing through *War Sirdar* and exploding beneath her. The 7100-ton *Hobart* jumped violently and was showered with splinters and seawater. One splinter about 30 centimetres long came through an open scuttle in the communications mess-deck and ricocheted around the bulkheads several times. Fortunately, the few men in the mess were flat on the deck and no one was injured.

War Sirdar was disabled and *Hobart* separated in a hurry and headed for open water. We needed sea room to manoeuvre in anticipation of further attacks. These did not eventuate, but *Hobart* had been prevented from topping up her fuel oil tanks. It was perhaps ironic that it was the aim of the Japanese pilot who put one of his bombs through the *War Sirdar* which saved us from a worse fate several days later.

A minute or two before the attack at Tanjong Priok, a lamp signal was received from Commodore Collins' shore headquarters (Collins was Commodore Commanding China Force and in charge of all British and Australian ships in the area). The signal instructed Captain Howden to take *Hobart*, *Perth*, *Exeter*, *Electra*, *Jupiter* and *Encounter* to Surabaya in east Java to join Rear Admiral Doorman's fleet. The British cruisers HMS *Danae* and HMS *Dragon* with the destroyers *Tenedos* and *Scout* were not ordered to go owing to their age and obsolescence.

Because *Hobart* was unable to complete refuelling in time, she could not sail to Surabaya and thus did not take part in the disastrous Battle of the Java Sea on 27 February. Instead, a Western Strike Force was formed consisting of *Danae*, *Dragon*, *Tenedos* and *Scout*, with *Hobart* in command. On orders from the Dutch Admiral Helfrich (operational commander of all Allied naval forces in the area) the Western Strike Force swept north to Banka on 26 February to intercept a Japanese invasion force believed to be heading for western Java.

No contact was made and *Hobart* retired with her consorts to Tanjong Priok. The situation there had become hazardous and *Hobart* was already monitoring transmissions from our sister ship HMAS *Perth*, who was engaged in the Java Sea battle, which saw half the Allied fleet lost and Admiral Doorman go down with his flagship. It was clear that if *Hobart*, *Danae*, *Dragon*, *Tenedos* and *Scout* were to escape from Java then we had to attempt a breakout without further delay.

Just before midnight on 27 February the Western Strike Force left Tanjong Priok for the last time. The Dutch destroyer *Evertsen*, a survivor of the Battle of the Java Sea, came with us. We searched northwards for Japanese forces, under orders to retire through the Sunda Strait if we sighted nothing by 4.30 am on 28 February. No contacts occurred, and the force passed through the Strait heading for Padang in western Sumatra to pick up more escapees from Singapore. *Evertsen* became separated from the force in the Strait during a squall, and at the time her situation was something of a mystery. She had in fact returned to Tanjong Priok and was shortly thereafter attacked by Japanese warships and driven ashore.

After the war it was revealed that the Japanese force we had set out to intercept in the Banka Strait area on 26 February was the Japanese Western Attack Group, under Vice Admiral Takeo Kurita. It comprised four heavy cruisers, three light cruisers, about 25 destroyers, the aircraft carrier *Ruyjo*, a seaplane tender and more than 50 transports and freighters.[3] Although Kurita's naval air arm had located *Hobart*'s Western Strike Force, and he had despatched two heavy and two light cruisers with three destroyer flotillas to intercept us, no contact was made. It is clear that this failure to make contact, with the failure of *Hobart*'s final search on the night of 27–28 February, were together a deliverance from certain destruction for our puny Western Strike Force.

Hobart arrived off Padang on 1 March and waited while the destroyers began embarking the evacuees. We accepted some 512 men, women and children from *Tenedos* and sailed immediately. Crowded with evacuees we headed for Colombo, reaching 29.7 knots and arriving on 4 March. *Hobart* was almost out of fuel oil, and the ship's food supplies had dwindled to the point where the cooks had to use great imagination in making tinned food palatable.

WHY WE SURVIVED

There is little doubt that *Hobart's* survival was miraculous, but two major factors contributed. First, there was the extraordinary skill of our much revered Captain Harry Howden; his superb performance as a cruiser captain undoubtedly saved our lives. Second, in all departments there was a high level of professional competence. *Hobart* had been operating in a war zone for a lengthy period with very few changes in her complement throughout this time. She was an extremely happy ship with a great team spirit.

Our cruiser's protection was vested in her armament, which comprised eight 4-inch high angle anti-aircraft guns, a main armament of eight 6-inch guns paired in four turrets, together with multi-barrelled pompoms and other close-range weapons such as Oerlikons. *Hobart* had no radar and depended entirely on her lookouts for detection of the enemy.

Considering that this ordeal was the heaviest and most concentrated aerial bombing the ship ever experienced during her illustrious career, the toll exacted was remarkably small. All damage was above decks, and restricted to such things as wireless aerials being carried away, railings cut and splinters through the funnels and other deck fittings, none of which impaired *Hobart's* fighting capability. A small number of the crew were slightly injured by splinters and only one man was seriously hurt when hit in the chest.

The ship returned to Sydney on 4 April 1942 and short leave was granted to all hands. Newspaper reporters were keen to hear of our exploits, especially as there had been unconfirmed reports and claims by the Japanese that they had sunk *Hobart*. In one of the many articles published, the *Adelaide Evening News* used the headline 'Hobart's Crew Tells of Their Escapes From Jap Bombs' and wrote how more than '50 South Australian members of the crew of the Australian cruiser Hobart are home on leave, satisfied that their ship has a charmed existence—and a wonderful captain'. *Hobart* was indeed a very 'lucky ship'.

10 'The Gunner'

J.E. Macdonnell and the face of naval battle

Peter Stanley

JAMES EDMOND MACDONNELL was born in Mackay, Queensland, in 1917 but soon afterwards moved to Toowoomba.[1] He entered the Royal Australian Navy at seventeen, having never seen the sea or a ship, apparently inspired by the stories of Robert Louis Stevenson. After serving in the permanent RAN from 1934 to 1948, in several ships and on active service, he became a journalist and freelance writer. Macdonnell remains one of Australia's most prolific novelists, having written over 200 books. This chapter will explore the relationship between Macdonnell's fiction and his naval service. It will reflect on the nature of that relationship and what we can understand of the experience of naval battle through studying it.

'QUICK-WRITTEN SOFT-COVERS': MACDONNELL AS FREELANCE WRITER

Macdonnell published his first stories during the war, in newspapers and pulp fiction magazines such as the *Pocket Book Weekly* and *Woman*, as well as a contribution to the first Australian War Memorial's naval 'Christmas book', *HMAS*.[2] His first book, *Fleet Destroyer*, described the service of HMAS *Nizam* with the Eastern Fleet. Its last chapter was written 'at sea

. . . on a filched signal pad at "B" gun' in the intervals between alerts during the raid on Surabaya. The official historian, George Hermon Gill, had read stories by the then Petty Officer in 1942 and had encouraged his writing. Gill wrote a preface to *Fleet Destroyer* praising Macdonnell's 'sensitivity [as] an interpreter'. His 'vivid touch gives life and colour to his writing. He has with the pen a flair that should carry him a long way'. *Fleet Destroyer*, Gill predicted, would be 'the precursor of more to follow'.[3]

He continued to publish colourful popular features in the Memorial's *As You Were* series in the late 1940s, both before and after leaving the Navy.[4] Gill may later have had reason to regret encouraging his protégé. In 1947 John Treloar, the Memorial's Director, had been concerned to read 'Challenge'—Macdonnell's speculative reconstruction of the *Sydney–Kormoran* fight—and badgered Gill about it. Although Gill's official history was still ten years away from publication, enough was known for Gill to be disturbed by Macdonnell's cavalier treatment of the facts relating to this sensitive subject. Gill soothed Treloar by stressing that Macdonnell was:

> liable, whilst writing in such a way as to suggest that he was an eye witness or is writing with some special knowledge, to let his imagination run away with him, and in doing so may be somewhat of an embarrassment.[5]

Imagination may have seemed a liability to an official historian, but it was clearly an asset to a freelance writer. After leaving the Navy Macdonnell worked for the *Bulletin* for eight years, writing its 'Personal Items' column, while also writing radio and screen scripts (*Into the Straight*, a racing story, was filmed in 1949). Macdonnell's first success was *Valiant Occasions* (popular accounts of naval actions of the Second World War which had originally appeared in the *Bulletin*), published by Constable in London in 1953. Macdonnell had published a dozen stories in the *Bulletin* between 1949 and 1953, but from the mid-1950s his principal work became the freelance production of fictional books, what he called 'quick-written soft-covers'.[6]

From 1956 the Sydney publisher Horwitz became Macdonnell's main publisher. They came together after his first wife, a commercial artist, delivered some artwork to the firm's North Sydney office. A casual enquiry, 'Do you know anybody who writes sea stories?', put Macdonnell in touch with the house which would publish most of his output, especially the novels of what became the 'Collectors' series' and the major achievement of his career.[7] Macdonnell was the most prolific

Publicity photo of J.E. Macdonnell. '. . . if a rush of recruits to the Senior Service results from the sale of this work, a grateful Public Relations Department can send its donation to me, care the publishers: if recruiting falls to an all time low, then I can only say the breed has changed.' *Bilgewater* by J.E. Macdonnell. (Horwitz)

of a 'stable' of war writers published by Horwitz, including William Bennett, Roger Hunt, Ray Slattery and John Wynnum.

These writers are today virtually forgotten, but at the height of his popularity Macdonnell at least was regarded as comparable to Morris West, Jon Cleary or D'Arcy Niland. He was enormously popular. His Horwitz softbacks sold about 40 000 copies apiece, with regular readers asking at newsagents and railway station bookstalls for 'the latest Macdonnell', irrespective of its subject or title. His hardbacks had sold 870 000 copies between them by 1960. *Gimme the Boats!*, his first fiction, collected from stories published in the *Sunday Herald* in 1953, sold over half a million copies by 1967. His books appeared in British and American editions and in translation in the Netherlands, West Germany, France and Scandinavia. By the late 1960s he was comfortably off, making $11 500 in 1967. (It is worth noting that this was three times the then current average male wage, and that at the time a Rear Admiral received about the same amount, so the Gunner had certainly made good.) Still, that the figure included the 500 suggests that every dollar counted: as a freelancer he was still writing to pay the bills.

This success was earned by hard, unremitting work. By 1960 he was contracted to produce twelve novels a year for Horwitz. From the late

1950s into the 1960s he published an average of about a dozen books a year. In 1968, his peak year, he published seventeen books. Macdonnell's service background enabled him to work as a freelance writer with rigid discipline. Described as being 'built for solid typing', he wrote 3000 words a day five days a week, stopping at the bottom of his tenth sheet of foolscap paper irrespective of the drama of the passage.[8] In his heyday in the early 1960s, he worked on the sun porch of his house in Avalon Beach, reading a few pages of Conrad to get into the mood. 'It's hard going', he admitted to John Hetherington.[9]

He needed to be disciplined and orderly, because he wrote in genres besides naval novels and (until 1968) under different names, so many as to make an exact count of his works impossible. His whole corpus amounted to perhaps a million words over a 40-year career. The attribution of novels he may have written under pen-names is confused.[10] Under his own name (and the pen-name James Dark in the United States) he published a dozen novels featuring the super-spy 'Mark Hood' who was, to paraphrase a reference work, an Oxford-educated American, debonair but a ruthless playboy.[11] As 'James Macnell' he certainly published four children's books, including *Captain Mettle, V.C.* and *Mettle at Woomera*.

During the 1970s his output declined to 6 books a year, followed by a long period of inactivity, with only two new books appearing between 1978 and 1984. In the mid-1980s he returned to four a year, and in 1988 published eight, although not all were necessarily written in that year. In this, Macdonnell's last full year of publishing, he seems to have realised that his career was coming to an end. His final titles suggest a presentiment that they would be the last: *Final Haven*, *In Close Waters*, *Long Leave*, *Short Cut to Hell* and *Strike That Flag*. In fact, however, they resemble his hastily-written earlier works. *Strike That Flag* actually begins 'It was a dark and stormy night'—although as Mrs Macdonnell notes, it was tongue-in-cheek. The books feature mainly 'Dutchy' Holland and Peter Bentley, but include for the first time explicit sex, reflecting changed notions of acceptability. Until the 1980s his novels were often seen in the mess decks of the RAN, although they are rarely found now, killed off by Tom Clancy clones and video cassettes. It is heartening that at the 2001 King-Hall Naval History conference an RAN Petty Officer told me that he had recently found one of his sailors reading one on duty. I hoped that he had let the sailor off lightly.

Macdonnell himself distinguished between his six 'serious' books— *Gimme the Boats!*, *Wings Off the Sea* (his novel of naval aviation in Korea), the Brady trilogy and *Valiant Occasions*—and his potboiling

Horwitz books. Except for the number of the editions of the Collectors' series on loyal readers' shelves, Macdonnell has sadly been denied the attention and respect he deserves.

'HE SPENT ALL HIS TIME WITH A NOTEBOOK': MACDONNELL IN THE RAN

Macdonnell joined the RAN as a 17-year-old in December 1934. Like his hero, Jim Brady, he soon became a Leading Seaman, in 1937, while serving in HMAS *Australia* in the Mediterranean. He was promoted rapidly; at 23 in July 1940 he was an acting Petty Officer in the cruiser HMAS *Canberra*. Like many of the fictional heroes he created, he became a gunnery specialist. From September 1941 to February 1942 he served in the sloop HMAS *Warrego*. He served in the corvette HMAS *Townsville* from February to December 1942, in the destroyer HMAS *Nepal* from May 1943 to September 1944 and in HMAS *Nizam* in 1944–45.

During the war Macdonnell served in the South Atlantic, the Indian Ocean and the Pacific theatre, but—from the perspective of an author who would describe naval warfare—he was unfortunate never to take part in a major action. He did not serve at all in the North Atlantic or in the Mediterranean (the setting of about a third of his books) and in the Indian and Pacific theatres mostly saw escort work. In 1944 *Nizam* was one of the four Australian destroyers providing the screen for the Eastern Fleet's raids on Sabang and Surabaya. This operation saw *Nizam* involved in no surface action, although it would form the basis of *Fleet Destroyer*.

In the course of writing this chapter I was fortunate enough to contact several of Macdonnell's former shipmates. Their recollections present a picture of a man marked out as different from his messmates. They describe him as, for example, 'not the most liked P.O. on board' possibly because he was 'pusser . . . strict, or by the book'. He was said to have 'carried out his duties in the real naval tradition, no beating around the bush'. Many shipmates knew of his literary inclinations: 'he spent all his time with a notebook and pencil in hand even when he was on watch'. One recalled him in HMAS *Townsville*: 'Whenever we weren't doing anything serious, we'd be aware of J.E.M. in the waist . . . doing some writing . . . a book, . . . a story for the newspapers'. 'Some of his stories', another man recalled, 'did not go over too well in the P.O.s' mess as he used names of some of his messmates in yarns about escapades ashore'.[12]

Macdonnell became an acting Gunner—a Warrant Officer—in February 1946, but his Record of Service was twice endorsed 'NOT recommended for confirmation'. There is no record of the reason for this dismissive attitude, although one former shipmate suggested that Macdonnell was involved in a collision at some point later in the war. His disappointment seems to have persuaded him to seek a second and more successful career as a writer. We can only speculate that a relationship may have existed between Macdonnell and his superiors of the kind which formed the dramatic basis of many of his novels. The difficulties of rising to commissioned rank from the lower deck preoccupied him as much as did the intricacies of gun laying: they are the mainspring of the Brady novels and of other books. It is plausible that his failure to gain acceptance estranged an intelligent, literate boy from the bush from the Navy which he had loved.

The public details of Macdonnell's naval service are cloudy, a consequence of the complexities of the Navy's rank structure, but also compounded by his ambition. Several reference works and the back-cover blurbs of many of his books give out that he became 'a commissioned gunnery-officer' and 'became lieutenant'. Although he was an acting Gunner, a Warrant Officer, he never became a Lieutenant and never appeared in the *Navy List* as such.

'THE GUNNER': MACDONNELL'S HEROES

Naturally, Macdonnell's naval novels relied heavily on heroic protagonists. These included the prim but courageous Bruce Sainsbury, VC, the rough diamond 'Dutchy' Holland of HMAS *Pelican* and Peter Bentley, captain of the destroyer HMAS *Wind Rode*, the central character of more of Macdonnell's books than any other. Charles Higham described the archetypal Macdonnell central character as 'an ordinary modest but rugged man with whom male readers can sympathise and identify'.[13] Some of Macdonnell's heroes were autobiographical or, rather, they contained autobiographical elements. Several of his protagonists mirror his own naval experience, in so far as they were commissioned from the lower deck. The hero of *Jim Brady, Leading Seaman, Petty Officer Brady* and *Commander Jim Brady* expresses this essentially social tension in its most extreme form. Higham described Brady as 'a physically strong bloke with an inferiority complex who comes from the lower decks [and] is suspicious of his fellow officers, but finally gets over all that and finds himself through proof of his courage in action'. Harold Thatcher, for example, is the hero of the story 'The Coward', set during the *kamikaze* attacks off Luzon. Thatcher is a gunner, a man like Macdonnell, who had 'hauled himself up through the hawse hole'.[14] Thatcher, in the manner of his fictional counterpart Horatio Hornblower, is contemptuous of his own fear but is admired by his shipmates as a hero. His death—in a direct hit on his directing station by Japanese shore battery—is described in graphic detail.

Macdonnell comes closest to telling his own story of the wartime navy in *The Gunner*, a Horwitz book and not one of the London-published hardbacks which he valued so much. *The Gunner* tells the story of two petty officers, Neil Lasenby and Jim Durham, who study their way, in the face of their First Lieutenant's animosity, into the commissioning course for gunnery officers. *The Gunner* reflects most clearly Macdonnell's achievement in rising from rural recruit to Commissioned Gunner. Lasenby and Durham represent a composite of his character, tastes and ambitions. They share his passion for gunnery and his enthusiasm for the historical novels of Rafael Sabatini, 'the old Sabbo', as Durham calls him. Sabatini (1875–1950) published over 30 novels. Macdonnell read them as a teenager at the height of Sabatini's popularity during the 1930s, a taste he carried with him into the Navy.

'IN B-GUNHOUSE': MACDONNELL'S DESCRIPTIONS OF NAVAL WARFARE

From the time of his earliest wartime writings Macdonnell drew upon and adapted his own naval experience, much of which went into the Brady series. In his preface to *Abandon and Destroy!*, set in the Mediterranean in 1941, he noted that 'few of the characters and incidents in this story are imaginary'. Later he drew less on memory and more on imagination. This produced some thin and sometimes silly plots. *Close and Investigate*, for example, has Peter Bentley's destroyer flotilla searching the Arafura Sea to sink a Japanese cruiser which was using a death ray to melt Brady's 'X' turret. The effect is bizarre, since all the details are correct, except for this clichéd science fiction fantasy.

Fantasy is perhaps the right word, because Macdonnell's novels constitute virtually an alternative or counter-factual history of the RAN in the Second World War. While for the actual RAN the war entailed much drudgery, bad luck and loss, in Macdonnell's war the picture was reversed. This suggests a reason for Macdonnell's popularity. Although the RAN made a substantial contribution to the Allied victory, with its ships seeing long and hard service, it was not often an exciting war. Australian ships took part in few major surface actions, some of which resulted in the loss of ships. Battles in which ships engaged enemy surface ships in ways which make good fiction were rare. Macdonnell's heroes, by contrast, took cruisers and especially destroyers into action against German E-boats and U-boats, and Japanese battleships, cruisers, destroyers and submarines, and almost invariably came off better. It was fiction, of course, but it was realistic fiction, what-might-have-been if only things had gone differently. Instead of long and gruelling patrols and tedious escort work, Macdonnell's ships were sent on secret missions. Instead of being sunk, they sank their adversaries. His hero Bruce Sainsbury sinks four U-boats in one day in the Atlantic. In *Circle of Fire*, 'Dutchy' Holland's destroyer HMAS *Jackal* sinks two submarines (one inside Darwin harbour) and takes on six Japanese destroyers, sinking one, while searching for a secret Japanese submarine base off the Philippines. In *Flotilla Leader*, HMAS *Wind Rode* sinks two Japanese destroyers. In *The Gun*, the corvette HMAS *Wattle* destroys another two. (Although Macdonnell had served in a corvette, HMAS *Townsville*, this appears to be the only novel which he set in one.) Macdonnell's fiction describes the war which many former sailors would prefer to have fought.

All the same, it would be unfair to write off Macdonnell as a hack wordsmith, spinning a dit for a dollar. At his best he could write powerful prose. This is most apparent in his hardback books, published by Constable and Dent in London. His most effective descriptions of naval warfare are therefore to be found in *Jim Brady, Leading Seaman* and in *Commander Brady*, and the best of his work is very good. Despite its prosaic title, the novel *Escort Ship* is a sustained and exciting description of a naval battle—a running fight between *Wind Rode*'s destroyer flotilla and a pursuing Japanese squadron—and as good as anything C.S. Forester wrote in *The Ship*. At the same time, the bad drives out the good. *Escort Ship*'s quality is submerged by the mediocre pot-boilers which outnumbered it.

His undeserved obscurity was a poor reward for the industry and commitment which he invested in his writing. It is our loss, but fortunately one able to be retrieved. In *Commander Brady*, for instance, Macdonnell, an author whose milieu is the masculine world of the mess deck and wardroom, produces a passage that is truly beautiful. Reflecting on how Brady's destroyer *Circe* was, paradoxically, 'an island of men, monastic, celibate', he perceives that it was yet 'populated by women, women who had never seen each other, and never would'.

HMAS *Jackal* takes on a Japanese carrier. '"Get that bloody Jap rag down. Hoist battle ensign!" And that was how the staggered carrier saw her—a midget, spitting, flinging white back over her bows, plunging in, and wearing, high at the truck of her foremast, board-hard in the fierce thrust of her passage, bright and proud in the searchlight's glare, the red white and blue of her belief.' *Under Sealed Orders* by J.E. Macdonnell. (Horwitz)

They were everywhere in the ship, these women. One, through the bosun's mate, commented caustically on the galley's cooking; . . . a woman in Brisbane and another in Broken Hill agreed that Ingrid Bergman was the finest actress on the screen. Another hummed, deep in the forrard magazine, a lilting love song she often sang over her housework. One of them stood beside the bosun's mate and made him lay his knife and fork down when his mouth was full; another wrapped a woollen muffler around the captain of B-gun's throat as he climbed the vertical ladder to take over the watch on his gun; and to another, a thin, work-worn woman on a dusty farm in the Victorian Mallee wheat-district, a stoker had made his last appeal when one of *Circe's* huge steel lifting tackles had fallen and crushed him against the port turbine: 'Mum', he had whispered, 'Mum . . .'.[15]

This is one of the most eloquent descriptions of the emotional world in which sailors live as one could ever read.

The strength of *Escort Ship* lies in its use of several minor characters to suggest the complexity of the men who make up the destroyer's crew. The novel focuses on Peter Bentley's astute use of gunnery and manoeuvre in and out of the flotilla's smokescreen to prevent the Japanese from overhauling the convoy it protects. The action is counterpointed by vignettes of Bentley's men. Perhaps the most incongruous character is Joe the Cook.

> The whole ship was shaking with her speed, but the silent men closed-up at their action stations were used to that. In the galley Joe the Cook, not smiling now, completed his last sandwich. They would not be needed just yet, but supper-time was approaching, and Joe the Cook knew well the feelings of hunger which replace tension in a man's stomach once the heat is off . . .
>
> Calmly and deliberately, feeling the deck quivering under his feet, he lifted the big pile of sandwiches and stowed them in a cardboard carton on the bench. . . . Then he put his steel helmet on, and, still in singlet and trousers, poked his head out through the galley door and took a look at what was causing all the excitement.[16]

Joe the Cook, having seen to his shipmates' needs, is the first man to die, struck in the face by a shell splinter as the Japanese cruiser finds *Wind Rode's* range. Macdonnell calls Joe the Cook into existence only to kill him at the first salvo. His purpose, though, is to portray the mutual bonds of support and obligation that criss-cross the ship, making individuals part of a wider and stronger whole. This is Macdonnell's skill in evoking battle at sea, representing it truly as a partnership between vessel and men.

Jim Brady, Leading Seaman is the only Macdonnell novel in which more than half the action takes place ashore, indeed hundreds of kilometres inland. It is the story of a boy from a Queensland town—Toowoomba—who in the late 1930s is inspired to join the Navy by an ex-Royal Marine. Macdonnell himself grew up in Toowoomba, and the novel is strongly autobiographical, evoking the world of rural Australia in the Depression, and written with unusual care and control. It is in the genre of a host of Australian country-child-comes-of-age novels or memoirs, from Gavin Souter's *The Idle Hill of Summer* to Don Charlwood's *All the Green Year*.

Like Macdonnell, Jim Brady joins the Navy in the 1930s, and is posted to an un-named Australian cruiser in the Mediterranean. By the time Italy joins the war in 1940 Brady is an acting Leading Seaman and on the way to becoming—like Macdonnell—a Gunner. Macdonnell's description of Brady's first action, against an 'Italian Battle Fleet', is some of his best writing. He provides a masterful description of what it felt like to serve in a gun turret in a warship in action.

In B-gunhouse, they felt the heel of the turn, and knew what it meant. Again Brady ran his eyes over his thirty-two ton charge, knowing that . . . he did it because of the familiar tightening of the skin of his face, the drying of his mouth, and the tension that was knotting in his guts.

Being normal men, Tug, at his cordite rammer, felt the same; Amos, clutching the trigger-guard of his Oerlikon on the starboard lower wing of the bridge . . . felt the same . . .

Fawkner pressed his earphones, tightening them against the whine of the pump, and listened.

'Enemy has opened fire,' he said briefly.

They stared at him, mutely pleading for information. Through his phones, through the tenuous lead running high up to the director, he was gifted with the divisional officer's eyes . . .

Even through the thick armoured walls of their turret they heard it—an approaching tearing sound, rising to a piercing shriek, and finishing abruptly.

'Over,' Fawkner muttered.

Over! Thought Brady. That meant they were in range of the battleships, but outside the range, if the silent breaches were indication, of their own eight-inch guns.

God, Brady prayed, why haven't we opened? He longed for the breaking of the tension, longed for the mind-filling action of loading and firing. . . .

Brady heard the cover of the voice-pipe slam shut, and straightened up. . . . The ship heeled, straight over sideways, under the punch of cordite, and the sea flattened into shuddering little ripples directly under her belching muzzles. She settled down to fighting, smoothly, automatically, with the facility of long training, all doubts of all men submerged in the prime need for concentration on their bellowing charges. . . .

In the middle of all this sweating toil, of men labouring and gasping and snatching a sweat-wiping hand across their streaming faces, and shadows leaping across the gunhouse as the electric lights flickered and shone under the shock of each broadside—in the middle of all this, sat Petty Officer Fawkner, aloof, watchful, out of it, at the same time as he controlled it, sitting on his wooden bench before the rangefinder, his hands clenched on its edge on either side of him, his head swinging from side to side, not a movement of the cordite-rammer or shell-hoist escaping his intense blue eyes. They had no idea of where their shells were going; had no time to think about it. The whole purpose of their being, the whole culminating reason for their months of training, was to feed shell and cordite into the gaping breeches and to keep the turret elevation and training pointers following the red pointers of the director far above them.[17]

To the layman this is a convincing passage. A former shipmate of Macdonnell's gave him 'top marks for his account of his first taste of action. I liked the strong command of important detail . . . and its understatement and lack of heroics made it completely believable'.[18] Authenticity mattered to Macdonnell. Frequently he complained of critics, often former sailors, who picked him up on minor technicalities—one said that he had described a destroyer as 'drinking fuel thirstily through a six-inch pipe'. The pipe, the critic objected, had a bore of only five and seven-eighths' inches.[19] Unlike his friend Carter Brown, Macdonnell remained wary of what a critic described as 'Monsarrat-like rollings around in the bedroom'. 'I hate writing sex material,' he confessed, 'it embarrasses me.'[20] What embarrassed him more, however, was getting technicalities wrong. 'You can have a hero making love 999 different ways,' he mused, 'but when you talk about the rate of fire of a multiple pom-pom in a Fleet destroyer . . . !'

Obviously Macdonnell's high output militated against his maintaining work of uniformly high quality. At worst, his 3000 words a day were mediocre. As with all writers, however, when he was writing of what he knew well, Macdonnell's naval material is assured beyond the merely technical aspects. It suggests a deep understanding of the nature of naval warfare.

Macdonnell appreciated that battle at sea was partly about machines, and he wrote knowledgeably about engines, signals and radar, but especially about guns and gunnery control. More than that, however, he understood how naval battle was about the collective. His description of the combination of the mechanical, electrical and human elements in a destroyer's fire control systems has, I believe, never been bettered. In *Gimme the Boats!*, he described the sensation of being 'the director layer of an eight-inch cruiser'. This was 'the man who squeezes the electric trigger, in whose fingers is culminated all the power, all the training and experience of 12,000 tons and seven hundred men'. Then, 'the sight of an enemy's masts . . . in the cross-wires of your sight like a spider in a web turns your guts to water and sends a paralysis creeping from your thighs upwards . . .'.[21] There is a strong sense of the collective effort in Macdonnell's evocations of naval warfare, and especially of the branch he knew best, the gunners and gunnery. 'They' in *Gimme the Boats!* are more than the men who load and fire the guns; they are also the gunnery director's crew: the director trainer, the phone-number, the indicator operator, the range-taker and the director control officer.

CONCLUSION

James Macdonnell's life and fiction present us with many conundrums. We have a competent and intelligent sailor who failed to gain the promotion he believed he deserved. We have a writer who produced some of the best prose on naval warfare, but also some of the worst. Above all, we have an author who could write realistically, truthfully, vividly and insightfully about naval battle, but who had not actually experienced the kind of ship-to-ship gun battles which form the staple of his fiction. In short, while we must allow that Macdonnell's naval training and service gave him extensive knowledge on which to draw a convincing picture, we must also acknowledge that essentially he relied on imagination. Those who have never experienced naval action can write about it—witness C.S. Forester and Patrick O'Brian. We have in James Macdonnell a naval novelist whose portrayal of naval battle is, at its best, based upon experience and deeply convincing but, like all fiction, is also based partly on imagination. Separating the real from the imagined in his writing presents us with a challenging task but one which is well worth attempting.

After spending his last years with his wife Valerie in Kuluin, Queensland, J.E. Macdonnell died on 13 September 2002.

11 | US submarines at war
The recollections of Motor Machinist's Mate Thomas R. Parks, USN

David Jones

THOMAS R. PARKS, Motor Machinist's Mate (as he became), USN, served in US Navy submarines for extended periods in the Asian and Pacific areas of operations in the Second World War.[1] His personal reflections provide us with an insight into the face of naval battle as experienced by a submariner. They also serve as a reminder of the strong links forged between Australia and the United States during the 1940s.

PEACE, WAR AND RETREAT

A native of San Diego with a family background in the US Navy, Tom Parks was born on 15 August 1921. He joined the Navy immediately upon leaving high school at the age of 18. After enlistment training he requested and received an appointment to the US Asiatic Fleet, where his older brother James was serving aboard the seaplane tender USS *Langley*. On arriving in the Philippines early in 1940, he was first assigned to the submarine tender USS *Canopus* and two months later to the submarine USS *S39*. Not all submariners first attended the submarine training school at New London, Connecticut, and Parks was one of those who went directly from the tender to on-the-job training. In *S39* he assumed duties as a fireman in the engine room, and became part of what was known aboard US submarines as 'the black gang'. *S39* was an old submarine of First World War design, launched two years before Parks was born.

The engine room in an 'S' or 'Sugar' boat was not large, but it was intimidating to someone whose previous mechanical experience had been limited to a Model A Ford. Still, the peacetime routine aboard *S39* was not onerous, with dives of one or two hours' duration just a few times a month and a full day's dive about once a month. As Parks recalled, 'Asiatic duty in those days before the war was good duty. We used to say "No strain in Asia" . . .'.[2] He and others aboard the American submarines in the Philippines believed that war with Japan would come eventually, but 'We weren't worried, though. We were complacent and convinced we'd dominate if Japan started anything. Actually, we underestimated their strength and ability, but what would a bunch of kids like us know anyway?'.[3]

For Fireman 1st class Parks, the reality of war first hit home during a major Japanese air raid on 10 December 1941, and it was a shock: 'The Japs bombed Cavite Navy Yard, and there were dead sailors and civilians all over . . . it was very unnerving. I felt anger, fear, frustration'.[4] The Japanese bombers departed, leaving the Navy Yard in ruins and over 1400 fatal casualties. Manila was declared open to the Japanese on 25 December 1941, and the American military forces remaining in the Philippines retreated to the island fortress of Corregidor at the entrance to Manila Bay. Here they fought on under siege. *Canopus*, with Parks back on board, was at Corregidor when a bomb hit her after deckhouse: 'Although it didn't kill many crew members, it destroyed most of my personal belongings as well as personnel records . . . All I had were the clothes on my back and my wallet'.[5]

Meanwhile the retreat of American submarines from the Philippines was underway. Tom Parks had missed *S39*'s first war patrol, but when she came in for re-supply he immediately rejoined. Her second war patrol lasted for just over three weeks and saw the submarine patrolling in the central Philippines without seeing much of the Japanese. *S39* concluded the patrol at Surabaya in Java which, in turn, fell to the Japanese early in March 1942. Parks takes up the story:

> I left *S39* there and was transferred to *Sailfish* . . . When I left Java on *Sailfish* the war was going very badly for us. The combined American, British, Dutch and Australian forces took a beating from the Jap. *Sailfish* commanded by Lieutenant Commander Richard Voge did get some hits on a Jap carrier but did not sink it.[6] During the remainder of the patrol we encountered no more enemy ships and we were ordered to

the West Australian port of Fremantle. After two months of war and running from the Japanese, coming to Fremantle and Perth was like entering Heaven. The people were friendly, were wonderful hosts and the Australian beer was outstanding. It was summer there and the weather was perfect. It reminded me of my hometown, San Diego, California, which is about the same north latitude as Perth is south latitude.[7]

Unfortunately the bad news did not end upon *Sailfish*'s arrival in Fremantle. While there, Parks learnt that his brother's ship, *Langley*, had been lost in action and that James was not among the survivors.[8] The loss had a deep and lasting effect on both Parks and his parents, but on this sad occasion he chose not to put his own feelings into words. The bad news continued into May:

> After a short stay in Fremantle we were ordered south to Albany. We made several patrol runs from there. The saddest was a supply mission to Corregidor. We offloaded most of our torpedoes and took on a load of 3-inch [76-mm] anti-aircraft ammunition and sacks of mail. Before we reached Corregidor we received the message that the fortress had fallen to the Japanese and we were ordered back to Fremantle.[9]

Sailfish had been at sea for two weeks.

> We could do nothing but turn back to Australia to offload the weapons and mail. Unloading that mail was a very poignant time and deeply affected us all . . . It was almost like carrying off dead bodies. For the first time we realised the Philippines were gone, and that if we were going to win this war, it would take a while. Our feeling that we'd kick 'em around was waning a bit.[10]

WAR PATROLS, REFIT AND TRAINING

Parks remained in *Sailfish* for over eighteen months, sailing on a total of seven war patrols through most of 1942 and 1943. Four of these patrols were from Australian ports to either South-East Asian waters or the Solomons. *Sailfish* returned to Pearl Harbor in January 1943 and proceeded to California for a thorough overhaul. This was Park's first sight of the continental USA in more than three years.

After her refit, *Sailfish* made patrols into Japanese home waters and the East China Sea. Parks left her in late 1943 for specialised courses on Fairbanks Morse diesel engines and subsequently stood by a new submarine, USS *Hackleback*, during her construction and commissioning at Portsmouth Navy Yard. By now a Motor Machinist's Mate 1st class, Parks remained with *Hackleback* during her first patrol in March 1945 to Japanese waters.

Much had changed in the underwater war since the end of 1943. American submarines reached the peak of their success in 1944, sinking more ships in that year than they had in all of the war up to that date. Japanese shipping had been all but driven from the seas. Parks, however, returned from *Hackleback's* first patrol exhausted:

> By now the Japanese navy and merchant marine were almost non-existent, so targets were hard to come by. Submarines now did a lot of rescue duty for B–29 bombers . . . Actually, it got really boring because there was nothing much to shoot at. When we returned to Midway, I was pretty burnt out. Besides, most of the crew were young . . . new sailors . . . and at age 24, after all my service, I was an old man to them.[11]

Leaving *Hackleback*, Parks transferred to the submarine base at Midway Island where he spent the remaining weeks of the war. He was discharged from the Navy in October 1945.

THE SUBMARINES

S39, the first submarine in which Parks served, was one of 51 'S' Class boats. She had a standard displacement of 854 tons, was 219 feet (66.8 metres) long and had been completed in 1923. By the time the Pacific War had broken out the 'S' boats were outdated. Because of an overall shortage in submarine numbers, however, the US Navy was compelled to use them in the front line in the Philippines, the Solomons and the Aleutians. Parks recalled life aboard *S39*:

> They weren't built with long range operations in mind so food storage and refrigeration was minimal. Fresh meats and vegetables were gone after a week at sea. There was no air conditioning and the boat really heated up in tropical waters. The ventilation system was very inefficient and there was no way to scrub the foul air. After ten hours submerged the air was REALLY foul . . . On an S-boat the mess tables folded up and were clipped to the overhead of the after battery compartment and only let down at meal time. If we wanted to sit and read someplace it was usually in the forward torpedo room. The berthing in the forward battery was very cramped and after the war started we took on extra personnel and there weren't enough bunks to go around so we had to

'hotbunk' i.e. sleep in the bunk of a sailor on watch . . . We didn't have good evaporators with which to distil fresh water and what we could distil was double distilled for the batteries which consume enormous quantities of water. A bath at sea was a few cupfuls in a bucket and sponge . . . There was only one head for the crew and it was smaller than a telephone booth. The waste was ejected by compressed air and it almost took an engineer to operate it without getting what we called a 'flareback' . . . Despite the lack of creature comforts we loved the ships and we felt that we were a breed apart.[12]

Transfer to the larger *Sailfish* brought a considerable improvement in Parks' living conditions. *Sailfish* was a modern fleet submarine of the *Sargo* Class: an early part of a continuous line of development which allowed the US Navy to mass produce more than 220 submarines to the same basic design. Tom's third submarine, *Hackleback*, was completed in November 1944 and belonged to the *Balao* Class, the pinnacle of the wartime development process.

> The *Sailfish* was 100 feet [30 metres] longer than the S-boats, had air conditioning, better food, better everything. It was palatial compared to *S39*. We normally travelled a long way on our patrols, as much as 5,000 to 7,000 miles round trip, sometimes all the way from Perth, Australia, north across the equator. Actually, much of our missions was spent going to and returning from our patrol areas. The submarine usually carried food for 75 to 80 days.[13]

Sailfish had a dramatic history before the Second World War had even begun. Launched in 1938, she had started life as the USS *Squalus* but during a dive on 23 May 1939 her main induction (the air intake for the diesel engines) failed to close, flooding her rear half and trapping her on the seabed at a depth of 73 metres. With 26 of her crew already dead, rescue efforts were put in train. Over the next 40 hours the remaining 33 crew members were rescued in the first successful use of a 'McCann' rescue chamber. *Squalus* was subsequently raised, repaired and returned to service under the name *Sailfish*.[14]

> When I reported aboard *Sailfish* there were three *Squalus* survivors in the crew. They never talked about their experience and we never pried. The general attitude of the *Sailfish* crew was that she was a lucky ship, having sunk once it was not going to happen again. That attitude was not shared by my parents. They were horrified by the news that I was going aboard *Sailfish*. Having lost one son in the war they were in great fear of losing another one. Fortunately for all concerned their fears were groundless.[15]

As the years passed Tom Parks came to walk the same path as his parents.

> When my oldest son went to Vietnam as an Army pilot I realised only
> then what my parents went through. A few years later my second son
> also went to Vietnam as a sergeant in the infantry and we weren't any
> better in dealing with it. Fortunately they both came home whole and
> well and mentally unscarred by their experiences.[16]

All submarine crewmen were required to be multi-skilled so that
they could perform any duty in any compartment of the submarine. In
S39 Parks qualified on the bow planes, stern planes and helm, stood
lookout watches and was assigned as a mess-cook before he was permitted to wear the dolphins of a submariner. Parks' specialised training and
role, however, was in the running and maintenance of the submarine's
diesel engines used for surface propulsion. These 'all had a maintenance
schedule which was religiously adhered to. Fuel injectors were cleaned,
tested and replaced if necessary. Main and connecting rod bearings were
checked for wear. Engine performance under load and no-load conditions was carefully monitored'.[17]

Between the wars the US Navy had difficulty in producing a
reliable diesel engine for submarines. Engines failed to deliver power to
specifications, were prone to breakdown and required long periods of
time spent in repair and maintenance. As a result the Navy requested
private industry to prepare fresh designs for a reliable lightweight and
high-powered diesel engine. Three firms answered the call, with very
different products.[18] In *Sailfish* and *Hackleback* Parks worked closely with
two different makes of diesel engine and was able to consider their
merits from his expert viewpoint. *Sailfish* was equipped with General
Motors (GM) diesels:

> They were a good engine but there were just too many moving parts
> and places to spring oil leaks . . . One serious fault of the GMs was
> 'swallowing' a valve. Sometimes a valve head would break off and jam
> between the piston and the cylinder head. Then the engine was out of
> commission until repairs could be made. This could involve replacement
> of the cylinder head, piston and cylinder. A submarine engine room is
> not the best place in which to perform such work.[19]

Aboard *Hackleback*, Parks worked with another reliable brand of diesel
engine produced by Fairbanks Morse.

> Their big advantage over the General Motors [engine] was the fewer
> number of moving parts . . . and they required much less maintenance . . .
> Their weakest point was the upper crankshaft which could and did break if

a careless throttleman was too slow in closing the outboard exhaust and flooded the engine. Water does not compress. If the crankshaft broke the engine was out of commission until the sub returned to base . . . I was fortunate in that I never experienced a major breakdown while on patrol.[20]

LIFE ON BOARD

Life aboard a submarine during the Second World War was unlike that in any other warship. Crews were confined within the pressure hull for the duration of a patrol and allowed on deck only for limited periods while on watch during surface-running. Stress levels remained high throughout the patrol as the boat was often operating alone in enemy waters. Even when close to home, the submarine was in danger of attack by over-enthusiastic units from its own side. Parks has described the experience of submarine life on patrol, as well as the relationship skills needed for shipmates to get along with each other:

> It WAS cramped on the ship and after a few days at sea it was very smelly. The battery acid fumes, diesel fumes, cooking odours and the smell of sixty-five unwashed bodies blended together in that essence only submariners know. We got along together living in this intolerable way because we knew we had to. There were occasional flare-ups of temper but they died down quickly. We used to engage in 'pinging'. This was the submariner's term for ragging or teasing a shipmate, getting its name from the sound of the active sonar or asdic. Pinging was never vicious and it helped to relieve the tension. If a man was unable to get along with his shipmates he was isolated and put into Coventry and immediately upon return to base was declared unfit for sub duty and transferred off the ship.[21]

The health of submarine crews was of vital importance to the effectiveness of their mission. As relief was a long way away, the crew depended upon their own resources:

> Serious injuries or illnesses were few on the boats . . . The submarine Pharmacist's Mates were exceptional men. Besides the regular Hospital Corps school they all received special training in medical practice for small independent commands. On *Sailfish* we had a seaman hurt in rough seas as we came through the [Great Australian] Bight. A wave came over the bridge and slammed him into a stanchion. His jaw was broken and he lost several teeth. The Pharmacist's Mate could not do

anything but administer pain medication. The man went to hospital aboard the tender when we arrived in Brisbane.

The most common ailment was the common cold. When we would leave on patrol someone always brought a cold with him and in that closed environment it spread like wildfire through the crew. Minor gastro-intestinal disorders also were quite common. Toothaches were another problem. Most of us were in or just out of our teens and problems with wisdom teeth were common. We had one sailor with a badly abscessed wisdom tooth. The Pharmacist's Mate lanced the abscess and packed it with sulphur. By the time the patrol ended the jaw was healed.[22]

Patrols might last for two months or more and were limited only by the amount of fuel and provisions able to be carried aboard. The unending cycle of watchkeeping, eating and sleeping reduced the normal rhythms of life to an even monotony:

To ease the boredom we played many games. In the crew's mess there was always some sort of game going on. We played poker, chess, checkers (draughts), cribbage and acey-deucy which is the Navy version of Backgammon. At the start of the patrol tournaments would be organised. Nearly everyone on the ship, officers included, joined in.

Later in the war we had a motion picture projector and movies were shown in the crew's mess. Most of the pics were second raters that never were big in the States but it was entertainment. We had a limited number of films so on a long patrol we saw them many times. We memorised the dialogue or sometimes the sound would be turned off and we supplied the dialogue and it wasn't suitable to be heard in a girls' school.

We also read a lot. The forerunners of today's paperback books were supplied to us free of charge and we literally devoured them. Some of the books which bordered on spicy were passed from hand to hand until they were falling apart. I always managed to find a bookstore in port and buy some books to take along. I generally bought poetry, Kipling, Tennyson, Byron, and books by the Brontes. It wasn't that I was any sort of intellectual but I knew those authors and poets from school days and they had staying power and that was important.

Despite all that was done to relieve the boredom a patrol run was not an experience which I would recommend to anyone. As someone once said 'It was hours and hours of boredom interspersed with brief moments of terror'. However, after many days and weeks of not sighting a target the sound of the general alarm and the cry of 'Battle stations' was almost welcome.[23]

THE EXPERIENCE OF BATTLE

Sailfish has been credited with sinking more than 40 000 tons of Japanese shipping during the war, including the escort carrier *Chuyo* on 4 December 1943 (after Parks had left). Tom Parks describes his experience of battle aboard the submarine:

> After a long and boring period the sighting of a target provided some excitement and when the word was passed to man battle stations there was a big adrenaline rush. Most of the crew did not know what was going on during the attack. The crew in the control room watched and listened as the attack progressed and the torpedomen had some clues from the number of tubes to make ready and the depth setting of the fish [torpedoes]. A few captains kept the crew informed but most didn't until the attack was over.[24]

One of *Sailfish's* more difficult missions was her sixth war patrol in September and October 1942, at the height of the Solomons campaign. Before leaving on this patrol the submarine's starboard propeller had been damaged and, although repaired before she sailed, it was still causing trouble.

> We got under way on September 12 to our patrol area in the Solomons. The damaged screw vibrated badly and we were all concerned that the Japanese would easily pick us up on their sound gear. We reached our patrol area on 16 September off the southern end of Bougainville just outside of Faisi. There were many Japanese targets and lots of destroyers and we were unable to make an approach. On 19 September we made an approach on a seaplane tender. Three torpedoes were fired, all misses. Either the target or an escort came back down the torpedo tracks and proceeded to harry us for about an hour dropping nearly 20 depth charges. We were pretty shaken up but no real damage. For the rest of this patrol it was one disappointment after another. We just couldn't get close enough to a target to fire. The noisy screw kept announcing us. We were depth charged several more times and had some near misses by bombs from enemy aircraft. On 19 October we received orders extending our patrol. We finally headed for Brisbane on 25 October arriving there on November 1st. We were in Brisbane for three weeks while we went into drydock for repairs to our screw and shaft. We all got 7 days leave and we needed it.[25]

In the South-West Pacific area, and particularly during the Solomons campaign, Japanese shipping was usually supported by a strong anti-submarine escort. A submarine's torpedo attack, whether successful or

Nittsu Maru sinking, 21 March 1943. 'Two torpex torpedoes hit, one under his bridge and the other under the mainmast. This ship went down vertically by the bow and was out of sight in three minutes 10 seconds . . . Two junks were nearby and they appeared to be heading to pick up survivors. Ordered battle surface to destroy the junks.' Commander D.W. Morton, USN, USS *Wahoo*. (NHC 80-G-60948)

not, was invariably followed by a counterattack from the escorts. Parks was on the receiving end of many depth-charge attacks.

> There is no other experience with which I can compare a depth charging. I experienced quite a few air raids in Manila and Surabaya, Java and they don't come close.
>
> The noise when a depth charge explodes is almost deafening. Water doesn't compress and the force of the charge hits the boat like a huge hammer. If the charge is close the click of the detonator pistol could be heard before the charge exploded. That was the time to be really nervous. The screws of the destroyer passing overhead could be heard if we weren't too deep. When the attacking escort was close and his sonar was on short scale rapidly pinging it could be heard inside the boat but as a general rule only the sonarman could hear it on his earphones.
>
> My battle station on *Sailfish* was the control room on the trim and air manifold. The atmosphere inside the boat during an attack was

stifling. In the tropics the sea water temperature would be in excess of 80 deg. F. [27 deg. C.] and the temperature inside the boat would sometimes exceed 110 deg. F. [43 deg. C.]. We would be rigged for depth charge with watertight doors and bulkhead ventilation flappers shut, all machinery, pumps and fans stopped. The captain would be at the plotting board plotting our escape manoeuvres. The sonarman would be giving him data on the attacker. Imagine a three dimensional chess board and you blindfolded. I think the greatest fear that we had was showing fear. The captain gave us our cue. He appeared calm and coolly gave orders.[26]

SUBMARINE COMMAND

Parks was in no doubt about the critical role of the submarine's captain. Alone and far from help in enemy waters, it was the captain who was responsible for all decisions and who led and inspired his crew. 'A submarine,' recalled Parks, 'is like a carefully machined weapon with all of its parts, i.e. the crew, in good working order but it is the captain's hand that holds the weapon without trembling and it is his finger on the trigger. The success or failure of a mission all comes down to one man.'[27] In his first three submarine captains, Parks was fortunate in serving with three of the best.

In *S39*, Parks served in peace and war under the command of Lieutenant-Commander J.W. Coe, USN. Both Coe, who was later lost in USS *Cisco*, and Parks' first captain of *Sailfish*, Lieutenant-Commander R.G. Voge, USN, had a strong influence on the future of the submarine war in the Pacific. Coe played a pivotal role in resolving the problem of deep-running torpedoes, a defect previously unrecognised by the US Navy, but revealed by failures in combat. He also pioneered the first successful 'down the throat' torpedo shot into the teeth of an oncoming target.[28] After *Sailfish*, Voge became Operations Officer on the staff of the Commander Pacific Fleet Submarines, playing a key role in formulating submarine strategy and operational planning for the remainder of the war.[29]

Voge's successor as captain of *Sailfish* was Lieutenant-Commander J.R. Moore, USN. As captain of USS *S44*, Moore had wrought some retribution for the loss of four Allied cruisers at the Battle of Savo Island on 9 August 1942 by sinking the Japanese heavy cruiser *Kako*.[30] For the first two years of the Pacific war, *Kako* remained the only major Japanese fighting ship to be sunk by an American submarine. Moore was in command of *Sailfish* during the worst depth-charging Parks ever experienced. This occurred on 25 June 1943 after the submarine attacked a three-ship enemy convoy escorted by warships and aircraft, and sank the passenger–cargo vessel *Iburi Maru*.[31]

> I especially remember 'Dinty' Moore. He was a great leader. Once off the coast of Japan we were subjected to a ten hour attack by three escorts who dropped over 70 charges. Captain Moore acted as if this were an exercise in escape tactics instead of the real thing. I was really scared and trying not to show it. I was staring at the captain wondering what we were going to do and he looked up, caught my eye, winked and grinned. I knew then that we were going to make it.[32]

Moore extracted *Sailfish* safely from this ordeal with only minor damage.

Parks regarded Coe, Voge and Moore as 'the finest skippers with whom I served'. But there were others whom he felt 'should never have

US submarine recovers Australian POWs (ex-HMAS *Perth*) from a torpedoed Japanese transport, 15 September 1944. 'I started to get involved [in the rescue], but my stomach couldn't take it. It was terrible. It was the first time most of us had seen the bloody side of war. I didn't want to see that. That's why I chose submarines. I went back up to the bridge and took over as officer of the deck.' Lieutenant Frank Fives, USN, USS *Pampanito*. (RAN)

been given command'.[33] One of the problems in US submarine organisation which was revealed in the glare of a real war was that too many submarine captains were unsuited to the role. The first wartime captain of *Sailfish*, Lieutenant-Commander M.C. Mumma, USN, had been one of the ablest of the Navy's submarine officers in peacetime, a strict disciplinarian and hand-picked to improve the boat's image after the *Squalus* disaster. Yet, during his first experience of depth-charging, Mumma 'went to pieces' and was forced to order his Executive Officer to take command.[34] Over-caution, failure to produce results and battle fatigue resulted in 30 per cent of American submarine captains being relieved of their commands in 1942 alone, and another 15 per cent in the following year.[35]

Sailfish's fourth wartime captain was also replaced, although according to Parks 'he was relieved before he could do any real damage'. Lieutenant-Commander W.R. LeFavour, USN, took over command of *Sailfish* in July 1943 for her ninth war patrol. The evidence suggests that the captain's behaviour made it an unproductive patrol and the Executive Officer, Lieutenant B.C. Jarvis, USN, was sufficiently concerned to raise the matter with his superiors.

> . . . Ben Jarvis was not alone in his assessment of LeFavour. The entire wardroom and 90% of the enlisted crew agreed. In one respect we should have liked his attitude. He was overly cautious to, as some thought, the point of cowardice. On at least one occasion he gave orders to turn away from a target for what reason we couldn't figure out. He was very cold and distant with most of the crew and all of the officers . . . It was disastrous for crew morale. Jarvis saw his duty as the senior officer next to the captain to bring the problem to higher authorities. This took a lot of courage on his part. Such action can wreck naval careers and I think this played a part in his not being selected for Admiral rank. LeFavour did go on to surface craft where according to [submarine historian Clay] Blair[36] he acquitted himself well.[37]
>
> At the time I disliked the man intensely but with the perspective of hindsight I can have a measure of sympathy for him. Being summarily relieved of command has to be a very traumatic experience for a naval officer.[38]

After the war was won, the different events and decisions shaping its course became better known, but at the time this broader strategic picture and the role of their vessel in it was information rarely available to the enlisted man. To the lower deck their officers and captain were their true leaders and the submarine was their world: 'As enlisted men we weren't privy to any command decisions . . . Except for [General] MacArthur and Admiral Lockwood I wasn't aware of any of the senior officers out there [in Australia]'.[39] To the men of the American submarine service their mission was simply stated. 'Find 'em, chase 'em, sink 'em'.[40] It was sufficient brief for the submariners to make a vital contribution to winning the war.

THE AUSTRALIAN CONNECTION

During 1942, Tom Parks spent four separate periods in Australia between war patrols in *Sailfish*. Initially arriving in Fremantle in March, he took periods of leave there and in Perth before his submarine went eastwards where it sailed on two patrols from Brisbane into the Solomons. His memories of Australia are overwhelmingly pleasant and satisfying. The tension of a two-month patrol was draining on submarine crewmen. Return to port was an opportunity for a well-deserved period of leave when they could unwind, relax and renew their strength for the next run.

Parks described Australians on both sides of the continent as the very epitome of hospitality. But there were differences: 'Perth was a great place to return to from a patrol run. There weren't too many American servicemen there and those who were there were mostly submariners and we were treated like visiting royalty'.[41] By contrast, 'There were thousands of US servicemen in and around Brisbane and the submarine sailors were outnumbered'. Nonetheless, Parks had a good experience of Queensland and retained some fond memories:

> At the time . . . [late 1942] the US Navy did not have things very well organised for submariners. However that was true wherever the subs operated. It wasn't until mid-1943 . . . that rest camps for submariners were really organised. With but few exceptions the rear echelon decision makers just didn't know how stressful submarine war patrols could be. As I remember it the City of Brisbane and its citizens did all they could to make our stay there a pleasant one.[42]
>
> Some of the big band leaders in the States joined the Service and organised bands. Dances were held in the town hall every weekend and we had a chance to meet some very nice Australian girls. I remember Newstead Park very well. When we came up the river returning from a patrol the people in the park, especially the children would wave and cheer. The Captain would salute them with the ship's whistle. It was as if we had come home and in a sense we had.[43]

Tom Parks (centre) with four shipmates from USS *Sailfish* on leave at Coolangatta on the Gold Coast in November 1942. 'So here we were in Australia, the promised land. What adventures it would bring none of us knew, but we were anxious to get started.' Lieutenant James Calvert, USN, USS *Jack*. (T. Parks)

When we were in dry dock I asked one of the yard workmen where he would go if he had a pocket full of pounds and a week in which to spend them. He came right back with Tweed Heads and Coolangatta. Five of us decided to go there but it wasn't easy. We could hire a car and driver but we needed a trip permit because we were going further than 25 miles [40 km]. The driver took us to the Transport office where I said that I wanted to go to a town near Coolangatta where my brother was stationed with a US Army artillery detachment and that I hadn't seen him for well over a year. I think the man at the office knew that I was lying but there was no way that he could check up on me so he gave us the trip permit. So it was off to Tweed Heads . . . We had an absolutely great time . . . When we got back to Brisbane we compared notes with the others some of whom went to Toowoomba and were just as enthusiastic about it as we were about the Twin Cities.[44]

Historical attention has been paid recently to conflicts between Australian and American servicemen in Australia. In Western Australia these tend to focus around the return of troops of the Second AIF from the Middle East in early 1942. In Brisbane there was the so-called 'Battle of Brisbane' which occurred over three nights beginning on 26 November 1942, which just happened to be the American Thanksgiving

Day.[45] During Tom Parks' four leave periods in Australia, however, he enjoyed generally good relations with Australian servicemen: 'I met a number of [Australian soldiers] while I was there and I was always treated as a friend'.[46] 'Admittedly there were some US sailors who behaved badly and there were some angry confrontations with Australian soldiers returning from the Western Desert campaign but for the most part it was a happy time for all.'[47]

Parks was not in port at the time of the Thanksgiving Day brawls in Brisbane, but he heard about them: '*Sailfish* departed Brisbane just a few days before Thanksgiving so I don't have first hand knowledge of the event. I remember sailors talking about it but at the time I was quite sure that they were exaggerating a lot in the telling and I don't know if the event made the papers in the States'.[48] He was in Perth when Australian troops returned from the Middle East, however, and it was there that he had his one and only altercation. To Parks it was very much the exception and more than redeemed by the support he received from two Australian seamen. The incident occurred on his final liberty, before *Sailfish* left on patrol on 22 April 1942:

> This really wasn't a good time to be going ashore as Perth was full of Aussie soldiers just returned from Tobruk and the North African campaign. The German propagandists had bombarded them with leaflets telling them how the Americans had taken over their country and their women while they were fighting and dying in Africa. When they got home they found a lot of the propaganda was true. They were of course highly pissed off and proceeded to take out their resentment on any American they could find . . . The Wentworth [Hotel] was my last stop on the way back to the ship. I was carrying a bundle of books and a good load of beer and when I went into the bar I saw that I had made a big mistake. The place was full of Aussie soldiers and sailors and not another American to be seen . . . I drank the beer and started to leave but with all the beer I had drunk and the state of my nerves I had an overwhelming desire to go to the head. When I went to the men's room three Aussie soldiers followed me and once in there started to give me a bad time . . .

The bullying had not yet come to blows when two Australian sailors entered.

> They said 'G'day' to the soldiers and sort of ignored me but they sensed what was going on. Then as they were standing on either side of me . . . the biggest of the two sailors put his arm around my shoulders and glaring at the soldiers said 'I don't give a ★★★★ what Navy we are in we

are all sailors aren't we.' . . . The soldiers decided that it might be better if they left . . . . Those two Aussie skimmers saved me from a bad beating and maybe even saved my life . . . The Aussies escorted me all the way back to Fremantle right to *Sailfish*. They were on a corvette tied up right across the Swan River from us.[49]

There was a sequel totally satisfying to all concerned: 'When *Sailfish* returned I found [the two Aussie sailors] and we put the local brewery on night shift. What a wonderful thing is the seagoing fraternity!'.[50]

CONCLUSION: THE SUBMARINE SERVICE YESTERDAY AND TODAY

These events, so central in Tom Parks' life, occurred well over half a century ago. Submarine technology has since then developed exponentially in terms of complexity and capability. Parks was still a modest man in his later years and had nothing but admiration for modern submariners: 'As difficult as it was to qualify back then [in 1940], it couldn't have compared to what is required of a submarine sailor on a nuclear submarine in today's Navy. These men are the best of the best'.[51]

There have also been changes in the makeup of submarine crews. Whereas during the war, African-Americans and Asians served aboard US submarines only as mess stewards, and the notion that women could crew submarines was unthinkable, these barriers have now fallen. Tom Parks saw the changes in a positive light: 'In the submarine service all that counts is the ability to perform. Any man regardless of the colour of his skin is accepted into full membership in that fraternity if he measures up'.[52]

I would suggest that all these changes are but matters of degree. There is a continuous line of experience stretching across the years from Tom Parks' day to the present. The similarities in submarine life are many and fundamental: the high level of technical skill required and the unforgiving nature of undersea operations; the need to get along with fellow crewmen in a very confined space on long voyages; the stressful nature of patrols in war or even in simulated war conditions; and the dominant role of the captain—all these factors are as relevant in submarines today as they were during the Second World War.

In conclusion, while the wartime presence of the US Navy's 'Silent Service' is not widely remembered within Australia today, American submarine veterans still feel a strong attachment. Let Tom Parks have the last word in reminding us of this bond: 'You are probably aware of this but it bears repeating. The official headgear of the United States Submarine Veterans of World War Two is modelled after the "Digger" hat complete with plume worn by Australian soldiers. This [is] because of the fond memories we all have of Australia'.[53] May those fond memories long continue—on both sides of the Pacific.

12 | The strain of the bridge

The Second World War diaries of Commander A.F.C. Layard, DSO, DSC, RN

Michael Whitby

PICTURE THE NORTH ATLANTIC on Saturday, 22 April 1944. Four frigates of the Canadian support group EG-9 were on an offensive anti-submarine sweep west of Ireland, along with the escort carrier HMS *Biter* and the British support group EG-7.[1] They had been out for eleven days, and had already destroyed one U-boat and made promising attacks on others. On the bridge of HMCS *Matane*, the senior officer of EG-9, Acting Commander Frank Layard, RN, was restless and uneasy. Put simply, he wasn't sure if he was measuring up. When HMCS *Swansea* and HMS *Pelican* had destroyed *U-448* after a four-hour hunt the week before, he wrote in his diary: '*Swansea* is certainly doing her stuff. Everybody on board here is desperately jealous—except me. My only reaction is one of fear and doubt whether in similar circumstances I would make a balls of it'.[2] As his diary shows, that was certainly what he thought he had done on 22 April:

> Not a very nice day with SW'ly wind force 6. We got an H/F D/F [high frequency direction finding] bearing at 5.15 and we weren't certain of distance [so] I turned the group to the bearing and steamed along it till 11.00 but saw and heard nothing. I planned my movements for the night so as to be in the eastern edge [of our patrol area] by about 0600 when

I was going to shape course for Loch Foyle but a signal arrived ordering us to operate with a Leigh Light Wellington aircraft during the night in another small area which quite upset my previous plans. We were just about in the middle of the area spread out in line abreast when at 2000 we got an A[nti]/S[ubmarine] contact to port. It was a cracking echo and very soon it became obvious that this really was a U-boat. I went slow, meaning to take my time, but the range closed very rapidly and I found myself in to about 300 yds with the bearing going rapidly right and the ship's head swinging as fast as possible to Std [starboard] to keep pointed. Suddenly, ahead appeared the swirl of the thing, which must have been very shallow. I was still worried that I was going to get so close as to lose contact before ready to attack when the periscope was reported just off the Std bow. I then got thoroughly rattled and in case he should fire a torpedo or gnat [acoustic homing torpedo] I reckoned I must go for him. Went full ahead and forgetting we were still in A/S contact dropped a pattern by eye, which as it turned out was a good deal too early. However, we picked him up astern and the other ships were now on the scene. *Swansea* then attacked and although we held him and so did [HMCS] *Stormont* for a time the A/S conditions, which were never good, suddenly became awful and we simply couldn't get our reverbs [reverberations] out at all and that was the last we heard of him. I started [an] Observant patrol and then a parallel sweep but it was dark soon after losing contact and if he got away he could make off on the surface.

I went through agonies of suspense and worry. What I've always dreaded has happened. We find a U-boat and I make a balls and lose it. It must be admitted the lack of daylight, the bad A/S conditions and the periscope all made it difficult but I feel I've let the ship and the group down and feel suicidal with shame.[3]

AN OFFICER AND HIS DIARY

In the annals of naval battle, few faces are as unmasked and as personal as that of Commander Frank Layard, as revealed through his diary. His impressions of naval life, of people, places and things, and of naval warfare are all laid out in stark detail. His diary is a truly remarkable document.

Layard got the idea of keeping a diary from his mother, and he believed it should contain everything of note. 'A diary is like a confessional', he wrote in later life, 'in that all one's sins and omissions are exposed and recorded.' 'Unlike the confessional, however,' he continued, 'the good is there as well as the bad and although in life there is much that I regret and am ashamed of, there are also some redeeming features and it is for the reader to form an opinion and to decide whether there is a reasonable balance between the debits and the credits.'[4] Layard wrote virtually a page a day from the time he entered the training college at Osborne as a fourteen-year-old cadet in 1913 to the time of his first retirement in 1947 (he served again during the Korean War). There is only one gap in 1919–20, when with hundreds of other young officers he was sent to Cambridge University to make good the education lost while serving at sea in the Great War. In a poem about this program the great Rudyard Kipling pleaded: 'Far have they come, much have they braved. Give them their hour of play'.[5] Layard probably played for he did not write.

This chapter focuses on Layard's sea-time during the Second World War—and he can be said to have had a good war—concentrating mainly on his command of the anti-submarine support group EG-9 during the challenging inshore campaign against the U-boats in the waters surrounding Britain. We can gain fascinating insights into the war at sea at perhaps the sharpest end—on the bridge of a warship—by analysing how Layard confronted a totally new type of anti-submarine warfare; how he handled people—Canadians—whom he had great difficulty understanding; and how he dealt with the strain of seemingly endless operations. Layard's brutal honesty gives us a near spotless window into the strain which accompanies naval command and reveals the burden of wartime operations on an officer who can be considered a fairly typical naval professional. His experience provides no great lessons, beyond how the average officer copes with the responsibility associated with command in wartime, although that, in itself, is worth understanding.

There is something else about the Layard diary. It presents a picture of an officer lacking in confidence, wracked by indecision and self-doubt. Yet, those who sailed with Layard paint a totally different portrait. They describe a professional with a cool, decisive demeanour; an effective leader whom they were proud to follow.[6] One officer referred to him as our 'beloved Captain',[7] and Lieutenant-Commander Allan Easton, an experienced RCNR officer who sailed with Layard as commanding officer of HMCS *Matane*, recalled: 'I respected his ability and admired his knowledge, yet I admired more his reticence in displaying it . . . I could have served no finer officer'.[8] Even the great U-boat killer Captain F.J. Walker, RN, evaluated Layard in 1942 'as a capable destroyer captain, who has shown marked coolness and good judgement under fire'.[9]

Layard can be likened to the duck who appears to move gracefully and calmly on the surface but is in fact paddling madly beneath. The contrast between what may be termed the 'inward' and 'outward' Layard

Commander A.F.C. Layard, RN, on the bridge of HMCS *Swansea* during the autumn of 1944. 'Once at sea, between God and the Captain there are no longer the many intermediaries found elsewhere in life. The Captain is the man to whom all turn in moments of crisis at sea and the man who has no one to whom to turn.' Lieutenant L.C. Audette, RCNVR, HMCS *Amherst.* (M. Whitby)

is very striking, and both must be considered when studying the man. When reflecting upon the pressures associated with command, the internal persona is as important as the external and it is the internal which will be featured most in this chapter.

LAYARD'S PROFESSIONAL FOUNDATION

Layard joined the Navy in 1913 because, as he recalled, his parents 'decided the little man was going into the Navy'.[10] 'I don't know that anything very much enthused me [about it],' he later explained, 'except that in those days the Navy was a great service and it was quite natural to want to belong to it.'[11] He served in the battle cruiser HMS *Indomitable* for most of the First World War, witnessing the Battle of Jutland from her foretop. Later in the war he transferred to destroyers, becoming a confirmed destroyer man, and loving the freedom and responsibility which service in such ships brought.

Throughout the 1920s, besides having some big ship time, he served as a First Lieutenant in destroyers in the Atlantic, Mediterranean and Far Eastern fleets. For reasons still unclear he decided not to specialise when a Lieutenant, choosing instead to remain a 'salt horse', but he seems to have been highly thought of. When his captain went down with pleurisy at Hong Kong Layard was appointed acting captain and entrusted with bringing the ship home to England even though there were relief commanding officers on station.

From September 1930 to December 1933, Layard, by then a Lieutenant-Commander, commanded three destroyers in the Mediterranean and Atlantic Fleets. He appears to have been an average commanding officer; a fairly good ship-handler, but one without panache; a level-headed leader, but one who could not be considered a hard driver. Steady and competent, he lacked the dash and aggressive confidence which characterised the more successful destroyer officers of the day. Promotion lists were short during that era of constraint, and when Layard was passed over for promotion to Commander for the final time in December 1933, he was devastated. He saw himself as a failure, pure and simple. After much reflection he decided to remain in the Navy, but was dismayed at how quickly he was pushed out of the mainstream. Instead of another destroyer command or a staff job in Gibraltar, as he requested, he was appointed physical fitness officer for the reserve fleet. This was followed by the command of a minesweeper, which was, according to one officer, 'the very scrapings of the barrel for the executive branch'.[12] In 1936 he was appointed to the Experimental Department at Whale Island, the Mecca of the Royal Navy gunnery world. There he did extremely well, showing an understanding of all things technical and becoming very comfortable with his surroundings, something ironic given earlier complaints in his diary about promotion lists being 'gunnery benefits'.

After the outbreak of war in 1939 Layard continually requested sea duty, but his pleas were turned down on the grounds that the work he was doing at Whale Island was too valuable. Finally, in July 1941, he was appointed commanding officer of the old lend-lease four-stacker destroyer HMS *Chelsea*. Except for an eight-month break in 1943, he was to serve at sea for the duration.

CONFRONTING THE WAR AT SEA: 1941–42

Although this chapter concentrates more on the latter part of the war, events in 1941 and 1942 provide interesting insights into Layard's encounter with the face of naval battle. One concerns his preparation for the job at hand. *Chelsea* was attached to the Western Approaches local escort force, operating out of Liverpool and shepherding North Atlantic and Gibraltar convoys in and out of British waters. Within a week of taking command of *Chelsea* Layard met his first convoy. 'It quite reminded me of the Grand Fleet at sea in the last war', he wrote.[13] On only his second voyage he was startled to learn that he would be senior officer of the escort (SOE). He had not been to sea for five years and his preparation for this job, and indeed for convoy escort in general, was practically nil. He received no formal training and did not even have the luxury of a 'shake-down' cruise in his new ship. All he could do was glance over convoy instructions and tactical manuals, and consult the experienced escort commanders among his extensive network of friends and associates. Even then he had difficulty absorbing the information he gleaned because simultaneously he was having to re-learn the job of commanding a ship.[14] It is fair to say that Layard was relatively lost during his first few weeks at sea, and he never really appears to have been comfortable over the next year.

Events after August 1942 typify the type of situation with which he had to deal. Layard had by then been appointed captain of the destroyer HMS *Broke*. While at sea with another convoy he was ordered to re-inforce convoy SC 94, which was under U-boat attack in the North Atlantic air gap. Again Layard was horrified to learn that he was to take over as senior officer. Upon joining the convoy he found it in complete disarray. After four days of attacks, six merchant ships had been sunk and two escorts damaged in encounters with U-boats. Faced with a tactical situation as murky as the thick fog shrouding the convoy, unfamiliar with the escorts now under his command, and with no opportunity to be briefed by the previous SOE or the convoy commodore, Layard was confronted with what can only be described as a desperate situation.[15] After about three hours with the convoy, and having had to make a myriad of decisions, Layard took over the bridge watch:

> It was very dark & when I took over I couldn't really make up my mind where we were. Then suddenly torpedoes were reported passing the ship & I saw one cross the bows from Starboard to Port & then on our Std. bow appeared the swirl of a U-boat, loud H[ydrophone].E[ffect]. also reported on the A/S. At that moment some ship to the Std. blew 6 blasts.[16] I didn't know where anybody was & I turned towards the U-boat & went on to 20 knots sweating with fear lest I was going to get across the bows of the convoy for whom I was heading directly or ram one of the escorts. I was quite unable to concentrate on the U-boat owing to this worry but found myself somehow pointing there. At close range we picked up good echoes & dropped a 14 charge shallow pattern. When it had gone I could only think of how I could turn before getting in among the convoy & had to give up all thought of the U-boat.[17]

This incident illustrates well the nerve-wracking experience faced by watchkeepers and captains of escort vessels manoeuvring in close proximity to a convoy at night while still in contact with the enemy. Layard was clearly unnerved, but although he considered his snap attack on the U-boat to have been unsuccessful, in reality *U-595* was badly shaken and forced to break off and return to base with heavy damage.[18]

The attacks on SC 94 continued over the next three days, and four more merchant ships were sunk. Afterwards, Layard, by then exhausted, despaired at how he handled the battle: 'Looking back on the whole thing I felt I'd made a thorough balls of both the night & the day episodes with which we'd been concerned & I felt depressed & fed up. There is no doubt about it, I'm not a man of action & when faced with an emergency I just can't compete'. Layard was being too hard on himself, but the mental strain associated with such responsibility was clearly immense. SC 94 was just one of many such episodes, and each time Layard put to sea with a convoy he agonised over the many command decisions which had to be made: Will I miss the rendezvous? Who should I send out on an anti-shadow sweep and how far should they go? What's our position? How long should I remain over the contact? Should I join the hunt? Should I stop and rescue survivors? Could I have done something differently? Was the loss of that ship my fault? Layard was surely not the only captain or SOE to suffer this angst, but his attitude contrasts starkly with the confidence that radiates from accounts (at least public accounts) by and of fellow escort commanders such as Gretton, Macintyre and Walker.[19]

Commander Layard with the other survivors of HMS *Broke* in Gibraltar, November 1942. 'It was perhaps appropriate that a gallant old veteran, who bore a name made famous by her predecessor in close action in the Straits of Dover in the 1914–18 war, should find a grave in the Mediterranean after having broken into a hostile harbour in the second.' Captain Stephen Roskill, RN, official historian. (M. Whitby)

In his self-recrimination over SC 94, Layard lamented that he was not a man of action. But the momentous events of 8 November 1942 show that this was not the case at all. During Operation TORCH, the invasion of North Africa, the destroyers *Broke*, with Layard in command, and HMS *Malcolm* were despatched to force the boom guarding Algiers harbour and land troops to take control of the port facilities before they could be destroyed by Vichy French forces. When *Broke*, with Captain H.L. Fancourt, RN, the senior officer of the operation embarked, and *Malcolm* made their first run in, they lost their bearings in the glare of searchlights so had to circle around again, all the while under accurate fire from coastal batteries. Layard wrote:

> Twice more we tried to find the entrance & failed both times. *Malcolm* 2nd time came under heavy fire & retired with 3 boilers out of action. We then stood well away & decided in spite of only now having ¹/₂ our force to have another shot. I had got the position of 2 buoys now taped, both burning dimmed lights. As we rounded the breakwater I felt quite

confident & in spite of Fancourt's advice to pull out again I went on to full speed & sure enough we were right & went slap through the boom like cutting butter.

Layard put *Broke* alongside in Algiers and landed his troops, but was forced to shift berths when the destroyer came under shellfire. When the new location was shelled, Fancourt decided correctly that their position was untenable and ordered Layard to withdraw. *Broke* was hit several times while escaping Algiers and the next day she lost steam and foundered in heavy seas. Layard and most of his crew were rescued by the destroyer HMS *Zetland*. Waking after his first sleep in more than 48 hours, the loss of *Broke* hit Layard hard: 'The more I thought about yesterday the more I felt I hadn't done all that I might have in shoring up & jettisoning more top weight & I got so depressed that I burst into tears . . . Reaction I suppose'. Today, this would be recognised as post-traumatic stress.[20]

Two aspects of the Algiers operation and its aftermath reveal something of Layard's character. *Broke* came under heavy fire and suffered nine killed and twenty wounded. It is normal to be curious about how one might react under fire, and Layard was no different. In his diary he recalled, 'I thought there was a rather unpleasant tendency [among some of the crew] to fall flat every time a rifle went off & I was delighted to find I didn't want to do it myself. I was simply overjoyed at finding I was able under fire to at least conceal any feelings of fright . . .'. This was not just self-serving—other officers remarked upon Layard's coolness under fire. Perhaps an even more courageous act occurred when he gave a personal report of his experiences to the irascible Admiral Andrew Cunningham, the naval commander for TORCH. 'I gave him an account of our little affair & told him the loss of the ship was due to a bad error of judgement on my part.' Cunningham's final report on the attack on Algiers reflected that honesty: Layard had performed gallantly under fire but had underestimated the damage to his ship and had been mistaken in not keeping *Broke* close by Algiers.[21] Despite this assessment, Layard's performance earned him a Distinguished Service Order (DSO) 'for outstanding zeal and enterprise'.[22]

LAYARD AND THE CANADIANS: COUSINS OF A KIND

War can bring together some strange bedfellows, and there is no question that Frank Layard and the Canadians he served with fit into this category. Layard began working closely with the RCN in

November 1943 and from February 1944, when he took command of the support group EG-9, he became totally immersed in the Canadian naval milieu, commanding Canadian sailors in Canadian ships. Although EG-9 was one of the more effective support groups in the inshore campaign, the buttoned-up Brit professional and the easy-going Canuck volunteers were not always a good fit. The relationship is worth exploring, though, since working with allies has always been a part of naval warfare, and the cultural differences between navies, and their different *modus operandi*, have an operational impact. Such differences also add to the burdens of command.

After losing *Broke*, Layard served for nine months in the Miscellaneous Weapons Division at the Admiralty working on projects such as HIGHBALL, the naval version of Barnes Wallis' dam-busting weapon. (Interestingly, because he lived in London during this appointment, instead of with his family in Prinsted, Hampshire, Layard had a fair amount of time on his hands and spent it reading every biography of Horatio Nelson he could find.) In the late summer of 1943 he was informed that he had been appointed to lead a new support group operating out of Halifax, a major convoy port in the western Atlantic. Although disappointed at the further separation from his family, he was glad to get back to sea and also to get the 'brass hat' of an Acting Commander. But from the start there were bad omens about service with the Canadians. When he dropped by Derby House in Liverpool to pay his respects to the CinC, Western Approaches Command, the Chief of Staff greeted him with 'What have you done to be sent out there?', which, Layard grumbled, 'seems to imply it is a God awful job'.[23]

Arriving at Halifax, Layard immediately suffered what we might now call culture shock. He was flabbergasted, for example, to observe a Canadian officer in a wardroom pick up a bone off his plate and start gnawing on it: 'A very nice chap but strange table manners'. The comparative dinginess of Halifax, its conservative liquor laws and the lack of culture in the sense that Layard appreciated it dismayed him greatly. But the institutional shock was even greater. The RCN had expanded 50-fold since 1939 and with that expansion had come severe teething troubles, both at sea and ashore. The greatest problem was with officer training. There were not enough regular officers to fill all the important positions nor a large reserve of experienced officers like Layard to call upon. Junior officers were being thrown into the Battle of the Atlantic with little experience and only the most basic training. On shore the RCN was simply overwhelmed. In 1939 it had barely the infrastructure to support a small force of about 3500 personnel, but by mid-war numbers had swollen to some 60 000.[24] Chaos and disorgan-isation were commonplace. Soon after arriving in Halifax, Layard went to see the movie 'Corvette K-225', a Hollywood propaganda film about the wartime RCN. 'Very good,' he wrote, 'but to my mind it depicted something so entirely different from the RN as to be almost completely unrecognisable. But of course the RCN is very different.'[25]

Layard took over the destroyer HMS *Salisbury* from Commander B.J. de St Croix, RN, whom he later referred to as the 'great Canadian hater'[26] and who had dubbed the RCN the 'Royal Chaotic Navy'.[27] Layard observed that 'The attitude in this ship initiated by the Captain is intensely hostile to the RCN. I think it is deplorable and I shall do my best to alter it'.[28] That he did, but he was never himself completely comfortable with Canadians. Consider a passage written on 21 March 1945, after more than a year's experience with the RCN, when he was temporarily riding in the frigate HMCS *Loch Alvie*:

> At about 1500 we shoved off [from Scapa Flow]. I've never been so ashamed of a ship's company. There were men in khaki trousers, in filthy duffel coats, sea boots, jerseys, mostly smoking and not one man in No 3s. The RCN [destroyer] *Iroquois* was on the other side of the oiler with every man in rig of the day. Thank God we were only seen by another RCN ship. I felt furious and also despairing because obviously apart from me there wasn't another officer who saw anything wrong with it. I told [the CO, Lieutenant-Commander E.G. Old, RCNR] that it was a bloody disgrace and spent a long time walking up and down after we had secured trying to think out what to do about it. My God if it had been my own ship . . . .[29]

Although Layard complained about his Canadians to the end, he realised he had to adapt to them and altered his leadership style to do so. Nor-mally a distant, hands-off captain, with the Canadians he became more involved in the day-to-day running of his charges. Due to the inexperi-ence of certain officers, and depending upon the effectiveness of individual ships—he ultimately rode in five different RCN frigates—he sometimes felt the need to fulfil the role of first lieutenant as well as of captain. He continually emphasised the need for training and took every opportunity for both individual ship and group exercises. He also assumed a mentoring role, educating his officers in the most basic skills associated with service at sea and officership. (This even extended to drinking, a favourite subject of Layard's. He constantly complained about Canadian sailors drinking to excess and on one occasion noted: 'I like to show in these ships that I can drink a lot without getting drunk'.)[30]

Perhaps the best indication of Layard's professionalism in this regard is the fact that he also worked hard to build bridges between senior British officers and the Canadians serving under them. In Plymouth in September 1944, after EG-9 had killed a U-boat in a particularly good attack, Layard persuaded the CinC Plymouth's Chief of Staff to come on board the frigate HMCS *Saint John* to say 'Well done'. 'I told him I thought the R.N. treated the R.C.N. unfairly—all criticism and no help and we'd never seen a senior R.N. officer on board.'[31] There were also problems in EG-9's home port, Londonderry, which was also home to Commodore (D) Western Approaches, Commodore G.W.G. 'Shrimp' Simpson, RN. As the senior officer responsible for RCN operational effectiveness in the eastern Atlantic, Simpson faced a significant challenge in transforming undertrained, poorly-equipped RCN ships into effective escorts. He could be quite scornful of Canadians, and although he reviewed operations with Canadian commanding officers upon their return to harbour, he rarely visited RCN ships. On one occasion Layard tactfully suggested to Simpson's Chief of Staff: 'what a pity it was [the Commodore] didn't try to get to know the Canadian COs better'.[32] Another time, he reluctantly went over Simpson's head to the CinC Western Approaches to ensure that his sailors could travel to England and Scotland for their leave, instead of being restricted to Londonderry where there was little for them to do but drink.[33] For his part, Simpson recognised the challenges that the Canadians posed to Layard. In his final evaluation of Layard, he wrote that he had performed '. . . entirely to my satisfaction. He has led with distinction a difficult team of individualistic Canadian officers'.[34]

Layard was completely professional in his approach to the Canadians under his command—something they recognised and deeply appreciated.[35] But having to work so hard at the relationship took a toll when he was already under heavy strain with the challenges of inshore antisubmarine warfare.

THE INSHORE CONUNDRUM

The Battle of the Atlantic has often been described as a game of chess, although it could be argued that convoy battles like SC 94 also had a large element of checkers in them. The inshore campaign was completely different and best resembles the board game 'Battleship', where players search a grid for the other's ships. Various tactics are used to find a contact among the maze of squares and once found a ship must be localised before final 'destruction' can be achieved. Then the search-hunt-localise sequence begins anew until all ships in the opposing 'fleet' are sunk. Luck, logic and patience are all keystones to victory.

A similar situation existed in United Kingdom waters from June 1944 until the end of the war in Europe. When the *U-bootswaffe* moved inshore in an attempt to thwart the build-up of materiel in Normandy, they let the convoys come to them, lying along the obvious coastal shipping routes amidst the thousands of wrecks which littered the ocean floor. *Rudeltaktik*—wolf-pack tactics—were not used, nor was there much occasion for communication between boats at sea and U-boat command in Berlin. The *Schnorchel* device (which by the late summer of 1944 was fitted to all U-boats deployed to inshore waters around the United Kingdom) negated the need for surfacing and transformed the U-boats into something approaching true submarines. For the Allies, the effectiveness of many of the weapons and tactics which had brought victory in the mid-ocean convoy war—radar, air power, HF/DF, code-breaking and evasive routeing—diminished in varying degrees as factors in anti-submarine warfare. Surface ships had to pick their way among the myriad wrecks and rock formations lying on the ocean floor, classifying each and every one and all the time subject to powerful tidal currents. It was painstaking work and revised search and localising tactics, equipment such as echo-sounders and the navigational device 'QH' (the naval variant of GEE) and accurate, up-to-date wreck charts became the new war winners.[36] As in 'Battleship', luck, logic and patience, above all patience, became the foundations of success.

Frank Layard's diary describes this battle well. EG-9 was at the forefront of the inshore campaign for its duration. The group's only real break, if it can be called that, came when it supported a Russian convoy in November 1944 (Layard's reaction to that was 'Ugh!!'[37]). The burdens associated with inshore operations fell heavily upon him and came from sources beyond U-boat hunting. In July 1944, for example, Layard's frigate HMCS *Matane* was severely damaged by a German glider bomb off Brest. In a splendid feat of seamanship—which doubtless he owed to his experience in *Broke* after Algiers—he coaxed the ship back to Plymouth where he was cheered ashore by his crew. Within a week he was back at sea in another ship. In fact, over the course of the inshore campaign, Layard rode in five different ships, sometimes double-hatted as both commanding officer and SOE. In each case he had to adjust to a new crew. 'I feel depressed and disheartened,' he complained on one occasion, 'and haven't the energy to start all over again in another ship.'[38] These and other causes aside, two sources of strain were particularly potent during the inshore campaign: tactical decision-making associated with inshore anti-submarine operations and fatigue.

Decision-making for senior officers in the inshore campaign essentially involved two concerns: classification and then prosecution of a contact. Consider this example of an all too typical day for Layard and EG-9:

> In the course of the forenoon a signal arrived ordering us to carry out a gamma search of 20 miles in our old position up and down from C. de la Hague to about the centre of the Channel. At about 1330 we turned to the E[ast] to get into our new position and almost at once picked up a contact. Ran over with the echo sounder and found it was definitely some thing on the bottom so went to action stations and attacked with H[edge]/H[og], which immediately produced oil. Meon and St. J[ohn] joined up while the attack was in progress and altogether we gave it 2 H/H salvos and 2 [x] 10 charge deep D[epth]/C[harge] patterns, but still nothing but fish and oil and the echo sounder trace looked nothing like a S[ub]/M[arine]. Reported I was attacking but thought it probably [a] wreck. After 3 hours I finally decided it must be a wreck as those attacks were accurate and must have killed it had it been a S/M and at about 1730 we all went on and took up our new gamma search at about 1900. I reported classifying it as wreck and was very worried when at about 2200 a signal arrived asking on what I'd based my classification and implying they thought I'd left it too soon. I was still further fussed when Cooke [the asdic control officer] reported to me that the paper speed on the echo sounder had been too slow and so the trace, which had influenced my decision quite a bit, was completely meaningless. Infuriating to have to signal that. To think I've done the wrong thing naturally puts me into an absolute lather.[39]

As Canadian historian Doug McLean has observed, 'EG-9 was one of many groups who learned the lesson of shallow water ASW the hard way in the difficult school of experience'.[40] It was a new game but, unlike his earlier service in the Battle of the Atlantic, Layard had at least as much experience and preparation to fall back upon as any other senior officer. Indeed in February 1944, harking back to his destroyer days in the Atlantic and Mediterranean fleets, he noted: 'this support group work is really much more like destroyer work—manoeuvres, signalling, etc.—and although I've been bred and borne to it those chaps [the other commanding officers of EG-9] haven't and a lot of training is required'.[41] This early experience served him well and, in conjunction with headquarters staff and other senior officers of groups, he developed operating procedures which proved effective.[42] When a contact was found, the first step was to check the wreck chart to see if it had already been classified as a known wreck. This took precise navigation and Layard quickly realised the value of the navigation aid QH, which gave accurate positions at virtually the push of a button. 'This Q.H. is a joy and delight', he noted on one occasion. 'Had a sniff round a wreck giving off oil on two occasions, on the N'ly leg and S'ly leg. Q.H. tells me at once it is the same contact and there is no movement.'[43] But it was seldom this straightforward. Few contacts could be readily classified, even with the help of QH and wreck charts, or by continual runs from a variety of angles using the echo sounder. Those about which there was any uncertainty were plastered with depth charges and hedgehog. 'One just has to attack every echo and there is <u>no</u> way of telling whether he is a S/M on the bottom or not.' Ships' hulls took a real pounding from the numerous shallow water explosions, but patience and 'stick-to-it-iveness', of which Layard had plenty, were the keys to success.

It was tedious, stressful work. Each contact required numerous command decisions, especially as to when to move on. 'We seemed to get a contact very nearly every ½ hour', he wrote in the midst of one patrol.

> Some were known wrecks and others needed investigation but I had to turn out for every one and fix the ship and decide whether or not to go on. This sort of thing is really exhausting but on the route between Hartland Pt. and Trevose Head where the bottom is littered with wrecks it happens unceasingly. Contact, investigate, check position, probably attack, examine result, classify . . . I shall be thankful to leave this patrol tomorrow and have a spell. It has been a particularly wearing 10 days.[44]

Despite the challenges of the inshore campaign, EG-9 had a good success rate. The group destroyed two U-boats and helped sink a third.[45] But the efficiency of the group and its commander is perhaps best exhibited by the almost surgical kill of *U-309* on 16 February 1945. At this time Layard was again double-hatted, serving both as senior officer and captain of the frigate HMCS *Saint John*, and was supporting convoys off the east coast of Scotland:

> We made Radar contact with our convoy N. of C. Wrath at about 0400 and took station in each quarter till daylight after which we took station ahead. It was misty and blowing a bit from the S.E. as we went through the Pentland Firth. At about 1430 when between No. 34 and 33 buoys we got an A/S contact while screening on the starboard bow of the convoy. We altered towards, ran over and got an E[cho]/S[ounder] trace

and as by Q.H. there was no plotted wreck in the vicinity I decided to give it a pattern and so we dropped 5, which immediately brought quite a bit of oil to the surface, so rather unwillingly, as I wanted to get on with the convoy, I returned and attacked again. After the 3rd attack I was just saying 'I don't think this is anything, do you?' when on steaming through the oil and explosion cafuffle [sic] we saw a lot of splintered wood work and some paper which, on fishing out of the water, proved to be bits of a German signal log!!!!

We lowered a boat and also picked up an aluminium flask and a tube of sorts marked in German 'Medical Stores Keil'. All this was most exciting and seemed to indicate that we were on a U-boat. Hoisted the whaler and carried out 2 or 3 more attacks before dark but nothing more came up except a great deal of diesel oil and splintered wood. I recalled [HMCS] Nene from the convoy and the two of us held contact all night. The whole thing seems such a complete fluke but at last one of the hundreds of contact we've obtained and investigated and attacked in coastal waters has proved to be the thing we've been looking for.[46]

Although Layard considered the kill a fluke, it was clearly testament to EG-9's skill and perseverance as U-boat killers.

SURVIVING THE STRAIN

Frank Layard was an old salt in a young sailor's game. He was, after all, in his mid-forties. In September 1942, sitting down for a glass of gin with two fellow destroyer captains, he complained: 'When I hear these young $2^{1}/_{2}$ stripers talk I realize what an awful old cup of tea I am by comparison'.[47] Layard was old and weary. In 1944 alone he was at sea for 211 days, almost two out of three, and it is clear that the pressures of war took a severe toll on him. The misery he felt before setting out for yet another patrol in February 1945 was apparent: 'Deep depression of course setting in . . . not to mention worry and nerves. Oh Dear, oh dear I sometimes feel I can't go on competing any more'.[48] And, seemingly, the war was going to last forever. On 19 April 1945—three weeks before the European war actually ended—he wrote '. . . it is obvious there is going to be no order to stop fighting and the Germans will continue to resist until every square mile is ours and that includes Norway and so it is still a long time before we can celebrate V.[E.] day'.[49] But even that would not be the end: '. . . then 2 or 3 years more fighting in the Far East. I suppose I shall have to do my duty and go out there if required'.[50]

German crew abandoning *U-175* on 17 April 1943 after an engagement with USCGC *Spencer*. Convoy HX 233 is on the horizon. 'The uncertainty along with the cold and discomfort is hard to take. Of course our job really is well done if we get most of a convoy through. But it's hard to sell that to the crew . . . they want excitement and battle. Well they got it. I bet the morale is better on this ship tonight than any in the whole damn navy.' Officer of USCGC *Spencer*. (AWM 304952)

Layard had sometimes considered relinquishing command of EG-9, but this feeling was driven by what he saw as his own poor performance. In January 1945, however, he considered stepping down because of fatigue and brought the matter up with a senior Canadian official. It was not until May 1945 that a relief was finally appointed but by then the war was won.

So how did Layard carry on? What got him through his entire war experience? Here was an officer, we now know, lacking inner confidence and full of self-doubt, who nonetheless performed long and arduous service. Many officers under similar strain suffered medical problems either during or after the war but Layard remained in excellent health. He lived until November 1999, dying just four days shy of his 100th birthday.[51] The physical and psychological ailments which ravaged so many other commanding officers who suffered strain and anxiety left him alone. Why?

Layard had an extensive personal network of fellow officers whom he had known through past service, and he took every opportunity to tap into it. Some, like Captain 'Jackie' Broome and Captain J.A. 'Bez' McCoy, served in important positions ashore such as Captain (D) Liverpool. Others like Captain Allan Scott-Moncrieff and Captain 'Sammy' Boucher (as well as Broome and McCoy) experienced similar service to Layard at sea. Whether it was exchanging gin in each other's cabins or getting together on runs ashore, Layard relied upon this band of brothers to give him the 'gen', and to discuss common experiences. Although he was usually in awe of their accomplishments (and they were all successful), their common experience probably reassured him that he was performing to expectations.

Layard also sought diversions. During layovers ashore he sought to go for long walks or to avail himself of local culture, whether inspecting old cathedrals or going to the theatre or a film. He was also a great socialiser who enjoyed impromptu parties and ships' dances. At sea, he always had a book going, and would grab a few minutes whenever possible to read modern novels, classics and even Shakespeare. He also enjoyed debating the events of the day—religion was a favourite topic—and he took great interest in the progress of the war, piping the news over the ship's broadcast system each day so that his crew knew what was going on.

Layard was also part of a devoted family circle. He and his wife Joan, herself an officer in the WRNS, were extremely close and he cherished her letters. In the most trying days of the inshore campaign, when he seemed to be close to the limits of endurance, he was fortunate enough to operate out of Portsmouth or Plymouth and was thus fairly close to his home in the small town of Prinsted in Hampshire, a boon of which he made good use. Gardening and playing with his two young children were a special joy. Even on layovers in Londonderry or Liverpool, he would bring Joan up and involve her in wardroom activities as a way of extending his naval family.

Certainly, Layard's diary was critical to getting him through. Keeping a diary was, of course, against regulations, and officers who served with him often observed him scrawling away at something—they didn't know what—at all times of the day and night. Quite simply, the diary was his release valve, his way of getting things off his chest. Without it, his mental anguish might have got the better of him.

More than anything, however, his professionalism got him through. Frank Layard had an unshakeable understanding of what his duty was, not only to his country or to the Royal Navy, but also to his profession as a seagoing officer. This was the foundation of his survival and success. This is what motivated him to try one more time to break through the boom into Algiers harbour, to work with and not against his Canadians and to persist in seeking to master the intricacies of inshore anti-submarine warfare. He was indeed full of self-doubt but, at the very least, his experience can provide comfort to those who similarly doubt their own abilities. There is another lesson to be learned from Layard's experiences, and an important one. Navies need traditional, thrusting heroes in the mould of the Johnny Walkers, the Philip Vians and the Andrew Cunninghams, but where would they be without a reserve of solid professionals like Frank Layard? They would be nowhere, and nothing.

Finally, to return to the attack on the U-boat in April 1944, with which we began, and which Layard believed he had botched. In 1986, after a reassessment by the Admiralty Historical Branch, he learned that he had destroyed *U-311* in that brief, wild engagement off Ireland. Once again, Frank Layard did far better than he gave himself credit for.[52]

13 | The pursuit of realism

British anti-submarine tactics and training to counter the fast submarine, 1944–52

Malcolm Llewellyn-Jones

BY THE MIDDLE OF the Second World War the Allies had mastered U-boat wolf-pack tactics in the North Atlantic.[1] The Germans sought to escape defeat by fitting existing U-boats with a *Schnorchel* breathing tube which enabled them to operate continuously submerged and thereby avoid air attack. These boats would be practically immobile, however, and in an attempt to recover the tactical initiative the Germans had for some time been developing U-boats with high underwater speed. As the war ended, it was known that this technology had fallen into Russian hands, so it was natural to assume that the Soviet Union would use it in a future war against the Western alliance.

This chapter explores the interrelated issues of realism in naval warfare training, the development of doctrine and tactics, and the interplay of the human and the technological (the 'art' and 'science') aspects of warfare. To do so it will concentrate on the warfare training given to British anti-submarine (A/S) escort groups and air squadrons, beginning with the system which contributed in no short measure to the mastery of the wolf packs. It will then describe how that system was institutionalised to cope with the new threat of the fast U-boat, first on the part of the German and then of the Soviet Navy. Notwithstanding the passage of time, the issues which arise have parallels with many which still confront modern navies. Although the terminology of today's 'revolution in military affairs' may have changed, there is actually little new in its concepts of sensor and information fusion and of integrating new technologies into weapons systems and command and control networks. Getting this whole context to work effectively remains the most significant challenge for any training regime.

WARTIME TRAINING AND TACTICS

Before the Second World War, Captain A.J. Baker-Cresswell, RN, an early escort group commander, observed that '. . . we had a very small [A/S] specialist branch, despised and ignored and practically never featuring in the promotion lists'. Another group commander, Captain C.D. Howard-Johnston, RN, put the issue in characteristically acerbic terms, pointing out '. . . that "Signals" was sought after for specialisation and no one dreamt of A/S as anything suitable for other than the Navy's idlers, drunks, etc.!'. Similarly, Commander Peter Gretton, RN, noted that '. . . generally, appointments to an escort vessel were looked upon as an invitation to give up all hope of further advancement'.[2]

The wartime expansion of the anti-submarine training organisation absorbed most of the available specialist A/S officers, leaving only a handful to command the escort groups. In consequence, these were mostly led by non-specialist officers, many of whom nevertheless became the more successful U-boat killers. When Howard-Johnston took command of an escort group at the end of 1941, he found that the convoy instructions book contained little tactical advice. Baker-Cresswell thought it was perfectly natural, therefore, for the first escort group commanders to create their own tactical instructions. As an A/S specialist since 1931, Howard-Johnston did just that, although according to Baker-Cresswell the instructions were so complicated that most of his group could not understand them. In contrast, Baker-Cresswell, a navigation specialist, deliberately kept his instructions very simple so that when new ships joined the group the rules could be quickly mastered. Such cases show how widely escort groups differed from each other in approach, and how each senior officer naturally believed his own tactical ideas were the best. This was to some extent an illusion because, as Commander D.A. Rayner, RN, recalled, the groups independently developed remarkably similar procedures, often differing only in the codewords used to execute them.

Individual ship training worked well at the working-up base at

Tobermory, but abbreviated wartime courses and the lack of a formalised system of group tactical training caused shortcomings that were most apparent in group tactical efficiency. Having to learn on the job, most senior officers had no real idea of what to do when their convoy was first attacked. Professor Patrick Blackett, Director of Naval Operational Research, highlighted the problem when he calculated some 60 per cent of shipping losses could have been avoided, at least in part, if the less efficient groups had been raised to the standard of the more effective ones.[3] Some of the better groups showed what could be done with a little imagination. Howard-Johnston, for example, played tactical games on his cabin table where he conjured different tactical situations with Dinky Toy ships, and all his escort captains (one of whom was Rayner) were encouraged to suggest tactical solutions. By degrees, these games welded Howard-Johnston's disparate group into a team, which could react instinctively and in concert, whatever the tactical situation. Baker-Cresswell took a slightly different tack to work-up his group and 'shake off the shore' after layovers between convoys. He organised half a day's tactical practice with the local Clyde submarines, in return allowing them to rehearse attacks on his escorts.[4] But these *ad hoc* arrangements were the exception rather than the rule.

The first element in the formalised remedy was the creation of the Western Approaches Tactical Unit (WATU) at Liverpool at the beginning of 1942. Here escort captains, and more especially group commanders, were instructed in agreed doctrine and allowed to practise it on the tactical floor. Captain Gilbert Roberts, RN, was the ideal choice to run the unit and cajole the groups into rough conformity.[5] Even so, WATU did not command universal approbation. Baker-Cresswell, although a long-time friend of Roberts, was not in favour of the unit. Nor would the highest-scoring U-boat killer, Captain F.J. Walker, RN, have anything to do with it, undoubtedly because he, like Baker-Cresswell and Roberts, was a self-assured and strong character who would have clashed with similar personalities dramatically.[6] Most officers, however, found WATU excellent value, because although Roberts was theatrical and irritating he made people think.[7] The doctrine in the 'Atlantic Convoy Instructions' was synthesised by Roberts from reports of proceedings, direct feedback from escort group commanders, tactical games at WATU and investigations by unit staff.[8] The advantage over the *ad hoc* individualistic training provided by some group commanders was that WATU could both analyse and fuse the experiences and lessons of many convoy operations.

The Instructions provided a common doctrine, so that escorts could be told what to do in a given situation quickly and concisely. But

Roberts did not try to impose a doctrinaire approach on tactics. On the contrary, captains and escort group commanders were encouraged to experiment with their own tactical schemes. Hence, while there were standard instructions, their application remained elastic. Roberts insisted that group commanders show initiative and, at all times, display tactical aggression, which in any case was Western Approaches' policy. He also insisted that his own staff display enthusiasm, zest and, above all, confidence to those who were at sea. In addition, he made sure that the content of the tactical games was constantly changing, both to keep pace with new enemy technology and tactics, and to maintain the vitality of the course. So, by the end of 1943, the school was investigating tactics against the *Schnorchel* boats and in shallow water operations. By 1944, although still teaching anti-wolf-pack tactics, WATU also included instruction in countering the new German Type XXI high-speed U-boats then working up in the Baltic.[9]

At the end of 1942, Captain Baker-Cresswell was appointed to organise and run an advanced training school for the tactical instruction of formed escort groups. He got started in early 1943 with tactical exercises centred around the yacht *Philante*. The yacht acted as a mock convoy, screened by one of the groups, with friendly submarines playing the part of U-boats. Because the group commanders knew their own ships' capabilities, Baker-Cresswell left them to carry out their own tactical plans, even refraining from imposing his own views at the post-exercise debrief. He saw his role as generating a realistic tactical setting, and to do this he relaxed safety rules considerably, often taking 'frightful risks' with the submarines.[10] It was just as well that experienced commanding officers were usually appointed to these boats.

Of course, the system was not perfect. When an operational research scientist, Professor W.M. McCrea, attended the conference at the end of a day's work, he saw that the exercises were reviewed on their merits, and that mistakes and difficulties were frankly discussed, but that some of the value in this approach was lost because no records were kept and the Training Captain in *Philante* changed fairly frequently. The Captain was not, therefore, in a position to instruct any of the groups, either from extended personal exercise experience or from accumulated statistics, as to which were the best tactics in a given circumstance. So, as Baker-Cresswell and his successor intended, each group learnt from its own exercises, but did not gain full benefit from the experiences of other groups. Consolidated operational experiences and lessons were instead issued in the Admiralty's 'Monthly Anti-Submarine Report', which seems to have been widely read.

With the introduction of escort carriers into the North Atlantic, steps were taken to improve the combined training of Fleet Air Arm (FAA) aircraft and surface forces. Starting in the spring of 1943, HMS *Biter*'s air group carried out a ten-day course, based at Ballykelly, in cooperation with the Londonderry training organisation. So successful was the experiment, and so obvious its benefits, that Admiral Sir Max Horton, CinC Western Approaches, petitioned the Admiralty to extend the scheme by setting up a combined A/S warfare training centre in Northern Ireland. In April 1943 a series of meetings was held to discuss the implementation of Horton's proposal. RAF Coastal Command aircraft from their Northern Irish bases at Ballykelly and Castle Archdale had already been carrying out occasional exercises with the Londonderry training submarines. It seemed natural, therefore, that Coastal Command should also participate in the new combined training school. It was agreed to base the new centre at the Naval Air Station at Maydown, close to the new tactical school at Londonderry. Horton sent Commander J.R. Phillimore, RN, recently promoted and appointed to Western Approaches as Staff Officer (Air), to start up the new school, sharing responsibility for the courses with Wing Commander F. Rump. The school was soon closely cooperating with the Training Captain in *Philante*.

For Coastal Command the combined course had less value, especially for those squadrons still conducting independent operations or already exercising locally with surface forces. Nevertheless, the course helped inexperienced aircrews brush up on what they had learned at the Operational Training Units, although Air Marshal L.H. Slatter, Air Officer Commanding 15 Group, thought some 'old timers' might see even this as a waste of time.[11] But the greatest value of the combined A/S school was in improving ship and aircraft communications and hence air–sea coordination, which was becoming increasingly important with the advent of the *Schnorchel*-fitted U-boats.

All tactical training at sea was underpinned by comprehensive harbour training, ranging from weapons drill to the sophisticated 'Night Attack Teacher', all under the control of experienced officers. This training, combined with WATU's basic lectures, provided the 'science' of A/S tactics. The 'art' came from free-ranging games on the WATU tactical floor, from the sea training with *Philante* and, above all, from actual contact with the enemy. The art and science of tactics constituted an interrelated dynamic, in which each enhanced the other and created a whole greater than the sum of its parts. In consequence, by 1944 the Western Approaches dictum of 'training and more training', emphasised almost to the point of obsession by Admiral Horton, really began to bear fruit. The training still concentrated, of course, on countering the *Schnorchel*-fitted U-boats, although Phillimore remembers staff discussions beginning on countering the new fast U-boats.[12]

THE FAST SUBMARINE THREAT

During the winter of 1943–44 the Admiralty's Naval Intelligence Department discovered that the Germans were developing a new U-boat with high underwater speed and sustained endurance submerged in an attempt to restore the mobility lost by the converted, *Schnorchel*-fitted U-boats. These new designs included the 25-knot Walter-turbine-powered Type XXVI and the hybrid 15-knot battery-driven Type XXI. To analyse this threat the British carried out various theoretical studies and games on the tactical floor at WATU, the results of which were confirmed during sea trials with the submarine *Seraph* in late 1944. *Seraph* had been converted into a 'high-speed' target capable of 12 knots submerged. As expected, the narrow searchlight sound beam of existing asdic sets made holding contact on *Seraph* very difficult in the highly dynamic engagements but the margins for error were much reduced when attacking with existing fixed-range, ahead-throwing weapons like Squid. The newly-formed 19th Escort Group had little success during the first week of the exercises, but improved rapidly thereafter. Some minor enhancements in the asdic gear helped, but it was apparent that continuous attack training was 90 per cent of the battle.[13]

As soon as the trials were completed, *Seraph* was pressed into the training of selected escort groups. This was expanded with the employment of two additional fast 'S' Class boats, *Sceptre* and *Satyr*, in February 1945. In these exercises individual escort group commanders continued to adapt tactics. The 'S' Class boats were excellent for attack practice, but their short high-speed endurance limited their use in tactical exercises. Search training was better carried out on the tactical table, although 'contact' was sometimes elusive. During such practice at Londonderry one senior officer, Commander A.F.C. Layard, RN, discovered how difficult it was to catch a U-boat capable of 12–15 knots, even with five escorts.[14] To enhance coordination, some group commanders were already experimenting with controlling the action from an improvised 'information centre' based in the navigation room, rather than from the bridge. Provided that a high standard of inter-ship communications and tactical plotting was maintained, this arrangement helped create a better mental picture of the engagement. Nevertheless, the bridge remained

The captured Type XXI electro boat *U-2518* at Dun Laoghaire Harbour in February 1946.
'[Against the revolutionary qualities of the new types of U-boat] the mighty sea power of the
Anglo Saxons is essentially powerless . . . It seems that the enemy has not yet found any
basically new means for locating and combatting submarines below the surface.'
Admiral Karl Dönitz, CinC, *Kriegsmarine*, February 1945. (M. Chapman)

the preferred command location for collision avoidance and for the
actual conduct of attacks.[15]

By the end of the war, training against the fast U-boat was clearly
well in hand, although it would have taken considerable time for every
escort group to practise and absorb the new tactics. Whether Horton
was correct in believing that hard-won experience would eliminate
the threat will never be known because, as one senior officer put it, the
ultimate 'blood and guts test' against the Type XXI U-boat never
occurred. With Germany's capitulation in May 1945, however, the
Admiralty assumed that this technology would pass to the Soviet Union
and it therefore became the benchmark of the submarine threat during
the early years of the Cold War.

POST-WAR DEVELOPMENTS

Seeking to capitalise on wartime experience, Admiral Horton issued a
paper within a month of the end of the war in Europe suggesting how

post-war A/S training should be developed.[16] Work was already in hand to continue and refine weapon and attack team training in harbour for individual ships' companies but Horton was emphatic that this program should be complemented by coordinated training at sea. Logically these practices should reflect the expected capability of the future threat—essentially, a submarine which could conduct an entire patrol submerged, with long submerged endurance at 15–20 knots and a high silent-running speed, which was able to dive to 1000 feet, and which was armed with anti-escort homing torpedoes. Although some preliminary training could be done with synthetic targets, Horton was convinced that they could never substitute for a real submarine. He reasoned, moreover, that these 'target' submarines must operate with the tactics expected of a future enemy—an enemy whose operations were likely to be very different from those of British boats.

From Horton's perspective, however, the fundamental difficulty in A/S training was the imposition of crippling safety restrictions. Night exercises with submarines had been conducted before the war (and more often than was generally known), but they were infrequent for safety reasons. Restrictions were relaxed and sometimes virtually abandoned during the war, but were certain to be re-imposed in peacetime. Such constraints tended to make A/S practice stereotypical and awfully dull. In addition, for most commanding officers, A/S exercises already lacked the excitement of anti-aircraft shoots. This was a real concern when promotion rested upon '. . . being seen to be doing your stuff'. Gunnery was highly visible, and 'made a lot of noise!'.[17] By contrast, often all that was seen during A/S practice was the submarine's smoke candle. Horton thought it necessary to overcome this sense of dullness if the Royal Navy was to make further great strides in A/S warfare.

One option was to carry out practice firings of A/S weapons, but submarine safety was still the prime consideration. As an example, while a ship could fire inert Hedgehog projectiles, the most effective weapon against deep-diving fast submarines was the Squid. Yet only unrealistic floating dummy projectiles were available for practice attacks with Squid. Measuring the success of an attack was also far less dramatic than when shooting down a practice air target. During the war, Captain N.A. Prichard, RN, Director of the A/S Division, had noted: '. . . the practical accuracy of an attack was easily tested by the admirably simple method of inspecting the surface of the water for the evidence of destruction'.[18] But in peacetime, no satisfactory method of assessing practice attacks had yet been developed. All tactical activity had to stop for measurements to be taken. This remained a problem into the 1950s.

Until mid-1944, the anti-U-boat campaign had been largely waged in the deep waters of the Atlantic. Here classification of submerged asdic contacts was relatively simple, because acoustic conditions were more stable and non-submarine contacts less numerous. But when the U-boats returned to inshore waters, the more difficult environment quickly exposed the limitations of classification techniques, despite most A/S training having been conducted in precisely the same areas! For training exercises, even in wartime, there was always the option to have the submarine fire a smoke candle when it was difficult to find, so that asdic contact could be gained and no training time 'wasted'. Realistic training in classification techniques, Horton emphasised, could only be conducted in a large area and with the hunting ships approaching from some distance. Unfortunately this kind of exercise took the most time and, consequently, had been the least practised.

The Admiralty had quickly appreciated the complexity of the operational problem, and Western Approaches Command had conducted improved training in searching techniques during the last year of the war. Horton suggested that similar training be continued as part of the post-war program and the attendant risk of wasting time be accepted. He believed, furthermore, that the focus should be on the tactical training of escort groups, the crucial value of which had been amply demonstrated. Officers with valuable wartime experience as escort group commanders would be available for some time to conduct this training and, ideally, they would use the exercise templates which had been developed by the Training Captain in Western Approaches.

Pre-war A/S doctrine had focused training on the coordinated escort screens used in the protection of fleet units, which were easier to practise than the looser type of cover used to screen a slow convoy. If post-war escort group commanders were to be trained realistically, however, then exercises with mercantile convoys had to be carried out. Horton believed that the obstacles to arranging them, even in skeleton form, had to be overcome if the lessons of the war were to be fully assimilated and applied. When it came to deciding what tactics should be taught, Horton reckoned that much information could be gleaned from wartime actions but the great variety of tactical situations experienced and now envisaged would require a good deal of analysis before the standard tactics—and therefore the most useful tactical exercises—could be formulated.

Successful wartime A/S actions were, of course, reported in detail. But much could also be learned from actions in which U-boats avoided the searching vessels. As the war ended, Captain Howard-Johnston, now

Director of the Anti–U–Boat Division, asked for three months to analyse every incident in which a U-boat had escaped. Unfortunately his Division was closed down and the analysis never done.[19] The Staff and Technical Histories were no help, since these were not issued until the early 1950s, and even then they concentrated on the German wolf-pack operations. As both Howard-Johnston and Prichard noted, in struggling with the new fast submarine, it was the last stage of the wartime campaign which was most relevant.

While the value of ship-borne and land-based aircraft in dealing with U-boats had been understood before the war, Horton believed their use had never properly been investigated. During the war, aircraft had no clearly developed tactics or weapons for attacking U-boats, and were woefully inefficient in communicating with escort vessels. These problems had been exacerbated by the wide dispersion of the main air and escort operational and training bases. It had proved practically impossible, for example, to arrange for ships' officers and aircrews to meet before or after operations, leading to misunderstandings and loss of efficiency. The answer had eventually been found in the provision of combined training at the joint A/S School at Maydown. 'It is clearly necessary from now on', Horton asserted,

> to ensure that the Navy, Fleet Air Arm and Coastal Command march together in the closest possible liaison in the development of A/S technique generally, and that tactical exercises which include the employment of aircraft are frequently carried out.[20]

This would only be feasible if the officers from both services lived and messed together at the main A/S training establishment. Flying officers could then easily go to sea, and ships' officers could fly in Coastal Command and FAA aircraft. So important was this program to Horton that he argued that nothing should be allowed to stand in its way.

Air Chief Marshal Sholto Douglas, Air Officer Commanding, Coastal Command, strongly supported proposals for joint training. Indeed a few days after a meeting called by Assistant Chief of Naval Staff (Warfare) Rear Admiral M.D. Oliver to discuss Horton's paper, Douglas expanded his ideas in a 'Memorandum on the formation of a combined A/S tactical school'. The aim of the school, he thought, should be to develop and teach combined tactics for both aircraft and surface forces. It must deal with the higher tactical training of formed units and not with individual ship or aircraft training. Douglas expected that some twelve or thirteen RAF squadrons would be trained annually, two at a time, during a six-week course. Captain Prichard, the Director of the A/S Division, likewise emphasised the importance of formed escort groups and their training in combined exercises with aircraft before joining major fleet formations. Echoing the consensus of the meeting, Prichard suggested that the school needed a nucleus of highly-trained staff, at least two ships to simulate a convoy and a permanent escort group for the development of tactics and training.[21]

Rear Admiral George Creasy, Flag Officer, Submarines, could not attend the meeting, although one of his staff put forward his views. Soon afterwards they were formalised in a paper on post-war A/S training in which Creasy, like Horton, concluded that the pre-war concentration on the screening of fast fleet units had handicapped analysis of convoy protection. In future, the submarine threat to trade needed to be better understood, and should be studied in conjunction with A/S defence. Creasy also recognised the vital need for at least occasional exercises with a convoy of merchant ships.[22] But he doubted whether aircraft could achieve significant success against the 'true' submarine of the future, and thought their A/S role would be subordinate to countering enemy reconnaissance aircraft working with submarines against convoys. Direct air attack upon shipping was also likely to increase, making it necessary for future training to include both anti-submarine and anti-air dimensions. The Air Ministry, later supported by the Admiralty, however, thought it better to avoid conflicting objectives and hence to confine training to joint A/S warfare.

CONSOLIDATION AND RESEARCH

Captains Howard-Johnston and Prichard wrote joint comments on the papers from Horton, Douglas and Creasy. Here, they believed, was a unified argument from the three authorities most intimately involved in A/S warfare. All three stressed the crucial need for a comprehensive organisation and agreed that wartime problems were the result of the RN's paying insufficient attention to submarine warfare during the inter-war era.[23] By late 1945, the Admiralty organisation was already being streamlined, with the amalgamation of the different A/S warfare areas into a single operational division—The Torpedo, Anti-Submarine and Mine Warfare Division—under Captain Lord Ashbourne, RN. The continuation of formed escort groups, the restructuring of the A/S Branch and the maintenance of a large reserve of trained men for future wartime A/S operations were all seen as vital. Training would be enhanced, Ashbourne observed, by the temporary continuation of a

Joint A/S School at Londonderry. None of these measures would be sufficient, however, if the more glamorous issue of fleet protection took precedence over the dull and difficult, but ultimately more important, defence of trade. Captain G. French, RN, Deputy Director of Plans, voiced the Naval Staff's opinion:

> . . . the root of this matter is a question of outlook and of the importance . . . attached to the adequacy of our A/S training and of trade protection exercises. . . . It is improbable that these will be given full weight unless there is a sufficiently powerful body of thought in the *Admiralty* organisation to insist upon it.[24]

In early 1946, Ashbourne went one stage further and proposed the establishment of the Joint Sea/Air Warfare Committee with both Royal Navy and RAF membership. The committee would hammer out joint policy on all matters connected with A/S warfare and make policy recommendations to the Board of Admiralty and Air Council through the staffs of the Admiralty and Air Ministry. (At their first meeting, in May 1946, the committee discussed a paper by Ashbourne, on the implications of the *Schnorchel*-fitted, fast U-boat.)

Post-war British A/S doctrine was rooted in the use of convoy for trade defence. Since submarines were less likely to be surfaced when operating against convoys, distant A/S forces were less likely to warn of, or hinder, a submarine's approach. Furthermore, modern submarines could probably attack from longer ranges outside existing A/S screens and, even if detected, would prove slippery customers to localise and attack.[25] These factors meant that A/S warfare around convoys would not only be more difficult, but also that the ideas of 'Attack at Source' and 'Transit Offensives', developed during the war, would have to be extended. Ashbourne thought these changes warranted careful study and a prolonged series of trials, but any solutions, he warned, would never be permanent. They were bound to be in a constant state of flux due to the interaction between developments in submarine and anti-submarine technology and operational methods.

Undoubtedly influenced by assessments from the Naval Intelligence Department, Ashbourne considered that future developments could be divided into two periods.[26] Basic research and technical investigations, he felt, should be directed primarily against the post-1950, or 'Long Term', problem. This was typified by submarines equating to the projected Type XXVI Walter U-boat design, which came closest to being a 'true submarine'. Training, however, should be directed against the 'Short Term' problem, up to 1950. This immediate threat was characterised by submarines equivalent to the wartime Type XXI U-boats. Ashbourne hoped that existing A/S ship gear would prove adequate to counter this threat without requiring major modifications, although he was less sanguine about airborne equipment. More research would be needed to confirm this analysis, although it could only be confirmed by sea trials against a realistic submarine target. Unfortunately, there seemed to be little prospect of obtaining a submarine capable of 15 knots submerged for some time. All the Type XXI U-boats in British hands proved unsuitable for trials without extensive refits, for which the resources did not exist. As a result, all work with the Type XXIs was abandoned in late 1945, with the one remaining specimen being lent to France in early 1946.[27] Other boats, such as the extensively converted HMS *Scotsman* and the Walter-powered HMS *Meteorite* (ex-*U-1407*), would not be available until 1948 at the earliest. In sum, for the foreseeable future the British would have to rely on the half-dozen converted 'S' Class boats available, on theoretical studies and on data from the Americans, who had two captured Type XXIs.[28]

THE JOINT ANTI-SUBMARINE SCHOOL

The primary arm for developing A/S doctrine and tactical training was to be the Joint Anti-Submarine School (JASS) at Londonderry, with contributions from the A/S schools at HMS *Osprey* and HMS *Vernon*. JASS was descended from the *ad hoc* wartime organisation made up of WATU, *Philante* and the joint school at Maydown. The new school would train formed units of ships and aircraft in the broader aspects of A/S operations, with an emphasis on joint tactics. The transition to peacetime training meant that resources were only sufficient to run 'experimental' courses from the end of 1945 until the beginning of 1947, at which point JASS was formally inaugurated under Joint Directors and full courses began.

The main course, known as the Joint A/S Unit Training Course, was six weeks long and attended by destroyer and frigate flotillas, together with naval and air force A/S squadrons. Units were already trained in their individual roles and the course aimed at providing a firm grasp of joint A/S tactics.[29] The emphasis was on tactical coordination, and lectures were illustrated by demonstrations on the tactical floor and reinforced by exercises at sea. A two-week Joint A/S Tactical Course was attended by commanding officers of Coastal Command stations, destroyer flotillas, escort vessels, submarines and air squadrons. One

Tactical floor at the Joint Anti-Submarine School, Londonderry. 'Useful harbour and sea training—that is, training which produces significant operational improvements—is dependent upon the combination of many factors whose connection is by no means always apparent. However, the most critical factor of all is agreed and practical tactical doctrine.' Commodore James Goldrick, RAN, Director General Military Strategy, ADF. (M. Llewellyn-Jones)

Canadian Officer, Acting Lieutenant-Commander H.J. Hunter, RCN, attended this course in 1947 and thought it gave '. . . an excellent appreciation of the submarine menace to our trade convoys' and that it emphasised '. . . the value of Air/Surface cooperation in combating this threat'. By sending officers to sea and to fly on exercises with their opposite numbers, Hunter thought the course achieved '. . . the object of showing air, surface and submarine officers the other side of the problem'.[30] JASS also ran a short course for students of the single service Staff Colleges, as well as the Senior Officers Technical Course which emphasised advanced A/S tactics and future developments.

The courses were supported by a permanent A/S Flotilla at Londonderry under Commander J. Grant, RN, who had served in *Philante* before being appointed Training Commander at the A/S School at *Osprey* in early 1944. His flotilla consisted of two destroyers and four frigates and, initially, two unmodified 'S' Class submarines. By 1947 the submarines had been replaced by modified fast 'S' Class boats, with the hope of at least one becoming a permanent fixture. The school also controlled a permanent Joint A/S Flight, with the RAF element at Ballykelly, initially with two Lancasters, a Warwick and an Anson flying classroom, and the FAA element at Eglington comprising Barracudas of No. 744 Naval Air Squadron. The JASS exercise areas encompassed the waters between Northern Ireland and Islay off the west coast of Scotland and extended 200 miles to the west. Nothing like this had been available to *Philante* and Maydown during the war. The JASS training courses culminated in advanced tactical serials involving both the permanent Londonderry forces and visiting units (the first of which was the 5th Destroyer Flotilla, sent from the Home Fleet in October 1947). Their training program, completed amidst realistic drizzly Atlantic weather, proved the value of close liaison between ship and air teams.[31]

FLEET TRAINING

When units returned to the fleet their training continued in major naval exercises, although these suffered from serious shortcomings, including the absence of fast submarines against which to practise. In an attempt to mitigate this problem, one early exercise adopted the idea of scaling down the ships' speeds. But this could not eliminate the problem of the relative time factor without equivalent changes to the screening distances, asdic ranges, and so on.[32] Any value gained from such exercises relied heavily on the participants' imagination and honesty and, in the end, it seemed best to relegate these problems to the tactical tables, as had been done during the war. A further difficulty was noted by Lieutenant-Commander Ian Purvis, RAN, during a liaison visit to Britain in 1949. There were many instances of ships' asdic equipment being unserviceable owing to poor maintenance. This problem was not confined to the Royal Navy but, in its case, stemmed from a lack of experienced ratings and the re-organisation of the A/S and electrical branches. It seemed to Purvis that the new, more advanced A/S equipment shortly to enter service would only exacerbate this problem.[33]

As Horton had warned, peacetime also saw rigorous imposition of the submarine safety rules which, unless relaxed, usually destroyed any vestige of realism and frustrated testing more adventurous tactics. These rules now included instructions specifically for exercises with fast submarines, relaxations of which could only be authorised by the Submarine Operating Authority, and then only if the submarine commanding officer had the necessary experience. Inevitably, as wartime commanding officers moved on to new appointments, the level of experience declined. Without the opportunity for realistic exercises, officers in the Admiralty doubted whether providing mercantile convoys for exercises would be worth the expense. Although many fleet A/S exercises were conducted, these mainly practised defence of fast military convoys or fleet units. Few, if any, exercises involved realistic convoy operations, and those that did concentrated on operational control of the convoys rather than their tactical defence.[34]

The first fast submarine for training was the USS *Trumpetfish*, deployed to Londonderry in May 1948. For two weeks, in poor asdic conditions, Captain Gibbs' 4th Escort Flotilla found *Trumpetfish* an extremely elusive target. Declaring the exercises at one point to be '. . . disastrous and profoundly depressing',[35] Gibbs' detection problems were compounded by the make-up of his flotilla. His fastest ships, the destroyers, were still equipped with depth charges, whereas the more effective weapon, the Squid, was fitted to the slower frigates. Participating aircraft fared little better, even though *Trumpetfish* frequently exposed considerable portions of her *Schnorchel* mast. The results were perhaps more worrying because the submarine was limited to 'mostly medium speeds' for many of the exercises, at times in compliance with instructions but also to conserve her battery. *Trumpetfish's* captain was also constantly worried about his navigational position and deliberately constrained his courses to avoid straying into shallower water. Even so, Don Smith, one of *Trumpetfish's* crew, remembers her bouncing off the bottom of the channel during some of the more energetic evasive manoeuvres.[36]

While these exercises were proceeding, the 6th Destroyer Flotilla under Captain Sir Charles Madden, RN, was beginning a work-up period at Portland with a fast 'S' Class boat. This was followed by a visit to the USN's A/S School at Key West in Florida, before the flotilla returned to Londonderry. Although by the spring of 1949 Madden's ships were highly efficient in dealing with fast submarines, exercises confirmed that—even in favourable conditions—current British equipment and weapons could achieve a kill rate of about 30 per cent, and then only if the target's speed was under 12 knots.[37] Moreover, all these exercises were heavily stylised, with the submarine's position known at the start of each serial. This was common practice at JASS, but it made the exercises most unrealistic in a wider tactical sense. Unusually, for the final training exercise during a course in early 1950, the submarines were given complete freedom of action. The post-exercise discussion revealed how effective the mere presence of aircraft had been in frustrating submarine attacks, even though they had achieved few sightings.[38]

Horton would doubtless have been impressed by the realism of this exercise, although the experiment does not seem to have been repeated. Worse, fast submarine training targets continued to be sparse. In 1950, for instance, Londonderry had two fast submarines for short periods only. Ironically, one was the Type XXI lent earlier to the French Navy and re-christened the *Roland Morillot*. Although she often had to conserve her battery, thereby restricting her top speed to 14 knots, she was still a difficult target to pin down. The captain of the destroyer HMS *Creole* noted that he spent some 90 per cent of his time in his operations room, but because there were up to four A/S ships involved in the close action, he still found it necessary to con the ship from the bridge. This he saw was quite unrealistic. In war, one or two ships would 'get on with it' and the others would remain nearby on a perimeter, allowing a captain to be constantly near the action plot, whether by day or by night.[39] Such exercises confirmed that the most effective way of dealing with a fast submarine was to control the entire A/S action, from detection to attack, from the operations room. This augured well for the new Type 15 frigate conversions with their improved weapons systems and internal facilities. The work-up with *Roland Morillot* also emphasised that good communications and an efficient action information organisation were crucial to the modern A/S battle.

TECHNOLOGICAL DEVELOPMENTS

Coastal Command was meanwhile introducing the new Avro Shackleton maritime patrol aircraft, the first British aircraft of its type designed specifically for the A/S role.[40] At last there was the space for the crew to operate efficiently while keeping a good lookout, a method which was still producing some 75 per cent of submarine detections during exercises.[41] By 1952, Coastal Command was undergoing a large expansion after the formation of NATO, and the number of crews passing through JASS's courses doubled. While these personnel had general experience in the A/S role, JASS was concerned that they lacked familiarity with their equipment and needed elementary instruction. FAA crews, by contrast, were better prepared, having already completed a three-month A/S course at Eglington.[42]

While visual sightings of the *Schnorchel* might be possible by day, the Shackleton had to rely on its radar at night. This was not nearly as effective as the high-powered anti-*Schnorchel* APS20 radar installed in the American-built Lockheed Neptunes also entering service with the RAF.

Post-war training in sea/air cooperation, Third Escort Flotilla and Coastal Command Lancaster of the JASS, Londonderry. 'This coastal [command] job, though less murderously expensive in casualties than some, was exacting, dangerous and highly skilled, and far too commonly tedious and unrewarding . . . That was part of the game, and what they did was as essential to victory as the breathtaking moments enjoyed by the few lucky ones who found and killed their prey.' Marshal of the RAF Sir John Slessor. (M. Llewellyn-Jones)

Even with these new aircraft, however, the chances of detecting a fully-submerged submarine were practically nil.[43] The only system available for this was the expendable sonobuoy, which acted as a remote acoustic sensor. These had been introduced prematurely in 1943 after inadequate trials and with over-optimistic ideas of their performance. In the early 1950s sonobuoy technology was still not sufficiently advanced for open-ocean searches. One Shackleton crew captain recalled reaching the night-time A/S exercise patrol area:

> We know that sinister steel shapes pass through these [Atlantic] waters mostly below, but occasionally on top. From our perspective, the ocean is very big and . . . [the submarines] are very small. They are also faster and much improved versions of the last war submarines. We know that

our chances of . . . finding one are remote because the more effective detection devices that we need are still undergoing development. If we get lucky, we might surprise one of them on the surface.[44]

If the aircraft could surprise the submarines on the surface, or when *Schnorchelling*, then they might attack with depth charges. While this method stood little chance of success, the tactic was often practised in training exercises.[45] Indeed the outstanding limitation of these anti-submarine aircraft (as indeed of the anti-submarine submarine) was the lack of a weapon which could destroy a fully-submerged boat. This problem would only be solved with the introduction of the air-launched lightweight homing torpedo. In the meantime much training concentrated on homing A/S ships on to their target for the kill.

By 1952 sonobuoy technology was improving sufficiently to give some hope of its capability for wide-area search, perhaps recovering some of the effectiveness lost when the U-boats first adopted submerged tactics in 1944. Training with sonobuoys in search patterns was tried at JASS, together with use of the new directional sonobuoys, which offered better fixing. It was hoped that these would allow crews to maintain contact for longer, to follow the submarine's manoeuvres more easily and therefore better home A/S ships.

New technologies to overcome the limitations of existing A/S equipment had been under development in the Royal Navy for some time. These culminated in 1949 with conversion of several wartime destroyers into fast Type 15 A/S frigates. The first two, HMS *Relentless* and HMS *Rocket*, could reach 31.5 knots and, with the combination of their new integrated Type 170 (Four Square) asdic, Limbo A/S mortar and planned 'Bidder' A/S torpedo, were expected to keep up with better and attack more effectively an evading fast submarine. By 1952 both ships had been allocated to Londonderry and were being put through their paces. The Admiralty, however, was struggling to keep even one fast submarine permanently on hand, and only HMS *Turpin* (a fast 'T' Class conversion) and *Scotsman* were intermittently available. Captain (D) Third Training Squadron, Captain M. Le Fanu, RN, reported that they had managed some duels with *Turpin* although, he wryly observed, she 'won on a technical knock-out'.[46]

These new ships with their more complex weapons systems presented further challenges to the training regime. The plotting tables in the operations room could now be fed continuously with up-to-date sensor information, but the A/S Control Officer was so busy controlling the Type 170 suite that he had '. . . a less clear mental picture of the submarine's movements' than officers in ships with the earlier and simpler Type 144 asdic. Worse, the asdic operators were mesmerised by the visual presentation during a long action, and often paid too little attention to aural detection and echo-quality. Correcting this tendency further occupied the Control Officer's time and limited the advice he could offer to his captain.

Nevertheless, the Type 15 frigate's excellent equipment and spacious operations room made the exercise of tactical command far more comprehensive and efficient. For the first time the operations room was the hub of the ship, and it was from here, below deck, that the captain conducted the battle. Moreover, with the all-round, variable range capability and integrated fire control of the Limbo mortar, the Type 15 was far more effective in attack than the older Squid-fitted ships. The Type 15's speed also gave it the legs to locate a submarine reported some distance from the convoy. But if the Type 15 carried the Senior Officer, and he were to hare off on chases or be immersed in close action, his control of the overall battle might be compromised. Perhaps, Le Fanu suggested, it would be better to put the Senior Officer in something like a *Loch* Class frigate with an enlarged Action Information Centre, thereby releasing the Type 15 for short-range searches and attack.[47]

CONCLUSIONS: THE PROBLEMS OF THE PURSUIT OF REALISM

The story of training to counter the fast submarine in the 1940s and early 1950s is a case study in the eternal problem of simulating the face of naval battle, of replicating the inherent complexity, confusion and danger of war conditions. The attempt to do so was, in the event, only partially successful. The Type 15 frigates and Shackleton maritime patrol aircraft constituted a watershed between wartime and post-war A/S developments. Although the new technology of the early 1950s could better cope with the fast submarine, the training needed for ships and aircraft was becoming ever more technical. This process had been gaining momentum even before the fast submarine threat was identified during the war. Fortunately for the British, wartime tactical training at WATU and Maydown and sea training with *Philante* had all emphasised the cooperative nature of A/S tactics and the importance of initiative, while down-playing the doctrinaire approach. Higher-level training had, in effect, concentrated on the 'art' rather than the 'science' of A/S warfare. As a result, when the threat began to change in 1944–45, the formal and informal elements of the training system could adapt with remarkable rapidity. As the war ended, the British sought to continue the methods which had proved so successful. They set up a senior inter-departmental committee to oversee developments, and proceeded to establish a permanent joint training facility at Londonderry.

While there was some progress in the crucial task of integrating policy with operations, systems and technology, the A/S organisation suffered from largely unavoidable limitations. Post-war safety restrictions inevitably affected the reality of exercises, as did the lack of ability to measure attack accuracy without interrupting the exercise. While more extensive training areas—without the restrictions of defensive mine-fields or enemy action—were available after the war, full benefit was rarely gained by allowing ships to carry out searches without prior knowledge of the submarine's start position. As a result classification techniques were not realistically practised. The desire to avoid wasting time in unproductive searches, together with parallel pressure to include unrealistic numbers of ships in close actions, also added to the lack of realism. But the fact that there was no fast submarine target until 1948 was the most serious limitation upon the pursuit of realism in A/S training.

14 | Command at sea in war and peace

An Australian experience during the Gulf War and after

Lee Cordner

Perhaps the hardest part of a naval career is that one's future hangs on a thread and there are more chances of that thread breaking than in most walks of life.

Vice-Admiral Sir John Collins, RAN

COMMAND AT SEA, the role of a warship's captain, remains today much as it has been for centuries. This is not to say, however, that the context of command has not evolved. Change has brought different factors and different challenges for commanders to face. Improvements in communications, for example, have given the commander at sea greater access to information and closer connectivity with headquarters and home than in the past. Of course, this means that more information has to be managed effectively, and its impact on both the commander and those he commands must be understood.

The captain of a warship is one of the last outposts of autocracy in a democratic society. He has, however, less autonomy today than in the past since his performance can be more readily monitored. Command at sea presents great opportunities but places considerable pressure on those who exercise it; pressure rarely found in other areas of human endeavour. The line between success and failure can be very fine. A poor decision, a poor judgement, or one piece of bad luck can destroy more than twenty years of a career and potentially the careers—and possibly the lives—of others.

The guided missile frigate HMAS *Sydney* (FFG 03) was under my command from 12 October 1990 to 29 April 1992. *Sydney* served in the 1990–91 Gulf War and in a subsequent operational deployment as part of the Maritime Interception Force (MIF) in the North Red Sea (NRS), enforcing United Nations Security Council (UNSC) sanctions against Iraq. HMAS *Adelaide* (FFG 01) was under my command from 16 May 1997 to 29 April 1999. *Adelaide* participated in several major exercises and deployments to Asia, including operations in Indonesian waters during the fall of the Suharto regime. For much of the period in *Adelaide*, I was the senior captain in the Fleet, and performed the role of Commander Task Group (CTG) during major exercises and operational deployments.

This chapter is a personal account of some of the challenges I encountered in command at sea and, in this context, I have used the male pronoun throughout because I am referring to my own experience. I do not claim to have been a particularly good or special commanding officer, although I was fortunate in the variety of experiences I encountered. I have attempted to be self-critical in my analysis. Reflection and the constant search for improvement are essential attributes for an effective commanding officer because, at the end of the day, we are only fallible human beings. This, therefore, is not an academically rigorous account. Its major analytical tool is personal reflection upon experience.

HIGH-STAKES LEADERSHIP: RUNNING A WARSHIP

Command is highly personal. The personality of the captain will, in time, be mirrored throughout his ship. Those who have commanded at sea will know the extent to which the ship is the captain and the captain is the ship. The captain lives alone on board RAN warships, following the Royal Naval tradition. He must largely keep his own counsel and find his own entertainment. The loneliness of command is an axiom of military life, and it can be particularly lonely when tough decisions are required.

The captain must think carefully about the example he sets. Every utterance and action will be scrutinised; he will be quoted and analysed. He should be impeccable in action and reaction while also being human and, above all, he must be genuine, as any pretence will soon be revealed in the course of a long deployment, particularly when he is placed under considerable pressure.

Australia's egalitarian ethos impacts on its naval culture by presenting interpersonal circumstances not generally found elsewhere. All on board see themselves and the captain essentially as equals. Yet they expect the captain to be different, to be competent, fair and above the pack but not aloof.

The captain must earn the trust and respect of his people. Australian sailors will not instinctively follow an officer just because he has been made their captain. They do not have to like him. Indeed, some inexperienced commanding officers have made the mistake of trying too hard to be popular, perhaps by avoiding tough or unpopular decisions or by becoming overly familiar with subordinates. Sailors will soon see through this approach. Once trust has been established, the ship's company will willingly follow and obey, sometimes displaying extraordinary loyalty and courage. The need for the ship's company to believe in the captain is significantly magnified during periods of great stress and danger, such as war.

PREPARING FOR THE GULF WAR

When I assumed command of HMAS *Sydney* in late 1990, fully one-third of the ship's company was also new to the ship, and we immediately began preparing for war. There was no doubt in my mind that war was likely, as news on the Middle East was increasingly bleak. I had only a few weeks to achieve several vital things: to evaluate the team I had inherited; to prove to the Maritime Commander (the Fleet Admiral) my competence to command in the most demanding circumstances; to establish my personality within the ship; and, crucially, to convince the ship's company that I was the right person to lead them into war.

The professional competence of the captain is crucial to the effectiveness of a warship. His skill as a naval tactician and, more importantly, how well he leads, motivates and inspires his people, is vital to success (and potentially to survival) for all on board. It was essential that a 'contract of trust' be established between the ship's company and myself. They needed to be convinced that the prospect of war was real and that I could bring them home safely, having acquitted themselves with pride and distinction. Conversely, they needed to be reassured that I had complete confidence in them.

Our training was thorough, demanding and realistic. *Sydney* had to attain war levels of proficiency in many facets of naval operations so as to be prepared for the uncertainties of the Gulf. The Nuclear, Biological and Chemical Defence (NBCD) and damage control requirements were particularly sobering. The Iraqis had a proven chemical warfare capability, which they had used to devastating effect on land against the Iranians and the Kurds. It was also assumed that they had a biological warfare capability. Added to this was the remote possibility that United States forces might use nuclear weapons to defend themselves if the Iraqis resorted to weapons of mass destruction. We trained for the extreme difficulty of operating in a tropical environment while wearing a chemical suit and gas mask. While I was confident that our equipment and training would ensure that most of us would survive, facing such weaponry was one of our most terrifying prospects.

The Prime Minister led the gathering of officials during an emotional farewell. My sense of responsibility for carrying the hopes and fears of our nation was magnified by the media hype. This was a period of great anxiety and uncertainty for our families and friends, who had to endure rampant media speculation while remaining in a society otherwise untouched by the prospect of war. Fortunately at sea we were unable to watch the 24-hour-a-day CNN coverage of the build-up to war.

One of my greatest concerns was the impact on our families of sensationalist reporting, or of major events being reported without any indication of the situation of the Australian ships, so before leaving Australia we established a family link organisation. I had observed this being used very effectively by the Royal Navy while on exchange duty during the Falklands War. Knowing that accurate and timely information was reaching our loved ones was important to morale at home as well as on board. Unfortunately the length of our deployment remained the subject of conjecture, and we departed with no idea of when we would return. We knew only that we would be away for many months, and certainly for Christmas.

THE GULF WAR

Sydney and *Brisbane* arrived in the Arabian Sea in December 1990, just as the focus and tempo of naval operations were changing.[1] *Adelaide* and *Darwin* had done exceptionally well in the MIF, whose task it was to interrogate and, if necessary, board and inspect shipping bound to or from Iraq. It was widely believed, however, that this phase of the operation had been completed. Certainly, as the Australian Task Group crossed the Straits of Hormuz and first entered the Arabian Gulf, a more intense phase of the operation began. We monitored frantic diplomatic activity as the United Nations deadline for the withdrawal of all Iraqi forces from Kuwait—15 January 1991—drew ever closer. A massive build-up of coalition forces around the Gulf continued and tension mounted as the possibility of an Iraqi pre-emptive strike was mooted.

Iraq had invested billions of oil dollars in acquiring an impressive array of military hardware. The Iraqi Air Force consisted of over 700 highly capable aircraft drawn from Western and Soviet sources and armed with an array of sophisticated weapons. These included the battle-proven Exocet missile, which the Iraqis had demonstrated their willingness and ability to use during the earlier Tanker War. The Iraqi Navy was less impressive, consisting of obsolescent ex-Soviet missile boats. Iraq also had large stocks of Scud ballistic missiles which could carry high explosive, chemical or biological payloads, large numbers of Chinese Silkworm anti-ship missiles (a land-launched Styx variant) and a considerable stock of sea mines, including modern Western ground mines and large numbers of Soviet moored mines. These latter mines floated near the surface and had an unfortunate record of breaking free in rough weather (or when freed intentionally) and of drifting down the Gulf.

This period of tension placed considerable pressure on *Sydney's* team. There was an atmosphere of excitement combined with fear and anxiety, but also the potential for boredom and complacency to set in during extended periods of patrolling. The challenge for the captain was to sustain a positive and confident atmosphere, while maintaining high levels of readiness and alertness during protracted periods of watching and waiting. We were well-prepared physically, our equipment was sound and well-maintained, and our training was first-class. But I also knew that we had to be prepared psychologically as we could soon literally be fighting for our lives.

Internal communications

I had already decided that constant and effective communication was vital within the ship. A well-informed ship's company which understood the wider political and military situation and our role within it would be better prepared for combat. The more they understood the need for high levels of vigilance, with a realistic appreciation of the risks, the better placed we all were to be self-disciplined and motivated in maintaining readiness and alertness. I addressed the ship's company every morning, and on the change of watch when events of significance occurred. I presented a personal overview of what was happening in the Gulf, of who or what was coming and going, and of any events or developments on the diplomatic front, as well as of news from home. This included candid explanations of the threats, along with a balanced view of the capabilities which the coalition possessed for dealing with them.

Twice every day I walked throughout the ship, no matter what operational imperatives contrived to keep me near the bridge and operations room, or how tired I felt. This gave me a first-hand feeling for morale and levels of readiness; and it enabled all members of the ship's company to see me regularly. They could ask questions and hopefully be encouraged by my frank and confident responses. I later learned that my internal broadcasts and visits were well-received. A sense of mutual trust, confidence and purpose developed in the ship's company—they felt included and 'in the know'. They were well-prepared psychologically because they knew what was expected of them and why.

Over-control

While the decision to communicate was clearly a successful aspect of my early period in command, another aspect of my performance, when analysed with the benefit of hindsight, was less so. It stemmed from my single-minded determination that *Sydney* and her entire ship's company would return to Australia intact having acquitted ourselves with distinction. I was 'driven' to this end. I had great confidence in our abilities and we prosecuted aggressively every task we were given, while volunteering for demanding and potentially hazardous missions for which we were well-prepared. I was, however, determined to ensure that we took every possible step to reduce the risks and in this I was partly inspired by a sense of history. I was very aware of the HMAS *Sydney* (II) tragedy in 1941. While the circumstances remain shrouded in mystery, there was considerable speculation that somehow *Sydney* had let her guard down. I was determined that I must not let that happen again.

The prospect of an Iraqi preemptive or retaliatory attack was real. In our damage control training we regularly used scenarios from USN experience in the Tanker War along with British experience in the Falklands. The fates of our USN sister ships, *Samuel B. Roberts*, which suffered massive damage after striking a mine, and *Stark*, which suffered extensive damage from an Exocet missile, were fresh in my mind.

I was also acutely aware of the responsibility of representing Australia and the Australian Navy. The combination of these factors led me to drive everyone on board, including myself, very hard. I was unremitting in my determination to maintain very high standards of readiness and alertness, which led to well-founded allegations of over-control. One of my Department Heads drew this to my attention in a frank, private conversation, which caused me enormous anxiety and soul-searching at the time. I knew, however, that I had to adjust counter-productive aspects of my leadership style and I will be forever grateful for the moral courage of that officer. The captain of a warship must have people around him who are prepared to give frank and fearless advice, but very sensitive personal advice about inappropriate or excessive behaviour on the part of the commanding officer is the hardest to give. The captain must create an atmosphere in which subordinate officers can offer such advice privately. He must also constantly review his own performance and be flexible as necessary.

The RAN Task Group slots in

At the height of the conflict, the massive coalition armada within the Gulf consisted of four aircraft carriers, two battleships, ten cruisers, more than 50 destroyers and frigates and over 100 logistic, amphibious and smaller vessels. Over 300 fixed-wing and 200 rotary-wing aircraft were deployed from these ships. The naval force was drawn from fifteen nations and the air and sea operations were conducted with a remarkably high degree of integration.

The RAN Task Group was highly regarded and highly sought after by USN Commanders because we were fully interoperable with high professional standards. The USN was short of escorts and the RAN had a reputation for getting the job done. The Australian Government had authorised our unrestricted commitment and the RAN Task Group slotted right in to contribute seriously to the USN-led coalition force.

MIF operations

Christmas Eve 1990 saw *Sydney* transiting the Straits of Hormuz at 30 knots. Although we had all thought MIF operations were over, Saddam Hussein was still intent upon winning the propaganda war by tempting the coalition force to overreact to a sanctions-breaking cargo vessel. *Sydney* was designated as the lead intercept ship in a group which also included several USN and RN warships. A rehearsal was held on Christmas Day in the Arabian Sea (my Christmas dinner was a turkey sandwich on the bridge).

Boarding *Ibn Khaldoon*, 26 December 1990. 'With surgical precision, two Iroquois helicopter gunships approached from up sun quickly positioning either side of the *Khaldoon*'s bridge wings . . . two Sea Knight helicopters dropped their cargo of US Marines on to the bow, a Lynx deposited British troops, and *Sydney* sent its boarding party by rigid inflatable boats.' Sub-Lieutenant Ralph Illyes, RAN, HMAS *Sydney*. (D. Illyes)

At dawn on Boxing Day we successfully intercepted the *Ibn Khaldoon* (alias 'The Peace Ship'). While loaded with prohibited cargo, the *Ibn Khaldoon* also had over 200 Arab women and children on board to maximise the propaganda effect. The boarding proceeded without major difficulties and no one was injured, although Iraqi authorities would later claim that excessive force had been used. *Sydney* led a similar successful boarding of an Iraqi tanker a few days later, which proved to be Iraq's last attempt to break the United Nations' embargo before hostilities broke out. *Sydney* arrived in Dubai in the United Arab Emirates on New Year's Eve for a well-earned break.

The tension builds

In early January 1991, *Sydney* was assigned an anti-air warfare station in the front line of the coalition forces as intelligence information suggested that the Iraqi Air Force might attempt a preemptive strike. We maintained very high levels of alertness, 24 hours a day. On

11 January *Sydney* was escorting the fleet tanker HMAS *Success* about 140 nautical miles from Iraq when a number of Iraqi aircraft went 'Feet Wet' (i.e. they left the coast) over the Gulf. They came close to Exocet release range from the northern-most USN frigate before being intercepted by combat air patrol fighter aircraft and turning away. We knew that the USN frigate had gone to 'General Quarters' and could hear the high-pitched voice of their Tactical Action Officer demanding permission to fire missiles. I recall thinking 'Maybe this is it', as we monitored the interaction on data link and voice radio circuits. There were similar Iraqi feints over the next few days.

I gave the ship's company a full briefing on what had occurred, concluding my summation by stating that a strike by aircraft armed with Exocets and other weapons could be attempted at very short notice. We had a newspaper reporter embarked at the time who wrote a very colourful account based on my briefing. I was grateful when he agreed to tone down his article so as not to alarm our families unduly.

On several occasions mines were found drifting in *Sydney's* recent operating areas. I adopted the practice, whenever possible, of shutting down the ship's gas turbine engines at night to allow the ship to drift with the wind and tide. This reduced the risks, as did vigilant lookouts and helicopter mine searches during daylight hours. In many ways the mine threat was more insidious than that posed by missiles and air attack. The majority of the ship's company slept below the waterline, so we knew that a mine strike would have devastating effects and could happen without warning. An air raid, on the other hand, would allow us several minutes to react, and we were well-prepared to defend ourselves.

The 15 January UN deadline came and went and we began taking Pyridostigmine Bromide (NAPS) tablets as prophylaxis against nerve agents, in addition to the cocktail of inoculations we had already received. These tablets had to be taken twice every day and at least 24 hours before exposure to nerve gas if they were to provide any protection. Gas masks were checked and the few beards remaining among the crew disappeared to ensure a good seal.

WAR COMES

Very early in the morning of 17 January 1991 the coalition force offensive against Iraq began. This was an awesome sight as we watched wave after wave of Tomahawk Land Attack Missiles (TLAMs) being launched from USN cruisers in our vicinity. The missiles were followed by waves of carrier-borne aircraft as the attack continued for several hours. A very tense period followed as we awaited anxiously the return of the aircraft and prepared for what all believed would be the inevitable Iraqi counter-attack. Fortunately, all the aircraft returned safely and there was no immediate response from Iraq.

We later observed a Scud missile streaking across the sky as additional carrier battle groups surged into the Gulf bringing extra escorting destroyers and frigates with them. These new units often did not understand the ambience of the Gulf scene so numerous false alarms were raised, which helped keep everyone on edge. During one such alarm I ordered *Sydney* to 'Action Stations'. USN units had reported a suspected Mirage F-1/Exocet attack, and flashes and streaks in the sky were reported by *Sydney* lookouts. These were later found to be USN aircraft returning to their carriers and dumping explosive ordnance.

Early on, Iraqi aircraft were detected flying down the coast of Kuwait toward the fleet. Coalition fighters intercepted them; a number

Tomahawk launch, USS *Princeton*, January 1991. 'Just before 0200 local time the Force Warfare Commander gave the order and a stream of Tomahawk missiles sped toward their targets in Iraq. We watched these missiles in awe. An unusual silence descended over the ship. We realised that the RAN was at war for the first time in twenty years.' Lieutenant-Commander John Vandyke, RAN, HMAS *Sydney*. (D. Illyes)

were shot down and the remainder fled. Several further attempts met with a similar response. After a few days, reports were received that large numbers of Iraqi aircraft had been flown to airfields in Iran, sparking concerns that the fleet would be subject to air attack from the Iranian side, despite Iranian assurances that the eventual total of 138 aircraft had been impounded.

Although there was deep hatred between Iran and Iraq, exacerbated by the slaughter of the Iran–Iraq War, the Americans were particularly concerned about Iran. The US aircraft carriers were vulnerable since they were operating in a very confined geographical area close to the Iranian coast and it fell to *Sydney* and *Brisbane* to screen the carriers from the Iranian side, which required us to maintain high levels of anti-air warfare alertness as well as a constant vigilance against small vessels. Dhows and other small craft had to be cleared away from the carrier-operating areas due to concerns about the possibility of a terrorist-type attack.

In late February *Sydney* was ordered into the far northern Arabian Gulf to join in the Combat Search and Rescue (CSAR) task. This involved rescuing Allied aircrew forced to eject while returning from missions over Iraq. Our helicopters were kept at immediate readiness for this task, which could involve rescuing aircrew either at sea or on land. We operated close to Kuwait and, in addition to the mine threat, were now within range of Iraqi Silkworm missiles. High levels of alertness were required as the ships used the radar-reflecting Hout oil rigs as a permanent missile trap. The northern Gulf was a very unpleasant place to be due to the persistent stench from oil slicks and the occasional decomposing body floating by. Added to this were the cold, dark 'nuclear winter' effects created by a blanket of heavy oil smoke from the extensive fires ashore.

We observed a large American and British Amphibious Task Group proceed into the northern Gulf and later learned that this was a feint to tie down Iraqi forces in Kuwait while the main offensive proceeded inland. Some ships from the Task Group continued into an area within ten miles of our position which, according to intelligence reports, was heavily mined. USS *Tripoli* (a helicopter carrier) and USS *Princeton* (an Aegis cruiser) struck mines. *Sydney's* Seahawk helicopter was first on the scene and ready to provide medical evacuation.

The Air Raid Warning remained RED (indicating that air/missile attack was in progress) as numerous Silkworm-related electronic emissions were detected. We heard a number of explosions including a loud and seemingly close explosion, accompanied by a bright flash, which rocked our ship. Debris with Chinese markings was later found in the vicinity, indicating that a Silkworm missile may have impacted on one of the oil rigs.

In this highly complex and constantly threatening environment *Sydney* maintained high levels of readiness around the clock for 47 days (as did *Brisbane*). The ship's company was divided into two equal teams, called Port and Starboard watches. A combination of fear, boredom, occasional interruptions to sleep, lack of daylight, the cocktail of drugs and extremely limited opportunities for rest and recreation caused continued fatigue. Gradually, but inexorably, the efficiency of all on board was affected. People became increasingly tired and short-tempered. Although it is difficult to assess in retrospect, we had probably moved into a potentially dangerous state of fatigue.

The captain's routine

Although not a watchkeeper I was constantly on call. A captain's sleep was frequently interrupted in the Gulf War environment. The sheer volume of shipping and air traffic created many situations requiring command attention. Modern communications, data links and the comprehensiveness of intelligence and surveillance information meant that there was a vast quantity of information to assess. The officers and sailors on watch could do this, and only called me with information of an urgent or important operational nature. Many of the calls came in the dark hours of the night, and it was essential that I could be instantly alert, able to assimilate information quickly, listen to the advice of my officers and make my assessment. I settled into an afternoon siesta routine, slept fully-clothed and supplemented the siestas and short periods of sleep at night with catnaps. Throughout this period I rarely achieved more than two hours of uninterrupted sleep.

Sydney proceeded to Dubai for three days' rest and recreation toward the end of the war, and I spent a couple of nights in one of the many four-star hotels. I felt in need of space away from the ship in which to unwind. I checked in and made a loose arrangement to meet some of the officers later in the evening for a drink. The fully-stocked cocktail bar, large bath and king-size bed all looked very inviting. I made myself a gin and tonic, which tasted exquisite after more than six weeks without alcohol. After a soak in the hot tub I lay down on the bed for what was intended to be a short nap. Twelve hours later I awoke, and realised that I had missed the evening's entertainment but felt mightily refreshed.

Commander Lee Cordner, RAN, on the bridge of HMAS *Sydney*, December 1990. 'As the operational tempo increased I noticed that the captain spent more and more time on the bridge or in the operations room. The captain's chair became not only the centre of his immediate command responsibilities, but also his office, dining area and bed.' Lieutenant-Commander Nigel Perry, RAN, Executive Officer, HMAS *Sydney*. (D. Illyes)

The homecoming

Sydney returned from the Gulf War in April 1991. I felt a strong sense of relief that our tour was over, but the homecoming was in some ways embarrassingly over the top. We were grateful for the recognition but bemused by all the fuss. We had done our job and there was no doubt of the reality of the risks we had faced, but because we had not lost lives or taken casualties there were some, particularly in the ex-service community, who felt that we did not rate the same status as those who had gone to war before. To some extent I was disappointed that we had not fired missiles and guns in anger, despite the fact that we had operated in the maritime front line of the war. But such was the nature of the conflict.

PREPARING FOR OPERATIONS IN THE NORTH RED SEA

After *Sydney* returned from the Gulf War she underwent a leave and maintenance period and a 57 per cent crew change. The situation in the Middle East had stabilised, but UNSC Resolutions against Iraq continued to ensure compliance with the terms of the cease-fire. In August 1991 *Sydney* was ordered to make preparations for a second deployment.

The news was greeted with mixed emotions on board. Many 'old hands' were less than enthusiastic at the prospect of spending a second Christmas away from home. They believed we had done our job during the Gulf War. Newly-joined members of the ship's company were generally excited at the prospect. Many felt that they had missed out on the Gulf War and were keen to prove themselves.

My main leadership challenge included bringing *Sydney* back to a war standard with little assistance from the Fleet trainers, many of whom were otherwise engaged. To a considerable extent I was put in the un-enviable position of being team captain, head coach and assessor. The work-up was made more difficult by some 'old hands' cynically questioning the need to undergo another broadly-based preparation for conflict. It was hard to convince them that the Middle East remained a dangerous and uncertain part of the world.

Readiness standards were achieved, but establishing the 'contract of trust' proved elusive until we were well into the deployment. A lesson here is that Australian officers and sailors will challenge conventional wisdom, which can be both a benefit for and an additional demand on leadership. Trust and support must be earned and require patience, careful communication and the will to persist. People must be convinced that the goal of their preparation is both important and necessary. The extraordinary levels of personal commitment needed to operate a warship at a high degree of proficiency cannot be attained until this conviction has been achieved. The captain must lead vigorously in this attitude and this task.

THE NORTH RED SEA MARITIME INTERCEPTION FORCE

In October 1991 *Sydney* began operations as the first Australian ship to participate in the North Red Sea Maritime Interception Force (NRS MIF). As the Australian Task Group Commander, I was given a concise operations order and rules of engagement that were both clear and expansive. During my farewell call on the Maritime Commander, he said he had complete confidence in me and would back fully any decisions I had to make. He then bade me farewell and wished me good luck, knowing he would not see me for six months.

While I relished the opportunity of independent command for such an important mission, the significance of my responsibilities took a little while to sink in. We were to represent Australia in a multinational operation thousands of miles from home with the eyes of the world upon us. It was during this operation that I would really come to understand the phrase 'the loneliness of command'.

We spent between ten and 21 days on station on average, boarding three merchant ships per day. We would then take a short break in an Egyptian or Saudi port (the options were few given our location). At first the task was interesting, but it soon became repetitious and routine. An attitude of 'This is boring' soon developed among the crew, along with 'Why do we need to maintain vigilance?'. But I knew we had to keep up standards and stay alert. We were in a potentially dangerous part of the world and the risks of our operations were greatly reduced by our remaining very professional and vigilant.

Keeping the ship's company interested and convinced of the need for high readiness became a challenge. We developed a close relationship with the American and French warships with whom we worked who had great respect for the aggressive and competent way in which we prosecuted our mission, and in many ways ours became a coalescing role. We encouraged short personnel exchanges between the other navies and tried to program unusual and fun exercises to break the tedium of the operational work.

The day before the first Middle East peace talks in late October the uncertainty of our circumstances was demonstrably sheeted home. *Sydney* was on station in the van of the NRS MIF patrol area when, without warning, several air contacts were detected by the alert team in the operations room. The contacts were closing very fast from the direction of Israel and Jordan. *Sydney* was immediately brought to Action Stations, not because we genuinely thought an attack likely, but to bring all the weapons and sensor teams to the highest state of readiness so we could respond if necessary. The aircraft swept west over the Sinai Peninsula before turning over the NRS and conducting a low pass over *Sydney*. We could clearly see the Star of David tail markings on the Israeli jets. The Egyptian Air Force responded by launching fighters from the Hurghada airbase to the west of our position. Simultaneously an Israeli patrol boat approached from the Straits of Tiran and passed through our force. The incident served to remind the ship's company where we were and how quickly things could change.

As this was our second Christmas in succession on operations we were given approval to proceed through the Suez Canal to Piraeus in Greece for rest and recreation. This was a great boost to morale and a welcome break from the tedium of the MIF operations. I again observed the heightening of emotions that separation from family during the Christmas period brought to the ship's company.

In all, *Sydney* safely boarded 219 merchant vessels of all types and sizes and of many nationalities. The boardings were conducted efficiently and effectively with minimum disruption to the vessels concerned, while scrupulously enforcing the UN mandate. At the end of my *Sydney* command I felt burnt out. Yet I was fortunate to have had the opportunity to command at sea during such a busy operational period.

HMAS *ADELAIDE*

On joining *Adelaide* in May 1997 I was dismayed to find tolerance of sub-optimal standards of maintenance and operational performance. There had been a significant turnover of personnel and little real teamwork was evident. My initial leadership challenge was to get *Adelaide* to an acceptable standard of readiness and to re-establish her in her rightful place as a leader in the Fleet.

On the basis of previous experience, I decided the best way to get results was to develop a sense of purpose and create some pressure to succeed. Many on board had become accustomed to the relatively easy pace of life in a ship in refit, others had not been to sea before and had no real conception of what it was all about. I agreed upon a program with the Commodore Flotillas (COMFLOT) to complete a full work-up in four weeks instead of the usual six. This would enable us to sail immediately on deployment to Southeast Asia, primarily to represent Australia at the Philippines Centenary International Naval Review, a considerable 'carrot'. But we had to achieve operational readiness standards first. Warships have no time to go home and train when an operational contingency or emergency arises.

Some experienced sailors on board and some Fleet staff felt the plan was overly ambitious and unachievable. I had to convince the dissenters that what we were about was important and necessary. The essence of creating a winning team was not to give up but to select achievable goals and press on.

We had some significant technical problems to resolve which almost derailed the plan and placed great strain on my engineering personnel. We performed poorly in a progress evaluation after two weeks at sea, and it was suggested that we were being impeded to some extent by a poor attitude. This was particularly evident among some senior sailors who were meant to be role models. I sat down with each group in turn and discussed the perception that some of them were letting the side down. Most were embarrassed that their loyalty, competence and commitment had been questioned and it was clear that they wanted to be part of something worthwhile. They wanted to be proud of their achievements.

The *Westralia* tragedy

Adelaide's achievement of the necessary standards would be a close-run thing. On the morning before the final readiness evaluation fate played a hand. *Adelaide* was 25 nautical miles to seaward of Fremantle, conducting Replenishment at Sea operations with HMA Ships *Success*, *Darwin* and *Sydney*, when we received the chilling news that the tanker HMAS *Westralia* was close off Fremantle and fighting a major machinery space fire. Details were sketchy at that stage but a fire in a tanker is one of the most frightening naval scenarios imaginable.

Adelaide assumed the role of On Scene Commander to coordinate support, and all ships were ordered to proceed at best speed to *Westralia*'s aid. The group's helicopters were brought to immediate readiness and other preparations made. As we closed I was able to speak with the Commanding Officer of *Westralia*. We knew each other well and I quickly understood the extent of the fire and offered him as much practical and personal support as possible.

Late in the day, with *Westralia*'s situation under control, *Adelaide* anchored in the lee of Garden Island. I received details of the loss of four lives and immediately briefed the ship's company. The naval community is a tight-knit one and the victims were well-known to many on board. We all felt that we had lost shipmates. Given the stress and emotion of the events of the day, COMFLOT asked me if we should defer *Adelaide*'s readiness evaluation. I decided that it was better to continue with the program than to allow people to dwell on the tragedy.

That evening I led a brief memorial service, as our Chaplain was still on board *Westralia* as part of the Critical Incident Stress Management debriefing team. The next day, after a flat start, the *Adelaide* team performed creditably. It was particularly noted that damage control incidents (battle damage, fire and flood) were attacked with considerable vigour.

A mixed-gender warship

Adelaide was my first mixed-gender warship and initially I felt some apprehension about this. Running a mixed-gender warship involves potential pitfalls if not managed correctly; indeed, equity problems sit alongside navigational incidents, loss of classified material and indiscretions with public monies as the major issues that can bring a commanding officer undone. I was determined to ensure an equitable environment in which all members of the ship's company could perform at their best. At every opportunity I reinforced the belief that every person had a valuable contribution to make. I required mutual respect for all, and expected every person to pull his or her weight for the good of the team.

The small number of equity-related incidents were addressed early and effectively. A mature and steady atmosphere was then considered normal, and after we had worked the ship up I was confident *Adelaide* could undertake any challenge. We could rise to a level of war-preparedness if required. Our performance was recognised with the award of the highly coveted Duke of Gloucester Cup for best ship in the Fleet in 1998.

PEACETIME EXERCISES AND DEPLOYMENTS

Even peacetime naval operations carry risks which place considerable and continuing pressure on commanding officers. Life at sea is demanding, and realistic training is essential. The slightest miscalculation can result rapidly in near misses or tragedy. There were a number of close calls during my period in command of *Adelaide*, which reinforced the need for command vigilance when manoeuvring close to other ships.

I was fortunate to be the Commander Task Group (CTG) during several major exercises and a number of deployments of groups of ships around Asia. The CTG role adds considerable pressures to the command of one's own ship. It requires planning and then implementation of the tactical or deployment plan, exercise or operation. Importantly, the CTG takes overall responsibility for the outcomes. These were often complex situations involving many ships and aircraft and thousands of people, perhaps operating in the confined waters of the Great Barrier Reef, Bass Strait or Southeast Asia. Managing personal fatigue was always a major consideration, as a CTG needs a clear head for running both the Task Group and his own ship. Many factors seemed to conspire against this and I catnapped routinely during the day or night, as I had during my *Sydney* command.

An example of the CTG's role in a real-world operation was in preparing to evacuate Australian citizens and others during the crisis surrounding the end of the Suharto regime in Indonesia. I was appointed as CTG and Naval Component Commander of a four-frigate force (HMA Ships *Adelaide*, *Newcastle*, *Canberra* and *Torrens*) and tasked to make preparations and stand by in Indonesian waters. We were subsequently informed that other nations' naval units en route to the area might also be placed under my tactical command.

We planned the naval aspects of the operation, which necessitated negotiating with Indonesian naval officials in Surabaya, since their co-operation would be essential to success. One of the first major tasks was to embark several additional helicopters flown into Surabaya from Australia and there were numerous legal, logistic and other matters to consider. All arrangements progressed satisfactorily, however, and the Task Group was soon ready in all respects to support an evacuation, having evaluated carefully the considerable potential risks and challenges of this operation. Fortunately the evacuation ultimately was not required.

CONCLUSIONS

Command at sea places extraordinary demands upon those who are fortunate enough to exercise it. Whether in war or peace the significant leadership challenges of developing and sustaining a high-performing team require skill and persistence. A 'contract of trust' between the captain and the ship's company must be established, so that psychological as well as physical preparations are sound. This is essential, since conducting operations in the harsh and unforgiving sea environment requires exceptionally high levels of commitment as well as fortitude from ordinary young men and women.

Routine challenges in command include long deployments away from base support, family and friends; sustained fatigue from sleep deprivation; and responsibility for the performance and safety of many young men and women and hundreds of millions of dollars worth of equipment. There are also exceptionally short decision timeframes, the outcome of which can mean life, death, or serious injury or damage, even in peacetime operations. The margins for error are small and the stakes can be very high. Mishandling an internationally sensitive diplomatic or operational situation can, for example, have significant national security and political implications. The modern commander has to guard against information overload and the behavioural pitfalls of autocracy, while dealing with the isolation of command.

In times of war the responsibilities are increased as fear, uncertainty and the penalties for mistakes are intensified. The strain on the commander of providing calm, decisive leadership in the dynamic and complex environment of modern, technologically-dominated warfare can be intense.

Despite the challenges, command presents considerable opportunities for professional achievement. Leading a high-performing team and participating in the development of excellent young men and women is highly satisfying. The considerable responsibilities, pressures and risks were, in my case, more than adequately offset by the ultimate self-actualising experience for a naval officer: command at sea.

Part III

The warrior and his foe

15 | The faceless foe

Perceptions of the enemy in modern naval battle

David Stevens

WRITING ABOUT NAVAL BATTLE, John Keegan has remarked that there is 'a profound and powerful set of values that inhibits the waging of maritime war, roughly summarised by the phrase "fellowship of the sea"'. What this implies, Keegan continues, 'is a code of mutual self-interest: today's well-found mariner is tomorrow's derelict, dependent for his life on the help of a passing stranger'.[1] In effect, there are times when the shared traditions of the sea have been accused of placing loyalty to one's profession and fellow professionals above loyalty to a nation or cause. Accustomed in peacetime to stand by any craft in distress, some sailors have admitted to a combination of 'awe and dismay' as they watched their warship destroy another vessel in battle.[2] Others, while willingly sinking enemy ships, claimed never to have felt animosity towards their crews, since 'every sailor wore the blue uniform with three stripes around the collar—a tie that bound us all'.[3]

Notwithstanding the power and significance of such cross-cultural bonds, there are those who would counter that war at sea is essentially about surprise, aggression and striking first. 'Fast-paced, deadly and decisive' is the description used by one recent exponent of naval tactics,[4] a detached and impersonal bias increased by continuing developments in

263

information and weapons technology. Senior thinkers and practitioners of maritime warfare have likewise rarely expressed sympathy with suggestions that concepts of morality might constrain naval operations. The American strategist Rear Admiral Alfred Thayer Mahan deprecated the view 'that the objects of a war are to be sacrificed to the preservation of life',[5] while Britain's Admiral Sir John Fisher proclaimed that the 'essence of war is violence' and that 'moderation in war is imbecility'. Although he was prone to exaggeration, Fisher's general rule was reportedly '(1) Give no quarter; (2) Take no prisoners; (3) Sink everything; (4) No time for mercy'.[6]

Clearly, the average sailor has little need to think in strategic terms, does not normally command a ship of war and can more readily indulge humanitarian ideals. But this apparent dichotomy between 'brotherhood' and 'ruthlessness' offers a clue as to how the psychological dynamics of war waged at sea are sometimes more complex than operations on land and in the air. Central to this issue is the manner in which the combatants perceive and treat their foe, not simply in terms of national stereotypes but also in the way context, culture and professional training influence attitudes. Despite the trend in postmodern warfare towards automated tactical processes, the spirit with which the enemy is engaged remains an important area of research and one which has seldom attracted in-depth study.[7] Lack of space prevents this chapter from offering a comprehensive analysis of human interaction in maritime conflict, but by shedding light on some aspects of Australian naval wartime experience it may provide a glimpse into the chaos.

'FOR THOSE IN PERIL ON THE SEA'

In the introduction to his classic novel *The Cruel Sea*, Nicholas Monsarrat—himself a veteran of wartime convoy work and frigate command—classifies the long and brutal Battle of the Atlantic as 'the worst of any war'.[8] The German enemy rates no mention in Monsarrat's *dramatis personae*, however, for as his title telegraphs, 'the only villain is the cruel sea itself'. The point is well made, for few professions require men and women to put themselves at hazard as consistently as navies do; and it is the idea of the uncompromising sea as the first and common foe of mariners which underlies any sense of fellowship. Man, after all, is essentially a land animal, and seamanship is not a skill acquired effortlessly. Generations of seafarers have used this contention to reinforce a sense of superiority over landsmen, most of whom seem sublimely indifferent to matters nautical. Naval professionals in particular feel themselves a breed apart, as a verse familiar to eighteenth–century seamen made clear:

How little do the land-men know
Of what we sailors feel,
When seas do mount and winds do blow!
But we have hearts of steel.
No danger can affront us,
No enemy shall flout,
We'll make our cannons right us,
So toss the can about.[9]

The key difference between the two environments is that, unlike the land, the sea is always in motion, and those who regularly go out in ships and experience the sea's many moods have grown accustomed to treating it with respect. Unforgiving of any human weakness, the ocean's unending motion puts great stress on men and equipment, while wind, water and hidden hazards have often proved more powerful opponents than the declared enemy. For good reason the wartime naval prayer makes no attempt to differentiate between friend and foe, beginning instead with a plea that God 'who rulest the waves of the sea . . . Preserve in thy gracious keeping all those who journey thereon'.[10]

The need to maintain professionalism as both seaman and warrior is the feature which most consistently distinguishes the sailor from the soldier. It is one of the ironies of the First World War that, while the Australian Imperial Force (AIF) suffered 65 per cent battle casualties, the Australian Navy lost far more men to maritime accidents and drowning than it did to enemy action. HMA Submarine *AE1*, which disappeared without trace or explanation in September 1914, was not only the Navy's first materiel loss in wartime, but also its worst single human disaster of the war. The maritime environment proved just as dangerous to Australian sailors during the Second World War. In June 1944 the requisitioned stores carrier HMAS *Matafele* disappeared with all 37 of her crew while on a routine passage through the Coral Sea, the vessel believed to have foundered in the unforgiving ocean swells. Almost lost was the destroyer HMAS *Nizam*, which was hit nearly simultaneously by a heavy squall and freak wave off Cape Leeuwin on 11 February 1945. She rolled more than 80 degrees to port, seemed to lie over for a second or two, and ten ratings were hurled or washed overboard and drowned.

The effects of a freak wave, however, pale in comparison with those of the small but violent typhoon which overtook the USN's Task Force

HMNZS *Kiama* in 'roughers'. 'I remember one night in the [Great Australian] Bight when we rolled past the inclinometer and kept going. I thought we were a goner. To be at sea in a corvette when the weather is bad is awesome. The tiny ship sinks into the trough as the wave towers over it, then rises at great speed to crest the wave. Despite the weather "normal" life still went on, ship and sailors to be kept clean, meals to be prepared and eaten.' Ordinary Seaman A. Grimmer, RANVR, HMAS *Ipswich*. (RAN)

38 in the Philippine Sea in December 1944. Buffeted by extremes of wind and sea, three destroyers capsized and sank with practically all hands, while five aircraft carriers, a cruiser and three destroyers suffered serious damage. In all some 790 men died and 146 aircraft were either swept overboard or written off through impact damage and fires. On the fringes of the tempest, HMAS *Quiberon* was badly battered, while her engineers found themselves on watch below for more than 30 hours 'as it was impossible to cross the weather deck'.[11] Seven years later, Typhoon Ruth, the most destructive storm of the season, struck the Allied fleet during the Korean War and severely disrupted air and surface operations. Australia's then largest warship, the 19 800-ton aircraft carrier HMAS *Sydney* (III), survived a night of terror which saw her pounded by huge waves, sending tremors from bow to stern and back again. Noise was everywhere, a combination of 'the boom of the wind, the creak of the working ship, the crash of mountainous seas against the ship's side, the hiss of spray on the deck'.[12] To add to the fears of all hands came the pipe 'Fire, fire, fire' as electrical equipment short-circuited. No personnel

were lost, but *Sydney* suffered far more damage in her brief encounter with the typhoon than came her way from the hands of the communists.

To be sure, according to the idealised and romantic view of naval service, the sailor's spirit is sustained by the special relationship evolved from the oneness of ship, sea and sky. Not atypical was the Australian seaman who explained that although he never quite conquered seasickness, there were still times when he could 'marvel at the magnificence of a stormy sea'.[13] There is doubtless real strength to be gained from the mariner's evocation of the ocean's 'magic, mystery and wonder', but this inspiration is generally tempered with reality.[14] After the tragic incident in *Nizam* many of her surviving crew suffered bouts of nervousness and insomnia and some suffered the after-effects of the shock for a considerable time.[15] Once deprived of his ship through accident or enemy action, the sailor is well aware of his exposure to a faceless elemental force which plays no favourites. Having escaped the sinking of HMAS *Perth* at the Battle of Sunda Strait, Chief Petty Officer Ray Parkin endured ten hours drifting alone in the dark before the glimpse of an island brought renewed hope. Yet, exhausted and half-blinded by fuel oil, he still faced a further demanding swim across a strong current which threatened to sweep him past safety and back into open water:

> Several times he thought how easy it would be to stop swimming. How comfortable it would be! . . . He knew something of the power of the sea because he had spent years on it, and he did not delude himself: there was the shore; here was he. Between them lay water—absolutely impersonal water—which did not care whether he lived or died; which was kinder and gentler to a lowly mollusc than to him.[16]

Some 100 *Perth* survivors doggedly made their own way ashore, albeit to spend more than three brutal years as prisoners of the Japanese, but they could at least be thankful that their ship sank in tropical waters. In the extreme cold of a North Atlantic winter a man in the water might measure his life expectancy in minutes. Indeed, a study of Canadian casualty rates during the Second World War found that the percentage of personnel seriously wounded or killed by the damaging action was usually less than 5 per cent.[17] The vast majority of deaths occurred afterwards, with the most important variables being the length of time taken for the ship to sink—the longer the time, the more orderly the abandonment allowing a greater number of lifeboats to be launched—and the period before authorities called off the search for survivors. British research held similarly that once a man had reached the relative sanctuary of a lifeboat or raft he was three-quarters of the way to safety.[18] More than 50 per cent of lifeboats adrift for more than 24 hours were recovered within five days and it was exceptional for a lifeboat not to be picked up within three weeks.

Such exceptions nevertheless occurred, particularly in the less-travelled expanses of the Indian Ocean, and hence longer-term endurance also depended upon good leadership and adequate fresh water. The presence of both these factors meant survival for the last 35 men of the liberty ship SS *Peter Silvester*, which was torpedoed 700 miles off Fremantle on 6 February 1945. Most survivors were recovered within a week of the sinking, but two lifeboats still remained unaccounted for when Australian authorities abandoned the search on 22 February. Another week passed before a warship on passage found the first of the missing boats. Its 20 occupants had suffered through two tremendous storms and had eaten the last of their meagre provisions four days before being recovered. The last lifeboat was not found until almost five weeks after the sinking, having sailed and drifted nearly 1100 miles. The fifteen men on board had run out of food after only 12 days and milk tablets a week later, after which they had been sustained on nothing but canned water and the occasional rain squall.

Conversely, a lack of both fresh water and adequate refuge was central to the tragedy which befell the men of HMAS *Armidale*. An attack on the corvette by Japanese aircraft in December 1942 left 102 survivors adrift in the Timor Sea with only a damaged motorboat, a badly holed whaler, a Carley float and a makeshift raft to support them. The motorboat and whaler attempted to reach land and were found after six and eight days respectively, but the 48 men left behind were never recovered. Conditions were extreme and even those rescued were already in an appalling state, severely dehydrated and collapsing as soon as they tried to stand up. A seaman in the rescuing ship HMAS *Kalgoorlie* described them as 'a pitiful sight' with 'sunburnt, blistered and ulcerated skin covered in caked fuel oil and salt. They were wrinkled up like prunes. Their rib cages stuck out. Some were bleeding from the backside. Their eyes were glazed, they were disorientated with very little recollection of what had happened . . .'.[19]

The combined enemies of the *Armidale* men were the merciless tropical sun, constant immersion and two equally frightening natural predators—sea snakes and sharks. The two-metre long sea snakes were both venomous and aggressive, uncaring as to whether they had coiled up on a live body or a dead one. Those survivors still strong enough to splash initially could frighten off the sharks, but they soon returned to nose around the dead and wounded. Often seeming to act in unison, the sharks circled the raft 'just like the Japs had circled the ship' and 'would attack almost as if they had been ordered in by the master shark'.[20] Sharks regularly feature in the tales of Australian sailors and although their reputation for viciousness is undeserved, comparisons with the human foe are common. Beaten by a school of sharks to the crash scene of an American bomber, HMAS *Kapunda*'s Sick Berth Attendant Mal 'Doc' Williams declared that he had doubled the entries on his 'list of hates': 'I now had two: Japs and sharks'.[21]

MOTIVATION AND CONTEXT

The majestic and powerful sea may been 'their great antagonist and arbiter of their destiny',[22] but it is against the ships and seamen of other nations that sailors are employed to fight. Australian sailors have always been volunteers, and the ramifications and varieties of human nature have meant that there has been no single motivation to join the wartime Navy. Although reporters and politicians might prefer simple moral and ethical values and clear distinctions between 'good' and 'evil', few sailors have demonstrated a close interest in a particular ideology. Of greater importance in the midst of combat was inculcation into a fighting service whose *esprit de corps* was founded on centuries of history and tradition. Personal identification with the Service and loyalty to ship and shipmates did far more to blend individual and group motives than any appreciation of the war's higher aims.

There were, of course, men attracted by the 'great object' in 1914 and 1939, those who believed that 'Our cause is just and God will help us'.[23] For most, however, such inspiration could be neither sustained in their own minds nor respected in an opponent. One anecdote told of a German officer after the Battle of Matapan who made the mistake of raising his arm and crying 'Heil Hitler' as he was recovered by a British destroyer. A brawny Australian seaman unceremoniously grabbed him and threw him back over the side. Before hauling the German in again the Australian wagged his finger and said with quiet determination: 'Remember to salute properly when you come over the side of a British ship'.[24] Another story related the strange legacy left by the ships' companies of HMAS *Shropshire* and HMAS *Hobart* after their post-war visit to the site of the Emperor Hirohito's summer residence. The smattering of English picked up by the children of the town thereafter included the cry: 'Down with the Emperor! Ned Kelly for King'.[25]

The irreverent sense of humour displayed by Australian servicemen has always been a great boost to morale and has often been used to defuse fear and anxiety. More revealing in the context of naval battle,

Naval Aircraft Mechanic Frank Eyck at Camp Blackhorse, Vietnam, 1968. 'As a young man I joined the RAN with the expectations of going to war and fighting ships, not people—not men and sometimes women. I was not prepared, nor trained for anything else. As professional sailors we were prepared to go wherever we were sent, but most were totally unprepared for the sights and conduct of our war.' Able Seaman Frank Eyck, RAN, Helicopter Flight Vietnam. (F. Eyck)

however, was one war-weary sailor's observation when, after enduring three years of fighting, he finally set eyes on the defeated Japanese:

> I could not picture those men as shining young heroes, full of enthusiasm for the Emperor. It was just not real.
>
> As for us we had seen too much dirt and filth, bad food and rough seas to be feeling very much at all. We hated the war. All we wanted was to win and get out of it—to be in the company of girls, to live normally instead of watching the sunrise and wondering whether that dive bomber was one of theirs or ours.
>
> We had no ideas of glory, we had fought as a team.[26]

Although they offer many of our best insights into the emotions aroused by enemy personnel, such face-to-face encounters were infrequent. It was in the nature of twentieth-century naval warfare to fight at a distance and, since most members of a ship's company worked below decks or encased in armour, it was easy to feel that war at sea was waged primarily against unseen enemy machines rather than against people. Indeed, after weeks, months, or perhaps years engaged in an endless cycle of watchkeeping, the 'enemy' was most often an abstraction, perhaps hated for every inconvenience, but rarely imagined as an individual. Generally it was only at the end of an action, when the defeated party was in need of rescue, that the faceless foe became human at last.

'THE HUNS'—1914–18

With close contact a rarity, sailors tended to form judgements about their adversaries on the basis of second-hand and often propagandist reports rather than personal experience. This is not to say that there was always consistency in perceptions of enemy personnel, or that every enemy vessel was merely accorded the characteristics of the opposing regime. Sailors are not such simple creatures. This point is well-illustrated by the contrast between Allied attitudes to the German commerce raider SMS *Emden* as opposed to the feelings expressed more generally about the German armed forces.

Throughout the First World War, Allied propaganda sought to portray the Germans as savage aggressors: '. . . fierce brutal hordes . . . who are ignorant or choose to appear ignorant of the first rudiments of honour and fair play'.[27] This approach focused on Germany's alleged litany of misdeeds and used unflattering comparisons with 'civilised' ideals to dehumanise the individual enemy serviceman. 'The German sailor,' one narrative stated baldly, 'is a foe without a vestige of chivalry, as it is understood by British seamen.'[28] Such simplistic portrayals made it easy to see the enemy as the embodiment of evil, and that they struck a chord within the Australian Navy was evident from early in the war. In May 1915 HMAS *Pioneer* destroyed a small enemy vessel found hugging the East African coast. The target was 'blown to bits' and there were no survivors. In describing the incident the editor of *Pioneer's* newspaper declared himself 'very sad when such awful loss of life occurs, but we are at war now and if we didn't annihilate these pestilential Germans our own lives would pay the forfeit'.[29]

Germany's adoption of unrestricted submarine warfare in 1915 helped to sustain this sense of outrage at what seemed a patently alien enemy. Upon hearing of the loss of women and children in the torpedoing of the passenger ship *Lusitania*, Stoker P.N. Faust of HMAS *Australia* (I) confided in his diary that 'this crime is the most murderous and is the biggest and most cowardly the world's history has yet known. My God it makes a man's blood stir up to think of it and to think we can coax them out of their burrow to drive them to Hell'.[30] Three years later, Rear

Admiral F. Haworth-Booth, Australia's naval representative in London, expressed similar disgust at the entire catalogue of U-boat attacks: 'such brutalities which have stultified every tradition of the chivalry of the sea, and made the name of our enemy stink in the nostrils of every true seaman'.[31]

Rather than hunting down and exterminating a hated enemy, however, during the last years of the war Australian ships were most often employed on monotonous patrol work. Here they endured all the misery of the wintry North Sea, made worse by the constant menace of U-boats and mines, but had little or no opportunity to fight back. In 1917 the men of HMAS *Melbourne* still professed a hope 'that the detested Huns would come out of their hiding places to receive their well-merited punishment' but 'were afraid lest the opportunity of avenging the deaths of murdered men, women, and children should never come'.[32] The ongoing public campaign of vilification had clearly been successful. Seeking action, some men transferred to the AIF in France, while others internalised their frustration. As the war drew to a close Yeoman of Signals C.F. Geary, in *Australia*, pasted a favourite poem into his diary:

> You spied for the day, you lied for the day,
> And woke the day's red spleen
> Monster who asked God's aid Divine
> Then strewed the seas with the ghastly mine,
> Not all the waters of the Rhine,
> Can wash thy foul hands clean.[33]

It is against this background of damning portrayals of German conduct and of promises of just retribution that the action between HMAS *Sydney* (I) and *Emden* in November 1914 stands all the more proud. Almost uniquely among the units of the German armed forces, *Emden*'s conduct received accolades from her enemies. Since the opening days of the conflict the general opinion in the Allied press had been that *Emden* was 'having a wonderful career' and that her actions against shipping and facilities were 'sportsmanlike' rather than indiscriminate. Admiration of *Emden* naturally centred on the character of her captain, *Korvettenkapitän* Karl von Müller, whose chivalrous behaviour was said to have ensured that no non-combatant life was lost during the raider's rampages. The London *Evening News* called him 'a brave, ingenious and courteous gentleman, [who] had treated his prisoners very well and played the game'.[34] A correspondent of *The Times* took pains to explain to his readers that von Müller's action in using a disguise (a false fourth funnel) during his operations was a legitimate ruse of war, not one of the treacherous methods commonly employed by the rest of the German armed forces.[35]

Discussing *Emden*'s successes in the same spirit as one might a brilliant innings at cricket matched the public expectation of the British (and indeed Australian) way of warfare. But the perception of 'war as sport' was an attitude not always comprehended by the Germans or even the other Allies.[36] The English had 'no real understanding of the war', *Emden*'s First Officer remarked later. 'With them it is not—as with us—a war of the people.'[37] Propaganda from both sides, however, seemed to agree that *Emden*'s men had displayed consummate bravery when faced with almost certain defeat. The *Daily Telegraph* reflected that 'It is almost in our heart to regret that the *Emden* has been destroyed',[38] while *T.P.'s Journal of Great Deeds of the Great War* observed 'Fortunately the hero of [her exploits] was not killed' in a battle that had 'set the odds . . . against him'.[39] Meanwhile German authorities ensured that the name would live on by christening a second *Emden* and allowing her to display an Iron Cross on her stemhead in honour of her illustrious predecessor.

One recent study has argued that laudatory descriptions of *Emden*'s conduct in the Allied press lent credibility to negative portrayals of other German activities—the exception that proves the rule.[40] It is noteworthy, nonetheless, that his opponents' professional admiration and respect for von Müller was not simply a construct of propaganda. The first of *Sydney*'s officers to board *Emden* after her surrender wrote to his father that he found the German captain to be 'a very fine fellow', while *Sydney*'s Captain Glossop, RN, thought so much of his opponents' gallantry that he let von Müller and his officers keep their swords. The care and consideration lavished on the German wounded by the Australians certainly helped to dissipate any animosity and demonstrated to both sides that the enemy might be human after all. Given the unusual opportunity to associate closely for a few days after their battle, officers in *Sydney* and *Emden* came to the joint conclusion that 'it was our job to knock one another out, but there was no malice in it'.[41]

'THE ITIES'—1940–41

The recovery and treatment of the *Emden* survivors reflected a mixture of respect and humanity, the latter reinforced by the ancient custom of mariners to rescue those they find shipwrecked—without consideration of circumstance or nationality. International Law has attempted to enshrine this obligation and, as early as 1907, Article 16 of the 'Adaptation to maritime war of the principles of the Geneva Convention (Hague X)' ordered that: 'After every engagement, the two belligerents, so far as military interests permit, shall take steps to look for the shipwrecked, sick, and wounded, and to protect them, as well as the dead, against pillage and ill treatment'.[42] Actual engagements with the enemy were so infrequent between 1916 and 1918 that it was not until the fighting in the Mediterranean in 1940–41 that the RAN had to face this issue regularly. Germany was again the principal enemy, but it was against the Italian Navy that Australian ships were first committed in action.

Initially, Australian sailors showed little respect for an enemy they variously described as 'Ities', 'Dagos' and 'Wops'. They were aware that the Italian Navy possessed some fine-looking ships, was numerically superior to the British Mediterranean Fleet and was likely to receive better air support, but morale in the Australian ships was high and bravado encouraged belief in an easy victory. Reflecting on Italy's chances on the day Mussolini declared war, a diarist in HMAS *Voyager* commented: 'If [they] have got any sense they won't leave Italy'.[43] The Australians often imagined the Italian fighting man as being somewhat ludicrous, perceptions which were largely shaped by memories of home, where the only Italians they were likely to come across were restaurateurs. When HMAS *Stuart* forced the Italian submarine *Gondar* to the surface in September 1940, the enemy crew were taunted by the sight '. . . of a row of grinning Australian sailors who lined the rails of the destroyer, some shouting "Waiter!" and others urging the Italians to "hurry on with the fish and chips, Guissepe [sic]!" '.[44]

The common refusal of Italian ships to seek battle except on their own terms, and their half-heartedness when they did engage, reinforced the generally low Australian opinion of their fighting qualities. Often Italian naval prisoners were found to be young conscripts, pulled out of merchant ships, fishing boats, or schools just weeks or days before their capture. 'Many of them had never seen a gun before' admitted one prisoner in excusing the performance of his compatriots.[45] Australians saw the Italians' lack of self-discipline as another sign of weakness. One of *Voyager's* petty officers noted with distaste the contrast within a mixed group of survivors from a mined transport ship: '. . . the Ities mostly howling and moaning while our own, most of them injured terribly, not saying a word'.[46] Mark Johnston has remarked how Australian servicemen have often seemed preoccupied with qualitative comparisons between themselves and their opponents.[47] The lack of professionalism apparent in their prisoners contributed to the feeling among Australian sailors that the Italians were an enemy somehow unworthy of their martial talents.

Australians admired 'guts', however, and when this trait was observed in an opponent ridicule might easily give way to comradeship.

On 27 June 1940, *Voyager* and four British destroyers sighted the Italian submarine *Console Generale Liuzzi* on the surface and sped in to attack. The submarine submerged, but depth charges forced her back to the surface where she fought a brief gun action before surrendering in a sinking condition. *Voyager* recovered 13 of the survivors, some naked except for their escape gear. After tending to their immediate needs with donated clothing, cigarettes, coffee and sandwiches, the prisoners were placed in a small compartment under armed guard. By the following day *Voyager*'s ship's company had determined that their prisoners were 'Not a bad lot . . . They showed guts by opening fire . . . and surprised us by their show of bravery.' For their part the Italians were pleased to find that the Australians did not kill without mercy—as their own propaganda had warned—and thereafter proved quite talkative. The Australian ratings soon found areas of common interest. One Italian had visited Hobart before the war in the cruiser *Raimondo Montecuccoli* and had a better knowledge of the local sailors' haunts than *Voyager*'s own reservists. These discoveries further cemented relationships, not for the last time leaving some Australians to wonder what war was all about. During the voyage back to Alexandria all the prisoners were observed to be 'happy and bright [and] enjoying themselves'.[48]

The encounter between the cruiser HMAS *Sydney* (II) and the Italian destroyer *Espero* on 28 June 1940 left an even greater impression upon the Australians. Having been engaged by several units of the British 7th Cruiser Squadron, the enemy vessel was already dead in the water when *Sydney* was detached to sink her. To the surprise of *Sydney*'s commanding officer, Captain John Collins, RAN, *Espero* elected to continue the fight and fired several shells and a torpedo at the approaching Australian warship. *Sydney* replied in kind until the destroyer was in flames and her men were seen jumping overboard. After waiting for the Italian to sink—her ensign still flying—Collins closed the position. It was by now completely dark, but through the blackness came the shouts and screams of the Italians. To one rating 'It was the most awful sound I have ever heard. The water seemed to be alive with men crying and moaning. It was our first real naval battle, and for most of us it was a terrible experience. One of the gunners of our ship was sick. I felt rather the same way myself . . .'.[49] A petty officer described in his diary how *Sydney* stopped for an hour and picked up 47 survivors: 'Some had lost arms or legs while others were badly burned and everyone was covered with oil fuel. They looked a sorry sight. Our doctors and sick bay staff looked after the injured while we led the uninjured to the bathrooms and scrubbed them clean again. Each man was given a good meal, hot coffee and a blanket then bedded down for the night'.[50]

Cries for help could still be heard and before leaving to rejoin his Squadron Collins ordered that an empty cutter equipped with oars, provisions and water be left at the scene. Collins later wrote that his response was in part motivated by the reactions of his own men who, having been impressed by the destroyer's fighting spirit, were reluctant to leave the Italians to their fate.[51] These feelings ran deep. One gunnery rating admitted that the one-sided nature of the battle had forced him to blot out thoughts of the enemy: 'If you'd started to think you'd have stopped firing . . . After the *Espero* was sunk there was no pride aboard the ship. I think as a matter of fact, that we were all secretly ashamed of ourselves, because the Italians had shown that they had more guts than we had'.[52]

To compensate, the Australians lavished even greater attention on their prisoners. The following day 'it was a common sight to see our chaps shepherding groups of the Italians round our ship, giving them all the cigarettes that they wanted and treating them to ice-cream and soft drinks from the Canteen'. One badly burned Italian became 'the most admired man onboard' when, after a pessimistic assessment by *Sydney's* surgeons, he showed unexpected progress. The Australians gave him a special cheer as he was hoisted ashore in a stretcher and an even louder cheer when he managed to raise an arm in acknowledgement. Such fraternal feelings were evidently reciprocated for, disconsolate at the thought of going to a prisoner-of-war camp, some of the Italians expressed a desire to stay on board *Sydney* since the crew were such 'nice people'. [53]

Concern for enemy personnel was dependent upon circumstance, however, with the survivors of a submarine's attack far less likely to be offered immediate assistance. Moreover, a victorious commander always had to keep in mind the additional dangers to which his vessel might be exposed. Looking back, Collins reflected that, in view of the submarine threat, he was running an unacceptable risk in recovering the *Espero* survivors, and that he would not have done so later in the war.[54] Presumably he had been influenced by the orders issued by Admiral Cunningham three days after *Sydney's* successful engagement with the cruiser *Bartolomeo Colleoni* in July 1940. The CinC was annoyed that *Sydney's* accompanying destroyers had lingered to pick up survivors instead of pressing on with the chase of the second enemy cruiser, *Banda Nere*. Not only had *Banda Nere* escaped, but Italian aircraft had attacked the stationary ships and badly damaged HMS *Havock*. As Cunningham pointed out, 'a destroyer with a large number of prisoners on board is bound to be considerably reduced in fighting efficiency'.[55]

Cunningham made it clear to his commanders that the rescue of survivors must never be allowed to interfere with the military necessity of destroying the enemy, but he was not above making concessions himself. Before ordering the sinking of the disabled Italian destroyer *Artigliere* in October 1940 he gave the enemy time to abandon ship and allowed HMS *York* to drop Carley rafts. Concerned that submarines might be about Cunningham did not delay further and only HMAS *Vampire* recovered survivors, but the CinC sent a plain-language signal advising the Italian Admiralty of the position of the remaining rafts. This action evoked a howl of protest in certain London newspapers which were concerned not only that Italian sailors had been saved 'to fight against us another day', but that the action might have attracted a larger enemy force. The monthly periodical *The Navy* rushed to Cunning-ham's defence:

The recovery of *Bartolomeo Colleoni* survivors, 19 July 1940. 'Difficult and distasteful as it is to leave survivors to their fate, commanding officers must be prepared to harden their hearts, for after all the operations in hand and the security of their ships and ships' companies must take precedence in war.' Admiral Sir Andrew Cunningham, RN, CinC Mediterranean Fleet. (AWM 002654)

His Majesty's ships in action do not make war with kid gloves. But nothing is going to stop British seamen from succouring other seamen in danger of drowning, even if they are enemies who have just been defeated, however these enemies might behave if the position were reversed. It is not kid-glove fighting to refrain from massacring the helpless. We should be proud of our seamen for that they behave like men and not like savages, rather than urge them to imitate actions that all condemn.[56]

This response might be dismissed as empty bluster, but Cunningham himself admitted that '. . . the instincts of the British race and the traditions of the sea produce in us all a powerful urge to rescue the survivors of sinking ships'.[57] It was a tradition, furthermore, understood and appreciated by the enemy, one who deeply respected their opponent and believed that 'while the war may have produced atrocities and excesses on land, at sea the British and Italian navies fought each other cleanly and without rancour'.[58] Displays of humanity should not be associated with weakness. Throughout the war the Royal Navy's (and, by long association, the Australian Navy's) fighting spirit rarely wavered and this attitude permeated all levels of command. By contrast, in the Italian Navy the existence of this *fratellanza del mare* ('fraternity of the sea') had more profound implications. Before the war a great many Italian officers regarded Britain as their friend and ally, and when war finally broke out they 'took up their duties in the appalling knowledge that Italy's only salvation lay in losing the war'. Few illusions about Germany existed and 'the Italian Navy's attitude throughout the war was basically, despite Fascist propaganda to the contrary, one of defeatism'.[59] The Italians fought not to win, but to survive for another day.

'THE JAPS'—1941–45

If the war against the Italian Navy could be considered a contest between like-minded enemies, both acting within an accepted set of rules and conventions, the campaigns against the Japanese are more generally understood as displaying atrocious behaviour on all sides. Paralleling the Germans' portrayal in the previous war, the enemy was perceived in Australia as culturally alien, but with the added dimension of a deep racial hatred. Much of the pervading atmosphere built upon white Australia's traditional fear of Asian invasion. According to one of the more measured wartime accounts, the Japanese were 'an aggressive and covetous people possessed of a sense of destiny and a desire for world domination'.[60]

Among the first Australian sailors to come face to face with the Japanese were those from the ill-fated *Perth*, and Ray Parkin records that what scant information he and his shipmates possessed when taken prisoner was not reassuring. He recognised it as propaganda, 'designed to make people in comparative safety hate the enemy enough to continue to prosecute the war without further hesitation', but of little use to those in the immediate presence of the enemy.[61]

Without doubt, the professional capabilities displayed by Japanese forces in 1941–42 came as a profound shock to the Allies.[62] Pre-war intelligence reports commonly suffered from a racial arrogance which allowed 'myth, prejudice, and wishful thinking' to replace empirical observation and analysis.[63] General Blamey was not alone in his view that the Japanese were '. . . a curious race—a cross between the human being and the ape',[64] and in the early days many Australian sailors referred to them as 'yeller bellies', a term which conveniently combined racial slur and connotations of cowardice.[65] Those ratings with Mediterranean experience might have looked on with bemusement, but declarations of 'Let 'em all come' and 'They'll *never* take Singapore' were widely recorded from among the youngsters in *Vampire*'s ship's company.[66] Such impetuousness from 'baby Nelsons' disappeared rapidly after they had witnessed the sinkings of HMS *Repulse* and HMS *Prince of Wales* off Malaya.

German Stukas in the Mediterranean were likened to '. . . fiends from hell let loose'[67] but, having experienced the first air raids on Singapore, one of HMAS *Bendigo*'s crewmen admitted in a letter that 'the Japs are worse, or rather better bombers than the Germans'. While the Germans 'might use more planes, they drop their bombs separately. The Japs come over and they all drop at the same time, so that their objective gets properly plastered. They are very accurate too and don't waste too many bombs'.[68] The Japanese followed up their assaults fast and furiously, demonstrating potently that their pilots 'were neither "partially blind" [nor] inefficient'.[69] Incessant bombing attacks became the hallmark of Japanese air superiority, and one chief petty officer in *Hobart* made no effort to disguise his feelings to a journalist: 'Who was it said these men had no brains, no machines, and they cannot fight anyway? You ought to hear the loud "Haw! Haw!" "Oh, yeah!" aboard ship when that subject is brought up'.[70]

Notwithstanding dramatic evidence of their professional naval mastery, the Australian public continued to believe that the Japanese were racially inferior, and most found it hard to accept that the enemy might share any redeeming characteristics with Australian servicemen. In June 1942 Rear Admiral G.C. Muirhead-Gould, RN, faced considerable public criticism after his decision to accord full military honours to the Japanese crewmen killed in the midget submarine attack on Sydney. In his defence, Muirhead-Gould argued that 'theirs was a courage which is not the property or the tradition or the heritage of any one nation: it is the courage shared by the brave men of our own countries as well as by the enemy . . .'.[71] How much Muirhead-Gould's tribute was motivated by a desire to alleviate the conditions of Allied prisoners of war and how much by his own sense of chivalry is open to debate. However, as news of enemy atrocities spread, Australians were even less inclined to recognise the Japanese as an honourable and gallant foe.[72]

John Dower has rightly pointed out that 'The propagandistic deception often lies, not in false claims of enemy atrocities, but in the pious depiction of such behavior as peculiar to the other side'.[73] Less attention, however, is paid to the reverse of the coin, and although many Japanese servicemen displayed a callous indifference to the suffering of others, there were exceptions. Chaplain J. Mathieson, RAN, credited the enemy destroyer which recovered him and 200 other *Perth* survivors with doing 'a sterling job':

> Most of those they rescued were in various stages of exhaustion from fuel oil, sunburn and exposure. They were decently treated, drops were put in their eyes, they were given tea, biscuits and cigarettes, and in the time they were in the destroyer and under naval control they were reasonably looked after.[74]

Another *Perth* sailor later recalled the apology and warning he received from the Japanese captain on leaving the destroyer: 'You put up a good fight. I am very sorry, but now you are to be handed over to the military'.[75] Even Japanese submariners—responsible for a number of atrocities against Allied merchant seamen in 1943–44—were at times capable of showing empathy for a fellow warrior. In March 1942 the submarine *I-1* captured five Australian soldiers, found fleeing in a canoe from Timor. Unable to accommodate them inside the hull, the crew quartered the prisoners on the upper deck, provided them with overcoats, and gave them drinks and tobacco. 'Samurai,' one Japanese sailor recorded in his diary, 'should have a feeling for one another.'[76]

In their treatment of a respected adversary Japanese and Australian sailors evidently shared some common ground, but there remained significant cultural differences. Most obvious was the cult of dying, encouraged by Japanese commanders, and illustrated by the enemy's general reluctance to be taken prisoner. On the night of 3 August 1943 HMAS *Stawell* ran across an armed Japanese barge off the coast of

Celebes, and after a short, sharp engagement left it sinking. 'What shocked and amazed me,' wrote Wireless Telegraphist Geoff Brooks afterwards, 'was the number of Japanese, clearly visible in the light from my Aldis lamp, swimming DOWNWARDS into the depths. I received such a shock at that sight that I yelled out to them, "That's the wrong way you stupid so and so's".'[77] *Stawell* had orders to take prisoners for intelligence purposes but managed to recover only one exhausted officer from the more than 20 survivors counted. It was at this point that several ratings demonstrated another common Australian characteristic, having unilaterally decided that resuscitation was of secondary importance to plunder. The Japanese 'had no sooner hit the deck before our souvenir hunters had stripped him of everything that they could'.[78] Only after the intervention of one of *Stawell*'s officers were most of his possessions returned. When he had recovered the prisoner made it clear that he expected to be executed but, as a sailor in HMAS *Goulburn* later noted in similar circumstances, '. . . for some reason we don't fight that way'.[79]

Australian sailors' feelings about fighting the Japanese were seldom straightforward. The crew of a Fairmile motor launch in late 1944 were pleased and excited at the prospect of 'an opportunity of "shooting up" a few Japanese' in an inshore raid. Catching the enemy completely by surprise they killed at least five troops with the first burst of gunfire, and the remainder—including at least one badly-wounded man attempting to crawl away—were shot dead as they attempted to escape. For good measure the Fairmile riddled the huts where the Japanese had been living with small arms fire and then, her work done, returned to routine patrols. Commando raids by parties of seamen landed from the Fairmiles were classified as even more 'thrilling' for the participants.[80] Nevertheless, such close-quarters fighting was comparatively rare and there is little evidence of the individual hatred and vicious 'kill-or-be-killed' psychology common among the forces fighting ashore.[81] From the relatively remote perspective of their mobile fortress home, sailors appear to have had more ambiguous attitudes. Some managed to combine pragmatism and compassion in equal measure. Wireman Jack Daven recalled his feelings after depth charges from HMAS *Lithgow* sealed the fate of the submarine *I-124*: 'I felt a bit sorry for them but they were the enemy'.[82] Likewise, when *Shropshire* opened fire on the battleship *Yamashiro* at the Battle of Surigao Strait, one of her upper-deck gunners admitted that he 'could not help thinking of the Japanese sailors being killed as hit upon hit was called: then their tracer shells came slowly towards us—two fell short and four passed over and it didn't take much to realise that the next could be "it" . . .'.[83]

Deliberately killing a helpless enemy raised a different set of ethical problems. It would be naive to think that members of the Australian Navy were incapable of atrocities, but they do seem to have been less susceptible to using the excuse of military expediency to justify slaughter. There is certainly no record of disregard for international law comparable to that displayed by Allied air commanders after the Battle of the Bismarck Sea in March 1943. On that occasion, having decimated a Japanese troop and supply convoy, US and Australian aircraft systematically searched the seas for enemy survivors and strafed every raft and lifeboat they found. RAAF squadron reports admitted that these follow-up missions 'were most distasteful for the crews involved', but remained a 'terrible yet essential finale'.[84]

Concepts of moral conduct undoubtedly were being stretched for RAN sailors as the increasingly desperate Japanese resorted to aggressive suicide tactics. During the Lingayen Gulf operations *kamikaze* aircraft caused many casualties in HMAS *Australia* (II) and HMAS *Arunta*.

'Path of the *kamikaze*' by Frank Norton, 1945. 'When a Zombie (suicide plane) comes hurtling at you, you've got to kill him, but very quick—or he'll kill you! . . . A frightful crash, and a bursting, flaming torch seemed to sear right across the cruiser's bridge . . . We gasped as the *Australia* seemed ablaze in the roar of the explosion.' Petty Officer Ted Mitchell, DSM, RAN, HMAS *Shropshire*. (AWM ART23056)

Shropshire was also present but despite similar attention managed to avoid being hit. Even so, the provocation was extreme. On 6 January the third *kamikaze* of the afternoon disintegrated under the fire of one of *Shropshire*'s 8-barrelled pompoms. The enemy pilot was blasted from the wreckage and at about 500 feet appeared briefly to hang beneath his parachute, '. . . a Jap very much alive, arms and legs spread wide, for all the world like a four-pointed star'.[85] There were some cries of 'shoot the bastard' to the pompom captain, but 'this did not occur and nor was it necessary'.[86] Before reaching the sea the Japanese slipped from his chute and disappeared below the surface.

In the heat of battle it was always possible that fear and stress might confuse judgement, but there were also times when sailors could feel far more detached from the killing. This was most obvious in some of the final campaigns against the Japanese, when there could be no doubt that the war was won. During the invasion of Tarakan in April 1945 Allied naval and air superiority was almost complete and there was little risk to the bombardment ships of enemy counter-attack. For some sailors the Japanese were clearly of a lower order than their fellow human beings, and watching them die had become almost a matter of light entertainment. Having described the idyllic weather and glassy sea 'usually found only in romantic novels of the South Seas', an observer in *Hobart* found 'life becoming much more interesting' when groups of escaping Japanese were encountered in rafts:

> A single one was spotted and approached by a destroyer. The Son of Heaven lost two sons or gained two, it all depends which way they look at it, because the two occupants immediately blew themselves up with hand grenades. The report from the destroyer was brief and to the point. 'Explosion observed on raft and now there are two very dead Japs'.
>
> Shortly after a speck in the distance was identified as another raft. This contained more Japs some of whom were not such conscientious objectors to the idea of being taken prisoner. One was a Naval Medical Officer who could speak English. He was the first to swim to the destroyer and his enticements persuaded four others to follow him. The others were left to their fate which appeared in the form of two of our planes. Probably the pilots appreciated the break in the monotony of the afternoon patrol and swooped in joyous dives over them. The lines of spray rising behind them as they rose from their dive left no doubt as to the fate of the remaining Japs.
>
> At approximately 1900 the 5 prisoners were transferred to the flagship—one wounded and 2 suffering diarrhoea (this is considered in the circumstances, very understandable).[87]

CONCLUSION

In 1940 an Australian journalist asked one seaman, a 'husky A.B.' in *Sydney* (II), how he felt during a naval engagement. The sailor replied with commendable honesty:

> . . . it's all sort of mixed up. Before the ship opens fire we are all keyed up. Sometimes you find yourself trembling, not with fear, but with the strain of waiting. Then when the action begins, it's all excitement. It's just as if you're taking part in the most exciting bit of some sporting contest, a football match or a swimming race. If you know you're hitting the enemy there's a feeling of elation, the same feeling as if you've kicked a goal in a football game. That wears off after a few minutes, particularly if your own ship isn't taking any punishment. Then you see the hits smacking into the other ship, with the flashes and the smoke and the glow of red-hot steel, and you begin to put yourself in the place of the other chap and try to think what you'd be feeling if you were at the other end. That's where discipline and training come in handy. For a brief period you feel that you want to stop firing. The feeling passes. You know that if you did the other chap would just belt hell out of you. So you continue belting away, but you do it mechanically. You don't even seem to think. The feeling of elation has gone, but it has been replaced by a sort of cold efficiency, and then you seem to do your best work . . .[88]

This is an eloquent description of the inherent motivation of the professional warrior, one for whom—as Samuel Huntington has argued—military quality is independent of the cause for which he fights.[89] Australian sailors were neither automatons nor naively idealistic. They were possessed, however, of a unifying sense of purpose and a skilled technical proficiency, both of which arose from a time-tested professional naval ethic. That this ethic also encouraged a sense of fraternity among seafarers is undeniable. Experiences were diverse and attitudes to the enemy varied considerably, but when given the opportunity sailors found it relatively easy to conceive of their foe as their fellow man and demonstrate humanity in the midst of the most inhumane of enterprises without in any way lessening their offensive spirit or resolution. Rather, it seems to have given naval personnel a clearer insight into the difference between military necessity and wanton violence under the guise of military expediency. In a profession that involves the management of violence, wartime conduct is the ultimate test. Throughout the wars of the twentieth century, the professionalism of Australian sailors ensured that the means they used against the enemy were justified, and that they remained capable and respected representatives of the Australian government and people.

16 | Stress in war

The warrior's confrontation with the spectre of Death

Colin A. Wastell

IN ONE OF his most powerful passages, Alan Walker, the author of the official volumes on Australia's medical services in the Second World War, describes the stress and shock experienced by the men of HMAS *Australia* during the Leyte Gulf and Lingayen Gulf actions in 1944–45. The ship was severely damaged twice, suffered more than 150 casualties in all and on one occasion was exposed to five straight days of *kamikaze* attacks:

> All on board had an acute consciousness of being subjected to a new type of warfare, the suicide bomber. There was a fearful atmosphere of uncertainty. The men felt that their ship was singled out for special attack—a counter-attack on *Australia* in a double sense. Even if an enemy plane were 50 miles away, they were convinced that, among dozens of ships, it was coming straight for their own. After these assaults many exhaustion states were seen: men lost their grip, and cried out that they could stand no more.[1]

Of course, the experience of men and women who go to war can never be truly represented by mere words. The horror and trauma which they experience are known only to those who have faced battle themselves.

To discuss the concept of 'stress in war' is therefore to some extent an affront to the experiences of these men and women. As such, the thoughts presented in this chapter are offered reverently and in humility, fully mindful of the sacrifice and fears of those who have suffered in the wars of the twentieth century.

'WAR TRAUMA SURFACES 55 YEARS ON'

It has been well over 50 years since the last world war. It therefore surprises some to hear of the emergence of war-related traumatic memories and experiences so long after the conflict. The 50th Anniversary of the end of the Second World War in 1995 was a time of celebration, or so it was for those who did not face battle. Such events for those who have experienced war are often the occasions when they are brought face to face with memories which are both horrific and painful. They also re-experience grief and loss. A 1996 AAP News report on the National Centre for Post Traumatic Stress Disorder (PTSD) in Melbourne noted that 'During last year's "Australia Remembers" commemoration and its heavy media coverage, the unit found in a number of veterans, symptoms previously held under check flared up'.[2] It is important to note two things in relation to this report. First, the media coverage seemed to force veterans to confront their memories of the horrors of war. Second, the symptoms did not appear suddenly. *The veterans had been holding them in check.* This is important as it speaks to the enduring cost of war to those who experience it. The price of holding these symptoms in check is, for many veterans, very high.

'War trauma surfaces 55 years on':[3] this headline appeared in the *Weekend Australian* newspaper in June 2001. The article described the increasing occurrence of long-delayed PTSD symptoms in veterans of the Second World War. These veterans were not remarkable in any particular way in terms of mental health history or particular war service. The question 'Why now?' was, however, of interest to the veterans as well as to the professionals who were helping them. There seem to be two important issues for these veterans. First, they are at a stage of life when they are reviewing their achievements; looking back over what they have done and what they have been through. This review process can often lead to the remembrance of experiences long denied during a person's life. The second issue is apparently associated with the ageing of the human body. The processes of memory and the various structures of the brain change during older age. The medical practitioner quoted in the *Weekend Australian* article stated that as people grow older there is 'a part of the brain called the hippocampus which starts to degenerate, maybe there's something to do with that'. The identification of certain brain structures as important to the emergence of these symptoms has been a recent focus of the study of the aftermath of stress in war.

THE SYSTEMATIC STUDY OF WAR STRESS

1914–18

The First World War must rank as one of the greatest acts of organised horror ever seen. The Western Front in Europe with its trenches of mud, the fields covered with wounded and the astounding casualty figures all have etched this conflict into the mind of anyone even slightly familiar with its history and detail. Along with this horror came two important developments for the study of stress in war. First, there was a developing interest in the long-term memory of the battlefield experience. This had begun in the mid-nineteenth century but by the early twentieth century was much more advanced. Better care of the wounded meant that greater numbers of soldiers survived their injuries and returned to civilian life or, if fit, to the battlefield. The second development was the emergence of a field of study focused on the aftermath of human disasters. In peacetime such disasters included train derailments or large-scale industrial accidents. As with battle casualties there were many survivors of these disasters and the medical and legal professions were engaged in trying to determine the nature of the injuries suffered and the best way to treat them in order to return people to their former lives.

The horrors of the First World War took their toll not only in terms of physical injuries but also in the emotional reactions that rendered some soldiers unable to fight on. These people now would be described as having PTSD. In the early part of the twentieth century various terms were used including 'shell shock', 'war neurosis' and 'nerves'. The British Army recorded 80 000 cases of war neurosis during the war and there were 200 000 war-related 'nerves' pensions being paid afterwards.[4] These are staggering numbers when one considers the likely rate of under-reporting of a problem which at the time was perceived as socially and morally disgraceful. It was therefore important to the British Army that a physical cause be identified. If a physical cause could not be found then it was believed there must be large-scale cowardice occurring which, in turn, gave rise to very worrying implications from the point of view of the national will in prosecuting the war.

Initially it was thought that war neurosis was the result of a concussion to the blood vessels in the brain.[5] The First World War saw artillery bombardment on a massive scale. Since the shock of exploding shells caused such an impact on the bodies and hence brains of soldiers, it was logical that the blood vessels of the brain might be damaged. The problem with this explanation was that symptoms of war neurosis were often found in soldiers who had not been exposed to shellfire. This meant that an explanation had to be found elsewhere. There was, some studies noted, very little war neurosis in three groups: prisoners of war; soldiers with very serious wounds; and officers.

These groups of servicemen had all seen combat and all been exposed to severe blast, yet they were noticeable for their lack of war neurosis. In line with the ethos of British society of the day, the lack of evident war neurosis among officers was used to assert that the affliction was the result of moral weakness. There were several substantial flaws in this assertion, not the least of which was the fact that medical practitioners of the time did not diagnose officers with the same disorders as enlisted men.[6] As an officer one just could not have war neurosis, as one was morally and constitutionally superior to the other ranks. This attitude was one of the most disturbing features of the British response to PTSD patients. Apart from the work of W. Rivers,[7] much medical treatment bordered on the cruel. It included harsh physical assaults, even electrocution, in attempts to return the patient to duty. Nevertheless, this period did see the beginning of systematic study of stress in war. The medical profession was confronted by many thousands of sufferers whose recovery was slow and in many cases minimal. (It is also worth observing that the other two groups with relatively little PTSD were men who were not going to return to combat and were therefore not seen as culpable for not rejoining the battle.)

Abram Kardiner

In the prevailing culture of severe treatment recommended by most of the medical profession for 'curing' war neurosis, Abram Kardiner stands out as a beacon of humanity. He treated United States veterans of the First World War, and his work with them was not only humane but also observant. He studied his patients carefully, listened to their stories of the horror of combat and began to form an understanding of war neurosis as a realistic response to that horror. He asserted that any man could break down in the face of the fear of death in battle and that war neurosis could thus be seen as a form of hysteria. In the early twentieth century, however, hysteria was viewed as a disease of women. Sigmund Freud was one of the early researchers and, as a result of his and others' work, hysteria became seen as a constitutional weakness. The symptoms of war neurosis did clearly parallel those of hysteria, but such a thought could not be entertained by the male-dominated medical profession let alone by the military establishment.

Kardiner noted that war neurosis consisted of four central experiences:

- an extreme physiological arousal leading to a lowered threshold to stimulation;
- a readiness for fright reactions;
- a sense of futility about life; and
- the subject acting as though the traumatic situation is reality now.[8]

These features are the central experiences for those who have experienced combat or the fear of combat. One of the puzzles of the First World War was the development of war neurosis among those who served far behind the front lines. Those who serve behind the lines nevertheless experience indirectly the horrors of war through the mediums of returning soldiers, the stress placed upon commanders and the anxiety of fighting a battle when one is unable physically to carry out the orders.

1939–45

The work of Kardiner and Rivers was largely unknown during the inter-war years; indeed, Kardiner's first work did not appear until the Second World War had begun in Europe. But improved medical procedures and the unwillingness of commanders to repeat the slaughter of the First World War meant that battlefield survival rates were further improved, and this resulted in an even larger number of combat survivors returning to civilian life. These returning servicemen and women carried with them the consequences of exposure to stress in war and captivity. The brutality of both major theatres of war left former prisoners of war and internees with deep psychological scars. Unlike First World War survivors, however, the memories of battle stress were close at hand for many involved in the assistance offered to returning service people and Second World War survivors were assisted with both treatment and re-education programs.

Two very important studies published in the 1940s are relevant to this present discussion: *War Neurosis* by R. Grinker and J. Spiegel and

War Stress and Neurotic Illness by A. Kardiner and H. Spiegel.[9] These works treat comprehensively the topic of war-related trauma. They also bear witness to the impact of non-battle factors on the recovery of survivors. Grinker and J. Spiegel, for example, noted that recovery was predicated on unit morale and leadership, and also revealed that recovery from the harmful aftereffects of battle stress did not depend on an individual's character or background, but on the features of the unit to which he belonged. This implies that battle stress reactions potentially can affect anyone—the very thought that the military establishment in the First World War was not even willing to entertain.

Kardiner and H. Spiegel took this research a step further. From their work with returned servicepeople they asserted that both resistance to and recovery from war neurosis was predicated on two specific features of the veteran's unit: the individual's experience of relatedness to his unit and his confidence in its leadership. Thus they held that an individual's ability to cope with battle stress is very much a matter of the unit's social conditions. A feeling of 'fitting in' and confidence in the commander are features that are very important from the point of view of unit morale. Training in weapons and tactics is integral to military thinking but in terms of the stress of war, however, Kardiner and Spiegel asserted that for tactics and weapons to be used effectively, the morale of the unit was critical, not secondary.

This is no surprise to the many naval veterans who bear witness to the importance of belonging to a 'happy' ship, or a crew's admiration for their captain for keeping them safe. As noted by Alan Walker, despite such factors as 'the fear inseparable from the trials of aerial attack, domestic anxieties and discontent engendered by monotony and lack of leave and other amenities', RAN ships in the Mediterranean maintained an excellent level of morale:

> In fact, the most uncomfortable and even dangerous surroundings were
> cheerfully borne over long periods when men were inspired by the
> challenging nature of their duties and by leadership of a high order . . .
> On the Tobruk run, even when there was the added burden of patients
> in fighting ships, no complaints were heard.[10]

Korea and Vietnam

The experience of stress in any war or conflict is confronting and ghastly. The importance of the campaign or its technical interest does not lessen the horror for those confronted by the prospect of death and their own mortality. The Korean and Vietnam Wars demonstrated the impact of public perception in understanding and dealing with battle stress. Coming so soon after the total engagement of the Second World War, the public view of the Korean War was often in terms of a 'police action' or 'minor conflict'. Even the term 'conflict' seemed to imply that it was not really a war, and Korean veterans progressively felt themselves to be 'forgotten'. From the point of view of the servicemen and women involved, however, it was always a war, and one which they could not help but remember.

The Vietnam War likewise was a police action or a conflict in the minds of the public, although it was in fact the longest war in which Australians have been involved as combatants. This war, however, was associated with a most significant change in social attitudes. Vietnam saw the emergence of large-scale contemporary disillusionment with war and added to the experience of battle stress another aspect: that of societal rejection. Having experienced the horrors of war these veterans were reviled by many elements of Australian society. The veterans of the World Wars returned home heroes. The veterans of Vietnam were treated as villains and the collective shame of their treatment is a social blight on Australia as a nation.

Moreover, the serviceperson returning to Australia from Vietnam often did so far more quickly than in previous wars. In the space of 24 hours a soldier could be back safely in Australia with all the unreality produced by such a transition. Where was the time to de-stress during a long voyage home or extended deployment on peacekeeping or occupation duties? The experience of stress in war was magnified for these veterans because they were left with a sense of rejection mixed with traumatic memories unmitigated by a transitional period before returning home.

REACTION TO COMBAT

The systematic study of stress in war is a very difficult activity, one best approached through studying the survivors of war. A great deal has been learned by means of this approach. One of the most comprehensive studies of stress in war to date has been conducted in the Israeli Defence Forces. This is a study of Israeli veterans of the Arab-Israeli wars of 1967, 1973 and 1982, which identifies a syndrome called 'Combat Stress Reaction'.[11] The study's findings indicate that the syndrome can occur in soldiers exposed to combat irrespective of their age or degree of success in previous combat. It is produced by a set of psychological processes which relate to the complex world of personal, societal and

Table 16.1 Symptom grouping in combat stress reaction

Group	Category	Features
A	Distancing	1 Psychic numbness
		2 Fantasies of running
		3 Engaging in thoughts of civilian life
B	Anxiety	1 Possibility of paralysing anxiety
		2 Fear of death
		3 Thoughts of death
C	Guilt and exhaustion	1 Loss of sleep
		2 Fatigue coupled with thoughts of poor performance
		3 Signs of weakness
D	Loneliness and vulnerability	1 Loss of friends/unit members/countrymen
		2 Recognition that in death one is alone
E	Loss of control	1 Weeping
		2 Screaming
		3 Range of impulsive behaviours, e.g. bursting into rage
F	Disorientation	1 Difficulties in concentrating
		2 Difficulties making associations that they 'should' know

Source: Z. Solomon, *Combat Stress Reaction* (1993).

physical factors. The syndrome consists of the six groups of symptoms shown in Table 16.1.

These six groups or clusters of symptoms are very informative in attempting to understand the nature of stress in war. They represent the central aspects of the process of experiencing and reacting to battle stress. There are those symptoms in which bodily aspects are uppermost; for example, paralysing anxiety, loss of sleep, bodily weakness and fatigue. The second set of symptoms focuses on the psychological reaction to the confrontation with death: fantasies of running, thoughts of death, loss of friends and difficulty in concentrating. Such experiences constitute the normal reaction to being confronted with an extreme threat to one's own life.

The Israeli study of reactions to these three wars, only a few years apart, provided an opportunity to examine such questions as whether personnel can be 'inoculated' against war stress. Is this possible? The answer would seem to be a very qualified 'yes'. Successful service in one war, however, did not indicate an immunity to combat stress reactions in subsequent wars. The key to the issue of psychological invulnerability did not appear to lie in the moral or heroic character of the individual.

THE PSYCHOPHYSIOLOGY OF TRAUMATIC STRESS

The search for the cause of traumatic stress reactions has taken two divergent directions. The early attempts of Mott and others to locate the cause in damaged blood vessels of the brain is an example of the physicalist approach.[12] Freud and his followers represent the second approach, locating the cause in unresolved Oedipal conflicts and other psychological concepts. The symptoms of traumatic stress reactions derive from both areas, however, and the psychological cannot be reduced to the physical. The issue of meaning in trauma reflects a process of a higher order than mere neuronal firings. But recent developments in brain-imaging techniques have allowed the study of trauma survivors and their brains' functions while they are recalling their traumatic memories.[13] When this is coupled with general work on the functioning of the brain a coherent picture emerges as to the origins and process of the traumatic stress survivors' experience.[14]

THE DEVELOPMENT OF THE HUMAN BRAIN

The evolution of the human brain has resulted in the establishment of three interdependent systems:

- the brain stem, responsible for internal regulation, e.g. of temperature and the immune system;
- the limbic system, responsible for internal responses to external stimuli (NB the amygdala), e.g. adrenalin release for fighting; and
- the neocortex, responsible for analysing the external world (NB the hippocampus), e.g. the site of rationality and will.[15]

The limbic system

The central role of the limbic system is as an unconscious guide for the emotions which stimulate survival behaviour. The amygdala assigns emotional significance and values to incoming neutral stimuli. Most human information processing is done out of awareness and unless the amygdala assigns feelings of threat, reward or novelty the incoming information is not registered consciously.[16]

To understand the role of the limbic system in the response to traumatic stress it is necessary to understand also the modern view of human emotion. Western thought has in many ways relegated emotion to a

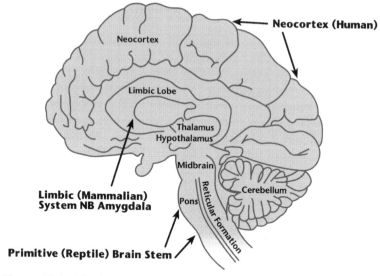

Figure 16.1   The human brain

position subsidiary to reason. This approach has been both challenged and rebuffed in the last 30 years by research showing that emotional processes are central to human functioning, not simply the handmaiden of thought.[17] For our purposes here, the following four findings are pertinent: the emotional system is separate from, although closely linked to, thinking or cognition; it motivates the individual to actions which assist survival; it plays both a facilitative and an inhibiting role in the cognitive processing of events; and it acts as an alert mechanism which is goal-directed.

Emotion is essential for survival and for learning.[18] The location of the emotional system in the limbic or mammalian section of the brain testifies to its primitive origins. The emotional system is hard-wired into the human body. The release of hormones is activated by emotional activity.[19] In situations of traumatic stress the intense emotional responses of fear or rage activate large muscle groups—the origin of the 'fight or flight' responses. The body is the initial site of the registration of traumatic stress, thus a body memory of the traumatic experience is formed. This physical memory is what serves a warrior well in repeated battles. When there is little time to think, the body takes over.

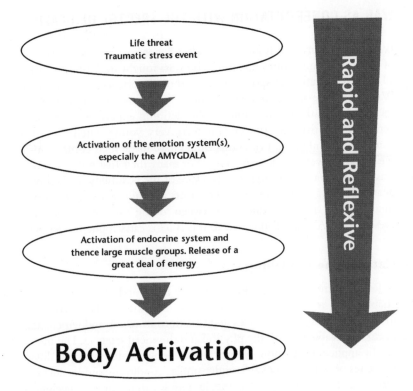

Figure 16.2 Automated traumatic stress response

For information to be stored in the long-term memory, the hippocampus must be engaged at the time of learning. The hippocampus is the main connection between the limbic system and the neocortex. High-level stimulation of the amygdala inhibits the operation of the hippocampus. Affect storms thus inhibit the categorisation and description of stimuli, perhaps to allow the brain and associated systems to concentrate on acts of survival without being distracted by higher-order thinking processes. Human beings react quickly and then seek to sort out what happened. Figure 16.2 represents the non-conscious route from 'life threat' to 'body response' and hence the laying down of a body memory. The process of understanding what happened comes afterwards, generally in a time of safety or a lull in the action.

WAR AS CONFRONTATION WITH THE SPECTRE OF DEATH

By its very nature, war results in casualties for at least one and usually all of the combatant groups involved. The wars fought by Australians have all involved death and severe injury (although fortunately in the Gulf War these were all suffered by the enemy). It is confrontation with this spectre of Death which is one of the defining experiences for many veterans. The majority of veterans were very young when they first went to war and in most cases this would have made their confrontation with death novel as well as shocking. For many their first military action was also when they became acutely aware of the possibility of their own death. These factors must be taken into account when considering the question of the distinction between 'doing one's duty' and self-preservation. A helpful approach to this issue is catastrophe modelling.

Catastrophe modelling

A full account of catastrophe modelling is beyond the scope of this chapter.[20] It is sufficient for our purpose to know that catastrophe modelling is a method of analysing situations in which sudden changes occur, applicable to both the physical and the social sciences. The model can be applied to situations where the following conditions apply: different states of being are possible under similar conditions; sudden changes can occur between states of being; hysteresis can occur, or a cycling of parts of the system under certain conditions; and divergence is possible.

The catastrophe model is best applied to situations where a state of flux exists as it proposes a way of understanding the sudden changes that occur in many physical and social contexts. Figure 16.3 illustrates one version of catastrophe modelling (the so-called 'cusp' catastrophe) in terms of a graphical representation. Control factors 1 and 2 are aspects of the situation of special importance in understanding that particular interaction.

As can be seen in Figure 16.3, under stable conditions change tends to be smooth. From point 'a' to point 'b' control factor 1 is relatively constant and so changes in control factor 2 produce smooth change. Similarly, for certain stable values of control factor 2, changes in control factor 1 produce smooth change. Catastrophe modelling becomes particularly valuable when we are trying to understand the conditions of a system under which sudden changes of state occur. In Figure 16.3, change from point 'c' to 'd' is smooth change but beyond 'd' a sudden fall occurs to 'e'. The important feature of this situation is that a reversal in

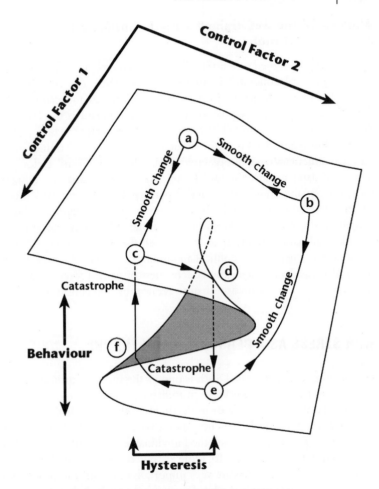

Figure 16.3   Continuous and discontinuous changes

Source: A. Woodcock and M. Davis, *Catastrophe Theory* (1978), p. 58.

value of control factor 2 does not cause the behaviour to revert to its former state on the upper surface, that is point 'd'. This is the hysteresis section of the diagram. In fact the relative value of control factor 2 must be reduced considerably before the behaviour will revert back on to the upper surface from point 'f' to point 'c'. The value of this model is in alerting the observer to the possibility that under certain conditions sudden changes occur and that the reversal of these changes is not a simple matter of a minor correction in a single control factor.

The case of the well-trained army becoming an out-of-control mob

Figure 16.4 is designed to illustrate the use of catastrophe modelling in a military–political context.[21] In many situations there can be a sudden collapse of governmental control of the armed forces, for example, the breaking under fire of Napoleon's elite Imperial Guard at the Battle of Waterloo, or the rise and fall of *juntas* in Latin America.[22] The example described in Figure 16.4 is of the sudden collapse of a well-trained army into a fragmentary and disorganised mob. The two control factors are 'perceived danger' and 'cohesion'. If cohesion remains relatively constant, the army remains an effective force as perceived danger increases (oscillation between points 'a' and 'b'). If, however, under conditions of high perceived threat cohesion diminishes, then there is a risk of collapse into disorder and panic (points 'b' to 'c' and then the drop to point 'd'). This model shows the need for political and military leaders to be proactive in times of crisis. To maintain the effectiveness of armed forces it is more important to address cohesion than to reduce the perception of danger.

WAR STRESS AS A PERSONAL CATASTROPHE

Confronting the spectre of Death is one of the most disturbing experiences of war. Many young Western military personnel have never seen a close relative or friend die or in death. How the individual reacts to a confrontation with death depends upon two important factors. The first is the sense of belonging which the individual feels towards a group. This has a number of elements. To some extent the values of the culture which the group embodies are very important in identification with the group or unit; an individual who does not hold to the beliefs and values of a group will find identifying with that group very difficult. On the other hand, the personal values of the individual may override the values of the group in a pro-social direction, for example, when an individual sacrifices their own life in order to preserve the lives of others. The second factor in confronting death is body readiness and associated body memory. If the individual belongs to the group then, when danger threatens, his automated response will be toward the preservation of himself and his group.

Figure 16.5 uses a catastrophe model to explore the situation in which an individual, faced with the prospect of their own death, nevertheless acts in the interests of others. The diagram illustrates the

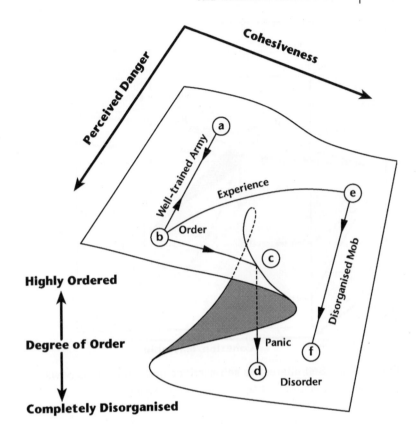

Figure 16.4   Social order vs disorder in times of danger

Source: A. Woodcock and M. Davis, *Catastrophe Theory* (1978), p. 122.

role of cohesion in the individual's response to the changing level of threat. Under low conditions of a 'sense of death', the degree of cohesion experienced by an individual is reflected in the extent to which they undertake pro-social actions. (The term 'pro-social' is used as an umbrella term for a range of behaviours, including supporting others in the unit and identifying with its general set of beliefs, such as the values of the nation to which the unit belongs.) As can be seen in Figure 16.5, a low 'sense of cohesion' or mateship will tend to be associated with self-interest being the predominant motive for the actions of those individuals.

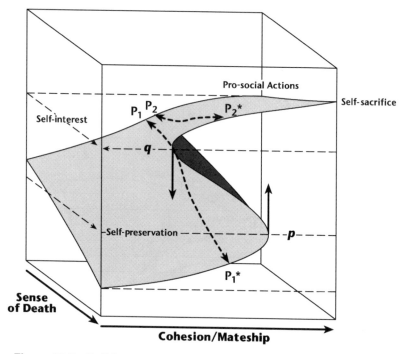

Figure 16.5   Self-interest vs self-sacrifice under the stress of war

Source: Adapted from J. Sashin, 'Affect tolerance: a model of affect response using catastrophe theory' in *Journal of Social Biological Structures*, 8:175–200, 1985, p. 182.

The situation changes drastically when the individual is confronted with the possibility of death. Notionally this would arise at the mid-point of the 'sense of death' axis. Here the activities of the individual with a low 'sense of cohesion' would not necessarily appear selfish. He or she may act in a manner which appears pro-social but which in fact harbours fears, or may contemplate actions which would be self-preservative at all costs. As the actuality of death confronts the individual, there is a point at which that person may openly act for his or her own self-preservation at the expense of others in the group. Those who are strongly integrated into the group will in all likelihood act in a self-sacrificing manner if called upon to do so.

Figure 16.5 offers a model of how to understand two features of human action under the stress of war. The first concerns instances in which some persons act heroically and others in a cowardly manner. The two points marked 'P_1' and 'P_2' represent two individuals who for all intents and purposes appear to be at the same point on the cohesion axis. Under the increasing stress of war, however, their actions diverge dramatically. 'P_1' pursues self-interest, 'P_2' self-sacrifice. Under extreme war stress these two individuals finish at points 'P_{1*}' and 'P_{2*}' respectively. The second feature concerns the sudden change in the actions of individuals who act initially in the interests of self-preservation, but then for no apparent reason act in a self-sacrificing manner. The key element here is that for 'P_1' the possibility exists of rapidly converting to self-sacrificing behaviour once the sense of cohesion increases to the point where the upward arrow occurs. Put more simply, once the individual 'P_1' recognises his connection to his mates, his actions may be very heroic indeed, even to the point of his own death. The individual 'P_2' is already acting for the good of his mates. If the sense of belonging or cohesion drops, however, then he may dramatically alter his behaviour and focus on self-preservation. The central determinant is the degree of cohesion and mateship, not the level of danger.

Catastrophe theory points us in the direction of social and biological processes. Faced with the threat of death, an individual's biology is triggered, resulting in the activation of the large muscle groups and associated body memory. Once this has occurred the individual enters an initially automatic, that is, non-volitional, process to carry out life-preserving actions in the most rapid fashion possible. These actions will, for those who are well-trained, be the standard procedures practised time and again in military units. These actions should not be the subject of contemplation but of rapid response. In war it is very often the case that 'he who hesitates is lost'.

The actions undertaken in a ship are directed towards the survival of the ship and its whole crew. Stories abound of fighting a ship so that the crew will survive and the interdependent nature of a ship and its crew reinforces the need to act in unison. Continuous training in damage control and in equipment and weapons handling reinforces the concept of acting as a team, as a cohesive unit. The body memory must be of actions which will assist the ship to survive. Fire-fighting teams on a ship are a good example of the team nature of survival at sea. The roles are distributed and yet clear. Whether fighting along a passageway or going down a hatch, procedures are designed so that the team always acts as a cohesive unit. This type of training is critical for the energised individual to be able to focus the activity of his large muscle groups in a manner which will best assist the survival of the ship and hence his shipmates.

Fire-fighting team in HMAS *Darwin*, training for Operation DAMASK, 1990. 'At times of danger and difficulty men always tend to act in accordance with habit and therefore if attention to duty and smart execution of orders are habitual in normal circumstances, men will act in the same way in times of stress. [Training] must aim to ingrain these habits thoroughly.' RN *Guide for Instructing Officers*, 1922. (RAN)

In individuals not well integrated into the ship's company these group survival procedures may be either poorly learned or subconsciously rejected and these are the people most at risk of pursuing self-interest at the expense of their shipmates. In times of grave threat they may be so influenced by the prospect of their own death that they lose connection with all other people. It is this loss of cohesion which motivates them to do things which they or others may later regard as cowardly. (It is sometimes said that the only difference between heroism and cowardice is the direction in which one is running.)

One example illustrates these concepts well. The story of 18-year-old Ordinary Seaman Edward 'Teddy' Sheean lives on as a supreme example of 'sublime and selfless heroism'.[23] On 1 December 1942 the Australian corvette HMAS *Armidale* was carrying out her mission of supplying Allied forces on Timor. During the afternoon the Japanese launched air attacks which fatally damaged the vessel. The captain ordered 'abandon ship', but as the survivors were trying to swim to safety, Japanese aircraft began strafing the crew. Sheean was a loader on the after 20-mm Oerlikon gun, and made for the side when the order to abandon ship was given. Upon seeing the harm being inflicted on his shipmates, however, he turned around and returned to his weapon. He strapped himself in and began firing at the Japanese aircraft, downing one and damaging two others. He was wounded twice, yet continued to fight to protect his shipmates as his ship sank.

What enabled Teddy Sheean to carry out this act of heroism? I would suggest that his body was so energised that he acted automatically, and that he was so focused on the action of shooting down the attacking planes that he did not even consider his own survival. The threat of death energised this man and his actions were for the welfare of others. Such a response defines heroism and selflessness in the face of death and can be produced only when the self is integrated into the group in a way which makes the group's survival more pressing than the self's.

'Ordinary Seaman Edward Sheean, HMAS *Armidale*' by Dale Marsh. 'None of us will ever know what made him do it, but he went back to his gun, strapped himself in, and brought down a Jap plane, still firing as he disappeared below the waves.' Ordinary Seaman R.M. Caro, RAN, HMAS *Armidale*. (AWM ART28160)

IN PEACE PREPARE FOR WAR

Recent progress in understanding the nature of the impact of stress in war has raised issues of which experienced naval and military men have long been aware—the value of realistic training and the importance of morale.

Training

The Falklands War is a recent instance of high-intensity naval battle. Ships and lives were lost on both sides. Interviews with ships' companies, from captains to ratings, mention time and again the importance of discipline and teamwork.[24] According to one interviewee, when his ship was on fire the fire-fighting teams went into action and it was 'just like Portsmouth' (the Royal Navy's fire-fighting training facility). It is the nature of naval training to be as realistic as possible as this enables the large muscle groups to attain a 'memory' of the sequence of actions, the weight and particulars of the equipment and a familiarity with the process, which can then be re-enacted automatically. This means that in an emergency, when the emotional system primes the individual for rapid reaction, the procedures necessary for survival are part of an automated response to danger.

Morale: cohesion and the sense of belonging

Arguably every sailor wants to belong to a happy ship. Studies in various countries, and especially in the Israeli Defence Force, have found that morale is not merely a social convenience but a capability essential.[25] From Kardiner's work onwards, the morale of the unit has been predictive both of its ability to manage stress in the midst of battle and to recover from the impact of stress.[26] We must recognise that the development of a sense of belonging and of unit cohesion are critical aspects of a unit's ability to function under battle conditions. It is the bonds of belonging which enable men and women to transcend the pursuit of personal survival and do the extraordinary things which are seen in battle. Such bonds also enable people to do the more ordinary things like fight fires and carry out their duty.

CONCLUSION

We must never lose sight of the strain suffered and the price paid by those who have experienced battle. The foregoing analysis is offered in the belief that those who have survived battle deserve our respect, our gratitude and our reverence. The thoughts outlined in this chapter are but the musings of someone trying to understand a noble and yet terrible part of human experience: the experience of the stress of war and of the face of naval battle.

17 | The face of the future naval battle

Peter Jones

DURING THE 100-PLUS years of Australia's national naval history there have been tremendous demands placed on sailors both in wars and other maritime operations. This chapter reflects upon the demands which will be placed on tomorrow's sailors.[1] To do this we must first consider the changing nature of naval warfare in the twenty-first century. This survey will be limited to a horizon of about 2020. Specifically it will deal with developments such as Network Centric Warfare (NCW), littoral warfare, changes in maritime capabilities and the efforts being made to transform navies, before examining the profile of tomorrow's sailor. Finally, it will consider what navies must do to ensure that this sailor can fight and win at sea.

TRENDS IN MARITIME WARFARE

For at least the last twenty years the major naval technological and conceptual developments have come from the US Navy, and it is there that we should look for a glimpse into the future. Over the last decade much has been made of the so-called Revolution in Military Affairs

(RMA).[2] Whether it is revolutionary or evolutionary is a moot point for others to argue. What is clear, however, is that in some fields, such as information technology, there have been leaps in capability which offer the warfighter the potential to do things very differently.

Network Centric Warfare

One such potential way is Network Centric Warfare (NCW).[3] NCW can be defined as 'the ability to network forces to obtain common and enhanced battlespace awareness (through information and sensor grids) and then use that awareness to maximum combat effect (through an engagement grid)'.

It has been suggested that combat data systems and tactical data links have been used at sea for about 40 years and that therefore so has NCW. This is only partly true, for it is through the ability to employ the common and enhanced battlespace awareness to maximum combat effect through such systems as Cooperative Engagement Capability (CEC) and fires coordination systems that NCW is really achieved. Before discussing NCW in detail, however, it is useful to have an appreciation of the main drivers. The three most important are resource constraints, threat systems and the information technology (IT) revolution.

Resource constraints, due mainly to technological and personnel cost increases, have meant that one-for-one replacement of capabilities will be more difficult to achieve in future (if indeed desired). At the same time the technical demands of operations have increased. This has served to drive the world's armed forces into combined (i.e., coalition) and joint operations as the norm.[4] In recent years it has also produced initiatives to better harness the combat power of the finite forces at a commander's disposal.

The second driver is the growing sophistication of threat systems. Considering first that familiar nemesis of the anti-ship missile, an Exocet missile travels at about Mach 0.8 (about eight nautical miles a minute). By 2020 ships may have to deal with scramjet missiles travelling at Mach 6–8 (almost 60 miles or 100 kilometres a minute). Such a threat will require full engagement or countermeasure cycles to be implemented in less than 60 seconds. To further complicate the future sailor's life, these new-generation missiles will probably be able to weave and will incorporate multiple sensors enabling them to distinguish ships from decoys. The use of stealth technology may also be incorporated into their design. The consequence of these technological developments is that there will need to be significant advances in maritime air warfare (AW) and in this arena NCW offers some particularly useful capabilities.

Undersea warfare (UW) will be no less challenging. Today's heavy-weight torpedoes have speeds of about 60 knots but they may be replaced in the next decade by more sophisticated 200-knot devices capable of being launched from much greater distances.[5] At the same time both nuclear and conventional submarines are becoming quieter and faster, with greater endurance and better situational awareness.

NCW offers opportunities both to exploit and nullify these advances. Indeed great care is needed not to focus too much on missile and torpedo lethality as such analysis can lead to erroneous conclusions. For example, significant advances are being made in phased array radar and long-range active sonar detection capabilities which receive far less attention. Yet it is how these complementary and competing technologies are tactically applied at sea by opposing forces which is and will be significant.

The final NCW driver is the enabling force of the IT revolution. Without the advances in real- and near-real-time wide bandwidth data transfer, the first element of NCW—increased battlespace awareness—could not be achieved. This data transfer not only increases scope but also variety of content. The IT revolution, for example, now allows greater access by ships and aircraft to databases ashore via satellite link. This is useful for intelligence purposes, target identification, engineering diagnostics, logistics and administration.

Technological advances have now reached the point where it is technically feasible to transfer raw radar and sonar data, enabling ships and aircraft to develop a shared composite picture and thus dramatically increase detection opportunities. This in turn allows better tracking and optimal engagement coordination against difficult targets. In a mature situation the sensor, weapon shooter and coordinator could all be part of different platforms. Indeed the sensor itself could actually consist of multiple platforms. This concept is the essence of CEC. To date, air warfare CEC has been successfully demonstrated at sea by the US Navy. The UW application of CEC is not far behind. The facilitation of this second element of NCW is central to its success but often overlooked amidst the proliferation of communications, surveillance and intelligence systems. CEC's tactical significance in both air and undersea warfare is the way in which it allows weapon engagements to proceed based only on a compilation of fleeting radar or sonar contacts. Such contacts may be all that can be expected from Mach 5 missiles or 200-knot torpedoes.

Another NCW development is fires coordination systems. The US Naval Fires Control System (NFCS), for example, will be an automated fires mission processing system. Designed to execute the land-attack mission, it will support extended-range gun munitions (ERGM), land-attack missiles, conventional ammunition and other new weapons systems, particularly those in support of forces ashore. NFCS will receive calls for fire, either electronically or by voice, will conduct target analysis and weapon target pairing, and digitally send fire missions to the appropriate weapons system(s).

The US Navy believes that a key operational benefit of NCW will be in the accelerated tempo of operations.[6] This will be achieved through a process of 'self-synchronisation'. The USN expects that tempo domination and high-speed operations will help it to achieve 'Full Spectrum Dominance', the elements of which are listed as 'Dominant Manoeuvre', 'Precision Engagement', 'Full-Dimensional Protection' and 'Focused Logistics'. Dramatic early results are expected in an operation, including the infliction of maximum enemy losses, the shortening of timelines and the locking-out of enemy options. The harnessing of NCW to achieve a twenty-first century *blitzkrieg* is encapsulated in the concept of Rapid Decisive Operations (RDO), currently being subjected to extensive experimentation under the auspices of the US Joint Forces Command.[7]

NCW offers opportunities and challenges and could potentially provide a significant competitive edge to any force. But it also introduces considerable complexity into an already difficult operating environment. It would be fair to say, however, that the force which is the smartest user of the IT revolution will probably be in the strongest tactical position.

NCW in littoral warfare

Nowhere are NCW advances more relevant than in relation to littoral operations. *Australian Maritime Doctrine* defines the littoral as 'those areas on land which are subject to influence by units operating at or from the sea, and those areas at sea subject to influence by forces operating on or from the land'.[8] Since the end of the Cold War the US Navy has refocused its attention upon the littoral and this interest has spawned many technologies and concepts. Extended-range guided munitions, for example, may allow a destroyer or frigate to engage a shore target at a range of about 60 nautical miles and at an accuracy of less than 30 metres. Missiles designed to engage shore infrastructure targets at longer ranges are also being developed.

Littoral warfare. 'The Navy has increased focus on joint operations in the littoral. Future warfare concepts rely increasingly on manoeuvre, tempo and shock to defeat numerically superior forces. These concepts envisage maritime forces providing protection and sustainment of embarked land forces while enroute and while the land forces remain in the littoral. In particular, surface combatants will play a dominant role in achieving area air battlespace dominance.' RAN Plan Blue, 2001. (RAN)

In contrast, the littoral is familiar waters for medium- and small-sized navies and, as such, it has strongly influenced their force structure and doctrine. One example is the heavy influence of littoral operations on the RAN's post-Second World War surface combatant designs.[9] Despite this interest, smaller navies have not always had the scientific and industrial resources necessary to develop systems optimised for inshore operations. It is, therefore, the USN's current interest in the littoral which has given or will give to smaller navies the systems they need to achieve greater influence on operations ashore. At the same time advances in stealth, radar, acoustics and other technologies are increasing unit survivability and effectiveness in this complex arena.

Naturally, for littoral warfare operational concepts to work, much greater integration is required between the three armed services. This fits in neatly with trends in army and air force concept developments worldwide. An Australian example is the Army experimental concept of Manoeuvre Operations in the Littoral Environment (MOLE). A key element of MOLE is the ability, where required, to configure lighter and more mobile land forces closely supported by maritime forces.

The littoral will be the ideal environment for the employment of Uninhabited Aerial Vehicles (UAV) and Uninhabited Underwater Vehicles (UUV), which will enter service in increasing sophistication over the next 20 years. Not far behind will come the Uninhabited Aerial and Uninhabited Underwater Combat Vehicles (UACV and UUCV). These assets will increase the battlespace awareness and combat options of the force. They will call for a new breed of surface combatant sailor and submariner to operate them—one whose computer gaming skills may finally become useful.

A significant result of the application of NCW is that the nature of task group operations will change. In particular, units that have traditionally operated at arm's length, such as submarines and maritime patrol aircraft, will often be integrated as key members of maritime task groups. This will have operational, doctrinal and cultural effects which will take some time to work through.

For tomorrow's sailor, NCW will create a more complex maritime operational environment where the tempo will vary dramatically. Not only will it include having to counter Mach 5 anti-ship missiles, but the maritime battlespace will be much greater in size than in the past and will encompass land-attack missions about a thousand miles away.

HIGHER-LEVEL CONCEPTS

While the concepts of NCW and RDO have the potential to change the nature of war at sea, there are other, higher-level concepts which may change the development of capabilities. This in turn will have an impact on the future sailor. These higher-level concepts include Effects-Based Operations (EBO), Concept-Led Long-Range Planning and the notion of Transformation.

Effects–Based Operations

In contemporary military strategic thinking there is a commonly held view that defence forces must move to EBO.[10] The US Joint Forces Command states that:

EBO is a philosophy that focuses on obtaining a desired strategic outcome or effect on the enemy, through the application of the full range of military and non-military capabilities at the tactical, operational and strategic levels. An effect is the physical, functional or psychological outcome, event or consequence that results from a selected action or set of actions.[11]

The perceived advantage of the EBO approach is well summed up by the US Navy, which believes that:

Effects Based Operations seek to defeat our adversary's strategy and resolve . . . [rather than] merely attrite his armed forces . . . new information technologies are enabling us to know our enemy, our adversary's strategy and operational doctrine, and our adversary's centers of gravity better.[12]

What will this mean for tomorrow's sailor? It is likely that tasks not traditionally undertaken by navies may enter their preserve. Information operations, asymmetric attack and cyber warfare may all become mainstream disciplines in the way that anti-submarine warfare and gunnery are today.

Concept-Led Long-Range Planning

In the twenty-first century, navies and the other service arms will struggle to develop and maintain sophisticated weaponry within tight budgets. In an attempt to improve the capability development and maintenance process some services are turning to Concept-Led Long-Range Planning.

Before describing this philosophy it is worth examining another planning challenge facing navies. How can they keep pace with technology in terms of acquiring relevant capability in a cost-effective way and ensuring that systems have the flexibility, through upgrades, to remain relevant during their service life? For example, it can take up to ten years from the point of deciding that a ship is required to the day it becomes operational. It will then remain in service for another 25 to 30 years. An Australian case study is the *Charles F. Adams* Class guided missile destroyer (DDG). The RAN's DDG requirement was first articulated in 1959 and the selected USN design had in fact been completed two years earlier. The third and last of the class, HMAS *Brisbane*, eventually entered service in 1967 and was not paid-off until 2001, after 34 years of service.[13] It was fortunate that the design of the DDG was exceptional, but not all designs are up to the challenge.

Concept for future Air Warfare Destroyer, 2002. 'Stealth technology is being applied to make ships less detectable . . . at the same time leaps in computer power are dramatically improving the performance of ships' weapons and sensors. These developments combine to make surface combatants more lethal and survivable both in the littoral and open ocean. Equally important are the tremendous advances in efficient hull form and propulsion designs.' RAN Plan Blue, 2001. (RAN)

The Concept-Led Long-Range Planning philosophy consists of a three-step process: (1) identifying future roles, missions, tasks and appropriate operational concepts; (2) subjecting these concepts to a rigorous experimentation; and (3) identifying the resulting capability requirements.

Transformation

A closely-related concept is that of Transformation.[14] This is seen as one way to help ensure that ships and aircraft are not built just for yesterday's war but have the flexibility to remain relevant throughout their service lives. Essentially, transformation envisages non-incremental changes in concepts, organisation, process, technology application and equipment through which significant gains are made in operational effectiveness, operating efficiencies and/or cost reductions.

Transformation aims to exploit more fully the information technology revolutions, but it is still early days. The US military is the first to adopt this course and, in what may be a blueprint for other nations, aims to:

- focus about 10 per cent of its effort on a set of very high leverage capabilities which enable new ways to fight;

- support this focus with another 10 per cent of effort to improve or accelerate critical complementary capabilities; and
- allocate the remaining 80 per cent of effort to maintaining existing, sound, and still relevant capabilities.[15]

How radical the eventual shake-up of the US military will be, especially after the events of 11 September 2001, is difficult to say, but in broad terms we can expect to see emphasis on: joint force integration; situational awareness and C4I (Command, Control, Communications, Computing & Intelligence) systems. This will require robust networks and high levels of interoperability; rapid response forces, including rapid logistical support; and long-range precision weapons.

A key element in both Concept-Led Long-Range Planning and Transformation is a more holistic notion of military capability. Traditionally naval capabilities have been ascertained by scanning the pages of *Jane's Fighting Ships* to see how many destroyers, submarines and so on exist in the fleet in question and what sensor and weapon fits they possess. In short, emphasis has been placed on platforms, equipment and, occasionally, logistics.

There is a growing realisation that military capability is much more than this which has evolved out of a greater understanding of the true cost of ownership—where the original cost of a platform is only a minor element in the through-life cost. Moreover, the sailor is a far more expensive capability component than in the past, that is, in terms of recruitment, training and retention.

Increasingly, therefore, defence forces are seeing capability not just as equipment and logistics. It is also personnel, organisation, training, support, facilities and doctrine.[16] This will have an impact on tomorrow's sailor because ships and equipment will take greater account of his or her needs and this, therefore, should provide more sustainable naval capabilities. It is just as well, because the demands placed upon tomorrow's sailor will at times be intense.

In 2001 the RAN moved further along the Transformation path when the Chief of Navy approved the Navy Innovation Strategy. This framework, which is aligned to other ADF developments, is the vehicle for achieving Concept-Led Long-Range Planning. In 2002 the RAN began exploring its *Future Maritime Operational Concept 2010* and its *Future Maritime Operational Concept 2020*, both of which will involve wargames, operational research projects and other studies.

The implications for future sailors of Transformation initiatives are that their ships and aircraft should have greater relevance, flexibility and operational effectiveness. Transformation could also change the structure and culture of the Navy.

A PROFILE OF THE FUTURE SAILOR

Having considered the likely nature of future war at sea, as well as the strategic and operational thinking underpinning future maritime operations, it is important to consider the profile of the future sailor.

The baby-boomers who now lead the Navy will, at the end of this decade, hand over the watch to Generation X. These younger sailors are those now attaining the rank of Commander or Chief Petty Officer. The attitudes and characteristics of Generation X and of the succeeding Generations Y and I are, naturally, different from those of their predecessors. Navies will have to adjust if they are to recruit and retain their services. Some would demur at the idea of navies bending to social change, yet historically navies have always done so—albeit with a time lag. Keel-hauling and flogging were done away with as a reflection of changing social mores.

So what are some of the issues navies may have to grapple with? Tomorrow's sailor will be less likely to be a 20-year career sailor. His or her period of service may shrink to as little as an average of five years. Training, maintenance and the systems themselves will need to be adjusted to take this into account. Lateral recruiting or even subsequent but not consecutive periods of service will need to be explored. Multi-crewing will likely become more widespread, with worked-up crews flying in and out and platforms remaining deployed. Some platforms are more suited to this concept than others and some of the more complex, such as major surface combatants, pose particular challenges.

The central importance of the sailor to the navies of the future is gaining long overdue recognition. This is reflected in the greater emphasis being placed on the sailor's requirements in the design of new ships. This new approach had its highest profile in the ill-fated USN DD21 (*Zumwalt* Class destroyer) Project. Despite its realignment into the DD-(X) program,[17] many of its personnel initiatives will be retained and are worthy of discussion here.

A key feature of the next generation of destroyers will be their smaller crew size. The DD21 envisaged a dramatic downsizing to about 95 personnel from about 350. The DD-(X) ship's company will initially be larger than 95, but thereafter will probably be reduced in size as automation progressively develops and practical experience is gained.

Operations Room, HMAS *Anzac*, 2001. 'The greatest single strength of the Navy is the calibre of its officers and sailors. Yet recruiting, training and retaining the right people will always be its greatest challenge. History shows that the best sailors invariably win the battle at sea. Maritime warfare in the twenty-first century is no different.' RAN Plan Blue, 2001. (RAN)

There are two key factors driving the reduction in crew size: personnel costs and the increasing difficulty faced by navies in attracting and retaining personnel for sea service. In the USN case it is estimated that personnel costs account for 40–60 per cent of the life cycle costs of a surface warship.[18] Hence to provide an affordable capability the USN must not only reduce crew size but also make training cost-effective. In addition, work practices and the working environment must be attractive to tomorrow's sailor. This is a daunting task. To achieve any success, people must be factored into the initial capability development. Some of the initiatives taken to do this in the case of DD21 were:

- Analysing all shipborne activities and reviewing how they can be made less manpower intensive. This has led to a new replenishment-at-sea system.
- Bridge and Operations Rooms layouts. In the latter the challenge is to take a wide bandwidth of data and provide it in a processed and comprehensible way.
- Virtually all components to have sensors linked to integral damage-control systems to reduce the need for manpower-intensive damage-control teams.

- Personnel to be monitored by the Reduced Ships crew by Virtual Presence (RSVP) system, which via Personnel Status Monitors (PSM) will monitor their location and physical status.
- Sailors to have a minimum accommodation level of a twin-berth cabin.
- Internet access for entertainment, training and education and satellite television and telephone access.

Many of these initiatives will be incorporated not only in DD-(X), but also in many new designs in the USN and other Western navies.

The future sailor will also be required to be multi-skilled. Manpower is being reserved for tasks in which people are indispensable, such as planning and decision-making, and the systems aboard ship are being designed to optimise the crew's ability to perform. Potentially, this will place considerable demands on the future sailor to absorb large amounts of data.

Battlespace awareness

A key factor in implementing both NCW and reduced crew sizes is effective human factors research. The USN is a leader in this area, but important work is being undertaken elsewhere. The Australian Defence Science and Technology Organisation (DSTO) has established a Future Operations Centre Analysis Laboratory to examine situational awareness in the military context. Early work suggests that developed situational awareness is a combination of technology and psychology.[19] Tomorrow's sailor will probably have been using computers since the age of three, and will be able to assimilate data differently to the old salts. There will be greater use of graphics, concurrent information and virtual Artificial Intelligence advisors. Clearly there is considerable potential to provide not only a more ergonomic Operations Room or Command Centre but also to optimise the presentation of data. The latter will depend on the degree to which information is processed and to which decision-making options are distilled and presented to the sailor.

Battlespace awareness is at the core of NCW thinking. If one has superior situational awareness then one is likely to have the winning operational edge. In the realm of NCW the theoretical aim is to create a transparent battlespace with resulting high-situational awareness. This requires high-quality communications links with mega-bandwidth. Indeed, some advocates of NCW believe that improved situational awareness is where the highest combat effectiveness pay-off can occur for the research and development dollar. Despite significant investments in this area, however, the transparent battlespace is likely to remain a distant goal.

CONCLUSION

Historical developments in warfare and their impact on the human experience of battle have highlighted two themes: first, technology has not mastered the sea nor insulated the sailor from all of its vagaries; and second, technology does not work all the time, especially at sea and if one has an enemy keen to ensure that it does not. We may therefore contend that the prudent cyber-admiral must ensure that he or she can operate in an environment of considerable uncertainty, and that doctrine should be developed sufficiently to allow for this.

Historically, the best-trained and led sailors have invariably won the war at sea, and the maritime war of the future is unlikely to be significantly different.

Notes

CHAPTER 1

1 M. Thwaites, *Atlantic Odyssey* (Oxford: New Cherwell Press, 1999), p. 11.
2 Quoted in J. Winton, *Cunningham: The Greatest Admiral Since Nelson* (London: John Murray, 1998), p. 303.
3 N. Monsarrat, *The Cruel Sea* (1951; reprinted Harmondsworth: Penguin, 1972), p. 445.
4 J.F. Calvert, *Silent Running: My Years on a World War II Attack Submarine* (New York: John Wiley & Sons, 1995), p. 93.
5 Quoted in M. Munthe, *Sweet is War* (London: Duckworth, 1954), title page.
6 W.P. Hughes, Jr, *Fleet Tactics and Coastal Combat* (Annapolis: United States Naval Institute Press (USNIP), 2000), p. 25.
7 R.H. Spector, *At War at Sea: Sailors and Naval Combat in the Twentieth Century* (New York: Viking Penguin, 2001), pp. 96, 165.
8 N. Miller, *War at Sea: A Naval History of World War II* (New York: Scribner, 1995), p. 11.
9 See Chapter 14.
10 Lieutenant-Commander Nigel Ward in M. Bilton and P. Kosminsky (eds), *Speaking Out: Untold Stories from the Falklands War* (London: Grafton Collins, 1990), p. 160. All ranks given are those held at the time of the events described.
11 J. Keegan, *The Face of Battle* (New York: Dorset Press, 1976, repr. 1986).
12 ibid., p. 15.
13 I am grateful to Professor David Horner for discussing this question with me.
14 See for example S. Hynes, *The Soldier's Tale: Bearing Witness to Modern War* (New York: Allen Lane, 1997), p. 25.
15 Cited in R. Holmes, *Firing Line* (London: Pimlico, 1985), p. 8.
16 See for example Holmes, *Firing Line*. A recent addition is M. Evans and A. Ryan (eds), *The Human Face of Warfare: Killing, Fear and Chaos in Battle* (Sydney: Allen & Unwin, 2000).
17 Paul Kennedy, 'The boundaries of naval history', Seventh Stephen Roskill Memorial Lecture, given at Cambridge University, 4 February 1997. (I am grateful to Professor Kennedy for providing a copy of this lecture.) Keegan applied the methodology of *The Face of Battle* to naval warfare in *The Price of Admiralty: The Evolution of Naval Warfare* (Harmondsworth: Viking Penguin, 1988). See also M. Middlebrook, *Convoy: The Battle for Convoys SC.122 and*

HX.229 (London: Allen Lane, 1976) and M. Middlebrook and P. Mahoney, *Battleship: The Loss of the* Prince of Wales *and the* Repulse (London: Penguin, 1977). Most recently there is Spector's *At War at Sea*. Valuable collections of firsthand accounts include J. Winton (ed.), *The War at Sea 1939–45* (London: Hutchinson, 1967); C. Howard-Bailey (ed.), *The Royal Naval Museum Book of the Battle of the Atlantic: The Corvettes and Their Crews: An Oral History* (Stroud: Royal Naval Museum/Alan Sutton, 1994); J. Thompson, *The Imperial War Museum Book of the War at Sea: The Royal Navy in the Second World War* (London: Sidgewick & Jackson/IWM, 1996); M. Arthur, *The True Glory: The Royal Navy 1914–1939: A Narrative History* (London: Hodder & Stoughton, 1996) and *The Navy: 1939 to the Present Day* (London: Hodder & Stoughton, 1997); and D. King and J.B. Hattendorf (eds), *Every Man Will Do His Duty: An Anthology of Firsthand Accounts From the Age of Nelson 1793–1815* (New York: Henry Holt & Co., 1997).

18 M. Hastings, *Going to the Wars* (London: Pan MacMillan, 2000, paperback edn 2001), pp. 108–9.

19 T. Lane, 'The human economy of the British Merchant Navy' in S. Howarth and D. Law (eds), *The Battle of the Atlantic 1939–1945: The 50th Anniversary International Conference* (London: Greenhill, 1994), p. 54.

20 Quoted in Lane, 'Human economy', p. 48.

21 Professor David Rosenberg, keynote address to the second biennial King-Hall Naval History Conference, Canberra, July 2001.

22 Surgeon Commander Rick Jolly in Bilton and Kosminsky (eds), *Speaking Out*, p. 128.

23 For example Thwaites, Monsarrat and J.E. Macdonnell (on whom see Chapter 10).

24 Hastings, *Going to the Wars*, pp. 272, 291, 320; Winton, *Cunningham*, pp. 233, 318; H. Nicolson, *Diaries and Letters 1939–45*, edited by N. Nicolson (London: Fontana Collins, 1967, paperback edn 1970), p. 170.

25 ibid., p. 43.

26 Rosenberg address.

27 Captain Jeremy Larken of HMS *Fearless* in Hastings, *Going to the Wars*, p. 380.

28 Rosenberg address.

29 Spector, *At War at Sea*, p. vii.

30 Dr Andrew Gordon, addressing the 2001 King-Hall Naval History Conference.

31 N.A.M. Rodger, *The Wooden World: An Anatomy of the Georgian Navy* (London: Collins, 1986). On naval warfare in this era see in general N. Tracy, *Nelson's Battles. The Art of Victory in the Age of Sail* (London: Chatham, 1996), and A. Lambert, *War at Sea in the Age of Sail 1650–1850* (London: Cassell, 2000).

32 These are rehearsed by Keegan, *Price of Admiralty*, pp. 60ff.

33 Second Lieutenant Lewis Rotely, quoted in Tracy, *Nelson's Battles*, p. 195.

34 See the account of Seaman William Robinson, aboard HMS *Revenge* at Trafalgar in King and Hattendorf (eds), *Every Man Will Do His Duty*, pp. 160ff.

35 T. Pocock, *Horatio Nelson* (London: Bodley Head, 1987), p. 327.

36 Spector, *At War At Sea*, pp. 180, 220.

37 A rare exception was the Royal Navy's boarding of the German prison ship *Altmark* off Norway in 1940.

38 Keegan, *Price of Admiralty*, p. 89.

39 Tracy, *Nelson's Battles*, p. 116.

40 Miller, *War at Sea*, p. 157.

41 Spector, *At War At Sea*, p. 100.

42 See Chapter 8.

43 Spector, *At War At Sea*, pp. 356–7.

44 Seaman Robinson in King and Hattendorf (eds), *Every Man Will Do His Duty*, p. 162.

45 W.E. Reeve, 'The scrap iron flotilla' in *Journal of Naval Engineering*, 38, 3, December 1999, pp. 461–71.

46 Spector, *At War At Sea*, p. 396.

47 King and Hattendorf (eds), *Every Man Will Do His Duty*, pp. 178–9.

48 I am grateful to Commodore James Goldrick and Captains Peter Jones, Peter Leschen and Richard Menhinick, all of the RAN, for the benefit of many conversations on the issues involved in surface warship command.

49 See Chapter 8.

50 Vice-Admiral Sir John Collins, *As Luck Would Have It: The Reminiscences of an Australian Sailor* (Sydney: Angus & Robertson, 1965), pp. 77–8.

51 See Chapter 4.

52 D. Horn (ed.), *The Private War of Seaman Stumpf: The Unique Diaries of a Young German in the Great War* (London: Leslie Frewin, 1967), pp. 197–200; Petty Officer Sam Bishop of HMS *Antelope* in Bilton and Kosminsky (eds), *Speaking Out*, pp. 118–19.

53 Admiral Sandy Woodward with Patrick Robinson, *One Hundred Days: The Memoirs of the Falklands Battle Group Commander* (London: Fontana Collins, paperback edn, 1992), p. 282.

54 Petty Officer Ken Enticknab in Bilton and Kosminsky (eds), *Speaking Out*, p. 111.

55 Spector, *At War At Sea*, p. 220.

56 Petty Officer Sam Bishop in Bilton and Kosminsky (eds), *Speaking Out*, p. 119; Chapter 3.

57 For example the damage to *Seydlitz* at Jutland. Spector, *At War At Sea*, p. 85.

58 As pointed out by a sailor in HMS *Arrow* in the Falklands. Hastings, *Going to the Wars*, p. 321.

59 Gordon Johnson, speaking at the 2001 King-Hall Naval History Conference.

60 Spector, *At War At Sea*, pp. 96–7; Holmes, *Firing Line*, p. 234.

61 For example, for the survivors of HMS *Antelope* aboard HMS *Intrepid*. Petty Officer Sam Bishop in Bilton and Kosminsky (eds), *Speaking Out*, p. 127.

62 Lieutenant-Commander Ward in Bilton and Kosminsky (eds), *Speaking Out*, pp. 165–6.

63 The words of a US destroyer sailor at Okinawa. Spector, *At War At Sea*, p. 308.

64 W.E. Reeve, veteran of the Australian destroyers in the Mediterranean in 1940–41, recalling unloading supplies in Tobruk harbour while under Stuka attack. In terms of going beyond this kind of acceptance and having

premonitions of death, the famous RAF officer Leonard Cheshire believed that such premonitions were defeatism and became self-fulfilling. M. Hastings, *Bomber Command* (London: 1979, Pan paperback edn 1981), p. 262.

65 As Keegan has pointed out in *Price of Admiralty*, p. 97.

66 Collins, *As Luck Would Have It*, pp. 148–9; Spector, *At War At Sea*, pp. 19, 89–90.

67 See Chapter 6.

68 Spector, *At War At Sea*, p. 209.

69 For the operational point about task groups see ibid., p. 286.

70 K. Poolman in Winton, *The War At Sea 1939–45*, pp. 95–101.

71 Surgeon Commander Jolly in Bilton and Kosminsky (eds), *Speaking Out*, p. 126.

72 There were 1828 sailors killed and 183 wounded in the evacuation of 16 500 troops. Winton, *Cunningham*, p. 221.

73 Spector, *At War At Sea*, pp. 168–84 *passim*.

74 ibid., p. 309.

75 Sub-Lieutenant Steve Iacovou in Bilton and Kosminsky (eds), *Speaking Out*, pp. 97–101.

76 D. Brown, *The Royal Navy and the Falklands War* (London: Leo Cooper, 1987), pp. 141–4; N. Friedman, 'Future C4I for smaller navies', in D. Wilson (ed.), *Maritime War in the 21st Century* (Canberra: Sea Power Centre, 2001), p. 156.

77 Middlebrook, *Convoy*, pp. 24–5.

78 Spector, *At War At Sea*, pp. 247–8.

79 T. Robertson, *Walker R.N.* (London: Pan, 1956, paperback edn 1958, reprinted 1973), p. 202.

80 See Chapter 12.

81 The number of British merchant seamen who died as crew of ships lost to enemy action in the Second World War has been officially given as 25 864. The casualty rate among all crews has been calculated as 25 per cent. C.B.A. Behrens, *Merchant Shipping and the Demands of War* (London: HMSO/ Longmans Green & Co., 1955), pp. 176, 178; Middlebrook, *Convoy*, p. 25.

82 J. Slader, *The Fourth Service. Merchantmen at War 1939–45* (London: Robert Hale, 1994), pp. 280, 282–3. The award of such decorations to naval personnel performing mine-disposal is another illustration.

83 Able Seamen John Courtney and Bill Williams, RANR. The first Australian serviceman to be decorated in the First World War, Lieutenant Thomas Bond, RANR, was awarded the DSO for his role in the same action. D. Stevens (ed.), *The Royal Australian Navy* (Melbourne: Oxford University Press, 2001), vol. III in *The Australian Centenary History of Defence*, p. 36.

84 Captain W. Tennant was the Senior Naval Officer ashore at Dunkirk. W. Lord, *The Miracle of Dunkirk* (London: 1983, Penguin paperback edn 1984), pp. 87–8, 92, 94, 96–9, 120–1, 144.

85 ibid., p. 272.

86 M. Hastings and S. Jenkins, *The Battle for the Falklands* (London: Pan, paperback edn, 1983), pp. 223, 225.

87 M. Stephen, *The Fighting Admirals: British Admirals of the Second World War* (Annapolis: USNIP, 1991), pp. 55, 58ff.

88 Collins, *As Luck Would Have It*, pp. 136–7.

89 Hastings and Jenkins, *The Battle for the Falklands*, pp. 106–7, 226.

90 Two examples from the Falklands are the difficulty in finding the effective word of command for troops of 2 Para to disembark from a landing craft at San Carlos and Major Ewen Southby-Tailyour's unheeded warning to Welsh Guards officers that the men aboard the landing ship *Sir Galahad* were in danger of air attack. Major Chris Keeble and Major Ewen Southby-Tailyour in Bilton and Kosminsky (eds), *Speaking Out*, pp. 208–9, 228ff.

91 See Chapter 5.

92 Lord, *The Miracle of Dunkirk*, p. 96.

93 Reeve, 'The scrap iron flotilla', p. 471.

94 Collins, *As Luck Would Have It*, pp. 92–3.

95 D.K. Brown, 'Atlantic escorts 1939–45' in Howarth and Law (eds), *The Battle of the Atlantic 1939–1945*, pp. 467–8.

96 Hastings, *Going to the Wars*, p. 319.

97 Lieutenant-Commander Patrick Kettle in Bilton and Kosminsky (eds), *Speaking Out*, p. 93.

98 Collins, *As Luck Would Have It*, pp. 95–6.

99 See Chapter 8. *Repulse* sank within eleven minutes of first being hit. Miller, *War at Sea*, p. 220.

100 M. Dewey, *Diaries, Letters, Writings*, edited by A.V. Grimstone, M.C. Lyons and U. Lyons (Cambridge: Pembroke College, 1992), pp. 143–4.

101 Slader, *The Fourth Service*, p. 282.

102 Spector, *At War At Sea*, p. 99.

103 Most British merchant seamen appear to have died during the time which elapsed between enemy action against their ship and assembly of survivors in life boats or rafts. Lane, 'Human economy', pp. 48–9, 50, 53, 56–7.

104 Captain Juan Antonio Lopez in Bilton and Kosminsky (eds), *Speaking Out*, pp. 85–6.

105 P. Cremer, *U-Boat Commander: A Periscope View of the Battle of the Atlantic* (English translation, Annapolis: USNIP, 1984), p. 67.

106 Calvert, *Silent Running*, p. 71.

107 Spector, *At War At Sea*, pp. 254ff.

108 I am grateful to Lieutenant James Lybrand, RAN for a briefing on the internal systems and fittings of HMAS *Waller*.

109 Cremer, *U-Boat Commander*, p. 23.

110 ibid., p. 84.

111 Calvert, *Silent Running*, pp. 67–70; Cremer, *U-Boat Commander*, pp. 57–8. On the terrors of being depth-charged and on submarine experience in general, see also the classic novel of submarine warfare by Lothar Gunther Buchheim, *Das Boot* (English translation 1975, paperback edn London: Cassell, 1999).

112 See Chapter 11. In the 1960s the USN began to install visual monitors inside its submarines which made the periscope view available to the crew. Spector, *At War At Sea*, p. 339.

113 Cremer, *U-Boat Commander*, pp. 97–102.

114 See Chapter 7.

115 Lieutenant-Commander Ward in Bilton and Kosminsky (eds), *Speaking Out*, pp. 159, 160.

116 Heavy casualties were expected largely due to Taranto being an experimental and unpredictable operation. In the event there were only two casualties among the striking force. Arthur, *The Navy: 1939 to the Present Day*, p. 66.

117 Spector, *At War At Sea*, pp. 329, 356.

118 Such as respect for the Argentinian pilots in the Falklands. See the remarks of several British pilots in Bilton and Kosminsky (eds), *Speaking Out*, pp. 142, 163–4, 167.

119 W. Lord, *Midway: The Incredible Victory* (Ware, Hertfordshire: Wordsworth Editions, 2000), p. 117.

120 For example aboard HMAS *Sydney* during the Korean War. The Australian Naval Aviation Museum, *Flying Stations: A Story of Australian Naval Aviation* (Sydney: Allen & Unwin, 1998), pp. 90–2.

121 Lieutenant-Commander Ward in Bilton and Kosminsky (eds), *Speaking Out*, pp. 165–6.

122 Flight-Lieutenant Ian Mortimer in ibid., pp. 142–3.

123 Admiral Sir Victor Smith, *A Few Memories of Sir Victor Smith* (Canberra: Australian Naval Institute, 1992), p. 31.

124 T. Lowry and J. Wellham, *The Attack on Taranto: Blueprint for Pearl Harbor* (Mechanicsburg, PA: Stackpole Books, 1995), pp. 24–5. For the recollections of Takeshi Maeda, a Japanese pilot who attacked Pearl Harbor, see S. Lunn, 'One moment of infamy', *The Australian*, Friday, 7 December 2001, p. 13.

125 Lieutenant Paul Holmberg, USN in Lord, *Midway*, pp. 169, 175.

126 Midshipman Charles Friend, RN quoted in Thompson, *The Imperial War Museum Book of the War at Sea*, pp. 98–9; Lieutenant-Commander Ward in Bilton and Kosminsky (eds), *Speaking Out*, pp. 162–3.

127 Spector, *At War At Sea*, pp. 200–1, 282–5.

128 The Australian Naval Aviation Museum, *Flying Stations*, pp. 96–7.

129 Arthur, *The Navy: 1939 to the Present Day*, p. 100.

130 As a naval officer in the Mediterranean, Nelson became involved in Italian diplomacy, ensuring Neapolitan entry into the war with France in 1793. Pocock, *Horatio Nelson*, pp. 107, 110. Commodore Matthew Perry, USN played a critical role in the opening of Japan to the West in the early 1850s. S.E. Morison, *'Old Bruin'. Commodore Matthew Perry* (Boston: Little, Brown & Co., 1967). Cunningham negotiated the peaceful disarming of the French squadron at Alexandria in 1940, avoiding the violence and loss of life which occurred at Oran. Winton, *Cunningham*, pp. 84ff.

131 Admiral Sir Max Horton, RN, was appointed C-in-C Western Approaches in November 1942 at the height of the Battle of the Atlantic. A.J. Scarth, 'Liverpool as HQ and base' in Howarth and Law, *The Battle of the Atlantic 1939–1945*, p. 247.

132 Rosenberg address.

133 See Chapter 4.

134 Collins, *As Luck Would Have It*, pp. 152–3.

135 Winton, *Cunningham*, pp. 136–9.

136 See Chapter 2.

137 Spector, *At War At Sea*, pp. 76–7, 86. See also J. Goldrick, 'John R. Jellicoe: technology's victim' in J. Sweetman (ed.), *The Great Admirals: Command At Sea, 1587–1945* (Annapolis: USNIP, 1997), pp. 383–4.

138 Winton, *Cunningham*, p. 55.

139 Commander Geoffrey Barnard, RN quoted in ibid., p. 142.

140 Hughes, *Fleet Tactics and Coastal Combat*, p. 27.

141 Admittedly, Collins on this occasion had a much smaller command than Jellicoe, but his mission involved HMAS *Sydney*'s cooperation with at least five other ships. Collins contrasted Cunningham's style with the very detailed orders issued by the US Navy during the Pacific War. Collins, *As Luck Would Have It*, pp. 84, 132; Spector, *At War At Sea*, p. 77.

142 Quoted in Pocock, *Horatio Nelson*, p. 157.

143 E.B. Potter, *Nimitz* (Annapolis: USNIP, 1976), p. 47.

144 C. Reynolds, 'William F. Halsey, Jr. The Bull' in Sweetman (ed.), *The Great Admirals*, pp. 486–7.

145 See in general Pocock, *Horatio Nelson*.

146 Winton, *Cunningham*, p. 383.

147 During the Dunkirk evacuation, Ramsay allowed Somerville to assume his duties while he rested. Lord, *The Miracle of Dunkirk*, p. 90.

148 Potter, *Nimitz*, pp. 47, 227–8.

149 See Chapters 4 and 12. See also Woodward, *One Hundred Days*, pp. 20–1.

150 Lieutenant James Munn, RN quoted in Winton, *Cunningham*, p. 188.

151 On these issues see Chapter 14.

152 He referred to Lieutenant John May, RN. Thwaites, *Atlantic Odyssey*, pp. 56–7.

153 Woodward, *One Hundred Days*, pp. 6–7.

154 On these factors see Holmes, *Firing Line*, pp. 115ff, 119ff, 125.

155 T. Parker, *Soldier, Soldier* (London: Heinemann, 1985), pp. 135, 166.

156 Holmes, *Firing Line*, pp. 360ff.

157 Bilton and Kosminsky (eds), *Speaking Out*, p. 217.

158 See J. Burke, *An Intimate History of Killing: Face-to-Face Killing in Twentieth Century Warfare* (London: Grant Books, 1999).

159 Holmes, *Firing Line*, pp. 376ff.

160 Commander Alan West, RN of HMS *Ardent* in Bilton and Kosminsky (eds), *Speaking Out*, pp. 107–8.

161 On soldiers under bombardment see Holmes, *Firing Line*, pp. 231–2.

162 ibid., pp. 159–60, 205, 223ff.

163 Spector, *At War At Sea*, p. 396. There can be exceptions; the crew's morale broke on the destroyer HMS *Verity* at Dunkirk and they had to be rested by Somerville. Lord, *The Miracle of Dunkirk*, p. 90.

164 Holmes, *Firing Line*, pp. 106–7.

165 Sir Max Hastings has made the point about the desert. Hastings, *Going to the Wars*, p. 232.

166 On this issue see Chapter 15.

167 Captain Brian de Courcy-Ireland, RN quoted in Arthur, *The Navy: 1939 to the Present Day*, p. 405.

168 Cremer, *U-Boat Commander*, pp. 38–40.

169 Middlebrook, *Convoy*, p. 37.

170 Woodward, *One Hundred Days*, p. 283.

171 See Collins, *As Luck Would Have It*, pp. 105–6. Cunningham believed himself lucky. Cunningham of Hyndhope, *A Sailor's Odyssey* (London: Hutchinson, 1951), p. 663. See also Chapter 11 and Cremer, *U-Boat Commander*, p. 66.

172 See Chapter 15.

173 Collins makes this point. Collins, *As Luck Would Have It*, p. 124.

174 See Chapter 6 and Collins, *As Luck Would Have It*, p. 80.

175 Cremer, *U-Boat Commander*, p. 43.

176 E. Smithies, *War in the Air. The Men and Women Who Built, Serviced and Flew Warplanes Remember the Second World War* (New York: Penguin, 1990, paperback edn, Harmondsworth: 1992), p. 45.

177 ibid., pp. 26, 45; G. Lyall (ed.), *The War in the Air 1939–45* (London: Hutchinson, 1968, Pimlico paperback edn, 1994), pp. 40, 46.

178 Smithies, *War in the Air*, pp. 41–3.

179 Hastings, *Bomber Command*, p. 191.

180 Calvert, *Silent Running*, p. 71.

181 Hastings, *Bomber Command*, pp. 191–2, 194.

182 V.M. Yeates quoted in ibid., p. 195.

183 Frank Baker quoted in Smithies, *War in the Air*, p. 36, his emphasis.

184 R. Hillary, *The Last Enemy* (London: Pan, 1969), p. 137.

185 Hastings, *Bomber Command*, pp. 193, 198, 199.

186 ibid., pp. 252–3.

187 ibid., pp. 184–6, 197.

188 ibid., p. 253; Holmes, *Firing Line*, pp. 14, 213–14.

189 Spector, *At War At Sea*, p. 254.

190 See Chapter 4.

191 See Holmes, *Firing Line*, pp. 270ff.

192 Calvert, *Silent Running*, p. 105.

193 ibid., pp. 165–6; Thwaites, *Atlantic Odyssey*, pp. 111–12.

194 Marine Chris White in Bilton and Kosminsky (eds), *Speaking Out*, p. 234.

195 Dr (then Lieutenant-Commander) David Stevens, personal communication.

196 *A Message From the Falklands: The Life and Gallant Death of David Tinker Lieut. R.N. From His Letters and Poems*, compiled by Hugh Tinker (London: Stackpole Books, 1982), p. 198.

197 Calvert, *Silent Running*, p. 63.

198 Spector, *At War At Sea*, p. 97.

199 Cremer, *U-Boat Commander*, p. 149.

200 On revenge see Calvert, *Silent Running*, pp. 69–70; Middlebrook, *Convoy*, p. 54.

201 Flight-Lieutenant Jeff Glover in Bilton and Kosminsky (eds), *Speaking Out*, pp. 154–5.

202 Captain J.A. Lopez in ibid., p. 86.

203 Tracy, *Nelson's Battles*, p. 195.

204 Spector, *At War At Sea*, pp. 181, 211.

205 See Chapter 8. See also M. MacPherson, *Long Time Passing: Vietnam and the Haunted Generation* (New York: Doubleday, 1984, Signet paperback edn, 1985), Part III.

206 See Chapter 16.

207 Spector, *At War At Sea*, p. 246.

208 See Chapter 11.

209 Woodward, *One Hundred Days*, pp. 177–8, 193.

210 Chief Petty Officer Ken Enticknab and Petty Officer Sam Bishop in Bilton and Kosminsky (eds), *Speaking Out*, pp. 114, 124.

211 H. Tinker, *A Message From the Falklands,* frontispiece.

212 Lieutenant-Commander Patrick Kettle, RN in Bilton and Kosminsky (eds), *Speaking Out*, p. 95.

213 T. Brokaw, *The Greatest Generation* (New York: Random House, 1998), pp. 281–5.

214 See the recollections of Marion Stock, a British staff nurse in the Falklands in Bilton and Kosminsky (eds), *Speaking Out*, p. 137.

215 For a case study of the problems involved in implementing an earlier technical revolution in naval affairs see Goldrick, 'John R. Jellicoe. Technology's victim' in Sweetman (ed.), *The Great Admirals*.

216 Rosenberg address.

217 K. Watman, 'Global 2000' in *Naval War College Review*, LIV, 2, Spring, 2001, pp. 75–88.

218 See Chapter 14.

219 Spector, *At War At Sea*, pp. 389–90.

220 R. Atkinson, *Crusade: The Untold Story of the Gulf War* (London: Harper Collins, 1994), pp. 13–17, 29–31.

221 See Chapter 14.

222 See, for example, ibid.

223 See Chapter 17.

224 *Mahan on Naval Strategy: Selections From the Writings of Rear Admiral Alfred Thayer Mahan*, edited with an introduction by J.B. Hattendorf (Annapolis: USNIP, 1991), p. xxx.

225 Robert F. Kennedy, *Thirteen Days: A Memoir of the Cuban Missile Crisis* (New York: Signet, 1969), p. 105.

CHAPTER 2

1 Vice Admiral Sir John Collins, *As Luck Would Have It: The Reminiscences of an Australian Sailor* (Sydney: Angus & Robertson, 1965), p. 88.

2 *The Fundamentals of British Maritime Doctrine*, BR 1806 (London: HMSO, 1995).

3 Villeneuve possessed a captured signal book and a contemporary text on naval tactics. See N. Tracy, *Nelson's Battles: The Art of Victory in the Age of Sail* (London: Chatham, 1996), pp. 180–1.

4   *Australian Maritime Doctrine, RAN Doctrine 1* (Canberra: Defence Publishing Service, 2000).

5   See A. Gordon, *The Rules of the Game: Jutland and British Naval Command* (London: John Murray, 1996).

6   B. Lavery, *Nelson and the Nile: The Naval War Against Bonaparte in 1798* (London: Chatham, 1998), p. 105.

7   Quoted in C. Oman, *Nelson* (London: Hodder & Stoughton, 1947), p. 517.

CHAPTER 3

1   R. Falkenberg, *Constantin von Hanneken: Briefe aus China 1879–1886* (Köln, Bohlau Verlag GmbH & Cie, 1998).

2   W.F. Tyler, *Pulling Strings in China* (New York: Richard R. Smith, 1930).

3   L. McGiffin, *Yankee of the Yalu: Philo Norton McGiffin, American Captain in the Chinese Navy (1885–1895)* (New York: E.P. Dutton & Co., 1968).

4   Falkenberg, *Constantin von Hanneken*, p. 349; the names of the foreign advisors have been Anglicised.

5   B.M. Blechman and R.P. Berman, *Guide to Far Eastern Navies* (Annapolis: United States Naval Institute Press, 1978), p. 76; quoting a 16 August 1905, edition of *Japan Mail*.

6   *Chinese Naval Encyclopaedia* (*Zhongguo Haijun Baike Quanshu*) (Beijing: 1998), pp. 226–7.

7   R.N.J. Wright, *The Chinese Steam Navy, 1862–1945* (London: Chatham Publishing, 2000), p. 14.

8   See T.L. Kennedy, 'Li Hung-chang and the Kiangnan Arsenal, 1860–1895' in S.C. Chu & Kwang-Ching Liu, *Li Hung-chang and China's Early Modernization* (Armonk, NY: M.E. Sharpe Inc., 1994), pp. 197–214; S. Spector, *Li Hung-chang and the Huai Army: A Study in Nineteenth-Century Chinese Regionalism* (Seattle, WA: University of Washington Press, 1964).

9   Jukichi Inouye, *The Fall of Wei-hai-wei: Compiled from Official and Other Sources* (Yokohama, Kelly & Walsh, 1895), p. 25.

10   Tyler, *Pulling Strings*, p. 41.

11   ibid., p. 38.

12   J.C. Perry, 'The battle off the Tayang, 17 September 1894', *The Mariner's Mirror*, vol. 50, no. 3 (August 1964), p. 247, quoting a 6 October 1894 article in *Eastern World*.

13   Tyler, *Pulling Strings*, p. 47.

14   A later description of this battle by Philo McGiffin clarified this as: 'Our actual formation, which has justly been criticized, was an indent or zig zag line, [with] the two ironclads in the center'. McGiffin, *Yankee of the Yalu*, p. 121.

15   Tyler, *Pulling Strings*, p. 49; *Chinese Naval Encyclopaedia* (*Zhongguo Haijun Baike Quanshu*) does not comment on this incident, see pp. 1271–2.

16   Tyler, *Pulling Strings*, p. 49.

17   D. Twitchett and J.K. Fairbank (eds), *The Cambridge History of China*, Volume 11: Late Qing, 1800–1911, Part 2 (Cambridge: Cambridge University Press, 1980), p. 106.

18   Tyler, *Pulling Strings*, p. 50.
19   For a description of the battle see Falkenberg, *Constantin von Hanneken*, pp. 349–59.
20   Inouye, *The Fall of Wei-hai-wei*, p. 25.
21   McGiffin, *Yankee of the Yalu*, pp. 64–5.
22   ibid.
23   ibid., p. 123.
24   ibid., p. 116.
25   ibid., p. 123.
26   Cited in B. Swanson, *Eighth Voyage of the Dragon: A History of China's Quest for Seapower* (Annapolis: USNIP, 1982), p. 110.
27   From an unidentified newspaper clipping, entitled '"Yang Wai" and "Metsuchina" Battle (1894)' provided to the author by Tony Dalton.
28   Chia-chien Wang, 'Li Hung-chang and the Peiyang Navy' in Chu & Liu, *Li Hung-chang*, pp. 248–62.
29   McGiffin, *Yankee of the Yalu*, p. 120.
30   Blechman and Berman, *Guide*, p. 79.
31   Tyler, *Pulling Strings*, p. 41.
32   Perry, 'The battle off the Tayang', p. 258.
33   B. Kaplan, 'China's Navy today: storm clouds on the horizon . . . or paper tiger?', *Sea Power*, December 1999.
34   Wang Cho-chung, 'PRC Generals call for reinforcing actual strength of Navy', *Taipei Chung-Kuo Shih-Pao*, 25 March 2001.
35   'Troops of China's three armed services are being assembled in Shantou', *Hong Kong Wen Wei Po,* 27 August 2001.
36   B. Elleman, 'Chinese 20th century naval mutinies: the case of the *Chongqing*' in C. Bell and B. Elleman (eds), *Twentieth Century Naval Mutinies: An International Perspective* (Newbury: Frank Cass, forthcoming).

CHAPTER 4

1   The author appreciates the access to personal papers given to him by Dr Maximilian Graf von Spee.
2   Agreements were concluded between the German government and shipping companies, chiefly for the fast postal steamers of the Norddeutsche Lloyd and the Hamburg-Amerika Line, whereby 20 ships were to become auxiliary cruisers in wartime.
3   'Auszug Operationsarbeiten des Kreuzergeschwaders, 11 April 1912–9 Oktober 1913', Bundesarchiv-Militärarchiv (German Federal Military Archive), Freiburg (BA-MA): RM5 2230, Bl.57. All subsequent 'RM' (Reichs-Marine) designations are from this archive.
4   See C. Dick, *Das Kreuzergeschwader. Sein Werden, Sieg und Untergang* (Berlin: 1927), p. 40.
5   Letter, Spee–Huberta v. Spee, 2 August 1914, Spee Papers: T27/7.
6   E. Raeder, *Der Kreuzerkrieg in den ausländischen Gewässern*, Bd.1, *Das Kreuzergeschwader* (Berlin: 1927), p. 75.

7   Japanese chargé d'affaires–Jagow, 17 August 1914, RM3/v 4578; also in RM3 6859, Bl.49. The full text of the Japanese declaration is in J. MacMurray, *Treaties and Agreements With and Concerning China, 1894–1919* (New York: 1921), Vol. II, No. 1153.

8   *Kriegstagebuch*, 'Betrachtungen' ('Observations'), 7 July 1914, Bl.1.

9   *Kriegstagebuch*, night 3–4 August, Bl.8.

10 *Report*, 14 October 1914, Australian War Memorial (AWM): AWM33/10/2.

11 Quoted without reference in Dick, *Das Kreuzergeschwader*, p. 100.

12 See C.E. Bean in Sir Charles Lucas (ed.), *The Empire at War,* vol. III (Oxford: Oxford University Press, 1924), p. 72.

13 'Bericht Marine-Assistenzarzt Dr. Dengel' in Dick, *Das Kreuzergeschwader,* p. 39.

14 Letter, Spee–Grete von Spee, 18 August 1914, T27/7. Berlin was mistakenly informed by the Stockholm embassy via London that the Australian Fleet had joined with the British in Chinese waters. Telegram, Reichenau–Foreign Office, 17 September 1914, RM3/v, 4578, Bl.47.

15 *Kriegstagebuch*, 4 August 1914, Bl.9.

16 Ambassador Erckert–Chancellor Bethmann Hollweg, 16 April, 18 May 1912; 16 October 1913, Politisches Archiv im Auswärtigen Amt (German Foreign Office Archive), Berlin: R16 680.

17 *Kriegstagebuch*, 1914, Bl.9, 14.

18 ibid., night 6–7 August 1914, Bl.10.

19 ibid., 15 August 1914, Bl.24.

20 See Raeder, *Der Kreuzerkrieg*, pp. 81–2. Communication within the German colonies was primarily by radio. There were high-power transmitters at Tsingtao, Yap, Nauru and Apia, and in 1914 another was being constructed at Bitapaka near Rabaul in New Guinea. At Angaur in the western Carolines, Truk in the eastern Carolines and Jabor in the Marshall Islands there were low-power transmitters in private control. A submarine cable connected Yap with Guam and thence the USA; with Shanghai and Tsingtao; and via Menado in the Celebes with cables to Europe.

21 *Kriegstagebuch*, Bl.15. 'Ambassador reports attack [on Tsingtao] feared daily', Bl.10.

22 ibid., Bl.19–20.

23 ibid. The radio stations at Yap, Rabaul, Nauru, Angaur and Apia all were destroyed or occupied within two months of the outbreak of hostilities.

24 Letter, Spee–Grete v. Spee, 18 August 1914.

25 *Kriegstagebuch*, Bl.21.

26 'Besprechung über Massnahmen gegen Japan', 17 August 1914, RM5 2292, Bl.37.

27 'Stellungnahme von B. und B.III zu der Frage "Was ist zu veranlassen auf das japanische Ultimatum"', 18 August 1914, RM5 2292, Bl.47.

28 *Kriegstagebuch*, Bl.20–1; also comments attached to RM5/v 2287, Bl.34, 'Aus Privatbriefen des gefallenen Kapitän z.S. Maerker, Kommandant S.M.S. "Gneisenau"', 14 August 1914.

29 A network of intelligence gathering agents was maintained in all ports by the Marine-Kriegsnacrichtenwesen (Naval Intelligence Service). These were

coordinated by local consuls, who held the Naval Code Books and liaised with visiting warship commanders.

30   *Kriegstagebuch*, Bl.20–1, 24–5. On American interests see S. Livermore, 'American strategy and diplomacy in the South Pacific, 1890–1914', *Pacific Historical Review*, vol. XII, March 1943, pp. 33–51.

31   'Aus Privatbriefen . . . Maerker', RM5/v 2287, Bl.34, op.cit.

32   *Kriegstagebuch*, Bl.26.

33   Letter, Spee–Huberta v. Spee, 18 August 1914, T27/7.

34   Letters, Spee–Grete v. Spee, 18, 29 August 1914, T27/7.

35   Letter, Spee–Grete v. Spee, 14 September 1914, T27/7.

36   Letter, Spee–Grete v. Spee, 1 October 1914, T27/7.

37   Letter, Otto–Grete v. Spee, 11 October 1914, T27/7.

38   Letter, Spee–Grete v. Spee, 13 October 1914, T27/7.

39   Letter, Otto–Grete v. Spee, 11 October 1914, T27/7.

40   Behncke–Pohl, 2 October 1914, RM5/v 4004, Bl.284; Pohl–Spee, 10 October 1914, RM5 2229, Bl.46; also 'Ganz Geheim', Behncke–Pohl, undated draft, Bl.19.

41   *Kriegstagebuch*, Bl.20.

42   See Raeder, *Der Kreuzerkrieg*, pp. 75–6, 110.

43   The two armoured cruisers were unsuited to extended operations without bases because of their high coal requirements. At 10 knots *Scharnhorst*'s daily consumption was 93 tonnes; in comparison that of the light cruisers was around 50 tonnes. At 20 knots consumption for the armoured cruisers rose sharply to 420 tonnes.

44   *Report*, 20 August 1914, National Archives of Australia, Victoria (NAA(Vic)): MP472, 6/14/6475.

45   Report in *New York Herald*, 16 December 1914.

46   Pohl–Spee, 10 October 1914, RM5 2229, Bl.46; Embassy Stockholm–Foreign Office, 26 November 1914, Bl.81.

47   Letter, Spee–Ferdinand v. Spee, 27 October 1914, T27/7.

48   Cited without reference in Dick, *Das Kreuzergeschwader*, p. 93.

49   Letter, Spee–Grete v. Spee, 27 October 1914, T27/7.

50   Letter, Spee–Huberta v. Spee, 27 October 1914, T27/7.

51   Letter of an officer in *Scharnhorst*, 2 November 1915, published in *Kieler Neueste Nachrichten*, 4 March 1915.

52   *Sydney Morning Herald*, 4 November 1935.

53   Otto von Spee, letter of 3 November 1914, published in *Kieler Neueste Nachrichten*, 20 April 1915.

54   Letter, Spee–Grete v. Spee, 2 November 1914, T27/7.

55   Letter, Spee–Grete v. Spee, 26 November 1914, T27/7.

56   *Sydney Morning Herald*, 4 November 1935.

57   Report of Consul-General Gumprecht in Valparaiso, Erckert–Foreign Office, 30 November 1914, RM3 3165, Bl.46.

58   F.W. Rasenack, 'Wie kam es zur Schlacht bei den Falkandinseln?', *MOH-Nachrichten*, Bd.9/12, 1960, p. 221.

59   Behncke–Pohl, 2 February 1915, RM5/v 4004, Bl.239.

60 Letter, Otto–Grete von Spee, 11 October 1914, T27/7.

61 Spee writing to his mother in 1898, quoted without reference in K. Middlemass, *Command of the Far Seas: A Naval Campaign of the First World War* (London: Hutchinson, 1961), p. 47.

62 Stubenrauch–Foreign Office, 11 December 1914, RM5 2229, Bl.95.

63 Sir Herbert Richmond, *National Policy and Naval Strength* (London: 1927), cited in Arthur J. Marder, *From the Dreadnought to Scapa Flow: The Royal Navy in the Fisher Era, 1904–1919*, Vol. 1, *The Road to War* (London: 1961), p. 367.

64 Viktor Valois, *Nieder mit England. Betrachtungen und Erwägungen* (Berlin: 1915).

CHAPTER 5

1 G. Blainey, 'A nation of islanders, we can hardly see the sea', *Weekend Australian*, 8–9 October 1988. He listed four main reasons. The first was a popular belief, especially among the young, that nuclear weapons had made navies outmoded. The second was that, because land-based conflicts had predominated in the four decades following the Second World War, public attention had turned away from naval power. Third, in Australia, this perception was reinforced by the nation's most recent experience of conflict, the Vietnam War. In Vietnam, the Army's operations, rather than those of the Royal Australian Navy, had received greater media attention, perhaps because men patrolling through jungles made better television than a destroyer executing a naval gunfire support mission. Finally, Blainey pointed out that a long period of relative peace on the world's oceans had disguised the importance of naval power. Ironically, this had led to a situation which permitted small nations, such as Liberia and Panama, possessing at best 'tinpot' navies, to have the largest merchant fleets in the world.

2 'Major-General Hutton on Australian Defence and the Military Forces', National Archives of Australia, Canberra Office (NAA(ACT)): A5954/69, 794/5.

3 Also accompanying the fleet were the transport *Kanowna*, the supply ship *Aorangi*, the collier *Koolonga* and the tanker *Murex*. See S.S. Mackenzie, *Official History of Australia in the War of 1914–18*, vol. X, *The Australians at Rabaul* (Sydney: Angus & Robertson, 1937).

4 The Germans expected the main Australian attack to be launched against the settlement of Herbertshöhe. The German operational plan, however, placed a higher priority on defending the wireless station, a strategic communications link for their East Asian Squadron. See 'Narrative of Events, Operations 11th, 12th Sept', 11 March 1915, NAA, Melbourne Office (NAA (VIC)): MP1049/1, 1915/079.

5 F.S. Burnell, *Australia v. Germany: The Story of the Taking of German New Guinea* (London: Allen & Unwin, 1915), p. 91.

6 See 'Seizure of the German Pacific possessions' in *Commonwealth Military Journal*, vol. 6, 1915, pp. 45–54.

7   Letter, Major P. Molloy to Naval Secretary, 20 April 1915, NAA(VIC): MP1049/1, 1915/079.

8   Apparently the mock attacks made by this aircraft were too realistic, as the Navy complained to the RAAF about the 'safety' of the attacks. See unnamed newspaper cutting, NAA(VIC): B1535/0, 754/4/29.

9   Admiral W. Ford, RN, 'Report on Combined Operations in Hobart to the Secretary of the Naval Board', 26 April 1935, NAA (Vic): B1535/0, 754/4/29.

10   N. Gow, 'Australian Army strategic planning 1919–39', *Australian Journal of Politics and History*, vol. 23, no. 2, August 1977, p. 171.

11   J. Robertson, *Australia at War, 1939–1945* (Melbourne: Heinemann, 1980), p. 7.

12   An account of Australia's last-minute defensive preparations in this area is given by M. Evans in *Developing Australia's Maritime Concept of Strategy: Lessons from the Ambon Disaster of 1942*, Study Paper No. 303, Land Warfare Studies Centre, Canberra, July 2000.

13   Major General S.F. Rowell, 'Long Range Planning for Offensive Action – Landing Operations', 13 March 1942, NAA(VIC): MP 1587/1, 289.

14   As part of long-standing agreements between Britain and Australia, the training and equipment of the two nations was standardised to meet the needs of cooperation in imperial defence. Australian forces used British doctrine manuals, generally without any alteration for local conditions.

15   Letter, Walker to Chief of Staff Combined Operations HQ UK, 24 March 1943, Public Record Office, London (PRO): DEFENCE 2/1045.

16   Letter, Walker to Chief of Staff Combined Operations HQ UK, 10 April 1943, ibid.

17   W.N. Swan, *Spearheads of Invasion* (Sydney: Angus & Robertson, 1953).

18   Major N.A. Vickery, 'Report on Naval Bombardment in the Lae Operations', 28 October 1943, Australian War Memorial (AWM): AWM 54, 505/7/18 Part 2, p. 1.

19   ibid., p. 5.

20   Captain K.A. Coventry, 'Aerial Observations and Control of Naval Bombardment—Aitape, July 1944', 11 August 1944, AWM: AWM 54, 603/6/1.

21   The full list of reasons is given in G. Long, *Australia in the War of 1939–1945: The Final Campaigns* (Canberra: Australian War Memorial, 1963), p. 505.

22   M. Uren, *1,000 Men at War: The Story of the 2/16th A.I.F.* (Melbourne: Heinemann, 1959), p. 229.

23   Long, *Australia in the War*, p. 506.

24   '3 Australian Ship Detachment Reports', 25 March 1944, AWM: AWM 54, 963/21/14 Part 1.

25   Commander A.V. Knight, 'Report of Proceedings *Westralia*', 1 June 1944, AWM: AWM 78, 363/2.

26   'Naval Requirements for AMF Units in Amphibious Operations', 30 June 1945, NAA(VIC): MP 1587/1, 289.

27   Rear Admiral Albert Noble, 'Action Report on Balikpapan-Manggar–Borneo Operations, US 7th Fleet', 30 August 1945, PRO: ADM 199/1516.

28 'Paper by DCNS, CAPT R. Dowling on the postwar defences of Australia', 27 October 1943, NAA(VIC): MP1185/8, 1855/2/549.

29 'An Appreciation by the Chiefs of Staff on the Strategical Position of Australia, February, 1946', NAA(ACT): A5954/69, 1645/9, Part I, p. 6.

30 The Chiefs' conclusions, based as they were on recent experiences in the Second World War, remain sound. The most significant conclusion of Millett and Murray's three-volume work, *Military Effectiveness*, which presents case studies of the performance of military organisations in the period 1914 to 1945, was that nations with a sound strategy could redress the tactical and operational deficiencies of their armed forces. Those nations with a faulty strategy, however, notwithstanding the battlefield effectiveness of their armed forces, were invariably defeated. See A. Millett and W. Murray (eds), *Military Effectiveness* (Boston: Unwin Hyman, 1989).

31 'An Appreciation by the Chiefs of Staff on the Strategical Position of Australia, February, 1946', NAA(ACT): A5954/69, 1645/9, Part X, p. 24 and Part XII, p. 27.

32 The Australian Naval Aviation Museum, *Flying Stations: A Story of Australian Naval Aviation* (Sydney: Allen & Unwin, 1998), p. 88.

33 N. Bartlett (ed.), *With the Australians in Korea* (Canberra: Australian War Memorial, 1960), p. 135.

34 'War Diary—Korean Operations', 72 CBAL Section, 31 October 1951, Naval History Directorate, Canberra.

35 The official history ascribes this innovation to Captain Harries, but it was actually an initiative of the Army CBALOs. See R. O'Neill, *Australia in the Korean War 1950–53*, Volume II: *Combat Operations* (Canberra: AWM and the Australian Government Publishing Service, 1985), p. 475. See the Australian Naval Aviation Museum, *Flying Stations*, p. 93.

36 ibid., pp. 86–7.

37 'Report, HMAS *Sydney* in Korean waters' by Major M.B. Simkin, Naval History Directorate, Canberra.

38 The Australian Naval Aviation Museum, *Flying Stations*, p. 101.

39 ibid., p. 100. These figures were compiled by the CBALS.

40 See Commonwealth of Australia, *Defence 2000: Our Future Defence Force* (Canberra: Defence Publishing Service, 2000), p. 47.

41 Lord Tedder, 'The unities of war' in E. Emme (ed.), *The Impact of Air Power: National Security and World Politics* (New York: Van Nostrand Company, 1950), p. 339.

42 P. Cosgrove, unpublished address to the AMPHIB 2000 Conference, Randwick Barracks Conference Centre, 22 June 2000.

CHAPTER 6

1 The most comprehensive account of the action is contained in A.W. Jose, *The Royal Australian Navy 1914–1918. The Official History of Australia in the War of 1914–1918*, vol. IX (Sydney: Angus & Robertson, 1928), pp. 150–207.

2   Cited in Jose, *The Royal Australian Navy*, p. 198.

3   Leonard Darby, 'Report on the wounded in the action between the "Sydney" and the "Emden"', *Journal of the Royal Naval Medical Service,* vol. I, July 1915, p. 228.

4   'Emden Diary', 9 November 1914, NHD: 372/45.

5   *Medical Officer's Journal,* HMAS *Sydney*, 1913–1919, AWM.

6   Darby, 'Report on the wounded in the action between the "Sydney" and the "Emden"', p. 230.

7   D. Steven (ed.), *The Royal Australian Navy* (Melbourne: Oxford University Press, 2001), vol. III in *The Australian Centenary History of Defence*, p. 40.

8   *Medical Officer's Journal,* HMAS *Sydney*.

9   Darby, 'Report on the wounded in the action between the "Sydney" and the "Emden"', pp. 231–2.

10 *Medical Officer's Journal,* HMAS *Sydney*.

11 ibid.

12 ibid.

13 ibid.

14 'Extracts from *Medical Officer's Journal*', NHD: 372/45.

15 ibid.

16 ibid.

17 ibid.

18 Jose, *The Royal Australian Navy*, pp. 192–3.

19 Cited in ibid p. 202

20 A.S. Walker, *Medical Services of the RAN and RAAF, Australia In The War Of 1939–1945* (Canberra: Australian War Memorial, 1961), pp. 2–3.

21 G. Bywater, notes in possession of author, January 1988.

22 Walker, *Medical Services*, p. 74.

23 Darby, 'Report on the wounded in the action between the "Sydney" and the "Emden"', p. 228.

CHAPTER 7

1   R.D. Layman, *Before the Aircraft Carrier: The Development of Aviation Vessels 1849–1922* (London: Conway Maritime Press, 1989).

2   N. Friedman, *British Carrier Aviation: The Evolution of the Ships and their Aircraft* (London: Conway Maritime Press, 1988).

3   Rear Admiral M.F. Sueter, *Airmen or Noahs: Fair Play for our Airmen* (London: Sir Isaac Pitman & Sons Ltd, 1928).

4   D. Macintyre, *Wings of Neptune* (London: Peter Davis Ltd, 1963).

5   H. Popham, *Into Wind: A History of British Naval Flying* (London: Hamish Hamilton, 1969).

6   R.D. Layman, *The Cuxhaven Raid* (London: Conway Maritime Press, 1985).

7   Captain S.W. Roskill, DSC, RN (ed.), *Documents Relating to the Naval Air Service 1908–1918* (London: Navy Records Society, 1969).

8   T.C. Hone, N. Friedman and M.D. Mandeles, *American and British Aircraft Carrier Development 1919–1941* (Annapolis: Naval Institute Press, 1999).

9   E. Arpee, *From Frigates to Flat Tops: The Story of the Life and Achievements of Rear Admiral Moffett 'The Father of Naval Aviation'* (USA: published and distributed by the author, 1953).

10   C.G. Reynolds, *The Fast Carriers: The Forging of an Air Navy* (Annapolis: USNIP, 1992).

11   RN Naval Staff History of the Second World War, *The Development of British Naval Aviation 1919–1945* (London: Historical Section of the Admiralty, 1954).

12   D. Young, *Rutland of Jutland* (London: Cassell, 1963).

13   H. Van Willigenberg, 'Graf Zeppelin afloat: Germany's aircraft carrier—what might have been', *Air Enthusiast Magazine*, Issue 92, 2001.

14   R. Jones, *Seagulls, Cruisers and Catapults* (Taroona: Pelorus Publications, 1989).

15   J.D. Brown, *Aircraft Carriers* (London: MacDonald & Jane's, 1977).

16   Popham, *Into Wind*.

17   Commander D.A. Hobbs, MBE, RN, *Aircraft Carriers of the Royal and Commonwealth Navies* (London: Greenhill Books, 1996).

18   J.D. Brown, *Carrier Operations in World War 2*, Volume 1 (London: Ian Allen, 1968).

19   J.D. Brown, *Carrier Fighters* (London: MacDonald & Jane's, 1975).

20   RN Naval Staff History, *Development of Naval Aviation 1919–1945*.

21   C. Shores, *Fledgling Eagles* (London: Grub Street, 1991).

22   T.P. Lowry and J.W.G. Wellham, *The Attack on Taranto: Blueprint for Pearl Harbor* (Mechanicsburg, PA: Stackpole Books, 1995).

23   Vice Admiral B.B. Schofield, CB, CBE, *The Attack on Taranto* (London: Ian Allen, 1973).

24   Friedman, *British Carrier Aviation*.

25   Hobbs, *Aircraft Carriers of the Royal and Commonwealth Navies*.

26   Commander D.A. Hobbs, MBE, RN, 'Ship-borne air anti-submarine warfare' in S. Howarth and D. Law (eds), *The Battle of the Atlantic 1939–1945: The 50th Anniversary Naval Conference* (Annapolis: USNIP, 1994).

27   J.D. Brown, *Carrier Operations in World War 2, Volume 2: The Pacific Navies* (London: Ian Allen, 1974).

28   R. Humble, *Fraser of North Cape* (London: Routledge & Kegan Paul, 1983).

29   Brown, *Carrier Operations in World War 2, Volume 2: The Pacific Navies*.

30   N. Polmar, *Aircraft Carriers: A Graphic History of Carrier Aviation and its Influence on World Events* (London: MacDonald & Co., 1983).

31   N. Friedman, *The Post-War Naval Revolution* (London: Conway Maritime Press, 1986).

32   J.R.P. Lansdown, *With the Carriers in Korea: The Fleet Air Arm Story 1950–53* (London: Square One Publications, 1992).

33   A. Gordon, 'HMAS *Sydney* in Korea: the firefly observer' in T. Frame, J. Goldrick and P. Jones (eds), *Reflections on the RAN* (Kenthurst: Kangaroo Press, 1991), p. 294.

34   N. Friedman, *US Aircraft Carriers: An Illustrated Design History* (Annapolis: USNIP, 1983).

35   The Australian Naval Aviation Museum, *Flying Stations: A Story of Australian Naval Aviation* (Sydney: Allen & Unwin, 1998).

36   D. Stevens (ed.), *Prospects for Maritime Aviation in the Twenty-First Century*, Papers in Australian Maritime Affairs No. 7 (Canberra: Maritime Studies Program, 1999).

CHAPTER 8

1   A story expertly told in J. Sumida, *In Defence of Naval Supremacy: Finance, Technology and British Naval Policy 1889–1914* (Boston: Unwin Hyman, 1989).

2   J. Hayes, *Face the Music* (Edinburgh: The Pentland Press, 1991).

3   For the strategic circumstances and the developing Japanese threat, see A.J. Marder, *Old Friends, New Enemies: The Royal Navy and the Imperial Japanese Navy*, vol. I, *Strategic Illusions, 1936–1941* (Oxford: Clarendon Press, 1981).

4   M. Middlebrook and P. Mahoney, *Battleship: The Loss of the* Prince of Wales *and the* Repulse (London: Allen Lane, 1977).

5   There is a good record of *Shropshire*'s service in the RAN from 2 December 1942–30 May 1947 in S. Nicholls, *HMAS* Shropshire (Sydney: Naval Historical Society, 1989).

6   The story of the *kamikaze* cult and its effect on US operations in the Pacific is told in D. and P. Warner, *Kamikaze* (Melbourne: Oxford University Press, 1983).

CHAPTER 9

1   R.A. Blain, 'Grim days in the Java Seas' in T.M. Jones and I.L. Idriess, *The Silent Service: Action Stories of the Anzac Navy* (Sydney: Angus & Robertson, 1952), p. 229.

2   Cited in L.J. Lind and M.A. Payne, *HMAS* Hobart (Sydney: The Naval Historical Society of Australia, 1971), p. 32.

3   See D. Thomas, *Battle of the Java Sea* (London: Andre Deutsch Ltd, 1968).

CHAPTER 10

1   Reference works give different dates of birth, some 11 March 1917; others, including his RAN personnel record (presumably based on his birth certificate), give 3 November 1917: the latter is correct. I am grateful to Mrs Valerie McDonnell for advising on this and several other points in a letter of 13 July 2001. Entries on Macdonnell appear in *Contemporary Author* (1969), p. 716; *Contemporary Author New Revision Series* (1983), p. 336; *Who's Who of*

Australian Writers; the *Oxford Companion to Australian Children's Literature*; and John Loder, *Australian Crime Fiction: A Bibliography 1857–1993* (Melbourne: D.W. Thorpe 1994).

2   'Petty-officer J.E.M.', 'Opening phase', *HMAS* (Canberra: AWM, 1942), pp. 163–5. Although according to his service record Macdonnell had left HMAS *Warrego* on 12 February 1942, his piece describes his part in the raids of 19 February. Former shipmates recall him as having written for the *Australian Woman's Weekly* also, but I can find no record of him having done so.

3   J.E. Macdonnell, *Fleet Destroyer* (Melbourne: Angus & Robertson, 1945).

4   Macdonnell concentrated at first on factual rather than fictional pieces. His *As You Were* contributions in 1946 alone include 'Prelude to invasion', pp. 11–13; '*Stuart* of Matapan', pp. 21–3; 'Timor evacuation', pp. 60–2; and 'Thumbs up!', pp. 173–4.

5   Gill to Treloar, 7 July 1947, official history correspondence, 1947–49, AWM: AWM 69, item 45/2.

6   J.E. Macdonnell, 'What you learn in the navy', *Bulletin*, 22 March 1961, p. 17.

7   ibid.

8   C. Higham, 'The fictionaires', *Bulletin*, 25 February 1967, p. 17.

9   J. Hetherington, 'A 12-novel-a-year-man', *Daily Telegraph*, 29 October 1960.

10 Macdonnell disclaims books published under several pen-names recorded in the National Library of Australia's catalogue, including Kerry Mitchell, James Workman, Noni Arden and Rebecca Dee. If titles by these writers are included, his output reaches over 250 novels, with 27 published in one year, 1963. If they are not by Macdonnell then the National Library's catalogue should be corrected.

11 Literary reference works mention Macdonnell superficially. Loder's *Australian Crime Fiction*, pp. 161–2, for example, repeats the error that he published under the pseudonym 'Mark Hood'.

12 I am grateful to the following former members of the RAN for sharing their memories of Macdonnell: John 'Nobby' Clarke (Kurralta Park, SA); Ashley Coleman (Mount Nelson, Tas); Shane Dooley (Tugun, Qld); David Jackson (Maroochydore, Qld); Frank Merry (Neerabup, WA); and James Stewart (Frankston, Vic). Macdonnell himself, as his wife put it, 'does not credit the "notebook on watch" comment'.

13 Higham, 'The fictionaires'.

14 J.E. Macdonnell, *Gimme the Boats!* (London: Constable, 1953), p. 208.

15 J.E. Macdonnell, *Commander Brady* (London: Constable, 1956), p. 71.

16 J.E. Macdonnell, *Escort Ship* (Sydney: Horwitz, 1960), p. 51.

17 J.E. Macdonnell, *Jim Brady, Leading Seaman* (London: Constable, 1954), pp. 249–53.

18 J. Stewart to author, 17 January 2001.

19 J.E. Macdonnell, *Bilgewater, or Meet the Navy* (Sydney: Horwitz, 1958).

20 Higham, 'The fictionaires', p. 17.

21 Macdonnell, *Gimme the Boats!*, p. 207.

CHAPTER 11

1   This chapter arises out of research conducted in conjunction with Peter Nunan of the Queensland Maritime Museum into the story of the American submarine base and the submarine task force established in Brisbane from 1942–1945. Thomas Parks was particularly supportive of the project, and open and clear in his memories of life as a submariner. I very much enjoyed my correspondence with Tom, and a strong friendship developed. Sadly, this was cut short when he passed away unexpectedly on 4 October 2000 in his 80th year.

2   T. Parks, Internet site http://www.geocities.com/Baja/Dunes/4791/submarines, p. 2.

3   Parks, in interview with J.F. Wukovits of *Military History Magazine*, http://www.geocities.com/Baja/Dunes/4791/interview, p. 2.

4   ibid.

5   ibid.

6   This was in fact the aircraft ferry *Kamogawa Maru* (6440 tons), torpedoed north of Lombok on the night of 2 March 1942. Her sinking was not confirmed until after the war. See J.D. Alden, *U.S. Submarine Attacks During World War II* (Annapolis: USNIP, 1989), p. 5.

7   Letter, Parks to author, 24 November 1999.

8   *Langley* was sunk by Japanese aircraft south of Java on 27 February 1942. Only 146 out of her total crew of 439 survived the sinkings, first of *Langley*, then of her rescue ship USS *Pecos* three days later. See W.G. Winslow, *The Fleet the Gods Forgot* (Annapolis: USNIP, 1984), pp. 232–40.

9   Letter, Parks to author, 24 November 1999.

10   http://www.geocities.com/Baja/Dunes/4791/ interview, p. 3.

11   ibid., p. 4.

12   Letter, Parks to author, 12 December 1999.

13   http://www.geocities.com/Baja/Dunes/4791/interview, p. 3.

14   See E. Gray, *Few Survived* (London: Futura Books, 1987), pp. 159–76.

15   Letter, Parks to author, 23 January 2000.

16   Letter, Parks to author, 31 January 2000.

17   Letter, Parks to author, 24 April 2000.

18   These three manufacturers were Winton, taken over by General Motors, Fairbanks Morse and Hoover, Owens, Rentschler (HOR). The HOR design proved highly unreliable and many of the twenty submarines originally fitted with these engines had them replaced by the more dependable General Motors or Fairbanks Morse models. See C. Blair, *Silent Victory* (Philadelphia: J.B. Lippincott, 1975), pp. 57–66, 263–6, 439–46.

19   Letter, Parks to author, 24 April 2000.

20   ibid.

21   Letter, Parks to author, 7 December 1999.

22   Letter, Parks to author, 23 January 2000.

23   Letter, Parks to author, 7 December 1999.

24   Letter, Parks to author, 23 January 2000.

25 Letter, Parks to author, 24 November 1999.

26 Letter, Parks to author, 2 December 1999.

27 ibid.

28 See T. Roscoe, *United States Submarine Operations in World War II* (Annapolis: USNIP, 1958), pp. 112–13, 145–6.

29 ibid., p. xvi.

30 See G.H. Gill, *Royal Australian Navy 1942–45* (Canberra: Australian War Memorial, 1968), pp. 136–56.

31 Blair, *Silent Victory*, p. 463.

32 Letter, Parks to author, 2 December 1999.

33 Letter, Parks to author, 30 November 1999.

34 Blair, *Silent Victory*, pp. 143–4.

35 ibid., pp. 361, 553.

36 ibid., p. 464.

37 Letter, Parks to author, 23 December 1999.

38 Letter, Parks to author, 17 January 2000.

39 Letter, Parks to author, 7 December 1999.

40 Letter, D. Smay to author, 12 May 2000.

41 Letter, Parks to author, 24 November 1999.

42 Letter, Parks to author, 30 November 1999.

43 Letter, Parks to author, 22 August 2000.

44 Letter, Parks to author, 24 November 1999.

45 See for example P.A. Thompson & R. Macklin, *The Battle of Brisbane* (Sydney: ABC Books, 2000); B. Ralph, *They Passed This Way* (East Roseville: Kangaroo Press, 2000), pp. 171–93; and P. Charlton, *South Queensland WWII 1941–1945* (Bowen Hills: Boolarong, 1991), pp. 24–6.

46 Letter, Parks to author, 7 December 1999.

47 Letter, Parks to author, 24 November 1999.

48 Letter, Parks to author, 7 December 1999.

49 Letter, Parks to author, 9 December 1999.

50 ibid.

51 http://www.geocities.com/Baja/Dunes/4791/submarines, p. 2.

52 Letter, Parks to author, 31 January 2000.

53 Letter, Parks to author, 30 November 1999.

CHAPTER 12

1 The author gratefully acknowledges the assistance of John Band, W.A.B. Douglas and The Canadian Battle of Normandy Foundation, Raymond Layard, Doris Whitby, Diane Graves, Lieutenant-Commander Doug McLean, and Matthew Sheldon and the staff of the Royal Naval Museum, Portsmouth.

2 Layard Diary, 9 April 1944. The originals of the diary are at the Royal Naval Museum, Portsmouth, although the copyright remains with the family.

3 Diary, 22 April 1944.

4   Layard MS, p. 1. This manuscript is a summary of the diaries, written long after the war, and is in the possession of the Layard family.

5   R. Kipling, 'The Scholars' in *Rudyard Kipling's Verse* (London: Hodder & Stoughton, 1966), p. 797.

6   This is derived from the comments and correspondence of several officers who served under Commander Layard, most notably Lieutenant-Commander John Band, RCNVR (Retd), who was his First Lieutenant in HMCS *Swansea*.

7   J.R.S. 'Broke, 1942', in *The Naval Review*, vol. 56, 1958, pp. 442–4.

8   A. Easton, *50 North: An Atlantic Battleground* (Toronto: Ryerson, 1963).

9   Captain (D) Liverpool, Form S-450, 26 November 1942. Layard's papers are in the possession of the family.

10   Details of Layard's career are from the diary and from a long hand-written MS Layard wrote in later life based on the diary. He also wrote a number of articles on his early naval service which appeared in *The Naval Review* in the 1970s. Accounts of some of his First World War experiences also appear in M. Arthur, *The True Glory: The Royal Navy, 1914–1939* (London: Hodder & Stoughton, 1996).

11   C. Whayman, interview with Commander A.F.C. Layard, 27 February 1992, Oral History collections of the Royal Naval Museum, also cited in R. Spector, *At War at Sea: Sailors and Naval Combat in the Twentieth Century* (New York: Viking, 2001), p. 36.

12   Commander J. Baker-Creswell, RN (Retd), to Vice Admiral Peter Gretton, RN (Retd), 5 October 1981 National Maritime Museum, Greenwich, Gretton Papers, vol. 23, Part 1, MS 93/008.

13   Diary, 28 July 1941.

14   Later Layard took the Western Approaches tactical course conducted by Captain Gilbert Roberts.

15   For SC 94 see Anti-Submarine Warfare Division, 'Analysis of U-boat operations in the vicinity of Convoy S.C. 94. 31st July–13th August, 1942', 15 September 1942; Captain (D) Liverpool, 'S.C. 94', 20 August 1942; 'Report of proceedings received from Commanding Officer HMS *Broke*', PRO: ADM 199/2007.

16   This was the corvette HMS *Primrose*.

17   Diary, 9 August 1942.

18   HMS *Broke*, 'Report of attack on U-boat', undated, National Archives of Canada (NAC): RG 24, vol. 11334, 8280-SC-94; *Befehlshaber der Unterseeboote* (German U-boat headquarters), War Diary, 8–9 August 1942, Directorate of History and Heritage (DHH), NDHQ, Ottawa: 79/446; and R.C. Fisher, unpublished MS, 'Fog of war: the battle of the Atlantic, summer 1942', July 1991, p. 98, Naval History Collection, DHH: 2000/5.

19   See P. Gretton, *Convoy Escort Commander* (London: Cassell, 1964); D. Macintyre, *U-Boat Killer* (London: Batsford, 1971); and A. Burn, *The Fighting Captain: Frederick John Walker and The Battle of the Atlantic* (Barnsley: Pen and Sword, 1998).

20   See also Commanding Officer Operation TERMINAL to Commander Eastern Naval Task Force, 'Operation "TERMINAL"—Report',

11 November 1942, and CO HMS *Broke*, 'Report of Proceedings', 11 November 1942, both PRO: ADM 199/204.

21   'Operation TORCH—Report of Proceedings', Naval Commander, Expeditionary Force, 30 March 1943, 3, PRO: DEFE, 2/602.

22   DSO citation. Layard Papers. The award was gazetted on 16 March 1943. Others in *Broke* were also recognised for gallantry, including two helmsmen who were both awarded the Conspicuous Gallantry Medal for remaining at their position even though being wounded and under fire.

23   Diary, 7 September 1943.

24   The RCN ultimately reached a strength of 90 000. For the effects of expansion on the wartime RCN see R. Sarty, *Canada and the Battle of the Atlantic* (Montreal: Art Global, 1999); M. Milner, *North Atlantic Run: The RCN and the Battle for the Convoys* (Toronto: University of Toronto, 1985); D. Zimmerman, *The Great Naval Battle of Ottawa* (Toronto: University of Toronto, 1989); and W. Glover, 'Manning and training the Allied navies' in S. Howarth and D. Law (eds), *The Battle of the Atlantic* (London: Greenhill, 1994).

25   Diary, 17 October 1943 (his emphasis).

26   ibid., 22 January 1944.

27   Layard MS, 1943, p. 66.

28   Diary, 11 October 1943.

29   ibid., 21 March 1945.

30   ibid., 15 August 1944.

31   ibid., 15 September 1944.

32   ibid., 28 December 1944.

33   This episode caused Layard great trepidation as he was an extremely loyal officer, indeed, his diary rarely contains any criticism of senior officers.

34   Commodore (D) Western Approaches, Form S-450, 25 June 1945, Layard Papers.

35   The devotion to Layard—and now to his memory—of those who sailed with him is quite remarkable. For a testimonial of his time in one ship in particular see F.M. McKee, *HMCS* Swansea: *The Life and Times of a Frigate* (St Catharines: Vanwell, 1994).

36   For the inshore campaign see M. Milner, *The U-Boat Hunters: The RCN and the Offensive Against Germany's Submarines* (Toronto: University of Toronto, 1994); W. McAndrew, D.E. Graves and M. Whitby, *Normandy 1944: The Canadian Summer* (Montreal: Art Global, 1994); D.M. McLean, 'The last cruel winter: RCN support groups and the U-boat Schnorkel Offensive', MA thesis (Kingston: Kingston RMC, 1992); and G. Hessler, *The U-Boat War in the Atlantic* (London: HMSO, 1989).

37   Diary, 21 November 1944.

38   ibid., 27 July 1944.

39   ibid., 1 August 1944.

40   D.M. McLean MS, 'A Canadian escort group in British waters: a history of Escort Group 9', Naval History Collection, DHH: 2000/5.

41   Diary, 12 February 1944.

42 Layard formed a particularly deep respect for the ability of Commander C. Gwinner, DSO, DSC, RN, SO of EG-1, with whom EG-9 often worked.

43 Diary, 6 July 1944.

44 ibid., 9 September 1944.

45 EG-9 is credited with destroying *U-247* on 1 September 1944 and *U-309* on 16 February 1945, but the group also played a role in the sinking of *U-1195* by HMS *Watchman* on 6 April 1945. EG-9 also destroyed three U-boats in the North Atlantic during March–April 1944.

46 Diary, 16 February 1945.

47 ibid., 1 September 1942.

48 ibid., 2 February 1945.

49 ibid., 19 April 1945.

50 ibid., 27 March 1945.

51 The author has had the good fortune to know two former captains of Canadian escorts in the North Atlantic, Allan Easton and Louis Audette. Both freely admitted that they suffered from ulcers—Easton's condition was so acute that he had to go ashore in 1944—and said that many of their colleagues had the same affliction.

52 For details of the reassessment see F.M. McKee, 'Some revisionist history in the Battle of the Atlantic', *The Northern Mariner*, vol. I, no. 4, October 1991, pp. 27–32.

CHAPTER 13

1 The inspiration for this chapter came from discussions with Commander Richard Compton-Hall, RN. My thanks go also to Michael Whitby, Joanna Taplin, Andrew Williams, Dominic Sutherland, John Guest, Doug McLean, William Glover, Peter Nash, Warwick Brown, John Salmon and George Karger.

2 Letters: Baker-Cresswell to Gretton, 5 October 1981; Howard-Johnston to Andrew Yates, 12 July 1980; and Howard-Johnston to Gretton, 28 September 1980, 'H-J' File, Gretton Papers, National Maritime Museum, Greenwich (NMM): MSS/93/008; D.A. Rayner, *Escort: The Battle of the Atlantic* (London: William Kimber, 1955), pp. 78–80.

3 'Note on certain aspects of methodology in operational research', P.M.S. Blackett, May 1943, Royal Society, Blackett Papers, File D.86.

4 Letters: Howard-Johnston to Andrew Yates, 12 July 1980; and Baker-Cresswell to Gretton, 5 October 1981, NMM: MS93/008.

5 E. Terrell, *Admiralty Brief: The Story of Inventions that Contributed to Victory in the Battle of the Atlantic* (London: Harrap, 1958), p. 149.

6 Letters: Baker-Cresswell to Gretton, 5 October 1981; and Howard-Johnston to Gretton, 28 September 1980, NMM: MSS/93/008.

7 See for example D. Macintyre, *U-Boat Killer* (London: Seeley Service & Co., 1976), pp. 121–2; R. Whinney, *The U-boat Peril: An Anti-Submarine Commander's War* (Poole: Blandford, 1986), p. 89.

8 Telephone interview with Lieutenant-Commander John Guest, RNVR, 14 May 2001.

9 'Western Approaches tactical policy', Admiral Max Horton, CinC, Western Approaches, 27 April 1943, RG 24, National Archives of Canada (NAC): File 307-0, vol. 11940, NAC.

10 Letter, Baker-Cresswell to Gretton, 5 October 1981, NMM: MS93/008.

11 AOC 15 Group, 10 December 1944, PRO: AIR 15/582.

12 Letter, Phillimore to author, 4 May 2001.

13 M. Llewellyn-Jones, 'Trials with HM Submarine *Seraph* and British preparations to defeat the Type XXI U-Boat, September–October, 1944', in *The Mariner's Mirror*, November 2000, pp. 434–51.

14 Diary, Commander Layard, 3 February 1945, Royal Naval Museum, Portsmouth.

15 'Remarks on *Philante* exercises, 29 July 1944', W.H. McCrea, 3 August 1944, PRO: ADM 219/142.

16 'Post-war A/S training', CinC Western Approaches, 1 June 1945, PRO: ADM 1/18221.

17 Interview with Commander Peter Richardson, 1 June 1998.

18 Minute by Captain N.A. Prichard, DA/SW, 7 July 1945, PRO: ADM 1/17590.

19 Howard-Johnston to J.D. Brown of the Naval Historical Branch, 24 February 1980, Howard-Johnston Papers, Churchill College Archive Cambridge (CCAC): HWJN.

20 'Post-war A/S training', CinC Western Approaches, 1 June 1945, PRO: ADM 1/18221.

21 'Minutes of meeting held in Admiralty on 4 June 1945 to discuss measures necessary for the coordination of requirements for combined air and surface anti-submarine training', 15 [June] 1945, PRO: ADM 1/18213.

22 'Post-war A/S training', Admiral (Submarines), 17 July 1945, PRO: ADM 1/20045.

23 'Post-war A/S training', [10 August 1945], PRO: ADM 1/20045.

24 Minute by D of P, 26 August 1945, PRO: ADM 1/20045 [emphasis added].

25 'Review of the problems of future A/S warfare' [December 1946], PRO: AIR 15/786.

26 'Russian naval tactics: proposed counter measures to Russian naval threat', 1946–1947, PRO: ADM 1/20030.

27 There may have also been a brief flirtation with the idea of obtaining one of the fast Japanese submarines.

28 'The development of A/S warfare', 4 May 1946, PRO: ADM 1/20960.

29 'Progress in underwater warfare, 1946 edition', PRO: ADM 239/420.

30 Letter, Hunter to CO RNAS *Eglington*, 24 February 1948, RG24 NAC: S-4973-30 Vol. 1, Vol. 1814, Acc. 83–84/167.

31 'Progress in underwater warfare, 1947 edition', PRO: ADM 239/421, p. 54.

32 'Report on combined air–sea anti-submarine exercise', CinC Home Fleet, 23 May 1946, PRO: ADM 1/19658.

33 'First Commonwealth TAS liaison meeting [10–20 October 1949]—Report by RAN representative', undated, NAA(VIC): MP 1185/8, 1846/4/343.

34   'Eleventh T.A.S. liaison meeting: minutes', Part 3, 'Exercise castinets', 9–11 September 1952, PRO: ADM 189/235.

35   'USS *Trumpetfish*, operations with Royal Navy forces off Londonderry, May–June 1948', 22 July 1948, RG 313, US National Archives (NARA): Box 96.

36   Email, D. Smith to author, 1 May 2001.

37   'The first experiences of A/S actions with intermediate (B) submarines: addendum to C.B. 04050(48)—progress in underwater warfare, 1948', PRO: ADM 239/423.

38   'Progress report—spring term, 1950 (9 January–31 March)', 25 April 1950, RG24, NAC: S-4973-30-1 Vol. 1, Vol. 1815, Acc. 83–84/167.

39   'Remarks on T.A.S. warfare—second thoughts from Londonderry', HMS *Creole*, 22 December 1950, Adams Papers (private collection deposited in Churchill College Archive Cambridge).

40   The carrier-based Gannet A/S aircraft was also in development at this time.

41   'Eleventh T.A.S. liaison meeting: minutes', Part 4, 'Progress at Londonderry', 9–11 September 1952, PRO: ADM 189/235.

42   'Joint Anti-Submarine School, Londonderry—progress report—summer term 1952', CinC Plymouth, 16 September 1952, PRO: ADM 1/23733.

43   Email, P. James to author, 15 August 2000.

44   Tony [Philip] James, 'Impressions of a night navex—1951' in *The Growler: Newsletter of the "Shackleton Association"*, Spring 2000, p. 15.

45   Email, Squadron Leader P. James to author, 14 June 2001.

46   'Eleventh T.A.S. liaison meeting: minutes', Part 4, 'Evaluation of fast A/S frigate conversions', 9–11 September 1952, PRO: ADM 189/235.

47   ibid.

CHAPTER 14

1   On naval operations during the Gulf War, see D. Stevens (ed.), *The Royal Australian Navy* (Melbourne: Oxford University Press, 2001); and E. Marolda and R. Schneider, *Shield and Sword: The United States Navy and the Persian Gulf War* (Washington, DC: Naval Historical Centre, 1998).

CHAPTER 15

1   J. Keegan, *Battle at Sea: From Man-of-war to Submarine* (London: Pimlico, 1993), pp. 2–3.

2   W.H. Ross, *Lucky Ross: The Autobiography of an RAN Officer—1934–51* (Carlisle, WA: Hesperion Press, 1994), p. 143.

3   Cited in M. Wiggins, *U-boat Adventures: Firsthand Accounts from World War II* (Annapolis: USNIP, 1999), p. 89.

4   Captain W.P. Hughes, USN, *Fleet Tactics: Theory and Practice* (Annapolis: USNIP, 1986), p. 7.

5   Cited in J.B. Hattendorf (ed.), *Mahan on Naval Strategy* (Annapolis: USNIP, 1991), p. xxx.

6   Admiral Sir R.H. Bacon, *The Life of Lord Fisher of Kilverstone* (London: Hodder & Stoughton, 1929), vol. 1, p. 171.

7   For a notable exception see M. Johnston, *Fighting the Enemy: Australian Soldiers and their Adversaries in World War II* (Cambridge: Cambridge University Press, 2000).

8   N. Monsarrat, *The Cruel Sea* (Harmondsworth: Penguin, 1951), p. 10.

9   N.A.M. Rodger (ed.), *Memoirs of a Seafaring Life: The Narrative of William Spavens* (London: The Folio Society, 2000, first published in 1796), pp. 86–7.

10   *Royal Australian Navy Prayers and Hymns* (Melbourne: Government Printer, undated), p. 14A.

11   J.H. Payne, 'A sailor's Odyssey', copy held by NHD.

12   R.H. Hain, 'Typhoon Ruth' in N. Bartlett (ed.), *With the Australians in Korea* (Canberra: Australian War Memorial, 1960), p. 225.

13   A.R. Grimmer, *A History of HMAS* Ipswich (Beecroft, NSW: HMAS *Ipswich* Association, 1993), p. 12.

14   B. Sheedy, *The War at Sea* (Dromana, Vic: Dromana Printing, 1996), p. 7.

15   A.S. Walker, *Medical Services of the RAN and RAAF, Australia in the War of 1939–1945* (Canberra: AWM, 1961), p. 161.

16   R. Parkin, *Out of the Smoke: The Story of a Sail* (London: The Hogarth Press, 1960), p. 1.

17   'Analysis of survival rates (RCN) during World War II', undated, NHD.

18   'What every shipwrecked sailor should know', in *The Argus*, 24 April 1943, p. 3.

19   Cited in F. Walker, *HMAS* Armidale*: The Ship That Had to Die* (Budgewoi: Kingfisher Press, 1990), p. 92.

20   ibid., p. 65.

21   M. Williams, *H.M. Australian Ship 'KAPUNDA'* (Beverley: Eureka Press, undated), p. 82.

22   J.E. Macdonnell, *Bilgewater, or Meet the Navy* (Sydney: Horwitz, 1958), p. 85.

23   Diary of CPO Whiting, 22 May 1941, cited in B. Whiting, *Ship of Courage: The Epic Story of HMAS* Perth *and Her Crew* (Sydney: Allen & Unwin, 1994), p. 12.

24   J.F. Moyes, *The Scrap Iron Flotilla* (Sydney: NSW Bookstall, 1944), p. 88.

25   Newspaper cutting in S. Nicholls, *HMAS* Shropshire (Sydney: Naval Historical Society, 1989), p. 216.

26   Williams, *'KAPUNDA'*, p. 120.

27   *The* Pioneer Observer, 1 May 1915, Naval History Directorate (NHD), Canberra: HMAS *Pioneer* file.

28   'War cruises of *Sydney* and *Melbourne*', unpublished manuscript, NHD, p. 247.

29   *The* Pioneer Observer, 1 May 1915.

30   Diary of Stoker P.N. Faust, HMAS *Australia*, 7 May 1915, NHD.

31   Speech by Rear Admiral F. Haworth-Booth, RAN, at a luncheon for the Rt Hon. Joseph Cook, contained in 108th Report of the Australian Naval Representative, London, 28 August 1918, NAA (VIC): MP 1049/1 1918/013.

32   'War cruises of *Sydney* and *Melbourne*', p. 247.

33   Diary of Yeoman of Signals C.F.G. Cleary, HMAS *Australia*, AWM: PR 82/72.

34   Cited in F.M. McGuire, *The Royal Australian Navy: Its Origin, Development and Organization* (Melbourne: Oxford University Press, 1948), p. 166.

35   See P. Cordier 'Knights, Huns, and the case of the *Emden*: images in British propaganda during the early months of the Great War' in W.B. Cogar (ed.), *New Interpretations in Naval History* (Annapolis: USNIP, 1997), p. 244.

36   ibid., pp. 239–41.

37   V. Mücke, 'The adventures of the *Emden* and her crew' in *The Naval Review*, undated, p. 77.

38   Cited in F. Forstmeier, *SMS* Emden (Windsor: Profile Publications, 1971), p. 22.

39   Cordier, 'Knights, Huns, and the case of the *Emden*', p. 236.

40   ibid., p. 247.

41   A.W. Jose, *The Royal Australian Navy 1914–1918. The Official History of Australia in the War of 1914–1918*, vol. IX (Sydney: Angus & Robertson, 1928), p. 567.

42   http://www.yale.edu/lawweb/avalon/lawofwar/hague10.htm, 15 June 2002.

43   Cited in R. Dymond, *The History of HMAS* Voyager *I* (Lucaston, Tas: Southern Holdings, 1992), p. 64.

44   G.H. Johnston, *Grey Gladiator: HMAS* Sydney *with the British Mediterranean Fleet* (Sydney: Angus & Robertson, 1941), p. 35.

45   ibid., p. 39.

46   Cited in Dymond, *HMAS* Voyager, p. 118.

47   M. Johnston, *Fighting the Enemy*, p. 4.

48   Dymond, HMAS *Voyager*, p. 71.

49   G. Johnston, *Grey Gladiator*, pp. 38–9.

50   Diary of Petty Officer John Ross, 28 June 1940, *Cerberus* Museum.

51   J. Collins, *As Luck Would Have It: The Reminiscences of an Australian Sailor* (Sydney: Angus & Robertson, 1965), pp. 80–1.

52   G. Johnston, *Grey Gladiator*, p. 41.

53   Ross, *Lucky Ross*, p. 145.

54   Collins, *As Luck Would Have It*, p. 81.

55   Letter, 22 July 1940, in M. Simpson (ed.), *The Cunningham Papers*, vol. I (Aldershot: Ashgate for The Navy Records Society, 1999), p. 120.

56   Cited in G. Johnston, *Grey Gladiator*, p. 120.

57   Simpson, *The Cunningham Papers*, p. 119.

58   'The Italian Navy' compiled in the office of the Director of Naval Intelligence, Admiralty, c. 1944, NHD: 211, p. 59.

59   ibid., p. 58.

60   *H.M.A.S.* (Canberra: AWM, 1942), p. 82.

61   Parkin, *Out of the Smoke*, p. 295.

62   See P. Lowe, 'Great Britain's assessment of Japan before the outbreak of the Pacific War' in E.R. May (ed.), *Knowing One's Enemies: Intelligence Assessment Before the Two World Wars* (Princeton: Princeton University Press, 1984).

63   J.W. Dower, *War Without Mercy: Race and Power in the Pacific War* (New York: Pantheon Books, 1986), p. 13.

64   ibid., p. 71.

65   *H.M.A.S.*, p. 199.

66   Quoted in T.M. Jones and I.L. Idriess, *The Silent Service: Action Stories of the Anzac Navy* (Sydney: Angus & Robertson, 1944), pp. 209, 210.

67   Whiting, *Ship of Courage*, p. 16.

68   'A letter from Singapore', author unknown in W. Eves (ed.), *HMAS* Bendigo *Corvette: By Members of Her Ships's Company* (self published, 1995), pp. 25–6.

69   J.F. Moyes, *Mighty Midgets* (Sydney: NSW Bookstall Co., 1946), p. 129.

70   Jones and Idriess, *The Silent Service,* p. 223.

71   Cited in D. Jenkins, *Battle Surface: Japan's Submarine War Against Australia 1942–44* (Sydney: Random House, 1992), p. 230.

72   See for example General Blamey's speech at the Japanese surrender. Cited in D.M. Horner, *Blamey: The Commander-in-Chief* (Sydney: Allen & Unwin, 1998), p. 555.

73   Dower, *War Without Mercy*, p. 12.

74   'Light cruiser: the last voyage of HMAS *Perth*', unpublished memoirs of Chaplain J.K.W. Mathieson, RAN, *Cerberus* Museum, p. 18.

75   R. McKie, *Proud Echo* (Sydney: Angus & Robertson, 1953), p. 84.

76   Combat Intelligence Center South Pacific Force, 'Extracts from diary of member of I-1', AWM: AWM 58-058.

77   G. Brooks, *'We Lived With Danger': A History of the Australian Corvette HMAS* Stawell *(J348) 1943–1945* (Canberra: Panther Publishing, 1994), p. 109.

78   ibid., p. 110. The officer's sword remained missing for many years afterwards.

79   Moyes, *Mighty Midgets*, p. 186.

80   ibid., pp. 83, 84.

81   Dower, *War Without Mercy*, p. 12; M. Johnston, *Fighting the Enemy*, pp. 95–102.

82   Letter, Daven to author, 1992.

83   S. Nicholls, *HMAS* Shropshire (Sydney: Naval Historical Society, 1989), p. 138.

84   Cited in L. McAulay, *Battle of the Bismarck Sea* (New York: St Martin's Press, 1991), p. 153; A. Stephens, *The Royal Australian Air Force* (Melbourne: Oxford University Press, 2001), p. 164.

85   Jones and Idriess, *The Silent Service,* p. 364.

86   Nicholls, *HMAS* Shropshire, p. 162.

87   'Personal narrative of part played by HMAS *Hobart* at Tarakan', by C. Phillips, entry for 26 April 1945, NAA(VIC): MP 1587/1 61C.

88   G. Johnston, *Grey Gladiator*, p. 41.

89   See S. Huntington, *The Soldier and the State: The Theory and Politics of Civil–Military Relations* (Cambridge, MA: Belknap Press, 1967), pp. 73–4.

CHAPTER 16

1   A. Walker, *Medical Services of the RAN and RAAF, Australia in the War of 1939–1945* (Canberra: Australian War Memorial, 1961), p. 161.

2   'Australia remembers 1945–1995', AAP News Service, 9 August 1996.

3   *The Weekend Australian*, 23–24 June 2001, p. 12.

4   A. Young, *The Harmony of Illusions* (Princeton, New Jersey: Princeton University Press, 1995).

5   F.W. Mott, *War Neurosis and Shell Shock* (London: Henry Frowde, Hodder & Stoughton, 1919).

6   Young, *The Harmony of Illusions*, p. 62.

7   ibid.

8   A. Kardiner, *The Traumatic Neurosis of War* (Washington, DC: National Research Council, 1941).

9   R.R. Grinker and J. Spiegel, *War Neurosis* (Philadelphia: Blakiston, 1945); A. Kardiner and H. Spiegel, *War Stress and Neurotic Illness* (New York: Paul B. Hoeber, 1947).

10   Walker, *Medical Services of the RAN and RAAF*, p. 160.

11   Z. Solomon, *Combat Stress Reaction* (New York: Plenum Press, 1993).

12   Mott, *War Neurosis and Shell Shock*.

13   B. van der Kolk, 'The psychobiology of posttraumatic stress disorder' in *Journal of Clinical Psychiatry*, vol. 58, 1997, pp. 16–24.

14   J. LeDoux, *The Emotional Brain* (London: Weidenfeld & Nicolson, 1998); M.C. Corballis, *The Lopsided Ape* (New York: Oxford University Press, 1991).

15   P.D. MacLean, *The Triune Brain in Evolution: Role in Paleocerebral Functions* (New York: Plenum, 1990).

16   LeDoux, *The Emotional Brain*.

17   R. Plutchik, *Emotion: A Psychoevolutionary Synthesis* (New York: Harper & Row, 1980); A. Damasio, *Descartes' Error: Emotion, Reason, and the Human Brain* (New York: Grosset/Putnam, 1994); A. Damasio, *The Feeling of What Happens* (London: William Heinemann, 1999); C. Magi and S.H. McFadden, *The Role of Emotions in Social and Personality Development* (New York: Plenum, 1995).

18   Damasio, *Descartes' Error*.

19   van der Kolk, 'The psychobiology of posttraumatic stress disorder'.

20   For a fuller treatment of catastrophe modelling see A. Woodcock and M. Davis, *Catastrophe Theory* (London: Penguin, 1978), and S. Guastello, *Chaos, Catastrophe, and Human Affairs* (Mahwah, New Jersey: Lawrence Erlbaum, 1995).

21   The example comes from Woodcock and Davis, *Catastrophe Theory*, pp. 121–30.

22   Guastello, *Chaos, Catastrophe, and Human Affairs*.

23   F.B. Walker, *HMAS Armidale: The Ship That Had to Die* (Budgewoi, NSW: Kingfisher Press, 1990).

24   Undated RN documentary.

25   Solomon, *Combat Stress Reaction*.

26   Kardiner, *The Traumatic Neurosis of War*.

CHAPTER 17

1 When using the term 'sailor' in this chapter it is implicit that this collectively refers to both officers and sailors.

2 For further discussion of the RMA a useful primer is K. Kak, 'Revolution in military affairs—an appraisal', Institute for Defence Studies and Analyses Website, http://www.idsa-india.org/an-apr-01.html. Another useful site is http://www.comw.org/rma.

3 For a more detailed discussion of NCW see D.S. Albert, J.J. Garstka and F.P. Stein, *Network Centric Warfare, 1999*, at the Website http://www.dodccrp.org. Also see http://www.usni.org/Proceedings/Articles98/PROcebrowski.htm.

4 Forces of two or more allied nations conduct 'combined' operations while 'joint' operations are those conducted by two or more services of one nation.

5 An illustration of this emerging capability is the Russian VA-111 Shkval torpedo.

6 For a good overview of the US vision of NCW, see V. Dutschke, 'Network-centric operations–naval operations in the information age', *Journal of the Australian Naval Institute*, Summer 2001–2002, pp. 4–9.

7 For more on the concept of Rapid Decisive Operations, see Website http:www.jfcom.mil.

8 *Australian Maritime Doctrine* (Canberra: AGPS, 2000), p. 154.

9 For examples of this influence, see D.M. Stevens (ed.), *The Royal Australian Navy* (Melbourne: Oxford University Press, 2001), Chapters 7–10.

10 For a fuller discussion of EBO, see 'US Joint Forces Command rapid decisive operations concept report FY 2001', November 2001.

11 ibid., p. B–2.

12 United States Naval War College definition of EBO, accessed at http:www.nwc.navy.mil.

13 R.N. Wallace, 'The Australian purchase of three United States guided missile destroyers: a study of the defence aspect of Australian–American relations', PhD thesis, Tufts University, 1980, p. 140.

14 J. McCarthy, 'Transformation study report', 27 April 2001, http://www.defenselink.mil/news/Jun2001/d20010621transrep.pdf.

15 ibid., p. 5.

16 In the ADF the fundamental inputs to capability are organisation, personnel, collective training, major systems, supplies, facilities, support, command and management.

17 See Website http://peos.crane.navy.mil for details of the DD21 and DD-(X) programs.

18 J.R. Bost, 'Optimizing manning for DD21', presentation to the RAN, 21 May 2001.

19 D.A. Lambert, 'FOCAL in 60', presentation to the RAN, 25 July 2001.

Index